The Essentials of Teaching in Secondary Classrooms

The Essentials of Teaching in Secondary Classrooms

A Basic Guide for New Teachers

M. Grace Mitchell
University of North Carolina at Charlotte

Upper Saddle River, New Jersey
Columbus, Ohio

Library of Congress Cataloging-in-Publication Data

Mitchell, Miriam Grace.
The essentials of teaching in secondary classrooms: a basic guide for new teachers / M. Grace Mitchell.
p. cm.
Includes bibliographical references and index.
ISBN 0-13-099074-4
1. High School Teaching—United States. I. Title.

LB1607.5.M58 2005
373.1102—dc22

2004048849

Vice President and Publisher: Jeffery W. Johnston
Executive Editor: Debra A. Stollenwerk
Editorial Assistant: Mary Morrill
Production Editor: Kris Roach
Production Coordination: Thistle Hill Publishing Services, LLC
Design Coordinator: Diane C. Lorenzo
Text Designer: Kristina D. Holmes
Cover Designer: Michelle Yandrich
Cover Art: Getty One
Photo Coordinator: Sandy Schaefer
Production Manager: Susan Hannahs
Director of Marketing: Ann Castel Davis
Marketing Manager: Darcy Betts Prybella
Marketing Coordinator: Tyra Poole

This book was set in 10/12 Garamond by Integra Software Services. It was printed and bound by Courier Kendallville, Inc. The cover was printed by Coral Graphic Services.

Photo Credits: Anthony Magnacca/Merrill, pp. 3, 83, 181, 221, 255; U.S. National Education Association, p. 33; Todd Yarrington/Merrill, p. 61; Scott Cunningham/Merrill, pp. 113, 245; Kathy Kirtland/Merrill, p. 149; Tom Watson/Merrill, p. 201.

Pearson Education LTD.
Pearson Education Singapore, Pte. Ltd
Pearson Education, Canada, Ltd
Pearson Education—Japan
Pearson Education Australia PTY, Limited
Pearson Education North Asia Ltd
Pearson Educación de Mexico, S.A. de C.V.
Pearson Education Malaysia, Pte. Ltd

10 9 8 7 6 5 4 3 2 1
ISBN: 0-13-099074-4

To my family of educators—Carlton, Miriam and Betty
with love

EDUCATOR LEARNING CENTER: AN INVALUABLE ONLINE RESOURCE

Merrill Education and the Association for Supervision and Curriculum Development (ASCD) invite you to take advantage of a new online resource, one that provides access to the top research and proven strategies associated with ASCD and Merrill—the Educator Learning Center. At **www.EducatorLearningCenter.com** you will find resources that will enhance your students' understanding of course topics and of current educational issues, in addition to being invaluable for further research.

How the Educator Learning Center Will Help Your Students Become Better Teachers

With the combined resources of Merrill Education and ASCD, you and your students will find a wealth of tools and materials to better prepare them for the classroom.

Research

- More than 600 articles from the ASCD journal *Educational Leadership* discuss everyday issues faced by practicing teachers.
- A direct link on the site to Research Navigator™ gives students access to many of the leading education journals, as well as extensive content detailing the research process.
- Excerpts from Merrill Education texts give your students insights on important topics of instructional methods, diverse populations, assessment, classroom management, technology, and refining classroom practice.

Classroom Practice

- Hundreds of lesson plans and teaching strategies are categorized by content area and age range.
- Case studies and classroom video footage provide virtual field experience for student reflection.
- Computer simulations and other electronic tools keep your students abreast of today's classrooms and current technologies.

Look into the Value of Educator Learning Center Yourself

A four-month subscription to Educator Learning Center is $25 but is **FREE** when used in conjunction with this text. To obtain free passcodes for your students, simply contact your local Merrill/Prentice Hall sales representative, and your representative will give you a special ISBN to give your bookstore when ordering your textbooks. To preview the value of this website to you and your students, please go to **www.EducatorLearningCenter.com** and click on "Demo."

PREFACE

The Essentials of Teaching in Secondary Classrooms: A Basic Guide for New Teachers is a methods textbook that represents the basics for anyone preparing to begin a career as a secondary teacher. It will be particularly helpful for those students in methods courses who will soon be student teaching. Likewise, it will be particularly valuable for newly employed, full-time professionals who have had little or no formal preparation as teachers. It is based on 25 years of experience working with new, unlicensed secondary teachers in public schools and with undergraduate and graduate students in teacher education programs.

The book is designed to be an overview of the most *essential* information needed for understanding the methods of teaching in secondary classrooms. Imbedded throughout is also a review of the important elements from foundations coursework that will help students see connections with all parts of their program. Often, students forget key concepts they learned in such required core courses as Foundations of Education or Adolescent Development—concepts they need to remember as they begin teaching. For those who have not been part of a program at all, the inclusion of this review provides a brief but critical introduction to important elements.

The text is designed for:

1. Students in teacher preparation programs in colleges and universities who are enrolled in secondary methods courses, serving as either a primary or resource text.
2. Students who are student teaching and need a resource that is a review of the basics.
3. The many new teachers who are populating classrooms in record numbers and did not have teacher preparation but need an overview of the essentials *now.*

This book is organized in such a way that new teachers can learn these fundamentals either in a general methods course or completely on their own, as they can engage in follow-up activities that can be completed with or without supervision. It cuts to the chase in a way that still reflects current research and national standards.

The Essentials of Teaching in Secondary Classrooms: A Basic Guide for New Teachers addresses the most critical topics in 11 chapters grouped into the following sections:

You: Your Role and Professional Environment

Your Students: Understanding and Working with Adolescents

Your Challenge: Effectively Teaching Secondary Students

Each chapter is written from the perspective of the readers. The first section focuses on the new teachers themselves—their role and the professional environment in which they function. The second section discusses students—their nature, issues related to managing their behavior, and those with special needs. The third section deals with the process of teaching secondary students effectively. Readers are encouraged to challenge themselves as they engage in activities and consider the advice and experiences of others whose views and suggestions are provided.

FEATURES

Some of the most distinguishing features of this text are the following:

- "Praxis Competencies" related to each chapter for passing the Praxis Examinations, which a majority of states require for teacher licensure.
- "Activities" that are self-directed for each section to help the teacher apply the content presented.
- "Reality Checks," which remind readers of the "truth" they must be aware of in dealing with certain situations, even if the "truth" doesn't always appear to be consistent with best practice.
- "Tips from the Trenches," which represent specific advice from veteran teachers regarding concepts presented in each chapter.
- A glossary that will define specific terms used in the book.
- Its ability to function as a handbook that the teacher can keep handy for quick reference.

The Essentials of Teaching in Secondary Classrooms: A Basic Guide for New Teachers is a practical resource to help new teachers become proficient in many of the basics of their craft. The book is written in a clear, reader-friendly manner where complex concepts are clarified for easier comprehension, and it represents only the most important elements of each topic that a novice teacher needs to know. Of course, the book does not intend to *replace* an in-depth teacher education program or even a secondary methods course. Rather, it will be useful as either a primary or supplemental text for such a methods course or a stand-alone resource for students. For those not yet part of a formal teacher education program, it provides a starting point as one begins to understand the complexity of teaching, and it stresses the need for continued study as these individuals embark on a lifelong journey of professional competence.

Acknowledgments

This book reflects the efforts and support of more individuals than there is space here to thank. However, I am especially grateful to the following people, who have been instrumental in helping me complete this project.

I want to thank the many teachers, student teachers, and students I have been privileged to teach, for the fine examples they are for our profession. Their suggestions, comments, and even their frustrations as they learned the ropes informed this book.

I want to thank Joy VanZandt, Mario DeMarco, and Mark Cavanaugh for their willingness to share their journey as beginning and alternative license teachers.

I want to thank my editor Debbie Stollenwerk, whose constant encouragement, insight, and support over the years have served as constant stimulation to keep at it.

I want to thank Paul Escott for his valuable editing suggestions.

Most of all, I want to thank my family and friends who wondered if I would ever finish.

Finally, I appreciate the contributions of the following reviewers who provided helpful comments throughout the project: Ronald Anderson, Texas A&M International University; Theodore E. Andrews, Southern Illinois University; Karen Bosch, Virginia Wesleyan College; Janet Boyle, Indiana University & Purdue University at Indianapolis; Leigh Chiarelott, Bowling Green State University; Noble R. Corey, Indiana State University; Carrie Dale, Baker College of Flint; Shirley W. De Lucia, Capital University; Janet M. Hamann, California State University, Bakersfield; Shirley Jacob, Southeastern Louisiana University; Nancy Kaczmarek, D'Youville College; Cynthia G. Kruger, University of Massachusetts, Dartmouth; Merry McCalley, California State University, Bakersfield; Eileen McDaniel, Florida State University; John McIntyre, Southern Illinois University, Carbondale; Jon S. Miller, Northern Illinois University; Sara Delano Moore, Eastern Kentucky University; Juan Munoz, California State University, Fullerton; Steve Neill, Emporia State; A. Y. "Fred" Ramirez, California State University, Fullerton; William A. Rieck, University of Louisiana, Lafayette; Patricia M. Ryan, Otterbein College; Kim Shibinski, Middle Tennessee State University; and George C. Willett, Southern Illinois University.

About the Author

Grace Mitchell has been in the field of education for 35 years, serving as a teacher, guidance counselor, and administrator in public schools at the secondary level. At the college level, she served as Director of Teacher Education at Davidson College for 9 years and continues to work with many colleges and public school systems in the area of teacher preparation. She is currently a faculty member in the Department of Educational Leadership at the University of North Carolina at Charlotte.

Brief Contents

CONTENTS

CHAPTER 5
Students with Special Needs 113

Part 3

Your Challenge: Effectively Teaching Secondary Students 147

CHAPTER 6
Planning for Instruction 149

PART 1

You: Your Role and Professional Environment

1

Your Role as a Secondary Teacher

When I was in college, I always thought it would be fun to teach for a while before I decided on a career. I needed a breather from the pressure of worrying about grades for a year or two. I knew I was good with kids and figured spending the day with them wouldn't be too different from when I was a "big brother" at camp. I also loved math and wanted to make them love it, too. The school schedule is great and I'd have a lot of time to do other things. I mean, how hard could it be?

First-year teacher

So you want to be a teacher. Why? What makes you think that this is the career for you? Before you go any further, it is absolutely vital that you take a long look at yourself.

This chapter will provide you with an opportunity to look at yourself as a new teacher and think about the qualities that will help you to become successful. You will explore some of your own personality traits and certain attitudes that will influence your work with students. Then you will consider how realistic you are, regarding your expectations of your students, your school, and the profession. You will also examine some of the basic premises of your current philosophical approach to teaching and how these notions affect what you do in your classroom. Finally, you will review ways to recognize your limitations and consider strategies to manage stress.

You: Why Do You Want to Teach?

You have spent a long time watching teachers and being guided by them. Few professions provide such an opportunity. Where else can you observe firsthand, for 13 years, the profession you choose?

But what did you learn? As you sat in your seventh-grade social studies class or your high school biology lab, what were you thinking about your teachers and their roles? You certainly saw how hard their jobs are; how many hours they spend before and after school preparing lessons, grading papers, working with individual students, talking to parents, and attending meetings. You also have heard over and over that they are not paid what they deserve for this dedication. Yet, at some point, you must have found yourself saying, "What a great job!" or "I would love to spend my career working with young people," or "I think I have some ideas about how to do this better than Miss Jones," or "I want to be a teacher just like Mr. Nazeer."

Regardless of what you were thinking then, what are you thinking now? Why does teaching appeal to you at this point in your life? It is important that you examine your motivation for choosing this career. After all, if you don't know why you are doing something, how can you tell if you should be doing it at all?

The Road to Becoming a Teacher

Most people are influenced to choose a career by things that have happened to them. Sometimes these things are very clear, such as an experience with serious illness that influences a person to become a doctor. Or decisions may be made for different kinds of reasons, such as when people choose professions that are lucrative simply because they want a particular lifestyle. Likewise, some may choose teaching because they encountered a teacher who made a difference in their lives. Others may see the profession as one that provides security and summer vacations. Still others may see the profession as a halfway house, something they can do until they decide what they really want to do.

It is possible to go into this—or any—profession for the wrong reasons. More than likely, you will not be happy as a person or effective as a teacher if this is the case. Some of the *wrong* reasons to choose teaching include thinking that (a) it is an easy job, (b) you will be able to go home every day at 3:00 p.m. and have your evenings and weekends free to do as you please, (c) you will have to concern yourself only with teaching lessons and will not have to face paperwork or additional tasks that seem unrelated to working directly with students, and (d) you have all the answers and can fix the problems that face schools today. Be advised that you are in for many disappointing days on the job if you enter the profession with any of these erroneous notions.

In examining why you want to become a teacher, take a minute to look at what experiences in your life have helped you to arrive at this decision (see Activity 1.1). What events in your past stand out as important in leading you to think that you will be a good teacher or a happy one? Looking at the person you have become is the first step in assessing yourself as a potential teacher. You need to review key events and how you handled

Self-Assessment: The Road to Becoming a Teacher

Autobiography

Write a complete autobiography of your life until now. Include descriptions of important people and events that you have experienced, in and out of school, especially ones that have influenced your decision to teach. What events brought out your strengths? Your weaknesses? When you have finished, reread what you have written and respond to the following question in three or fewer sentences: "Why do I want to be a teacher?"

them (or didn't handle them) as you were growing up and to remember the role of influential people who helped you. You will then be able to analyze some of your own motivations for wanting to teach. You will also need to isolate strengths and qualities that can be assets when you are in the business of helping others to develop.

Fortunately, most effective secondary teachers who have had successful careers as educators went into teaching for the *right* reasons. Research indicates that the four most common reasons cited by good teachers for wanting to teach are that they: (a) genuinely like young people and want to help them learn and grow, (b) have a desire to impart knowledge about a subject they love, (c) have an interest and excitement about the process of teaching, and (d) have a desire to perform a valuable service for society (Myers & Myers, 1995). Others, especially minority teachers, say that they want to "make a difference" in the world and describe their decision as a vocational "mission" to help their communities (Gordon, 1993).

Reality Check 1.1

Two things you want to remember. First, some of your reasons for going into teaching may be more noble than others. So what? Don't waste time worrying at this point that you may not be doing this for the *right* reasons. Just be aware of what some of them are. Saving the next generation may not have been the number one reason you chose teaching. But keep in mind that many excellent teachers entered the profession for purely pragmatic reasons. They accidentally saved the next generation on the way to paying the rent.

Second, no matter whom you have in mind as your ideal teacher and no matter how much like that teacher you think you are or can be, accept that it may take you a while to get there. Right now, you are a hybrid consisting of your own style, the imprints of teachers you have observed, and the teacher you want to be. It will be helpful, however, to keep that mental image of your ideal teacher in your head as you begin. It can serve as a centering buoy when things get rough during those first months. When necessary, ask the image, "What would *you* have done here?"

It is also true that many see the profession as offering job stability, and to a great extent, it does. Entering teachers also say that they find the field exciting and challenging and like the work conditions, such as academic vacations and being able to start each year with a brand-new group of students. Do these reasons sound similar to your own? Most beginning teachers also say that they were inspired by at least one favorite teacher. Who was yours?

Qualities of Effective Secondary Teachers

Members of every profession have certain qualities and characteristics that tend to make them successful in their respective fields. Counselors need to be good listeners, executives need leadership skills, policemen need to be able to make quick decisions, and attorneys need to be able to create clear arguments on behalf of their clients. Likewise, there are particular qualities teachers must have if they are to be successful. Before discussing these, take a minute to complete Activity 1.2.

There are many qualities that are present in excellent secondary teachers. Most understand their students, know where they are developmentally and have concern for their welfare. They are sympathetic and empathetic when dealing with their students' problems. At the same time, they also know that students need consistency. They know when

ACTIVITY 1.2

The Qualities of a Good Teacher

List at least seven qualities of a good teacher. Then indicate beside each, on a 1–10 scale, the extent to which you think you have this quality, from 1 (*a little*) to 10 (*a lot*).

Fill in the columns with names of two of your favorite teachers and indicate the extent to which they have the qualities that you have named.

Quality	Degree to Which *You* Have the Quality	Teacher A	Teacher B
1.			
2.			
3.			
4.			

It will be helpful if you discuss what you discovered with someone else. More than likely, you found that the traits you like in your favorite teachers are also ones you have, to a great extent, yourself. Maybe not. What will you learn from this?

to be firm and when to be flexible. But they are predictably firm about some things and predictably flexible about others. Secondary students respond best to consistency. Jan, a second-year teacher, is always consistent in applying rules for assignments. She reports that her students know that she never accepts term papers late, "and they don't ever ask for extensions."

Lee Canter (1994) said that high-performing teachers *are knowledgeable and passionate about the subject matter they teach and want to impart a love of their field to their students.* They are enthusiastic instructors who inspire their students to want to know more. Moreover, these teachers understand the curriculum and how their subject fits into the total program. They look for ways to integrate their course material with that of other subjects. They keep abreast of current trends in their discipline and look for ways to enhance their own expertise.

The best teachers constantly *study teaching.* They know how to teach and are always looking for better ways to make their lessons interesting. They are able to organize their instruction into coherent and stimulating lessons and activities that reflect an awareness of developmentally appropriate tasks. They have high standards for their own performance in the classroom as well as the performance of their students. They have excellent planning skills and are flexible. These teachers are enthusiastic learners themselves and focus their energies on identifying and emphasizing the unique talents of their students.

The best secondary teachers *create an atmosphere conducive for learning.* They are fair and are good managers of the classroom environment. They understand how to do their jobs and are secure in their ability to do them well. They have a sense of humor and strive to foster joy about learning and excitement about their subject in their classes. The room is full of posters, bulletin boards, and artifacts designed to stimulate an interest in the content taught. Does this sound like the teacher you want to be?

What Will Make You Successful?

Successful teaching at the secondary level today depends on your ability to do five important things, each of which will be discussed in more detail in later sections of the book.

Understand Yourself

To be successful in this career, it is very important that you understand who you are and why you want to teach. You must be a secure person, one who is emotionally mature and able to accept the volatile nature of adolescents.

Accept and Like Teenagers

You will need to be patient and realize that most of what teenagers do and say is a reflection of their developmental stage. But most of all, you must be able to enjoy them for who they are.

Be Knowledgeable in the Content You Are Teaching

It is absolutely critical that you know as much about your content area as possible. Secondary students need teachers who are able to field questions about topics they are reading. You need to know enough about your subject to be able to provide anecdotal information that will fill in the gaps and round out a class's understanding of a concept. This requires more than just having read the text the night before or glancing over the "Questions for Thought" in the teacher's edition. Secondary students can easily tell if you are just winging it or if you have a deep and significant understanding of what they are studying.

Students want to see their teachers as experts in their fields, whether or not they are. This does not mean that there will not be questions you can't answer. There will always be. But how you respond to them is key. Do you look frantically to find the answer in the teacher's guide? Do you dismiss the question as off the topic at hand? Or do you respond comfortably to such questions, stimulated yourself that someone has offered an insightful idea from which you all can learn? At the very least, they want you to appear comfortable and competent with the subject matter—with what you know and don't know. Obviously, this presents unique challenges if you are teaching out of your field, as many beginning teachers are (Ingersoll, 1999).

You should also develop a plan for your own supplementary reading during the year that will keep you informed about your field and enable you to reach beyond the usual resources to enrich your classes.

REALITY CHECK 1.2

You may be thinking that it's all you can do just to keep up with the reading and planning for the next day. You will want to forget supplementary reading and exploring areas of your content that might take time you don't have. Sorry, but it's a necessity if you truly want to be an excellent teacher. Do you want to go to a doctor who hasn't kept up with the latest surgical procedures since he graduated from medical school 20 years ago?

You may not be able to work in much time to do this at the very beginning. But it is a fact that many beginning teachers think they have the time to sit in the teachers' lounge watching television or reading the paper because they have prepared the next day's lesson. They assume they don't need to do more preparation because only this section of content will be covered. Remember that your goal is to become knowledgeable in your content at a deeper level. Read. Research. Go beyond the lesson at hand. You owe this effort to yourself and to your students. Just a few minutes several days a week over a period of time will help.

Know How to Teach

Dismiss the notion that if you have a degree in the content you are teaching or have some expertise in the field in another way, that it is enough to be a good teacher. Everyone has had teachers who were clearly very bright and knowledgeable but who simply couldn't teach. What good is their knowledge in the classroom? Therefore, you must understand the process of teaching if you are to be a success. Studying teaching principles in a formal teacher education program is often the best way. But reading the many available resources (such as this one) will also be helpful in guiding you. Some of the ways to enhance your own development as a professional will be discussed in a later chapter.

Be a Good Multitasker

Teachers have shattered the myth that you can do only one thing well at a time (see Figure 1.1). You will get used to listening to a student's explanation about his misplaced assignment while you are writing a note for someone to go to the office as you stand outside your door on hall duty, putting out your hand to slow a running student. You will find yourself teaching the class while operating a slide projector, adjusting the temperature in the room, noticing two students who are passing a note, and moving toward a student who is talking.

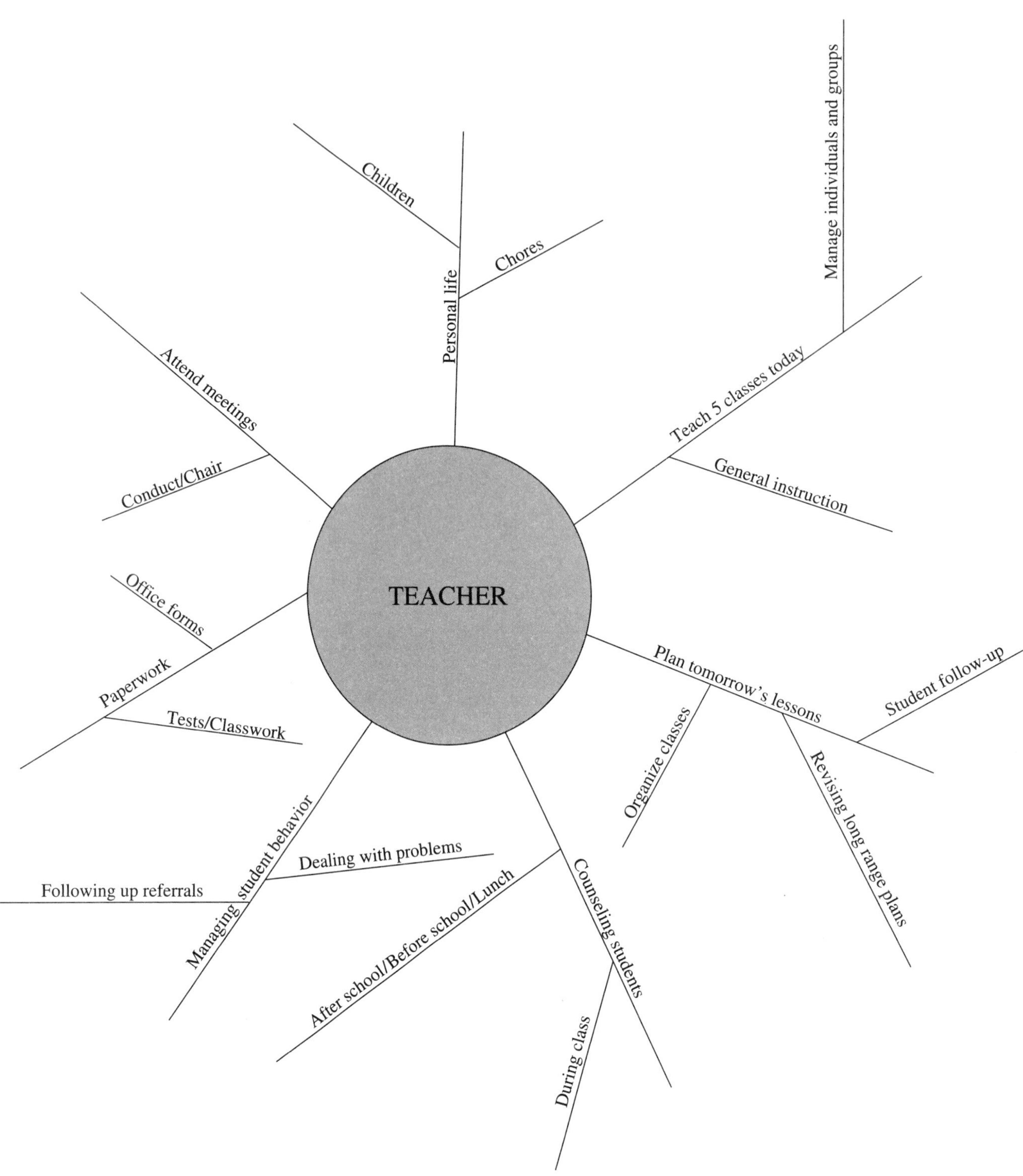

FIGURE 1.1 Typical Teacher's School Day
Portrait of a Multitasker

You can train yourself to see and respond to things that can be handled with your feet while your eyes and hands are doing something else. All part of the job.

Self-Assessment: How Do Your Personality and Attitude Affect Your Teaching?

Your Personality

Think back to your days as a secondary student. What exactly do you remember about your teachers? Was it that stimulating lesson about the causes of the Great Depression? How about that interesting class when you spoke only Spanish all period? You probably don't recall specific content. If your memories are about what happened in your classes at all, more than likely they are about some unique quality of a teacher—the more bizarre the better. It might be the clothes Miss Edwards wore, the fact that she would take the sleeves out of her blouses for spring and put them back in for the winter. Perhaps it was Mr. Peters's ability to write math problems from one end of the board to the other without pausing, using both his left and right hands. At class reunions held years after graduation, Elaine, a veteran teacher, still laughs at Mrs. Kazmarak's habit of catching students looking at the clock and asking them the same question: "Time will pass, will you?" (She now does this in her own class.)

True, there was learning taking place, whether or not some were aware of it, but it is also true that most secondary students remember their teachers as people long after they have forgotten what they studied in their classes. Regardless of how unique their teachers were and how unusual their personalities, there are some teachers with traits that most students respond well to in all circumstances. These teachers have personalities that are characterized by *confidence*, *respect* for themselves and for the students they teach, and *passion* for their subjects.

At this point in your life, you probably think you know yourself pretty well, and maybe you do. However, for many, this complicated profession you are entering may bring out another personality you never knew you had. At the very least, the constant demands of working in a labor-intensive situation for eight hours a day may strain your ability to project certain positive qualities and may even bring out characteristics you would rather not be evident. This is unavoidable. How many professions do you know where a *daily* requirement is to interact in some meaningful way with 50–150 people, monitor their personal and academic progress on an individual basis, and satisfy both parents and administrators at the same time? In addition, as a teacher, you will "perform" for eight hours a day as you present engaging lessons you spent hours preparing for up to five different audiences (classes). Tired yet?

As you begin this profession, your "teacher personality" will emerge—in essence, a slight modification of your own. True, you are still basically you. But it is useful to focus on who you are when you are not under this pressure if you are going to develop aspects of your personality that will help you as a teacher and play down those characteristics that will not.

It is also important to understand how you are perceived by others. Personality traits affect everyone's professional interactions, no matter the occupation. How others (students, parents, peers, and administrators) see you is absolutely key to your success in this field, more so than in some others. You don't have to relate well to your plumber or even to your attorney, although it helps. You just need for that person to get the job done. But unlike the plumber who needs to fix a pipe, or an attorney who needs to be an advocate for a client, you are in the business of working with students in two ways: academically, moving each student from point A to point B, and personally, helping multiple "clients" to grow up.

As a teacher, you can't always get your job done unless you pay some attention to the critical factor of your personality. If students see you as unapproachable, they will not ask questions. If they see you as someone who is easy, they will not give your class (or you) the proper respect.

Mr. Vicks, a third-year teacher, commented that he had never realized how dogmatic he appeared to students when he began teaching.

> When I was in college, I was president of my dorm and was always considered to be the one to get things done. I organize things very well and am good at giving precise directions. I have always received a lot of praise for being this way and considered it a strength when I began teaching. I am very specific about how I want assignments done and because I take the time to explain them carefully, I don't have too much patience when my students don't do them exactly right. I always thought I was just being clear about what I wanted them to do. Since they never asked me any questions, I thought they understood what to do. But when students in all of my classes turned in poor work and began to refer to me as "Hitler," I had to think about that. Once I asked my college roommate what he thought I was like in college. He told me my friends called me "Generalissimo"! I realized that one of the problems my students were having could actually be me! I needed to adjust my approach.

At this stage in life, more than likely, you go about living on automatic pilot, rarely giving much thought to habits that represent who you are. Becoming more aware of yourself will help you to determine how to use or modify your own personality in your teaching. This does not mean that you will attempt to psychoanalyze yourself in any depth—as if you could. You are simply in search of some general truths that you want to consider before you begin teaching. You can gather important information in several ways that will involve some reflection on your part. You must also seek the insight of others. There are also many individual inventories and tests (such as the Myers-Briggs Type Indicator®) that are available and very informative to help you to learn some things about yourself. No one is suggesting that you can, or even should, try to *change* your personality. But focusing on aspects that help you or hurt you can only make your performance as a teacher more effective.

Figure 1.2 may help you to get you started.

When you looked at the brief descriptions of your type, did you tend to agree or disagree with what you read? Were there implications regarding the general approach to teaching you will probably take? Are there things that could be problematic for you? For example, if you were described as an INTJ, what implications for working with teenagers are there if, in fact, you do see yourself as critical, serious, and highly independent? Does this mean that you are most comfortable with lectures and highly structured methods? If so, how naturally will you be drawn to using methods with your classes that involve group work or discussion, methods that have proven to be developmentally appropriate and effective with secondary students? Remember, there are no "good" types or "bad" types. All of the types have advantages and disadvantages at certain times for working with certain students on certain tasks. The important thing is to look for ways to adapt your personality as much as you can to accommodate the many personalities of your students. Keep in mind that, although you may be predominantly one type, your class represents individuals of *all* types.

You've had a chance to look at how you see yourself. Now take a look at how others see you. Be brave! Activity 1.3 on page 13 will provide important information.

REALITY CHECK 1.3

Face it. You're normal. People don't want to hear the truth about themselves. Yet, if they listen with an open mind, they usually learn something. The students could care less about your ego—they are too busy trying to preserve theirs. If they think you are a stuffy, condescending teacher, they'll let you know in many different ways. Hear it from someone who likes you first, and try to pay attention to ways you can modify your demeanor. Likewise, if there are things about you that you simply can't—or don't want to—change, that's fine, too. Just go into the classroom aware of yourself and how you can use your good traits and play down your bad ones.

Your Attitude

Attitudes are a fundamental part of a person's personality. The dictionary defines *attitude* as "the manner of acting, feeling, or thinking that shows one's disposition or opinion" (*Webster's New World Collegiate Dictionary*, 2000, p. 91). Secondary students pay extraordinary attention to a teacher's attitude.

Ryan and Cooper (1992) said that there are four major categories of attitudes that affect teaching behavior: (a) the teacher's attitude about herself, (b) the teacher's attitude toward the students, (c) the teacher's attitudes toward peers and parents, and (d) the teacher's attitude toward the subject matter. Clearly any predisposition teachers demonstrate in these categories that is positive and uplifting will enhance their

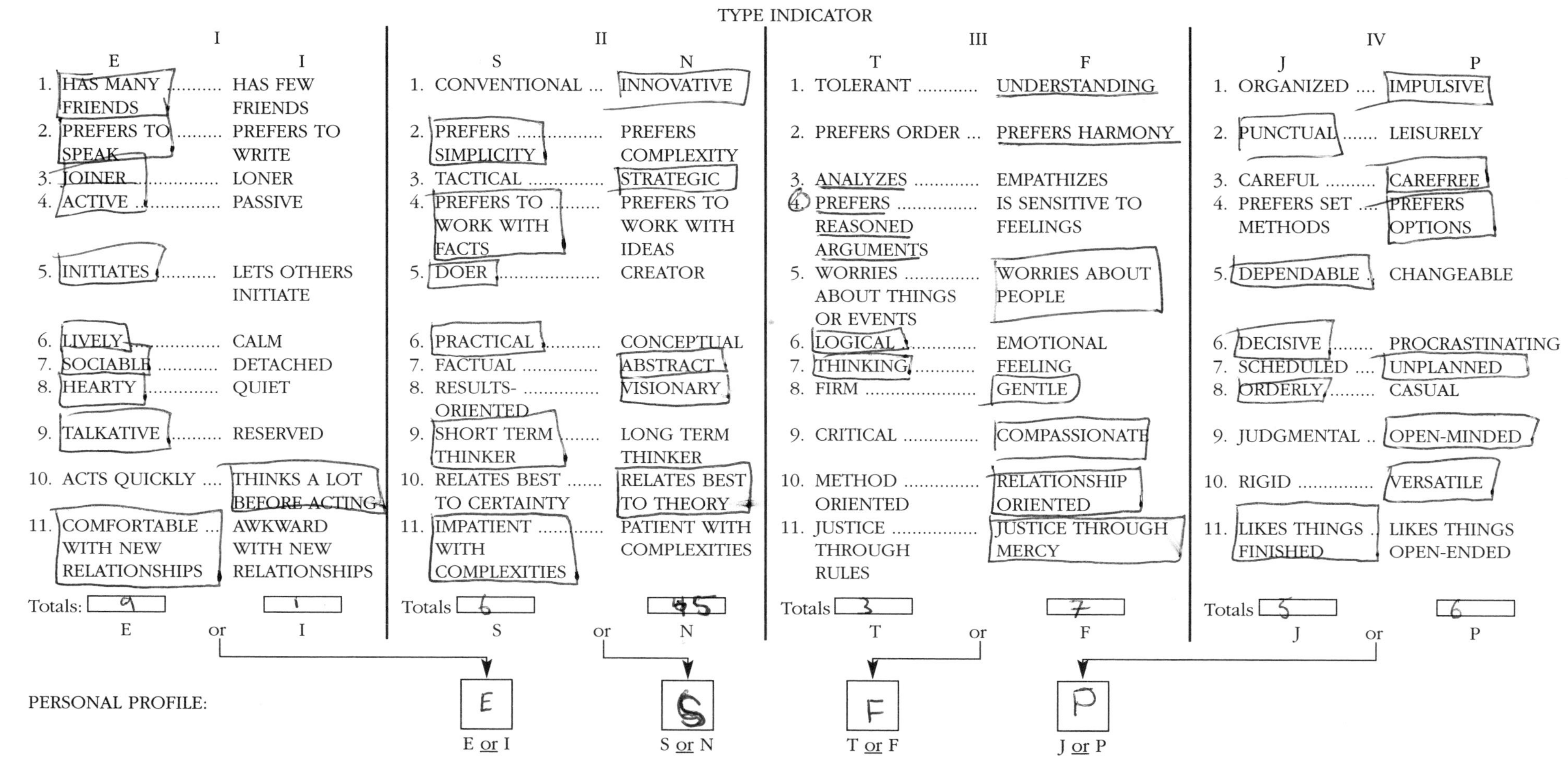

Directions: 1. For each pair of words/phrases in columns I–IV, circle the word or phrase which best describes the way you usually see the person being rated.
2. In the box at the bottom of each column, enter the number of circles in the column above.
3. On the lower section of the sheet, enter in the 4 personal profile boxes the letter from each of the four columns.

TYPE INDICATOR

	I		II		III		IV	
	E	I	S	N	T	F	J	P
1.	HAS MANY FRIENDS	HAS FEW FRIENDS	CONVENTIONAL	INNOVATIVE	TOLERANT	UNDERSTANDING	ORGANIZED	IMPULSIVE
2.	PREFERS TO SPEAK	PREFERS TO WRITE	PREFERS SIMPLICITY	PREFERS COMPLEXITY	PREFERS ORDER	PREFERS HARMONY	PUNCTUAL	LEISURELY
3.	JOINER	LONER	TACTICAL	STRATEGIC	ANALYZES	EMPATHIZES	CAREFUL	CAREFREE
4.	ACTIVE	PASSIVE	PREFERS TO WORK WITH FACTS	PREFERS TO WORK WITH IDEAS	PREFERS REASONED ARGUMENTS	IS SENSITIVE TO FEELINGS	PREFERS SET METHODS	PREFERS OPTIONS
5.	INITIATES	LETS OTHERS INITIATE	DOER	CREATOR	WORRIES ABOUT THINGS OR EVENTS	WORRIES ABOUT PEOPLE	DEPENDABLE	CHANGEABLE
6.	LIVELY	CALM	PRACTICAL	CONCEPTUAL	LOGICAL	EMOTIONAL	DECISIVE	PROCRASTINATING
7.	SOCIABLE	DETACHED	FACTUAL	ABSTRACT	THINKING	FEELING	SCHEDULED	UNPLANNED
8.	HEARTY	QUIET	RESULTS-ORIENTED	VISIONARY	FIRM	GENTLE	ORDERLY	CASUAL
9.	TALKATIVE	RESERVED	SHORT TERM THINKER	LONG TERM THINKER	CRITICAL	COMPASSIONATE	JUDGMENTAL	OPEN-MINDED
10.	ACTS QUICKLY	THINKS A LOT BEFORE ACTING	RELATES BEST TO CERTAINTY	RELATES BEST TO THEORY	METHOD ORIENTED	RELATIONSHIP ORIENTED	RIGID	VERSATILE
11.	COMFORTABLE WITH NEW RELATIONSHIPS	AWKWARD WITH NEW RELATIONSHIPS	IMPATIENT WITH COMPLEXITIES	PATIENT WITH COMPLEXITIES	JUSTICE THROUGH RULES	JUSTICE THROUGH MERCY	LIKES THINGS FINISHED	LIKES THINGS OPEN-ENDED
Totals	9	1	6	45	3	7	5	6
	E or I		S or N		T or F		J or P	

PERSONAL PROFILE: E (E or I) S (S or N) F (T or F) P (J or P)

FIGURE 1.2 Personality Preference Profile

ESFP

BRIEF DESCRIPTIONS OF THE SIXTEEN TYPES

E N T J
Intuitive, innovative ORGANIZER; aggressive, analytic, systematic: more tuned to new ideas and possibilities than to people's feelings.

E S T J
Fact-minded, practical ORGANIZER; aggressive, analytic, systematic: more interested in getting the job done than in people's feelings.

I N T P
Inquisitive ANALYZER; reflective, independent, curious: more interested in organizing ideas than situations or people.

E S T P
REALISTIC ADAPTER in the world of material things; good natured, tolerant, easygoing: oriented to practical, firsthand experience; highly observant of details of things.

I S T P
Practical ANALYZER; values exactness: more interested in organizing data than situations or people: reflective, a cool and curious observer of life.

E N T P
Inventive, analytical PLANNER OF CHANGE; enthusiastic and independent: pursues inspiration with impulsive energy, seeks to understand and inspire others.

E S F P
REALISTIC ADAPTER in human relationships; friendly and easy with people, highly observant of their feelings and needs: oriented to practical, firsthand experience.

I S T J
Analytical MANAGER OF FACTS AND DETAILS; dependable, decisive, painstaking and systematic, concerned with systems and organization: stable and conservative.

I S F J
Sympathetic MANAGER OF FACTS AND DETAILS; concerned with people's welfare: dependable, painstaking and systematic: stable and conservative.

I S F P
Observant, loyal HELPER; reflective, realistic, empathic: patient with details, gentle and retiring: shuns disagreements: enjoys the moment.

I N F P
Imaginative, independent HELPER; reflective, inquisitive, empathic, loyal to ideals: more interested in possibilities than practicalities.

E S F J
Practical HARMONIZER and worker-with-people: sociable, orderly, opinioned: conscientious, realistic and well tuned to the here and now.

E N F J
Imaginative HARMONIZER and worker-with-people; sociable, expressive, orderly, opinioned, conscientious, curious about new ideas and possibilities.

I N F J
People-oriented INNOVATOR of ideas; serious, quietly forceful and persevering: concerned with the common good, with helping others develop.

I N T J
Logical, critical, decisive INNOVATOR of ideas; serious, intent, highly independent, concerned with organization, determined and often stubborn.

E N F P
Warmly enthusiastic PLANNER OF CHANGE; imaginative, individualistic: pursues inspiration with impulsive energy: seeks to understand and inspire others.

FIGURE 1.2 Personality Preference Profile *(Continued)*

From *People Types and Tiger Stripes,* 1993, by Gordon D. Lawrence. Used with permission. Center for Applications of Psychological Type, Gainesville, FL, p. 14.

ACTIVITY 1.3

Reflect and Share: Personality Feedback

Warning: Not for the Fainthearted!

Directions: Identify two people who know you well, preferably people who have seen you in a variety of situations. These need to be people who will not be afraid to tell you the complete truth. You and your relationships with them need to be strong enough to withstand the absolute truth or the exercise is a waste of time. Hard as it may be to do it, there are rewards for really paying attention to this.

Part A: (1) Ask each of them separately to complete Part A for you regarding some of your personality traits. Be sure to choose people who will be honest with you. (2) Complete Part A yourself, being as honest about your characteristics as you can. (3) Share and discuss your findings with each other.

Part B: (1) List your areas of strength—things that you learned about your personality that will help you to be effective as a teacher. (2) List areas of concern—things you learned about your personality that might hinder your effectiveness. (3) Describe a strategy that will help you to maintain an awareness of these personality traits and how they might impact your teaching.

Part A General Observations of __________'s Personality

1. List five (or more) words that describe his/her personality.
2. List three (or more) of his/her *best* personality traits.
3. List three (or more) of his/her most problematic personality traits.
4. Describe a situation that would bring out the best in him/her. Why?
5. Describe a situation that would bring out the worst in him/her. Why?
6. Other observations/comments.

Part B

Personality Trait	Areas of Strength	Strategy to Use to Maximize My Effectiveness
1.		
2.		
3.		

Personality Trait	Areas of Concern	Strategy to Address
1.		
2.		
3.		

When you have completed the sheet, take time to share openly what you see. Remember to keep an open mind and to be receptive! The comments may feel like criticism but this person is trying to help you. If you are working with an honest person, you may hear more than you ever wanted to know about yourself. Remember, it's nothing compared to the feedback about yourself that you will inevitably get from your students!

effectiveness as educators whereas negative attitudes will impact the students and their learning in an unproductive way.

Your attitudes become a part of everything you do and say and secondary students will become aware of your attitudes very quickly, no matter how hard you try to hide them. They notice a friendly hello in the halls or a tendency to avoid eye contact. They are so sensitive to what they perceive as a teacher's attitude that it affects their entire feeling about you and the class, often more so than does what is actually said or done. When asked, students will say "She doesn't like me," or "He only believes the smart students are worth talking to," or "She doesn't like jocks." It doesn't matter whether students are correct in their assessment; they believe it and their responses to you and to your class are based on their perceptions.

Research clearly indicates that teachers' effectiveness is directly related to the teachers' views of themselves, their students, and their profession (Edwards, Green, & Lyons, 1996). The best way to deal with your attitudes is to first be aware of what some of them are (see Activity 1.4).

Activity 1.4

Personal Attitude Inventory

Directions: The following are some indications of attitudes that you might take into your classroom as you begin teaching. Indicate on the checklist below the extent to which you agree or disagree with the following statements about yourself.

Your attitude about yourself	**Agree**	**Neither agree nor disagree**	**Disagree**
1. I will be a good teacher.	✓		
2. I am a competent person.	✓		
3. I have never attempted anything I haven't been able to do.	✓		
4. I am a successful person.	✓		
5. I am strong.	✓		
6. I am creative.	✓		

Your attitude about students	**Agree**	**Neither agree nor disagree**	**Disagree**
1. Students are motivated to learn.	✓		
2. Students want to work hard.		✓	
3. Students want fun teachers.	✓		
4. Students will take advantage of "nice" teachers.			✓
5. Students need structure and rules.	✓		
6. Students will do anything for a grade.			✓

(Continued)

Your attitude toward parents	Agree	Neither agree nor disagree	Disagree
1. Parents are supportive of teachers.			
2. Parents want their children happy, no matter what.			
3. Parents do not understand schools.			
4. Parents put too much pressure on their children for grades.			
5. Parents are demanding.			
6. Parents are uninvolved with their children's education.			

Your attitude toward your subject matter	Agree	Neither agree nor disagree	Disagree
1. I know the pertinent content I will be teaching.			
2. My subject is the most important one my students will take.			
3. There is not enough time allotted for my subject.			
4. I read widely about my content area on my own.			
5. I hope that I don't have to teach this subject again.			
6. I usually have to explain to others why my subject is important.			

As you considered these statements, did you begin to see some patterns emerge in certain areas? For example, consider your responses in the section "Your attitude toward your subject matter." What could you say about your attitude toward your own teaching assignment this year if (a) you hope you don't have to teach this content again, (b) you think it is not that important to the students anyway, and (c) you have never read much about this content? Do you think that these attitudes will be apparent to your students? How would you describe your attitude relative to *all four* categories listed above? Can any of your attitudes get in the way of your being an effective teacher? List ways you will keep them from interfering with the effective job you want to do.

Your Expectations: What Do You Think Being a Teacher Will Be Like?

What You Can Realistically Expect from the Profession

Most people who enter the teaching profession have very strong opinions about what good teaching is. Because every citizen in our country has been required by law to be exposed to schools, almost everyone is a self-described expert on what needs to be done in the classroom. As the teacher at the beginning of this chapter said, "How hard could it be?" But as anyone who has spent much time in schools can tell you, teaching is much more complicated than it looks.

Most people entering the profession bring with them not only their own experiences, but images from movies and television. Inspirational teachers routinely are put on pedestals because they change students' lives forever. The exciting news is that in real life, this is often true. This is one of the few professions in which you actually can have the kind of impact on someone's life that you dream of having. It is unrealistic, however, to enter a classroom fresh from a viewing of *Dead Poets Society, Lean on Me,* or an episode of the television show *Boston Public* and think that's what it's going to be like every day. Radical changes can and do happen, but just as a family physician may save the life of a patient in his office, many of his days are spent giving physicals and dispensing antibiotics.

Likewise, most of what a teacher does every day is routine. For every student who says, "Yes! I've got it! Thank you!" you will have 10 students who want to know if this assignment is "for a grade." Often, new teachers expect that they are going to be able to create the most perfect, stimulating lessons possible every day. They envision poignant one-on-one conversations with students after class in which they will explore some idea inspired by the lesson with an adoring teenager who will hang on their every word. Teachers seek these highs every day, and when they occur, it is magic. But most of the time you will be answering questions about the homework that was due the day before or a missed test. That's OK—that's what you do for a living and most of what you will do is mundane. Every day and each encounter don't have to be inspiring to be valuable.

New teachers also usually expect that there will be a community of colleagues in their field who will be a constant source of stimulation and support and from whom they can learn. This is a realistic expectation. It does happen quite frequently. Teachers often make and maintain lifelong friendships with their colleagues, even after they change schools or move out of town. Teachers know that their profession is not an exact science. What works for one group may not work for another. They use everything and everyone to find suggestions about how to tackle a difficult concept, a reluctant student, or an unreasonable parent. Most people in this profession are happy to share their time, their ideas, and their resources with colleagues. Everyone has the same objective: to help students succeed. You will find this profession to be one of team players.

You may find yourself reluctant to ask other teachers for ideas or help. You are not alone. Sometimes it may be a matter of not having the time. Other times it may be your pride or not knowing whom to ask. Forget those excuses. Teachers love to talk about what they do. There is a wealth of assistance down the hall and countless ideas next door you can borrow. Go ahead—ask! Don't feel embarrassed. Next week, the teacher next door will be coming to you!

REALITY CHECK 1.4

Rather than embrace the profession as it is, some new teachers come expecting to rescue it—they have heard the profession is in deep trouble and needs to be saved. There has been so much negative media attention that it is not surprising that many have the impression that teachers are failing to educate anyone. Teachers know that society doesn't treat the profession with the respect it deserves, and they live with that reality every day. Ironically, some of them don't even respect the profession themselves, agreeing to some extent with people who say "those who can, do, and those who can't, teach." Often, teachers add to these perceptions by talking freely about the aspects of their jobs that cause them the most concern—most of which have nothing to do with the process of teaching or working with the students. Such talk is rampant in teachers' lounges, often the only place available during the day for some to vent frustration. True, like all professions, this one can disappoint even the most optimistic novice. However, you can avoid this by being realistic as you begin and weighing negative comments you hear carefully before you let them affect your views.

Never forget that the public schools across the nation vary widely in terms of what they are able to provide for students. Obviously, the wealthier communities have the latest technology and well-funded programs as well as the personnel and volunteer pool to ensure their students' success. Other schools are severely underfunded and operate daily with broken windows and poor heating systems. They invariably have an overworked staff, limited resources, and few opportunities for enrichment (Kozol, 1991). Many in these situations feel that they have traded their dream of teaching for a reality of social work.

The following are some things you will find if you teach in a public school in the United States:

- You can expect that the condition of your school and the quality of the personnel will reflect the economic level of the community.
- You can expect that, in spite of what you have read and no matter where you teach, most schools have teachers, administrators, and staff who love students and are working very hard to do a good job for them. In some situations, this is true in spite of inadequate funding.

- You can expect a profession that is filled with opportunities for your own intellectual and personal growth.
- You can expect that, especially in today's economy, there is rarely enough money in the staff development budget to support your own continued professional enrichment activities such as attending conferences and so forth. This situation is improving in many places, however.
- You can expect to meet a plethora of state, local, and national standards before your state will issue a teaching license to you.
- You can expect that your teaching license must be current in accordance with the local and state guidelines where you teach. This may mean additional hours of college credit or the equivalent in related activities such as staff development programs.
- You can expect that you are entering a profession that represents a giant bureaucracy. Public schools are government agencies that have numerous guidelines and procedures that you will be expected to know about and to comply with.
- You can expect to be entering one of the most noble professions that exists.

REALITY CHECK 1.5

If you are like most beginning teachers, you will not take the time to find these guideline books and to read them. Mistake! There is good information for you that will help you to understand the environment in which you work, the expectations your employers have for you, and where in the school and school system you can find human and other resources. Some schools have a thorough orientation period where you will review the contents of such documents, and may provide them online. Others have nothing in this regard. Take the initiative yourself. You will be glad you did.

Specific professional expectations will vary. It is important for you to become knowledgeable about what is expected from you as a teacher in your particular school district. It is also true that some systems are more diligent than others in terms of educating their new employees about expectations. Regardless, you will still be expected to know what you are to do. Protect yourself. Ask questions and read teachers' manuals and guidelines from your school system and state. Begin your new career with your eyes wide open.

What You Can Realistically Expect from Your School and School System

Your school system operates as an agent of the state. Therefore, you can expect that state guidelines will be the basis of programming, procedures, and policies. Local systems do, however, have the flexibility to supplement their curriculum when funds are available and the community supports it. The state curriculum guides as well as other information are usually available at each school. If not, they will be in a central location for all teachers to use.

In addition to the many guidelines from the state and learned societies, most systems and the schools within those systems have additional and very specific guidelines for their teachers to follow. They are usually compiled into handbooks and are often distributed to new teachers at the beginning of the year. You will be expected to familiarize yourself with the contents.

How autonomous will you be? Will the administrators in your school leave you alone to teach the way you think is best? Will they serve only in an advisory capacity? In one sense, you will find that there is the opportunity to close your door and conduct your class the way you want—within certain parameters. Ultimately, the other side of that door represents several audiences to whom you must be accountable: the parents of your students, the guidelines of the state and local school system, and, most directly, the administration in your own building. The research is contradictory when examining how all of that translates into real autonomy, and it also depends on how you define autonomy. This is predictable when you consider the different assumptions and priorities of both teachers and administrators, all of whom function in a top-down bureaucracy (Ingersoll, 1994). Clearly the principal who is concerned about getting everyone out on the football field for a required monthly fire drill during fifth period sees things differently from the teacher who is trying to give her class an important test.

However, at the very least, Cox (1995) suggested that teachers and administrators in many schools are merging their interests and responsibilities on a regular basis. Now, more than ever, closing that door and dealing in a world of your own with only your students is a fantasy from the past. Increasingly, teachers are being asked to assume roles as leaders in their schools. Educators agree that teachers must be the central element in school reform and must take the primary responsibility for creating better ways for students to learn (Lambert, Collay, Deitz, Kent, & Richert, 1997). During the next decades, your school system will be encouraging you to take on the additional role of school reformer. You'll be asked to expand your skills and help to solve the larger problems your school system faces. Some systems are more progressive in this arena than others, of course. Linda Darling-Hammond (1997) reported that, although schools are asking teachers to design new educational goals and take the lead in reform, many teachers don't know how to do this and do not get the support they need to make this happen.

Your school system will also expect you to be a positive role model for your students and to conduct yourself in an appropriate manner at all times. Teachers are judged by public opinion, and this is a conservative field. It may seem unfair that you must be more careful than the local banker about where you do certain things on your own time—and it is. Have you ever noticed that when that banker is arrested for driving under the influence, it is not in the newspaper? When a teacher is arrested, it is front-page news. Of course, you are *legally* allowed to do many things on your own time that some of the parents of your students would rather their children's teacher not do. You also have rights regarding academic freedom. And although your school system can't legally fire you for conducting yourself in an imprudent manner, you may be viewed as a problem by many parents as well as school administrators. It is wise to pick your battles carefully. Your overall success as a teacher can be compromised if you decide that your personal life is simply no one's business but yours.

What You Can Realistically Expect from Your Students

Students, like all human beings, are complex individuals. This is especially true for teenagers. They are at a difficult time in their own development. In short, they are so often confused about who they are that they must constantly challenge who *you* are as they sort things out. One minute they sound as if they have truly become adults, rationally articulating coherent and insightful arguments about the subject at hand or the world situation. The next minute, they are emotional and immature, screaming that you and every other adult they know is unfair. Thus, it is best to be prepared for almost anything as you attempt to work with these young people.

Generally speaking, you can expect some of the following to be true of most adolescents you will be dealing with.

- They are smart. Their generation has been showered with luxuries and state-of-the-art entertainment, which has resulted in an impressive level of perception about the world. Don't let this fool you. While they may know the intricacies of programming elaborate computer data for games, they are still young people who have a lot to learn. They need to face the challenges of growing up—let alone all you have to teach them about language arts or algebra.
- They have become harder to educate. Because they have been exposed to many things, it will not be easy to impress them. You'll lose them with an uninspired lecture. This is primarily for two reasons. First, they hold adults in less awe than previous generations did and are more honest in saying so. Your words, especially if they think there are too many of them, are not necessarily perceived as pearls of wisdom. Second, they are used to things coming to them at a rapid pace and in an entertaining manner (Sousa, 1998). After all, this is the generation that is used to seeing life crises described, addressed, and solved in 30-minute television shows. They like drive-through service. They are also increasingly dependent on external sources for stimulation, and they want instant gratification from these sources. It's no wonder they complain that school is "boring" (Heath, 1994).

But learning isn't always quick—it takes time. By the time they get to you in secondary school, especially high school, where the content has become more complicated, many of their teachers will have tirelessly worked for years to make this process "fun." At this point, these students are realizing that for many classes (hopefully yours), they must actually *study.* Some will even like it!

- They want teachers who are people they can look up to and respect. The old advice not to smile till Christmas isn't totally wrong-headed. They want friendly teachers but ones who will hold the line and not allow them to get away with too much. This doesn't mean that you can't be responsive. By all means you should be. But they don't need you as a friend—they already have friends. Instead, they need someone to admire, a role model, a guide. Rather than trying to be their friend, help them to make friends. Remember the three Fs: be *f*air, *f*irm, and *f*riendly.
- They want you to be very knowledgeable about your subject. They are looking for challenge, no matter what level they are on at the time.
- They expect you to want them to succeed and to help them to do so. This will probably mean extra time one-on-one with someone who is having a problem—during lunch, before school, after school. You'll get used to that.
- They expect you to care. There is an old saying that is very true: "Students don't care how much you know until they know how much you care." You can show that you care without becoming someone who takes on too many of the students' responsibilities for their problems. Students also see how much you care when you attend after-school functions and sporting events. When they see you in the stands, they know that this is a choice for you to be there. It means even more that you took the time to show interest in them as people – not just as students in science class. Theodore Sizer (1996) said that teachers should "practice caring rigor and rigorous caring" (p. 96).

REALITY CHECK 1.6

It is natural to face a group of adolescents and assume that they are you, just a few years younger. Unless you are in your early twenties, they are not. Things change rapidly in the world and after only a few years out of college, you may find yourself saying, "I feel so old!" Don't assume that the secondary experience of today's students means that the schools and standards are going downhill. Give students credit for negotiating their world at least as well as you negotiated yours. Teenagers have always been interesting and complex. They still are—that much hasn't changed.

Expectations of You: How Do Professional Standards Affect Your Development as a Teacher?

Like most other professions, the field of education is guided by standards. *No matter where you teach, you will be expected to know and to demonstrate competency in meeting certain standards.* You will be expected to know what the standards are and to comply with them. There are usually two levels of standards. First, there are those that inform the general practice of teaching, ones that would apply to all content areas. Second there are content-specific standards that relate to your specific discipline (to be addressed in Chapter 6). All of these standards reflect what your state and your local school system have determined are necessary skills to be an effective teacher.

The standards that inform the general best practice in teaching and that will be of most use to you at this point are the INTASC core principles. The Interstate New Teacher Assessment and Support Consortium (INTASC) is a consortium of state education agencies and national organizations dedicated to the preparation and professional development of teachers. These standards represent what all beginning teachers should know, be like, and be able to do if they are to be effective teachers, regardless of their particular subject or grade taught. These standards inform how teacher education programs and professional development are implemented. These core principles are as follows:

Standard 1: Content Pedagogy. The teacher understands the central concepts, tools of and structures of the discipline(s) he or she teaches and can create learning experiences that make these aspects of subject matter meaningful for students.

Standard 2: Student Development. The teacher understands how children learn and develop, and can provide learning opportunities that support their intellectual, social and personal development.

Standard 3: Diverse Learners. The teacher understands how students differ in their approaches to learning and creates instructional opportunities that are adapted to diverse learners.

Standard 4: Critical Thinking. The teacher understands and uses a variety of instructional strategies to encourage students' development of critical thinking, problem solving, and performance skills.

Standard 5: Motivation and Management. The teacher uses an understanding of individual and group motivation and behavior to create a learning environment that encourages positive social interaction, active engagement in learning and self-motivation.

Standard 6: Communication and Technology. The teacher uses knowledge of effective verbal, nonverbal, and media communication techniques to foster active inquiry, collaboration, and supportive interaction in the classroom.

Standard 7: Planning. The teacher plans instruction based upon knowledge of subject matter, students, the community, and curriculum goals.

Standard 8: Assessment. The teacher understands and uses formal and informal assessment strategies to evaluate and ensure the continuous intellectual, social, and physical development of the learner.

Standard 9: Professional Development. The teacher is a reflective practitioner who continually evaluates the effects of his/her choices and actions on others (students, parents, and other professionals in the learning community) and who actively seeks out opportunities to grow professionally.

Standard 10: School and Community Involvement. The teacher fosters relationships with school colleagues, parents, and agencies in the larger community to support students' learning and well-being.

Source: The Interstate New Teacher Assessment and Support Consortium standards were developed by the Council of Chief State School Officers and member states. Copies may be downloaded from the council's web site at www.ccsso.org

Which of these areas represent the most challenge for you now?

Your Philosophical Approach: What Do You Believe About Students and Teaching?

A wise person once said, "We see the world not as it is, but as *we* are." Our thoughts about the world and our views about how things work in life are the very core of what we are about. Like our attitudes, these basic beliefs shape us and are reflected in the way we respond to everything. As teachers, what we truly believe about students, learning, and the entire process of teaching comes through with each assignment we make; every lesson we prepare; and every interaction we have with students, parents, and peers.

Clearly, every individual has his or her unique take on the world, and the philosophical underpinnings we each have are the result of our own experiences and backgrounds. Our particular approaches to the world naturally affect our teaching, just as they would affect any profession we choose. Understanding our own philosophical orientations as well as the philosophical orientations of those around us who think differently helps us to see other points of view in situations. In education, this is a necessity.

There are as many philosophies as there are human beings; any attempt to group them into defined categories with complete accuracy is futile. But the exercise of exploring some of the most common predispositions is useful as we try to understand our own perspectives.

Even though we recognize the uniqueness of every person's philosophy, research and trends over time reveal that there are several general prevailing philosophical approaches to teaching that are evident today. Four will be discussed briefly here. They can serve as broad benchmarks from which we can refine and understand our own views. Before discussing them, it will be useful for you to examine some of your own philosophical notions in Activity 1.5.

Where do you stand? Look at the five groups and see where you have the most circles. If you are like most people, you have circled items in several categories, which means you have an eclectic philosophical approach.

Before you read a brief description of the basic tenets of these categories, determine which group(s) are most compatible with how you feel today. Keep in mind, you may and probably will alter your view with time and experience. For now, label the categories as follows:

Group A	Progressive
Group B	Educational Conservatist
Group C	Social Reconstructionist
Group D	Educational Humanist
Group E	Vocationalist

Brief Descriptions of Prevailing Philosophical Approaches to Teaching

There are really four basic schools of thought (with many subsets) that represent the predominant philosophical approaches to teaching today (Lucas, 1984). They are educational conservatism, educational humanism and progressivism (combined), vocationalism, and social reconstructionism. To understand some of the characteristics and the fundamental differences of the respective schools of thought, we will consider each one briefly in its purest form. Remember that it is rare to see any one philosophical approach that does not have some traits of other approaches. Most philosophies, like most people, are combinations of several orientations. Therefore, as with all philosophical ideas, there are many variations of each type, and many people find that no one descriptor sums them up accurately. There are also many approaches not addressed here at all. It will be to your advantage to seek opportunities to learn more about the various philosophies of education. You may be thinking, "What does this have to do with how to teach?" The simple answer is, *everything*! While it may appear on the surface not to have any direct bearing on your teaching, the truth is that it does—in more ways than you know.

Remember, no one of these or any other philosophy or approach is "bad" or "good." All have particular characteristics that simply represent a person's predisposition. Understand something about them, and not only will you be able to work with people whose ideas may seem like they are from another planet, but you may learn to see things differently yourself in the process.

Educational Conservatism

The fundamental ideas of educational conservatism are based on the premise that the school plays a key role in preserving the culture of the past and in transmitting it to future generations. (The term *educational conservatism* should not be confused with political conservatism.) Educational conservatists contend that there are some facts, concepts, and values that are essential for everyone to know, no matter what he or she chooses to do in life. The curriculum should consist minimally of an emphasis on basic academic skills that all students should master, regardless of interest. Instruction is content centered. Teachers have certain knowledge that they must impart and that students must master.

There are related approaches that are subsets of educational conservatism as well. Essentialists such as William Bagley in the 1930s stated that it is the conservative function of education that is most significant during times of change. Teachers should have as their

Activity 1.5

Determining Your Own Philosophical Approach

Directions: You are beginning your career with some ideas and assumptions about education as a field and the process of teaching and learning. Read the following statements and circle all the statements in each group with which you agree.

Group A

1. Education should be active and related to the interests of the student.
2. Learning through problem solving should replace focusing on subject matter.
3. Education should be life itself rather than a preparation for living.
4. The teacher's role is not to direct but to advise.
5. The school should encourage cooperation rather than competition.
6. Only democracy permits and encourages the free exchange of ideas, which is necessary for real development.

Group B

1. Learning, by its very nature, involves hard work and often reluctant effort on the part of the students.
2. The initiative in education should lie with the teacher rather than the student, because the student needs the guidance and control of adults if he or she is to realize maximum potential.
3. The heart of the educational process is the absorption of prescribed subject matter.
4. The school should retain traditional methods of mental discipline.

Group C

1. The main purpose of education is to assist in social reform.
2. Educators should be committed to helping students see themselves as proactive members of society.

3. The way of the future is for all societies to be genuinely democratic.
4. Teachers should persuade students in a democratic way to see the need for reform in our society.
5. The means and ends of education must be reorganized with respect to the findings of research.
6. The child, the school, and education itself are shaped largely by social and cultural forces.

Group D

1. The basic goal of education should be to promote each individual's self-development—moral, spiritual, emotional, and intellectual.
2. Schools should not infringe on the rights of each person as an individual.
3. Not everyone needs to acquire the exact same skills, values, competencies, or knowledge.
4. The most valuable ends of learning are those that have been freely chosen by those involved.

Group E

1. Education should provide every high school graduate with a marketable skill and assured entry into further training.
2. Students who left school prior to graduation should get equivalent experience provided by the public schools.
3. Schools should offer career education orientation, with subsequent guidance, counseling, and placement services to all students at all levels.
4. The goal of education should be the replacement of traditional general education with career education.

primary purpose providing the time-tested classic knowledge that has been proven to be important over the long haul. Many of the traditional approaches embody the ideas of the educational conservatists.

The following characteristics are evident in schools where educational-conservatist ideology is the foundation:

1. Teacher-centered instruction
2. Rigorous academic instruction
3. Traditional teaching methodology (such as drill and Socratic discussions of important books other than textbooks)
4. Self-contained classrooms
5. Strict discipline, sometimes with corporal punishment
6. Dress codes
7. Frequent homework
8. Competency-based assessment and evaluation

Educational Humanism/Progressivism

Not to be confused with the term *secular humanism*, educational humanism (root word *humane*) is based on the needs of the person. It is totally child centered. The term affirms the sanctity of the individual and the importance of self-directed human development. Educational humanists believe that teaching should promote self-actualization and individualization, using methods of instruction that provide maximum freedom for self-initiated, self-directed learning. John Dewey is often referred to as the father of this school of thought. He believed that teachers were facilitators of learning and that students only truly "learn by doing." In the 1970s, the term *open education* became more prevalent. An extreme example of this was Summerhill in England, which was a complete form of open education. The students chose their own curriculum and decided where, when, and even if they wanted to study. Instruction took place in small groups or one-on-one. Thus, learning was intensely personal.

The term *progressivism* is closely linked with educational humanism. It originated as more of a social movement that fostered such initiatives as the kindergarten in the early part of this century. Francis Parker, who stated that the true purpose of education is the development of the human being, and William Kilpatrick, who was the organizer of the "project method," were progressives. As with John Dewey, their emphasis on hands-on methodology is key. The teacher is a guide.

Constructivism is a current approach that is rooted in the ideas of educational humanism and the belief that children and their needs are at the center of all instruction. Constructivism is not so much a theory about teaching as a theory about knowledge and learning. It represents a synthesis of cognitive psychology, philosophy, and anthropology. Constructivism defines knowledge as temporary, developmental, and socially and culturally influenced. Constructivists, therefore, maintain that knowledge cannot be objective. These classrooms are based on problem-solving and hands-on activities—working with concepts already known to create new constructs. Increasingly, these teachers are creating a new context for learning where the students are central to instruction (Lambert, Collay, Deitz, Kent, & Richert, 1997).

We see the following characteristics in schools where humanist principles are paramount:

1. Child-centered instruction
2. Learning situations that are organized mutually by the teacher and the learner
3. A nurturing and supportive learning climate
4. Emphasis on developing a genuine concern and respect for the worth of others

5. A school program that is experience centered
6. Student involvement in the evaluation process
7. Multiple learning options for students
8. Teaching and learning focus on the students' real concerns

Vocationalism

Those who are advocates of vocationalism suggest that the most important purpose for education is to prepare students for the world of work. The overall goal is to ensure that young people have useful skills and the ability to make a living and to serve the needs of society. This was an understood need long before we had our current system of schooling. For centuries, apprenticeships were the primary method of instruction. Young people worked side by side with those who had mastered a craft, and learned by watching and then doing under the direct supervision of someone who could show them how.

The vocationalist approach has its roots early in this century when many business leaders believed that full-scale industrial education should be introduced into schools. In 1906, the National Society for the Promotion of Industrial Education (NSPIE) was founded. The purpose was to promote the establishment of institutions for industrial training and to influence the public schools to assume a major responsibility for job preparation. Charles A. Prosser, the executive secretary of the NSPIE, saw the primary role of schools as to prepare children for useful service. As time went on, the comprehensive high school offered a compromise with vocational preparation as a part of the prescribed course of study. Today it represents an important element of the curriculum.

The following fundamental principles are the roots of vocationalism:

1. Coursework is practical in nature.
2. Vocational education should enjoy equal status with academic education.
3. Vocational education must be integrated with academic education.
4. The curriculum offers exploratory and advanced vocational courses.
5. Teachers have expertise in the trade and the skill areas they teach.

Social Reconstructionism

Social reconstructionism is education for human survival. Many say that formal education should be above politics and that schools should avoid divisive issues. However, social reconstructionists believe that at no time have schools been isolated from current trends in society. Thus, schools should perform the social service of helping students to learn to resolve monumental issues. In some ways, schools practice this philosophy all the time. There were increased numbers of fatalities on our highways, so the schools began to have driver's education classes. Concerns about teenage pregnancy resulted in classes on sex education. Business and industry contribute "free" materials to schools every day with obvious agendas. It makes sense to many to use the schools this way. After all, you have young, impressionable people assembled en masse and exposed to information. What students learn in schools has a direct impact on society. Therefore, schools have the potential for helping to bring about social change.

There have been many advocates of this philosophy during this century. George Counts (1969) claimed in the 1930s that the schools were in the grip of reactionaries and that educators needed to face social issues. He felt that apathy was the real problem. Likewise, Harold Rugg (1933) said that schools are not "forward-thinking" and are obsessed by the halo of the past. He advocated a curriculum that would arise out of the problems and issues that directly affect society. John Childs (1956) went even further. He stated that schools should not serve the current social order. Instead of teaching students *how* to think, he said they needed to teach them *what* to think.

Later in this century, we have seen new phases of social reconstructionism, many preferring the term *futurism.* Alvin Toffler's *Future Shock* (1970) promised a more detailed agenda as he recommended that the role of education should be to serve as an adaptive mechanism for the social system and for the individuals within it. He and many others agreed that it is a hard thing to shift education into the future tense but that a failure to do so could be disastrous.

The following are some of the basic components of the social reconstructionist approach:

1. Courses devoted to war and peace, leisure, ecology, and social planning
2. Open discussions that invite students to share ideas
3. Problem-based curriculum

The philosophical orientation people have becomes very clear when they are trying to work together and agree on a project. A beginning middle school teacher once remarked how striking the different perspectives were when she attended her first Parent Teacher Student Association (PTSA) executive meeting as a faculty representative. Two of the officers were clearly educational conservatists, another was an educational humanist/progressive, and the fourth was an ardent social reconstructionist. They were involved in a discussion of how to spend money from the latest fundraiser. The educational conservatists argued strongly for a structured supplementary reading program for the entire school that would culminate in formal debates about key ideas. The money would be spent for the books, and a committee of teachers and parents could design the format for everyone. "This will raise the test scores because it will help all of our students read more critically," one said. The educational humanist wanted to let the student government decide. "This is their project—they worked for it and should have the last word on how the money is spent." The social reconstructionist wanted to organize a community campaign for the homeless, using the proceeds as seed money. He stated, "When are these students ever going to become socially conscious if we don't encourage their involvement in community as part of their education?" People's philosophical foundations may not be as clear in all settings as they were in this one. But being aware of where others are coming from will help you to understand their motivation better.

Developing and Refining Your Philosophical Orientation

Developing a focused description of your educational philosophy is about as easy as describing in twenty-five words or less your philosophy of life. Many teachers go their entire careers without ever asking themselves what they truly believe. It is true, however, that teachers who can articulate some of their beliefs are more intentional about the work they do with students and are more effective. As you are starting your career, take this opportunity to name and claim what you think about schools, teaching, and students (see Activity 1.6).

Developing Your Philosophical Approach

List 10 things that you believe at this point about schools, teaching, and students. Keep the list and at the end of this book, refine it, making adjustments and additions where needed. During the school year, at the end of each quarter, refine the list again. At the end of the year, organize your thoughts into a coherent statement of your philosophy. Find a colleague to discuss it with and ask for feedback.

Your Concerns: What Should You Keep in Mind as You Begin?

Before you begin to prepare for this new adventure, take a deep breath. Think about what you know about yourself as well as why you are going into teaching in the first place. What are some of your attitudes toward teaching, students, parents, and the process of instruction? What is your role, your purpose, as you work with these students at the most difficult time in their development?

You will have more to deal with than you can possibly imagine when you begin school. Most people will find the number of details overwhelming if they do not focus carefully on taking one step at a time. As one beginning teacher put it, "I don't know what I don't know yet." A first-year teacher once shared that his system provided a week of preparation and staff development days prior to the arrival of the students. Although he had been through student teaching and knew something of what to expect, he found that after gathering his textbooks and planning his first day, he just sat in his room for the rest of the week, not really knowing where to begin. One week into the semester, he realized how much there was to do and longed to have just one of those days back to catch up. When you have read this book, hopefully you will have many ideas of what you need to be doing to prepare for that first day with the students.

In the meantime, there are some things you will want to keep in mind as you begin to think about your first year.

Recognizing Your Limitations

No matter how excited you are about all the things you are going to do with your students this year, there are some important things you need to remember.

You are not superhuman. You will undoubtedly have more things that you want to do than you have time for, more ideas for lessons than hours to prepare them in, and more students than you can properly give attention to. There are only 24 hours in a day, and you will need to learn early about the basics of time management. Often, new teachers find themselves spending every waking hour at school or at home thinking about school. And at the beginning of the year—until you get things under control—this may be necessary. However, for the long run, this is a mistake. Your students need, as much as anything else, a balanced person who has a life outside the classroom. You will be able to give them more and better attention if you are rested and have had a good weekend.

You will not be able to reach every student. That's not to say that you shouldn't try. The very nature of teaching is heavily dependent on the nature of the relationship that you have (or don't have) with your students. It is unreasonable to expect that any person would have a completely comfortable and rewarding relationship with every other person. Teachers often feel that they must be all things to all people. And to some extent, it is your job to try to be. Talk to other teachers to get information and ideas you otherwise have not considered. But don't hold yourself responsible for total success with every student.

You will not be able to solve every problem. Most schools have numerous resource people either on-site or within reach by phone. Learn early where to go for help. When students want to confide in you, it will be flattering and your helper tendencies will kick in. It will be tempting to listen for hours to a student who is a victim of abuse or who is pregnant, but unless you have special training to do so, you are not the person who should be counseling this student. Refer him or her to the proper personnel who have the resources to provide focused, serious help.

No matter how hard you worked on a lesson or how long you spent searching for the perfect video or the most exciting resource, some lessons will simply not be successful. And there will always be a reason. Maybe the class's attention is on that week's big football game; perhaps you didn't realize they had not had some necessary background information before you could cover this material. It doesn't matter. It happens to everyone. Your job is to reflect on why things went the way they did and do better next time.

Managing Stress

Stress can be defined as anything that causes your body to react physically or psychologically. Stress by itself is neither good nor bad—the key is how you respond to stressors in your life. Bad stress usually arises when we feel out of control. Subtle pressures build up and can overwhelm us. Over time, we can become so stressed out that we are unable to function well or at all. Good stress, on the other hand, may provide us with just enough adrenaline to see the same situation that caused bad stress as a challenge. In the field of education, there will be numerous opportunities for stress to play a factor in your day. Thus, it is critical to pay attention to stress and note when, why, and how it is affecting you (see Activity 1.7).

While many of these findings will come as no surprise to you, you may find the following thoughts on teacher stress interesting. Consider as you read how these facts apply to you.

1. Those with moderate numbers of students experience less stress than those with large class loads.
2. The older the teacher, the less the stress.
3. The more experienced the teacher, the less the stress.
4. Females experience more stress than males. This is in large part because they are less able to depersonalize than males are.
5. Elementary teachers experience less stress than secondary teachers, and they generally feel more accomplished.
6. Those who have a solid personal life that is most important to them are less stressed than those who focus totally on their jobs. (This will depend, of course, on the quality of their personal life.)
7. Those whose higher order needs (social, self-actualization, etc.) are met at school are less stressed at work than those whose needs are not met at school.
8. Those who experience a lot of peer support experience significantly less stress.
9. Those who experience a lot of administrative support experience significantly less stress.

Reality Check 1.7

Except in unusual circumstances, notice that almost *half* of these findings will apply to you (items 1, 2, 3, and 5). The other half might also apply to you, depending on your school and personal situation. This is a major wake-up call. It doesn't have to mean that you will be completely stressed all the time, but there are definitely external factors that suggest you will need to learn to deal with stress.

Activity 1.7

Self-Appraisal: How Does Stress Affect You?

Directions: Answer "yes," "no," or "sometimes" to each of the following. Although your responses may vary depending on the situation and circumstances at the time, try to determine which response is usually true for you.

1. I am organized.
2. I don't procrastinate.
3. I choose my friends carefully.
4. I take care of myself physically.
5. I eat the right foods.

(Continued)

6. I exercise regularly.
7. I get enough sleep.
8. I develop good plans to deal with my life.
9. I am aware of my strengths and weaknesses.
10. I don't say yes to everything that comes up.
11. I have good routines.
12. I have a good sense of humor.
13. I express myself when I am upset.
14. I am flexible.
15. I don't try to do everything myself. I will ask for help.
16. I seek spiritual nourishment.
17. I actively work to improve myself.
18. I know how to slow down.
19. I am good at making decisions.
20. I stand up for myself when I feel I am being mistreated.

Count how many items you responded "yes" to. Decide if you think you have enough of them to be able to respond well to potential factors that can result in bad stress. If at least half of your responses are not "yes," you need to look carefully at how you are managing certain potential problems in your life as a teacher.

Take time to consider potential stressors in your life as you begin teaching. What will be your plan to manage those issues?

Make a list of potential stressors with corresponding management strategies.

Pay careful attention to which stressors you indicated could be problematic. Remember that, right now, before the school year has swept you into a frenzy, they may seem manageable. Keep your list in front of you as the year progresses, noting how you said you would handle the various items on it. And then do so.

TIPS from the TRENCHES

The following are suggestions beginning teachers say they wish they had when they began teaching. Consider them as you think about your role as a secondary teacher.

1. *Be patient*—especially with yourself as you are learning about your students and about teaching.

2. Expect that your students will be curious and interested in your personal life. They will bombard you with a variety of questions, such as where you live, what you like to do on the weekends, and whom you date. Usually, the younger you are, the more interested they are in these things.

3. *Dress professionally.* The students notice what you have on more than what you are saying, especially if you are a woman. Too many teachers dress as if they were working in the yard. Respect yourself, your students, and the job you are doing by paying attention to your appearance. Unless there is a special occasion that warrants it, never wear jeans.

(Continued)

4. *Listen to your students.* Don't assume your students will learn the way you learned, think the way you thought when you were their age, or believe what you believed when you were a secondary school student. Some things never change with time, but many other things do. You'll never really know what's real in their lives unless you hear them when they speak.

5. *Project a positive attitude as much of the time as possible, regardless of how you feel.* Yes, it can be faked. Practice. You don't have to keep a perpetual smile on your face, but a pleasant demeanor will go far with students as they try to decide how approachable you are.

6. *Work harder with those students to whom you are not particularly drawn.* Spend more time trying to understand them and their personalities than with those it is easy to be with and to teach. These students are your biggest challenges and most likely need your help the most. It's not always easy, but it's your job.

7. *Keep an open mind about* everything *related to this profession.*

PRAXIS™

Overview

Most states require the Praxis Series tests as part of their teacher licensure process. The tests are part of an Educational Testing Service (ETS) program that is also used by colleges and universities to qualify individuals for entry into teacher education programs. There are three levels of assessments: ones designed for (a) when you enter a college-level program, (b) when you complete your college program, and (c) when you enter the field and your first year of teaching. You will need to find out from your local school system licensure representative and your state department which tests (if any) you will need to take.

Praxis I: Academic Skills Assessments are designed to be taken early in your career to measure your reading, writing, mathematical, and listening skills. The Reading and Writing tests are available in two formats. The paper-based Pre-Professional Skills Tests (PPST) are 1-hour multiple-choice tests. The Writing test includes both a 30-minute multiple-choice and a 30-minute essay section. The Praxis I Computer-Based Tests (PI-CBT) in Reading, Writing, and Mathematics have computer-delivered questions that require selecting single or multiple responses, highlighting or reorganizing information, or providing constructed response (essay). Each test session is two hours long to allow sufficient time for tutorials on computer use, the test itself, and the collection of background information for score reporting. The Listening Skills Test is a 1-hour test with multiple-choice questions based on recorded segments. See the *Registration Bulletin: Your Guide for Registering for the Praxis Series* for detailed information about these tests.

Praxis II: Subject Assessments measure your knowledge of the subjects you will teach. They include (a) Subject Assessments/Specialty Area Tests that test your general and subject-specific pedagogical skills and knowledge; (b) Multiple Subjects Assessment for Teachers (MSAT), which was developed jointly by ETS and the California Commission on Teacher Credentialing; and (c) Principles of Learning and Teaching (PLT) tests, which use a case study approach to measure your general teaching knowledge at three grade levels: K–6, 5–9 and 7–12—one of which you will probably take, depending on your area of assignment. The tests feature constructed-response (essay) and multiple-choice items.

Praxis III: Classroom Performance Assessments are used to evaluate all aspects of a beginning teacher's performance in the classroom. These assessments are conducted in the teacher's own classroom by local trained observers who use a set of consistent, reliable, and nationally validated criteria. These assessments are usually administered during the first year of teaching.

More than likely, if you have a college degree and are working on licensure, most colleges will waive the Praxis I requirement. However, the chances are very good that if you are in a state that requires the Praxis Tests, you will be required to take and pass the Subject Assessment Tests. ETS provides a Web site with all current, pertinent information regarding these tests. *Test-at-a-Glance* booklets are also available without charge to help you prepare for Praxis I and Praxis II assessments. The booklets are grouped by subject area, and their main purpose is to familiarize you with the structure and content of the test(s) you will be taking. They provide descriptions of the tests, sample questions with answers and explanations, and tips on preparing for the test. You may contact ETS for the booklets or to get more information either by calling 609-771-7395 or e-mailing praxis@ets.org.

Praxis Competencies Related to Your Role as a Secondary Teacher

Most of the specialty area tests and Praxis I will not have questions that *directly* relate to topics addressed in this chapter—your role as a secondary teacher. These tests focus more specifically on issues related to teaching practices and content addressed in later chapters in this book. However, there may be several questions that reflect these issues on the PLT test and, perhaps more indirectly, questions from your Specialty Area tests. These will be most evident in your constructed response or essay questions. These may focus on such topics as teacher self-evaluation and how understanding your own attitudes and approaches may or may not enhance instructional effectiveness. There may be questions that reflect your understanding of the need to focus your attention on interpersonal relations.

Sample Question

You have four very shy students in your fifth-period social studies class. You have decided for the next unit to assign students to cooperative learning groups to address certain issues. Each member of each group will then present a portion of the total product to the class. You have spent most of your class periods lecturing and are now concerned that this new approach, while educationally valid, may not ensure that the students will get the information you want them to have. You are also concerned that the shy students will not participate fully since they seem much more comfortable with lecture. But your supervisor has suggested that you expand your teaching methods, so you are willing to try.

1. How will you ensure that the shy students will benefit from your plan?
2. Describe three other methods you might try instead of lecture and cooperative learning.
3. Describe three ways you will ensure that the information in your unit will be covered to your satisfaction.
4. Describe two reasons that your supervisor might think that the methods should be expanded. Is the lecture method not effective? Why or why not?

Notice that this particular question requires you to consider some things about interpersonal relationships (Question #1—ensuring the success of the shy students) but also asks you to incorporate what you know about methodology. Question #3 might be answered in terms of how a teacher might plan the lesson or how a teacher's own personality reflects a preference for methods such as lecture that allow the teacher to be in "control" over each activity. In later chapters, you will see how some topics are addressed by themselves (such as classroom management and methodology) rather than in combination with other topics, as in this example.

Suggestions for Further Reading

If you have time to read only one book . . .

Jackson, A. W., & Davis, G. A. (2000). *Turning points 2000: Educating adolescents in the 21st century.* New York: Teachers College Press.

Kottler, E., & Kottler, C. J. (1998). *Secrets for secondary school teachers: How to succeed in your first year.* Thousand Oaks, CA: Corwin.

Other excellent sources . . .

Marsh, D. D., & Codding, J. B. (1999). *The new American high school.* Thousand Oaks, CA: Corwin.

Ryan, K., & Cooper, J. (1995). *Those who can, teach* (7th ed.). Boston: Houghton Mifflin.

Sizer, T. R. (1996). *Horace's hope: What works for the American high school?* Boston: Houghton Mifflin.

References

Agnes, M. (Ed.). (2000). *Webster's New World College Dictionary* (4th ed.). Cleveland, OH: IDG Books.

Canter, L. (1994). *The high performing teacher.* Santa Monica, CA: Canter Associates.

Childs, J. L. (1956). *American pragmatism and education.* New York: Holt Rinehart and Winston.

Council of Chief State School Officers. (1992). *Model standards for beginning teacher licensing assessment and development: A resource for state dialogue.* Washington, DC: Author. http://www.ccsso.org/content/pdfs/corestrd.pdf.

Counts, G. S. (1969). *Dare the schools build a new social order?* New York: Arno.

Cox, P. W. L. (1995). The teacher in the high school of the future. *Clearinghouse, 69*(2), 80–83.

Darling-Hammond, L. (1997). *Doing what matters most: Investing in quality teaching.* Kutztown, PA: National Commission on Teaching and America's Future.

Edwards, J., Green, K., & Lyons, C. (1996, April). *Teacher efficacy and school and teacher characteristics.* Paper presented at the annual meeting of the American Educational Research Association, New York, NY.

Gordon, J. A. (1993). *Why did you select teaching as a career? Teachers of color tell their stories.* Educational Resources Information Center (ERIC) Clearinghouse (ERIC Document Reproduction Service No. ED383653).

Heath, D. (1994). *Schools of hope: Developing mind and character in today's youth.* San Francisco: Jossey-Bass.

Ingersoll, R. (1994). Organizational control in secondary schools. *Harvard Educational Review, 64*(2), 15–172.

Ingersoll, R. (1999). The problem of underqualified teachers in American secondary schools. *Educational Researcher, 28*(2), 26–37.

Kozol, J. (1991). *Savage inequalities.* New York: Crown.

Lambert, L., Collay, M., Deitz, M. E., Kent, K., & Richert, A. E. (1997). *Who will save our schools? Teachers as constructivist leaders.* Thousand Oaks, CA: Corwin.

Lawrence, G. (1993). *People types and tiger stripes* (3rd ed.). Gainesville, FL: Center for Applications of Psychological Type.

Lucas, C. J. (1984). *Foundations of education: Schooling and the social order.* Upper Saddle River, NJ: Merrill/Prentice Hall.

Myers, C. B., & Myers, L. K. (1995). *The professional educator: A new introduction to teaching and schools.* Belmont, CA: Wadsworth.

Rugg, H. (1933). *The great technology.* New York: John Day.

Ryan, K., & Cooper, J. (1992). *Those who can, teach* (6th ed.). Boston: Houghton Mifflin.

Sizer, T. (1996). *Horace's hope: What works for the American high school.* Boston: Houghton Mifflin.

Sousa, D. (1998). The ramifications of brain research. *Educational Leadership, 55*(1). Alexandria, VA: ASCD.

Toffler, A. (1970). *Future Shock.* New York: Random House.

2

The School Environment

I'll never forget my first day. After spending six years behind a desk, I was leaving the "real" world to begin a career as a secondary teacher. When I arrived at 7:00 a.m., the whole building was already buzzing with activity. Students were everywhere—talking, singing, and slamming locker doors. Teachers were frantically answering questions, copying handouts, and trying to get things ready for first period. The phones in the office were ringing off the hook and guidance counselors were registering lines of nervous new students. It was exhilarating! This is the "real" world!

First-year teacher

This teacher is absolutely right—secondary schools are the "real" world. What other institution in our country is so inclusive? Rich, poor, smart, not-so-smart, motivated, disengaged—they are all there together. After high school, they may return to their own neighborhoods, their own "social classes," where most will stay for the rest of their lives. But for now, they are all one group, a microcosm of our society—a subset of the public. They work, play, fight, date, and grow up together under one roof for four years, bringing perspectives, concerns, and the many expectations they and their parents want the school to fulfill.

You teach a small segment of that public. Wouldn't it be great if the only two things you had to be aware of were the students in front of you and the lesson you have so carefully planned? It's not that simple. Dismiss any fantasies that you can close the door to your room when the bell rings and ignore events in the hall, the rest of the school, the community, or the nation as a whole. Within your own classroom, those students you face reflect influences and pressures that will affect you and your lessons in many ways. Some of those pressures are direct, some are indirect; some of these influences you can control, others you cannot. It will be important that you learn which is which. As you face the very political world of education, remember that you can make a difference with your students no matter what the conditions of your particular school climate if you understand what is influencing that climate and learn how to work within it.

This chapter will help you to understand some of the basics about the secondary school environment itself, beginning with a brief overview of the institution's development and the nature and organization of today's secondary schools. Then you will get a sense of what makes them run, how they are funded, what legal issues they (and you) face, and what makes them effective. The chapter concludes with attention to the influences you will need to recognize to be successful. These will include outside influences, such as national trends, and inside influences, such as the leadership in your school, the quality of the academic programs, and the curriculum.

American Secondary Schools: How Did They Get to Be the Way They Are?

The comprehensive secondary school is a relatively new phenomenon. If you are to understand it as an institution, you will need to learn a little about what happened as it evolved and how it got to be that way before you arrived on the scene. We will begin with a very brief historical overview.

The Recent Development of the Secondary School

The secondary school as we know it today resulted from dramatic changes in secondary education, changes that occurred during the nineteenth century. For most of that time, secondary schools were institutions for boys, but girls were later admitted. These were specialized schools, preparing students for particular vocations, but they became comprehensive. Eventually assuming the traditional college-preparatory functions, they became universal schools for all American youth.

In the late 1890s, a movement to consolidate rural schools gained momentum and many new secondary schools were built. Until this time, secondary education was available for wealthy boys, with doors closed to the common people. As the economy changed and the percentage of young people needed for farm labor decreased, more teenagers could attend high school. Other reasons for an extension of secondary schools were (a) the spread of elementary schools and the need to prepare teachers as part of the secondary school experience, (b) the support of the press and labor organizations, and (c) the gradual growth of equality between the sexes (Gutek, 1991; Webb, Metha, & Jordan, 1999).

The American secondary school emerged over a period from the 1890s until the 1920s, reflecting shifts in the social and economic patterns in a more urban nation. There were increasing concerns about what a secondary school should do and whom it should serve. Should it continue to prepare college-bound students, or should it provide a more pragmatic background for those not going to college? To respond to these questions, the National Education Association established the Committee of Ten in 1892. Charles Eliot of Harvard chaired the committee, which consisted mostly of college presidents and professors who were asked to examine the relation between the secondary schools and colleges. The committee's position developed around two basic concepts: (a) an earlier introduction to the fundamentals of several subjects in the upper elementary grades, and (b) no differentiation between subjects or teaching of college preparatory and non-college-preparatory students. This report reflected the higher education perspective and bias of its members and demonstrated the tendency of colleges to dominate secondary schools. Although the committee said that high schools didn't exist specifically for college preparation, its report clearly was most concerned that subject matter be suitable for entrance to college (Gutek, 1991).

Secondary schools were, however, from the beginning of this century, a higher "common school." The old common schools had been elementary schools "devoted to the cultivation of literacy, numeracy, and citizenship" (Gutek, 1991, p. 55). Common schools, normal schools (teacher-preparation institutions), and secondary schools developed together during the nineteenth century and were closely related. Often only those with the approval of colleges were considered worthy of the name "high school." It was resistance to this elitist idea, the broadening of its curriculum, and the establishment of an earlier alliance with the elementary schools that made the American high school.

The greater part of this revolution occurred early in the twentieth century when high schools changed into a true higher common school. Until about 1920, the high school was still regarded as a selective institution. In *The Selective Character of American Secondary Education,* George S. Counts criticized the secondary school for primarily serving the upper socioeconomic classes (Counts, 1922; Gutek, 1991). This was true, according to William French (1957), for three reasons: (a) immigrants from southern and eastern Europe were not traditionally encouraged to attend high school, (b) the cost of education—books, supplies, transportation, clothes, lunches, and so forth—was prohibitive, and (c) rural areas lacked a financial base to support secondary schools.

In 1918, the National Education Association (NEA) established the Commission on the Reorganization of Secondary Education to reexamine the purpose of the secondary school. The commission produced The Cardinal Principles of Secondary Education, which stated that the task of secondary schools was not merely to prepare a select few for college but also to prepare the general population for life. It emphasized such curricular priorities as health, command of fundamental processes, vocational preparation, citizenship and worthwhile use of leisure time (Webb, Metha, & Jordan, 1999).

By the 1930s, a forerunner of what we might recognize as the comprehensive secondary school of today emerged. It offered a wide range of courses to an increasingly diverse student population. Although college preparation was still a function of these schools, more and more programs were available for youth whose formal education would end on graduation (Gutek, 1991).

Between 1900 and 1920, students were attending school in record numbers. Grades 7 through 12 were usually spent in a secondary (high) school. New buildings were needed; thus, for initially practical reasons, junior high schools were established (Rich, 1992). At the same time, however, there were loftier arguments for such a change. Educators influenced by John Dewey and other progressives offered a psychological rationale for making the first three years of secondary school separate. They maintained that, developmentally, students at this age were going through unique physiological and social changes. These could not be addressed adequately in the high school setting. Therefore, this plan would provide a better overall transition, offering such innovations as guidance services and exploratory courses.

In the 1960s, the middle school emerged as a refinement of the junior high school. Advocates claimed that there was still a need to provide even more focused attention to this age group in all respects. The junior high school, they insisted, was too much of a "little (junior) high school." They went on to argue that high schools couldn't provide

Activity 2.1

My School and the One Where I Teach

1. In one page, describe the middle school you attended or the school you graduated from. What was it like? Consider the students, the teachers, the community, the curriculum, the extracurricular activities, and anything else that made it unique.

2. Now take some time to find out about the school where you will be teaching. Interview an administrator and the faculty member who has been there the longest. What changes has the school been through? What things about its past will be useful to know?

3. List at least four ways that your school and the one you will teach in are different and four ways they are the same.

enough differentiation in instruction and attention to issues related to personal growth and development for young adolescents. The middle school concept received popular support and still remains the most current model for educating students in grades 6 through 8.

Growth and development of secondary schools during the decades since then have continued—both because of and despite many pressures they still experience today. High schools still have some influence on the curriculum of middle schools. Colleges still tend to influence the college-bound curriculum, and businesses still influence the vocational track in high schools. Every constituency in society wants the schools to do a better job of promoting its particular agenda. Because of the nature of what schools do, this may always be the case.

The Nature of Today's Secondary School

Demands by society have pressured schools to become all things to all people. Everyone has an opinion about what schools should do and how they should do it, and citizens are not reluctant to express their views often and loudly.

Americans have had good reason to be proud of their secondary schools, enrolling more youth for longer periods of time than any other country. Since the 1960s, more than 90% of 14–17-year-olds have been enrolled in high school. More than 70% graduate and an additional 20% finish high school through GED programs, half of those enrolling in postsecondary education programs (Berliner & Biddle, 1997). Going to college and beyond has become part of the life experience for numerous Americans. The egalitarian ethic has truly found fulfillment in America's schools.

Yet, during the same century when American successes are so outstanding, public schools have been subjected to harsh criticism for failing to provide educational opportunities to everyone, for being unable to eliminate illiteracy, for democratizing at the expense of academic standards, for failing to teach useful subjects, for being costly. Each success has been countered by a complaint.

This tension between pride and criticism has been a central feature of American education in the 20th century. It reflects the intense investment of the public in the success of the schools and the desire of the educators to try to accommodate everyone. Secondary school teachers know this firsthand. They know that their classrooms are avenues of social and economic mobility whose primary purpose is to enhance equality of opportunity for each student. Egalitarian aims lead to an emphasis on policies to improve access to education, more equitable distribution of resources, and curriculum and teaching styles adapted to individual needs.

An opposing view of schooling stresses meritocratic standards. It emphasizes selectivity and the academic quality of educational experience and deemphasizes the egalitarian responsibilities. Critics of this view feel that this way of thinking has resulted in high schools being places that stifle creativity while they foster competition, conformity, and intolerance—attitudes already rampant in society (Hardy, 1999). Teachers deal with this constantly as they wrestle with the pressure to raise test scores and expect more and more from their students. They ask themselves if they are really being asked to teach tests or students.

Still another set of expectations for the schools stresses the resolution of social problems. Americans have been particularly intent on trying to resolve social dilemmas through educational programs. Immigrant assimilation translates into bilingual education. Economic and labor problems lead to a focus on work training opportunities. Alcohol abuse, automobile accidents, and sex education all become the schools' responsibilities, resulting in these respective curricular emphases becoming part of health classes and drivers' education courses. As educational purposes become all-consuming, the schools are left in the uncomfortable position of being criticized both for not doing enough and for doing too much!

Powell, Farrar, and Cohen (1985) provided an excellent description of the high school environment when they compared it to a shopping mall. Like shopping malls, secondary schools accommodate a wide range of "customers" with different tastes and purposes. They can select from an amazing number of products (courses) and services (career counseling, health services) that are conveniently arranged in one place with ample parking and transportation. Teachers often regard themselves as salespeople, trying to attract students to their classes. Of course, there are always students who browse and never buy and others who avoid the mall altogether. This comparison is still very accurate, maybe now more than ever. Theodore Sizer noted in 1996 that very little had changed in many of the high schools he studied in the early 1980s.

Secondary schools offer numerous courses, sometimes several hundred, from which students can choose. In most situations, days flow in an atmosphere of "controlled chaos," with many customers wanting attention for a variety of purposes at all times. Every person in the school has his or her own schedule, needs, and plans for being there. Many students spend twelve or more hours at school if they are involved in extracurricular activities. Most schools, even the ones that have fewer resources, are self-contained "cities," complete with a "food court," and constitute the entire world of many of their students. To say the least, it's a labor-intensive, high-energy environment. Take your vitamins.

Teachers such as the one at the beginning of the chapter find the atmosphere "exhilarating." Others think it overwhelming. Regardless of your or anyone else's impression of the total atmosphere, you, like your students, will find your own order, place, sense of purpose, and structure within it.

Facing a New Century: Current Changes and Challenges for Secondary Schools

According to Paul George and Kenneth McEwin (1999), high schools face a substantial transformation in the next decade. In 1996, the National Association of Secondary School Principals issued a report, "Breaking Ranks: Changing an American Institution," the most recent attempt to reorganize the comprehensive secondary school. There were six primary theme areas.

1. Personalization—encouraging high schools to break into units of no more than 600 students so that teachers and students could know each other better. Teacher-advocates (advisors) as well as more individualized curriculum planning would be incorporated.
2. Coherency—urging secondary schools to focus on an interdisciplinary, integrated curriculum that would help students see coherence in their learning.
3. Flexibility—modifying the Carnegie Unit, with longer school years and schedules for teachers and students that would provide more options.
4. Technology—including technology in all aspects of teaching and learning.
5. Professional development—improving the effectiveness of educators.
6. Leadership—enhancing productive leadership within the school.

Scheduling Adjustments: Making the School Day Reflect the New Priorities

In an effort to make large secondary schools feel smaller, reformers have paid careful attention to academic learning time as a critical element in student achievement (Carroll, 1990). In the 1980s, many school districts raised graduation requirements, narrowed the curriculum to basic courses, and increased the number of class periods each day. Many schools found that the longer day was too expensive and students were unhappy about fewer elective choices. Some school systems created "schools within schools" and "academies within schools" to provide specific curricular emphases for smaller numbers of students with particular interests and needs. Things also changed from more, shorter instructional classes to fewer, longer blocks, resulting in "block scheduling" (George & McEwin, 1999; Jones, 1995; Rettig & Canady, 1996).

The two most commonly used block schedule models are the 4 × 4 semester plan and the alternate (AB) schedule. The 4 × 4 model usually offers 90-plus minute classes with students taking four courses each day and teachers teaching three each day, using the fourth block for planning. Students can complete a course in one semester, meeting daily. In the alternate day (AB) schedule, the courses run all year (Jones, 1995; Rettig & Canady, 1996).

Another model, the Copernican Plan (Carroll, 1990), is also used, but much less often. This approach utilizes the "macroclass," in which students take one course at a time, attending a 4-hour class every day for 30 days, or taking two courses for 60 days. Included in the day might be time for a seminar to help students integrate knowledge, to take electives, and to provide for teacher planning. Among the advantages are a reduced student load and fewer course preparations.

These and similar models have resulted in improved attendance, more focus on the part of the students, less stress, more personal attention by the teachers, and fewer discipline problems (Kadel, 1996; Rettig & Canady, 1996). No one plan is perfect, of course, but these positive results have prompted nationwide interest in block scheduling in some form. It has been estimated that more than half of the secondary schools in the United States are using or planning to use some variation of block scheduling (George & McEwin, 1999; Rettig & Canady, 1996).

You are entering the field at a time when major shifts are occurring in the secondary school. Many significant and systemic changes reflect a sincere desire by educators to respond to the needs of their students. Depending on when you graduated, the school you teach in may look very different from the one you attended (see Activity 2.1 on page 36). It needs to be if it is going to serve a changing society with a more diverse, complex, and demanding population (see Activity 2.2).

Activity 2.2

School from a Student's Perspective

Do you really want to know what school feels like to a student? Become one for a day. Yes, try it. You will gain more insight from this simple exercise than you imagined.

Directions: After following prescribed school district guidelines for visiting schools, go to the guidance office and randomly select the schedule of a student you do not know. Take a few minutes to review his or her cumulative folder to understand something about the person. Plan to follow the student's schedule for an entire day, including lunch. (You will need to talk to each teacher prior to the exercise to ask for permission to do this.) Sit in the back of the room and try to look unobtrusive. It will be most helpful if the student does not think he or she is being watched.

Observe how different his or her classes are, how the student functions in each, how he or she relates to the teachers and the other students. In the end, how do you feel about a day from the student's perspective? Were you stimulated? Bored? Tired? What did you learn that can help you as a teacher?

School Operations: How Do Public Schools Run?

Approach to Governance

Governance arrangements establish the rules of the game. They determine through statutes; collective bargaining; and other legal agreements, regulations, and court rulings who is responsible and accountable for what within a school system. In the education system, the real work of learning happens in the classroom, the interaction between teacher and student. But as the Committee for Economic Development noted in 1994, this interaction does not happen in isolation. Decisions made by those outside the classroom such as principals, school boards, and state and national governing officials greatly impact what goes on in each classroom (Report of the National Commission on Governing America's Schools, 1999).

This is a nation of "little red schoolhouses," a country that likes direct local control of its education system. Basically, the closer to home the control of a school, the better most Americans like it. Unlike the countries in Europe with more nationally centralized bureaucracies, most of the authority over schooling is delegated to the states. This traditional approach has been the predominant mode of public education governance for the last century. It does have advantages, such as providing a mechanism to deal with a large and diverse clientele, standardizing the allocation of resources, and making fair distribution of services across the state (Ziebarth, 1999).

There are those who feel that the traditional bureaucratic structure does not provide the flexibility, adaptability, and creativity that are now necessary for schools to get the job done. New approaches in governance are being tried out that include increased deregulation, site-based management, and charter schools (semiautonomous schools established by parents, teachers, or community groups; Ziebarth, 1999). The trend of the future is that there will be more and more decentralization in education governance during the next decades. Clearly, Americans are facing critical choices between two very different systems of school control: the continuing of the current (traditional) system, and moving to a more decentralized (privatized) approach (Bauman, 1996). This major, systemic shift will require some adjustment on everyone's part.

Governance at the State and Local Levels

The jury is still out in terms of how effective these relatively new attempts at decentralizing education governance are. But clearly, the trend toward decentralization is in full swing. For now, the states are still ultimately in charge—ironically, even if to grant permission for various initiatives that represent decentralization. The state school boards still delegate much of the responsibility for implementing state policies to the local education agencies (LEAs). This is why most procedures that are followed in school systems are usually state mandates.

For example, the state may say that a certain number of physical education units is required of all high school graduates. But a particular school system within that state may choose to increase the requirement for its students. That's fine, as long as the state's minimum requirement is enforced. States also determine other areas such as curriculum guidelines, teacher licensure requirements, and testing procedures for students and teachers. The structure of state bureaucracies varies somewhat; Figure 2.1 is an example of a typical organization.

Public schools are government agencies, an arrangement based on the idea that schools are for the public good (Myers & Myers, 1995). Therefore, at the top of the organizational chart is the U.S. Constitution, followed by the three branches of the state government. State boards of education are selected by various means. They may be appointed by the governor, elected by one or more of the houses of legislature, or some combination of both. Sometimes they are elected by the citizens of the state. Their job is to regulate educational practice in the state and serve as advisors to governors and legislators regarding educational business. They do such things as establish requirements for homeschooling, adopt textbooks, establish minimal standards for student performance, and

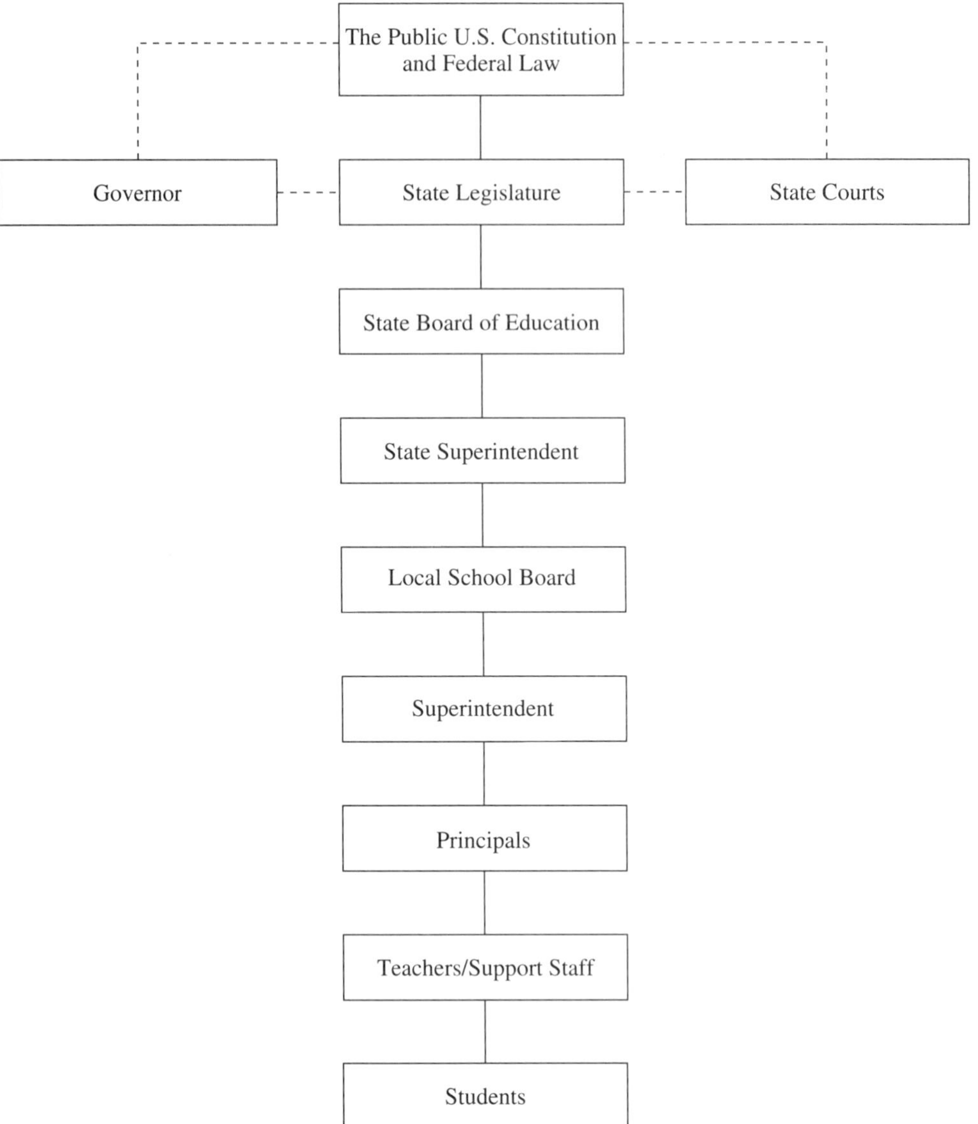

FIGURE 2.1 Typical Organization of Public Education at the State Level

regulate what teachers must do to get and keep their jobs (McNergney & Herbert, 1995). State education departments carry out the state's education business. Each is directed by a chief state school officer, often called a state superintendent or the superintendent of public instruction.

At the local level, school systems are controlled by local school boards. These are your employers. These boards are elected or appointed citizens who provide advice and permission regarding the operation of the public schools. Because education is a power reserved to the states, local school boards are also agents of the state. These boards are the policy-making committee for the public schools and have been a critical part of the history of public education. Nationwide, there are about 15,000 local school boards and 95,000 local school board members, 96% elected by their communities (Resnick, 1999).

School boards represent the best example of lay members of the community coming together to shape a vision for a school district. They have the authority to establish schools and select the system's executive officer (the local superintendent). They also set policy that will affect the operation of the schools in their districts. Their decisions reflect the priorities of the public they serve.

Next in line is the local superintendent, who has a difficult and challenging job. He serves at the pleasure of the school board and faces issues such as strategic planning for the system, assessing educational outcomes, administering special services, and negotiating labor contracts (Hanson, 1991). The superintendent must do this as well as many more time-consuming and energy-draining tasks and somehow keep everyone happy—parents; his staff; other personnel; and his "bosses," the school board. It's no wonder that the average length of time superintendents stay in their jobs is 5.5 years nationally and only 2.5 years if they are city superintendents. A superintendent works with assistant superintendents and other staff to carry out his or her duties. See Figure 2.2 for an example of how a local school system is organized (McNergney & Herbert, 1995).

On a daily basis, the most important person to you (after the student, of course) is the principal. This person is responsible for managing the everyday operation of the school, which includes everything from handling discipline to dealing with staff and teachers, implementing rules, balancing the school's budget, and maintaining the physical facility. The principal also sets the tone for the school and shapes the environment you will work in. Because the principal's relationship with teachers is such an important key to the school's effectiveness, he or she, maybe more than any other one person in your school, will impact, in some way, everything you do.

Funding Schools

The money used to finance public education comes from taxes levied at the national, state, and local levels. On average, the federal government provides 6.6%, the state provides

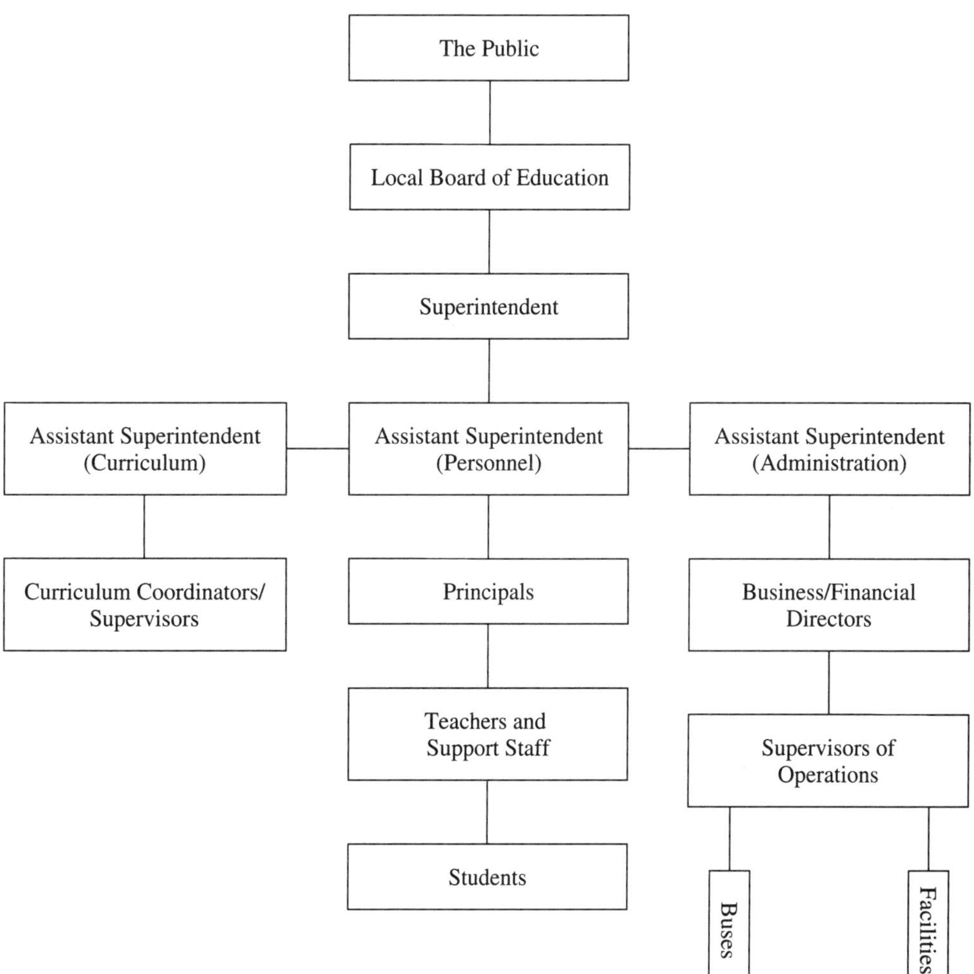

FIGURE 2.2 Typical Organization of a Local School System

45.8%, and schools receive approximately 47.6% from local funds (U.S. Department of Education, 1997). Basically, three types of taxes are levied: property taxes, sales and other user taxes, and income taxes. Clearly, most of the money comes from the local and state levels, which explains why there is such a wide range from state to state and community to community in terms of resources for schools. Jonathan Kozol (1991) has written extensively about the "savage inequalities" that exist between school districts. This is because local governments depend mostly on property taxes and sales taxes. If a community does not have a large tax base, obviously it doesn't have enough money for state-of-the-art schools. But the community down the road might have a lot of money for its schools. Thus, the disparity. This is also a reality for states, which rely on sales and income taxes. Poorer states have less money for schools. Per-student expenditure ranges from approximately $3,732 in Utah to $10,153 in New Jersey (U.S. Department of Education, 1999). The legislature of some states such as Washington provides the majority of funding to address inequities. Finally, the federal government, which provides the smallest percentage of funding, relies on income taxes.

In recent years, debate has sharpened on the funding of schools. Since the beginning of public school history, financial trends reflect taxpayer resistance. This has often been connected to increasing demands for accountability, with the effectiveness of public education being based on objective (testing) results.

Many current debates relate to tuition tax credits and vouchers, examples of the controversial idea of school choice. Naturally, given that schools deal with the children of the public, there will be those who feel that they are not getting what they should from the public schools. These parents want assistance in sending their children to a private school of their choice. Tuition tax credits allow parents to claim tax deductions for part of the tuition they pay to send their children to private schools. Likewise, many advocate the use of educational vouchers, which allow parents of school-age children to be given a voucher or flat grant that represents a student's estimated educational cost or portion of the school budget to be used at any school of their choice (private or public).

Generally, public opinion supports efforts to improve education through reforming the existing system rather than creating any alternative approach. Americans do support, however, under certain conditions, the idea of experimenting with different possibilities on a smaller scale. For example, a majority of Americans like the idea of a parent being given a voucher to pay part of tuition at a private or church-related school, but not the total payment (Report of the National Commission on Governing America's Schools, 1999). Most research offers conflicting evidence regarding success with vouchers, although low-income minority students reflect significant increases in parental satisfaction and participation. There is still little information, however, about the effects of tuition tax credits. Regardless, these and similar initiatives will continue to be controversial topics and will have major ramifications for the funding and future of public schools.

Legal Considerations

The increasingly litigious nature of our society makes professional liability something that all educators need to think about. The courts are full of lawsuits in which someone, usually a parent, complains that a teacher or a school system has not lived up to appropriate performance standards. Litigation also occurs when someone (usually a student) was damaged in some way. You have probably read about cases of parents suing school systems because their children graduate and cannot read.

Fortunately, things like this don't happen often, and you probably will not have to face such a scenario. What will you do if it does happen? Although most school systems should have adequate liability coverage, a situation may arise when this isn't the case. You may want to consider whether you want additional coverage. If so, professional liability coverage is available in two ways. First, many professional organizations' dues include liability insurance as a benefit. Second, an education association may sponsor some insurance program in which members may participate if they wish. For example, some organizations charge as little as $70 a year for $1,000,000 of liability coverage.

What kinds of things can get you into trouble? Actually, quite a few things, and most of them you might not ever think twice about. For example, can you get into legal trouble for giving a student an aspirin? Quite possibly, especially if he is allergic to aspirin. This is why you are not allowed to do so. Obviously, everything you may need or want to be aware of cannot be addressed here, but the following lists sample areas of general concern to teachers relative to what is legal and what is not:

REALITY CHECK 2.1

You are probably thinking, "Legal issues are not going to be a problem for me. I've got more important things to do to get ready for tomorrow." Famous last words. The best way to be sure it will never be a problem is to go into your teaching situation with your eyes wide open. There are a couple of ways to do it. First, most of the important things you will have to know are compiled for you by most school systems in a nice policy handbook somewhere. Read it! Second, attend any workshops or classes that your system offers on this subject.

Teachers' Rights

1. Standardized tests for teacher licensure have been found *not* to be discriminatory (*U.S. v. South Carolina,* 1978).
2. Contracts signed when you are hired are legally binding.
3. Tenure prevents teachers from being dismissed without cause and requires due process. "Cause" is defined by the state. The usual reasons are incompetency and insubordination (*Board of Regents of Colleges v. Roth,* 1972).
4. Teachers have the right to belong to unions.
5. The law prohibits teacher strikes in most states.
6. School boards may establish leave policies for pregnant teachers but the policies may not contain arbitrary leave and return dates.
7. Dismissal of a teacher because of physical impairment or contagious disease is unconstitutional (*School Board of Nassau County v. Arline,* 1987).
8. Teachers have academic freedom and may express their opinions as long as school operations are not disrupted (*Kingsville Independent School District v. Cooper,* 611 F. 2nd 1109 (5th Cir. 1980).
9. Employers may use affirmative action plans to increase the number of minority employees.
10. Restraint on a teacher's behavior (dress, immorality) depends on whether it impairs the teacher's effectiveness (*Board of Trustees of Compton Junior College District v. Stubblefield,* 94 Cal. Rptr. 318, 321, 1971).
11. Teachers can be sued if a student is injured while in their care if negligence can be proved (*Biggers v. Sacramento City Unified School District,* 25 Cal. App. 3rd 269, 1972).
12. Permission slips do not release teachers from legal responsibility.
13. Teachers are required by law to report suspected cases of child abuse to authorities.
14. Educational malpractice has not been supported by the courts.

Students' Rights

1. Nondisruptive expression is protected by law (*Tinker v. Des Moines Independent Community School District,* 1969).
2. School newspapers can be regulated by school officials (*Hazelwood School District v. Kuhlmeier,* 484 U.S. 260, 1988).

3. School suspensions are legal if due process is followed (California Education Code, sections 48900 and 48910).
4. Search and seizure is legal if reasonable cause exists (*New Jersey v. T.L.O.*, 1985).
5. Corporal punishment is not cruel or unusual punishment and is permitted *where allowed by law*. In other words, it is still legal in some states (*Ingraham v. Wright*, 430 U.S. 651, 1977).
6. Parents and students (when age 18) have access to their own school records (*Family Educational Rights and Privacy Act, Buckley Amendment*, 1974).
7. Students are required by law to attend school.
8. Most states allow homeschooling.
9. Organized prayer in schools is illegal, although silent, individual prayers are allowed in some states (*Wallace v. Jaffee*, 1985).
10. The courts say it is legal for students to choose not to say the Pledge of Allegiance (*West Virginia State Board of Education v. Barnette*, 319 U.S. 624, 1943).
11. Public schools are not required to teach creationism, because such teaching would advance a religious doctrine.
12. It is legal for students with AIDS to attend school under certain conditions (*Chalk v. U.S. District Court Cent. District of California*, 1988).
13. Teachers may not administer medication to students.

Obviously, there are numerous specific laws, rulings, and statutes that exist relative to education and your responsibilities as a teacher and they change. By the time you read this section, some of the sample rulings just mentioned may have been reversed! Although it may feel like it at times, it is not necessary for you to become an attorney to teach. Doug Punger, a veteran school system attorney who works regularly with new teachers, says that there are *categories* of legal considerations with which you need to be familiar. They include the following critical areas:

1. Constitutional Laws—These include understanding the First Amendment and how it will apply to freedom of speech, the press and association. You will also need to understand laws that address freedom of religion, search and seizure, equal protection, and due process under the 14th Amendment.

2. Federal Statute Laws—These deal with the particulars of Title IX, which includes discrimination statutes, sexual harassment (and your duty to protect students from this), the Family Rights and Privacy Act, and the Individuals with Disabilities Education Act (IDEA), which will be discussed more fully in Chapter 5.

3. State Laws—Every state has specific statutes that address such issues as your legal duties as a teacher, discipline procedures, as well as suspensions and expulsions.

As a teacher, you will often find yourself facing a decision about whether to use copyrighted materials. It is important that you observe the copyright laws, which are federally mandated. The "fair use" doctrine allows for the nonprofit reproduction and use of certain materials for classroom purposes without the permission of the owner of the document if it meets the criteria for "brevity, spontaneity, and cumulative effect" (Webb, Metha, & Jordan, 1999, p. 394). It is your responsibility to be aware of these potential legal concerns.

REALITY CHECK 2.2

Face it, your school system will do almost anything to avoid a legal situation. School administrators and elected officials don't want trouble. This is not to say they will not back you if you find yourself in a precarious situation—more than likely they will. The best advice is to know your rights and your students' rights and follow the law.

Your Situation: What Other Influences Will Affect Your Teaching?

Not surprisingly, you are entering a very political world where many people want to influence and/or control what you do. While this is true of many professions, it is especially true of teaching. After all, as stated before, these are *public* schools and John Q. Public wants to be heard with respect to how its youth are educated. Dealing with, listening to, and, in some cases, responding to the priorities of a variety of constituencies—either directly or indirectly—will be part of your job.

REALITY CHECK 2.3

True, you do have to listen to almost everybody's opinion. It's part of your job. However, you need to remember two things before you begin to think of yourself as a doormat.

1. *You* are the professional. If the opinion of a layperson is counter to what you know to be professionally sound, stick to your guns. Don't give away the power that you have been hired to exercise. Just be polite and be willing to consider the other person's view. In most cases, others will respect your judgment.
2. *You* are also part of the public. Your opinion as a person is as valid as anyone's. Besides, you are the teacher.

You will find that it is often harder to do this if the person who is criticizing you is (a) older than you are, (b) has an abrasive style, or (c) has influence in the school or community. It won't be easy, but don't let any of these factors keep you from doing what you think is best. Once people learn that you are not going to back down, they will respect you more.

Layers of Influence

You will find that you are at the center of many layers of influence (see Figure 2.3). Depending on where or what you teach, they may feel like layers of pressure. For example, the drivers' education teacher will more than likely hear from fewer parent groups than the social studies teacher whose students are studying the historical and current activities of the KKK.

In most cases, the closer to you the layer is, the better chance you stand of influencing what goes on in your school or classroom. But it is also true that the closer the layer is to you, the more directly you will feel the pressure from certain influences.

Consider the following situation.

Jane, a first-year social studies teacher was faced with several parents who wanted her to use a certain supplementary reader that advanced a particular political ideology. She angered the parents when she explained that this particular book was inappropriate to assign for the entire class not only because it did not follow the state-mandated guidelines, but also because some students and their families might find the material offensive. She attempted to appease the angry parents because she wanted good relations and also because they had considerable influence in the community. So she added an assignment option indicating that any personal reading their children wanted to do would be accepted as extra credit.

The parents were still not satisfied and began a campaign to discredit Jane as a teacher. They lobbied the school board to modify the local curriculum to allow the inclusion of such materials throughout the system. The administration wanted to please the parents and encouraged Jane to "try to work something out" (although they declined to say what that would mean). Jane was convinced she was right and had been more than fair. Disappointed that her principal did not support her, she stood her ground, determined not to allow the parents to tell her what materials to use. After many heated discussions, which involved local politicians and attorneys, the school board voted to support Jane. But the issue had taken its toll on her, and she left the school district to teach elsewhere the next year.

Usually disagreements like Jane's do not get so uncomfortable. As a teacher, however, you must understand that all of the stakeholders in what goes on in your classroom do need to be heard. Their motivation varies. Some are well-intentioned people who have a mission. Some are genuinely interested in the welfare of their own children and the success of the school program. Others like the feeling of power that comes from pushing their agenda. Regardless, they know that the school is one audience that must be responsive. Learn which groups you should work with and which you should send down the hall to an administrator, whose job it is to manage such people.

Sometimes when the issues are big, you will feel like you are in the eye of a hurricane as you go about your daily work, with weighty, possibly dangerous, influences swirling

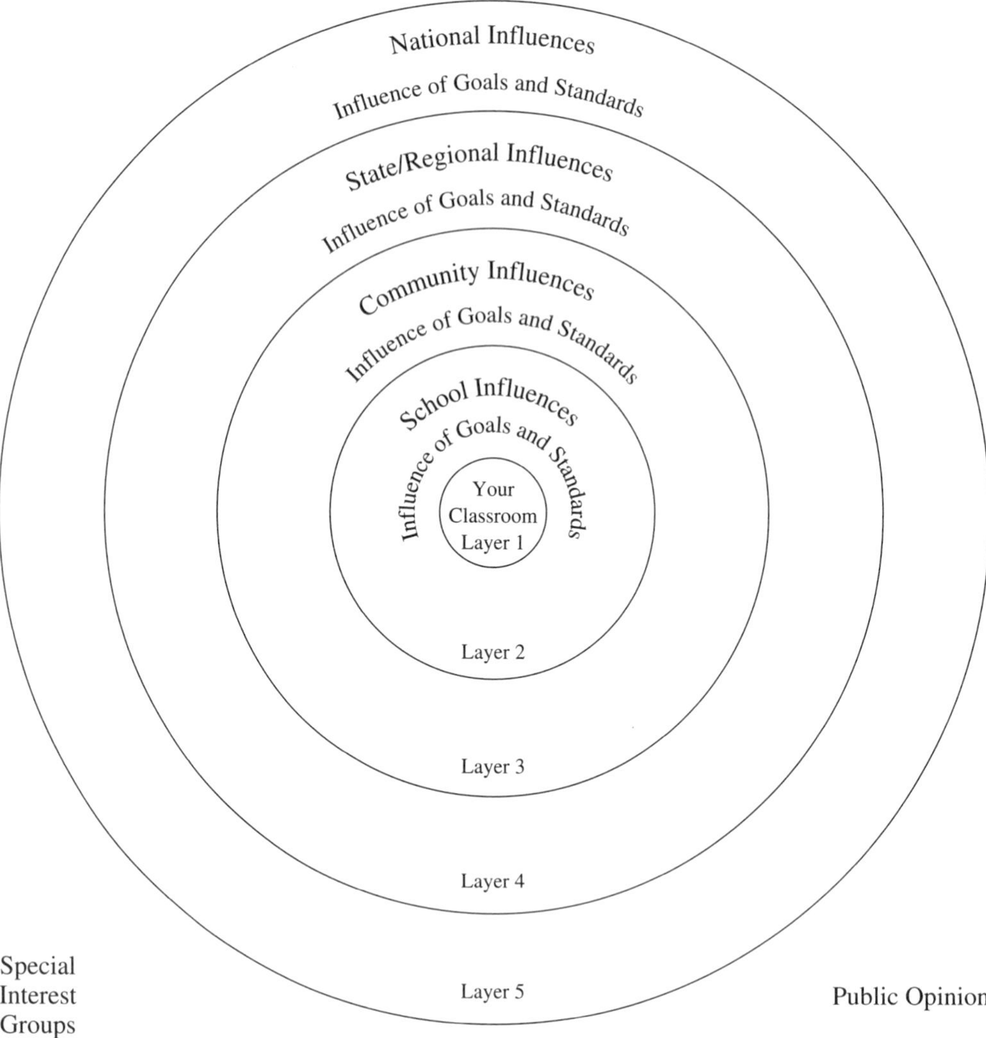

FIGURE 2.3 Layers of Influence

REALITY CHECK 2.4

You are not alone as a teacher—especially when things like this come up. Use the expertise and advice of administrators, veteran teachers, and even representatives from your professional organizations—people who can guide you through difficult political situations that arise. When possible and appropriate, let them handle it—at least until you know your way around the school and community better. They usually can navigate these treacherous waters easier than you can for two very good reasons: (1) they've had more experience, and (2) they usually know the players well.

around you. Some of these layers of influence are close to home (parent pressures and lack of administrative support such as Jane faced), and others seem far away (national trends in the field). But for the most part, these influences are just subtle realities you need to understand your job in the context of.

Layer 5—The National Scene

Let's begin with Layer 5, the most distant layer: the national influences. We all know that the condition of education is always a major concern of most Americans. Interestingly, while parents in recent surveys give their own children's schools high marks, they think very little of the nation's schools (Report of the National Commission on Governing America's Schools, 1999). Therefore, what better campaign issue for someone seeking the presidency? In recent administrations, it is becoming a predictable priority for candidates to address education. It's politically prudent to address an issue most Americans want fixed. After all, they have been repeatedly bombarded with stories from the media about how their schools are failing. Education is one area each president thinks can be greatly improved in his administration.

REALITY CHECK 2.5

Don't believe everything you read. Yes, while no one with a pulse will disagree with the statement that the schools in general need improving, there are many excellent schools in the nation that are doing an outstanding job. For an enlightening description of the other side of the story, read David Berliner and Bruce Biddle's *The Manufactured Crisis: Myths, Fraud, and the Attack on America's Public Schools* (1997).

Basically, this is a good thing. While it has been historically true that the states exercise most of the control of public schools in our country, this trend does mean that education is getting much needed attention at the national level. Presidents' plans do set a tone for the nation and influence what states, and ultimately your local school board, do.

You may be familiar with some of the initiatives of recent administrations. In 1990, President George H. W. Bush, in his State of the Union Address, called for the adoption of the following six goals:

1. By 2000, all children in the United States will start school ready to learn.
2. By 2000, the high school graduation rate will increase to at least 90 percent.
3. By 2000, American students will leave Grades 4, 8, and 12 having demonstrated competency in challenging subject matter that includes English, math, science, history, and geography; every school in the United States will ensure that all students learn to use their minds well so that they may be prepared for responsible citizenship, further learning, and productive employment for our modern economy.
4. By 2000, the nation's teachers will have access to programs for the continued improvement of their professional skills and the opportunity to acquire the knowledge and skills needed to instruct and prepare all American students for the next century.
5. By 2000, students in the United States will be first in the world in math and science achievement.
6. By 2000, every adult in the United States will be literate and will possess the skills necessary to compete in a global economy and exercise the rights and responsibilities of citizenship.

President Clinton, in 1994, with the "Goals 2000: Educate America" Act, reiterated a commitment to these goals, adding two more. They are:

7. By 2000, every school in the United States will be free of drugs and violence and will offer a disciplined environment conducive to learning.
8. By 2000, every school and home will engage in partnerships that will increase parental involvement and participation in promoting social, emotional, and academic growth of children (Earley, 1994).

Likewise, President George W. Bush announced within the first week of his administration his plan for bipartisan education reform that he described as "the cornerstone of my administration." He called for solutions based on accountability, choice, and flexibility in federal education programs in the No Child Left Behind Act of 2001 (NCLB Act). The act includes increased accountability for states, school systems, and schools; greater choice for parents and students, particularly for those attending low-performing schools; more flexibility for states and local education agencies in the use of federal money; and a stronger emphasis on reading, especially for younger children.

Lofty goals. And as you know, many of the ones in former administrations were not completely achieved. But they provided a set of guidelines that have indeed affected how schools have done business for the last decade. They all stress *accountability.* As a teacher, you will directly feel the push for accountability from the national level down to your very own classroom in a variety of ways. This push is often manifested in the national and state standards that are in place to guide your performance as a teacher (discussed in Chapter 1). The influence of these standards is constant and cannot be overemphasized. Likewise, the need for accountability is evident in the goals set by numerous people and agencies—from presidents to local school boards. *The impact of these standards and goals and the accountability they require permeate every layer of influence.* They are designed to have a positive effect on your classroom. The current goals outlined by George W. Bush will influence schools in the years ahead. Once goals are articulated, there is always a better chance of progress. And we have seen progress.

Layer 4—The State Scene

As previously indicated, the states have most of the control over the public schools in our nation. Since there is no mention of education in the U.S. Constitution, it is considered to be one of the powers reserved to the states by the 10th Amendment. Therefore, all state constitutions specify that the legislature has the power to establish and maintain public schools, although states may not enact laws that violate anything in the Constitution (Webb, Metha, & Jordan, 1999). Usually you will see this translate into state requirements for obtaining your teaching license, curriculum guidelines, testing requirements, and your professional behavior (see Activity 2.3).

The primary functions for the state-level agency include:

- Implementing the state board's policies for operating the state's K–12 schools.
- Monitoring the schools in accordance with legislative mandates.
- Being an advocate for public education.
- Providing information about the schools to the state legislature and public.
- Providing technical assistance to public schools.
- Collecting data about the schools.
- Disbursing state funds for the operation of local school districts.

State departments also have regional offices in areas that are spread across the state. These offices are an attempt to assist school districts in implementing guidelines and procedures and to involve the local school districts more closely in the decisions made at the state level. There are opportunities for teachers from many school districts across the state to serve on committees at the state level. Unless you choose to involve yourself in this way, this layer will seem very remote to beginning teachers.

ACTIVITY 2.3

Examining the "Professional Code of Conduct" for Your State

You are expected to conduct yourself in certain ways as a teacher. Every state has guidelines that you should be aware of and they should be readily available for you to see. Examine the Professional Code of Conduct and Ethics for your state. An administrator at your school should be able to tell you where to find it, and it can often be found online. Discuss the implications of each point with a mentor or veteran teacher.

Layer 3—The Community Your School Reflects

It is impossible to separate the community from the institutions within it. The high school is the centerpiece of many communities and may even be the finest building in town. It reflects the values and priorities of the people who live there. It also represents the socioeconomic context within which the school must operate. It is critical that you understand where your students are coming from—what kind of cars they drive, what they do for fun. Do they go to school in the neighborhood they live in or are they transported across town? Paying attention to socioeconomic diversity among your students will help you to become aware of their frames of reference when you teach. For example, you won't make the mistake, as one teacher did when explaining the mathematics of interest payments, of referring to buying a Mercedes to students whose families can barely afford a car at all.

Likewise, you need to understand the general values and political climate of the community and school district. Is this a very conservative area of the state or a very liberal one? Are the people well educated as a group or do they have little education? What do most of them do for a living? Is this a white-collar, blue-collar, or mixed community? How diverse is the population? What can you find out about the local school board and its effectiveness? Finding answers to all of these questions *before* you start teaching will help you to make your lessons more relevant and help you to avoid saying things that will offend students and parents and ultimately make your job harder (see Activity 2.4).

It is a natural tendency for all of us to teach with a frame of reference that resembles where we went to school ourselves. Perhaps when you dreamed of teaching, you pictured communities like those you grew up in. It is also true that stereotypical images of what the other side of the tracks must be like can be misleading. Observing what is really the case will help us to keep from imputing into our students images that may represent the media's interpretation of certain student populations rather than what is real.

It is also important to remember that students in most classrooms today are from several different neighborhoods. No matter how small your class roster, you will have socioeconomic and cultural diversity within every group you teach.

ACTIVITY 2.4

A Trip Through the Neighborhood

Directions: Get a map of the neighborhoods your students live in from the person in charge of transportation in your school. Plan to spend an afternoon driving through the neighborhoods where your students live, following the bus routes of your students. You may even prefer to ride with one of the bus drivers as he or she is driving the route. Pay close attention to the following and complete this chart. Keep it in your desk so that you won't forget what you observed.

Describe the following:

The types of neighborhood(s) your students come from

What you observe people doing

Proximity to malls, landmarks

How well maintained the streets and homes are

Other observations

Based on what you have seen, make a list of things you will need to incorporate into your teaching, as well as things you will want to avoid incorporating into your teaching.

Special Interest Groups, Public Opinion, and the Media

As we have discussed, since public education seems to be everyone's concern, you need to be aware of the fact that certain groups will exert pressure to advance their cause. These *special interest groups* may be well meaning, but they always have an agenda. They are organized, focused on their goals, and are knowledgeable and well connected. They get things done. They advocate many activities designed to exert control over curricular, instructional, and governance issues in public education (McNergney & Herbert, 1995). Some of the prominent ones include the American Civil Liberties Union (ACLU), the Anti-Defamation League (ADL) of B'nai B'rith, Daughters of the American Revolution (DAR), National Association of Manufacturers, and the National Organization of Women.

Schools are also influenced by teachers' organizations. The NEA, with over 2 million members, and the American Federation of Teachers (AFT) have influenced the priorities of schools for years in many productive ways.

Public opinion does influence public education. It's unavoidable. The press, which is in a position to influence public opinion, has tremendous power in our society. It watches governmental and education leaders so that they do not cheat the people, and the simple act of watching and reporting can be extremely persuasive. This is a good thing—most of the time. Not only does the press provide information about what's going on in the schools but it can serve as part of the instructional process as well. Remember those ever-popular *Weekly Readers* and *Junior Scholastic?* Educational television now helps educate young people as well.

Layer 2—Your School Environment: Who's Who in Your School

Finally, a little closer to home, a segment of your environment that will have a major influence on you: your school. How does it feel? What are its problems? Are you part of those problems or part of the solutions? Are you a positive contributor to the atmosphere?

Recent trends have been to shift decision-making responsibilities from school boards and superintendents to the school level. This is usually referred to as site-based management (SBM). The idea is that those closest to the students (the principals, teachers, and parents) will have the greatest ability to improve student performance. The school would have greater independence but also have more of the responsibility for the results. Sounds good—but the results have varied and studies have not been able to confirm that this method is as effective as had been hoped. This is primarily because of the great variations in how SBM has been implemented (Report of the National Commission on Governing America's Schools, 1999).

The biggest factor within the school that will affect you and your success as a teacher is the other people with whom you work. It is important to get to know these people and what they do, to know best how they can help you to do your job. You will find the following people in most high schools.

Supervisory Personnel

The Principal This is the most important person; he or she has the ultimate responsibility for everything that goes on at the school. This is probably the person who interviewed and hired you. If so, he or she has faith in your ability to do the job well. This means you already have an advantage. Keep in mind that principals oversee the instructional program and the physical facility, they evaluate teachers and staff, they solve countless problems, and they generally address anything that needs fixing in the building. In other words, they are busy people. They must also attend countless meetings that take them off campus and deal with most of the public relations issues that arise. While it is true that the principal is an excellent resource for you, try to avoid running to him or her with every question—big or small—that arises. There are almost always other people to ask.

The Assistant Principals There is usually more than one assistant principal at most secondary schools, and their responsibilities vary. One may be in charge of curriculum; another may handle transportation, textbooks, and discipline ("buses, books, and butts"); and so forth. These people often have been assigned most of the hands-on administrative work for the school by the principal. They can answer almost every question you may have and solve your discipline problems, and they will probably be the ones to evaluate you. Like the principals, they're busy, but don't hesitate to ask them for help if you need it.

Reality Check 2.6

Sad to say, but much of what administrators think of you is based on how often they see you needing help with discipline. Sending students too often gives them the impression that you don't have control of your class. Unfortunately, as a beginning teacher, you may need to do this more than you will have to later. They know this. Just try to make careful decisions about when to ask for help, and look for ways you can handle problems on your own—especially when they are small.

Support Personnel

Guidance Counselors Most secondary schools have several guidance counselors whose job it is to advise students, keep permanent records, and refer students for special services. Most of these people got into the field because they wanted to help students with problems. Unfortunately, what many find is that, in addition to dealing with student issues, they have a tremendous amount of paperwork—completing college recommendations, adjusting schedules, and even creating master schedules (when the assistant principals in the school aren't assigned this task). Many complain that although they do discuss student concerns, they do not have the time to do as much of this as they would like. They are the keepers of most of the information about students, however, and can answer most questions about their problems, history, and placement in special classes. They are also excellent interpreters of test data.

Curriculum Coordinators These resource people usually coordinate all aspects of the curriculum. They often work with teachers in gathering resources and materials for teaching the curriculum and materials for units. In some cases they also work with students' schedules. They can be excellent observers and can offer good feedback on strategies that will work with certain student groups as well.

School Psychologists Most schools have one school psychologist who serves as a resource for students who have special needs. This usually means they are in charge of testing these students and referring them for placement. They also serve on the school service teams who monitor the progress on these students once placed. They are a wonderful resource, but are often spread very thin. It will often be difficult to get too much time with them.

Social Workers Most schools also have at least one social worker who works with the guidance counselors and the psychologists to gather information that will be helpful in making instructional and placement recommendations for students. Most teachers do not deal directly with social workers, but they are available to answer questions if needed.

Content Area Supervisors (Central Office Staff) Most school systems, especially if they are large, have resource curriculum specialists for each content area taught. They are usually housed at a central location and are available to provide help for your teaching of a specific area.

Peers Other teachers, including your departmental chairperson, are usually your *best* sources of immediate support. Most school systems now assign a mentor to beginning teachers, and mentors can be very helpful. If yours is not, identify another teacher who can serve as someone you can talk to about concerns.

Support Staff Secretaries, custodians, cafeteria workers, school nurses, and resource officers all have important jobs that are key to the effective running of the total school program. Get to know who they are and speak to them by name when you see them. One last reminder: anyone who has worked in a school will tell you that the school secretary usually runs the place. Make this person your friend!

A word about extracurricular activities. Think about your days in secondary school. What do you remember? If you are like most people, probably the most important part of your life as a teenager was what you did *outside* of class. Extracurricular activities play a critical role in the total school experience. Students know teachers are interested when they

ACTIVITY 2.5

Observation of an Extracurricular Activity

Choose any extracurricular activity that interests you. Observe it at practice and in competition at least once. Make a point of talking to your students who participated after the event. If your schedule permits, consider becoming an advisor or coach for the activity. If you find yourself too overwhelmed to do this your first year, consider making it a priority for your second year. You will be glad you did!

choose to spend time with them outside of class. And you will find that you enjoy them even more when you get to know them in another, more relaxed, setting (see Activity 2.5).

Layer 1—Your Classroom

Mr. Cervantes teaches 10th-grade English and prides himself on his room. In fact, even though he has been teaching only three years, his room is rapidly becoming a legend at his school. Students tend to linger after class and come back in the afternoons and at lunch. They just like to be there and often comment on what they see. It's wall-to-wall color. One wall is covered with posters depicting movie versions of the novels his students read. One wall is a giant display of student essays, many with accompanying pictures, sketches, or other artwork. Another wall is designated for poetry and other student work and changes every few weeks. Students are encouraged to post their own poetry here as well. Across the top of the room is a timeline of events and information about authors and their writings.

There are three centers in the room, which Mr. Cervantes changes every quarter. Each of these centers is a hands-on place where students can go to do things. One center highlights some aspect of the diversity his classes represent. At these centers, he makes a point of observing important holidays from a variety of cultures as well as providing suggestions for supplementary reading, highlighting current events, and spotlighting important men and women from other countries. Another example is a music center with headphones where songs (poetry put to music) are available. Students are also encouraged to put their own poetry to music. Another center is a computer station with instructional software available, and students are encouraged to do individual research online. The room demonstrates a serious respect for the classroom environment and his students. It's alive and relevant to them—a fun place to be.

What does your room look like? Remember, this is your world for 8 hours a day (often longer!). Not everyone likes to put the time into it that Mr. Cervantes does, nor do you have to. But you should make it a place you and your students enjoy coming to each day.

ACTIVITY 2.6

Planning Your Classroom

Spend some time thinking about how you want your room to look. Consider the things just mentioned as you make your plans. Sketch out several floor plans for your students' desks. Remember that the plan you design is not written in stone—you can revise all year long. In fact, some teachers rearrange the room at the end of each quarter just to keep the students interested. It also makes them feel like they are getting to start over.

Sad to say, but many secondary, especially high school, teachers ignore the physical environment, leaving the room devoid of any attractive features, with no areas of interest and little, if any, color. Think about it—don't *you* want an interesting place to spend part of your day in? If you don't think students notice, take a look at their lockers or their rooms at home. How many have covered them with pictures and other meaningful decorations?

Your room can actually be a teaching tool, one where you can not only brighten the class aesthetically, but provide additional information with posters and artistic displays of content the students are studying. One of Mr. Cervantes's students commented that he had learned the eight parts of speech because it had been the subject of an amusing bulletin board with the Simpsons reviewing basic grammar. The organization of the room can supplement what you want to accomplish (see Activity 2.6).

According to Cooper et al. (1999), there are four key elements to keep in mind as you arrange your classroom.

1. The order of your desks. Do you want rows? Groups? Stations? You must consider what type of activities you will be having the students engage in, how you can keep areas free for walking around the room, and where you want your desk. Experiment with several options.
2. An area designated for storage and materials needed for the classes you teach.
3. Nothing in the room that will distract students from the lesson or that will create noise or diversions from the tasks at hand.
4. A plan for maintaining the room so that the next class will be able to enter a well-organized space, not one that will take the first 10 minutes of the class to get ready and clean up from the last one.

Secondary school teachers should also consider additional factors. For example, how are the papers and projects from class to class to be stored? Should you have some centers or stations around the room, places where students can do independent work if they finish assignments early? One social studies teacher has both a "Current Events" station and an "Extra Credit" station (both set up at all times) where students do additional activities. There's no magic formula for creating a great environment—it really doesn't matter what you choose to do. A lot will depend on your own personality and subject matter. The important thing is to give some thought to it and make your environment part of your planning. As you deal with all the influences in your field that you *can't* control, here's one that you *can*. Welcome your students into your world!

Effective Secondary Schools

Considering all of the influences that secondary schools have swirling around them, what makes a school effective? In recent years, quite a bit of research has been conducted to determine the answer to this question. The following findings have been consistent regarding some elements that are common to effective schools. As you read this checklist, rate your school from 1(*worst*) to 10 (*best*) on each item. What conclusions can you draw from this?

Effective high schools have:

1. Strong leadership, with a principal who
   - Is assertive as an instructional leader
   - Is goal and task oriented
   - Is well organized
   - Conveys high expectations for students and staff
   - Has well-defined policies that are clear and well communicated
   - Visits classrooms frequently
   - Is highly visible and available
   - Provides strong support to teachers
   - Is adept at parent and community relations

2. A positive environment that includes
   - An orderly school climate
   - Clear, firm, and consistent discipline procedures
   - A cooperative atmosphere
   - Few classroom interruptions
   - Parental involvement in student learning
   - Positive community relations
   - Adequate facilities and resources
   - A well-kept school facility
3. Competent teachers who demonstrate
   - High verbal and conceptual ability
   - Concern for upgrading professional skills
   - Knowledge of content taught
   - An understanding of the principles of learning
   - An understanding of the characteristics of students
   - Lessons with more time actively teaching
   - Assignments with less busywork
   - Planning with more learning activities
   - Lower absenteeism
4. An effective instructional program that
   - Is goal oriented
   - Is assessment driven
   - Provides immediate feedback to students
   - Is appropriate for the learners served
   - Includes an emphasis on basic skills
   - Demonstrates continuity of instruction across grades
   - Includes effective grouping for instruction
5. Assessment and revision that include
   - Ongoing assessment of student progress
   - Communication of progress to students, parents, and community
   - Periodical evaluations on total school effectiveness
   - Instructional improvement with shared responsibility
   - A focus on problem identification
   - Indicators of a dynamic program open to improvement

So, how does your school stack up? Based on the scores you gave it, which areas seem to be its strengths? Its weaknesses? Complete Activity 2.7 to help you further determine what you can do to make your school environment the very best it can be for your students.

ACTIVITY 2.7

General Observation of School Climate

Directions: Schedule an appointment to talk with an experienced faculty or staff member at your school whose judgment and opinion you trust. Ask for a tour with this person of the entire building, asking this person to comment on the quality of (a) leadership, (b) overall school environment, (c) instructional personnel, (d) instructional program, and (e) assessment procedures that exist. Discuss his or her observations in terms of how he or she agrees or disagrees with what you have seen. Summarize your discussion and list some changes you think would make the school better.

(Continued)

Summary of Observation

	What he/she observed	What I observed	Recommended changes
Leadership			
Overall school environment			
Instructional personnel			
Instructional program			
Assessment			
Other?			

TIPS from the TRENCHES

The following are suggestions teachers wish someone had made to them when they began teaching.

For understanding the world of education . . .

1. Do the activities suggested in this chapter. They actually do help you to understand better the world you will be entering.

2. Read as much as you can about the governance, funding practices, and legal issues in education. Although it is a start, there is not enough in this chapter for everything you need to know. You will definitely be affected one way or another by what is happening in these areas on a regular basis.

3. Follow the local and state news to stay abreast of what's happening in your community relative to education and your school system specifically.

For understanding your school environment . . .

4. Find a place in the school that is your "home." If you have your own room, that's great! Many new teachers, however, travel from room to room and have only a corner of a room as their office. Make it as comfortable as you can.

5. As soon as you begin teaching, identify a person to be your resource, one who appears to be in the know. This may be a veteran teacher or an administrator. Decide that this will be the person to whom you will go to get questions answered most of the time.

6. Definitely ask questions about your school until you understand how it functions. Ask about the students, the facility, the chain of command—everything.

7. Go to workshops that relate to understanding your environment. For example, many systems offer workshops about legal responsibilities and so forth.

8. Get involved with your school. The unhappiest new teachers, especially ones who leave the profession, often report that they feel isolated and that no one is interested in them. Take the initiative to get to know others and become a part of things.

9. Take time to talk to the staff in your school. Find out what they do and something about them personally. It doesn't have to be a formal interview, but these conversations will go a long way to improving your working relationships with them. Remember, the school secretary and the custodians have the keys to the kingdom. Make friends with them as soon as possible!

10. Create your own world—a classroom environment you can look forward to spending 8 hours a day in.

PRAXIS™

Praxis Competencies Related to the School Environment

The Praxis examination will have few, if any, multiple-choice questions that directly relate to your school environment or the issues addressed in this chapter. It is more likely that your knowledge of these things will enable you to answer with depth a variety of essay or constructed-response questions. For example, if you are asked about ways to work with a student who has a certain problem, your knowledge of who is who in the school will enable you to direct the student or parent accordingly.

Likewise, understanding some of the basic legal rights that you (or your students) have may provide you with a relevant perspective in an essay. For example, if you are asked about how to evaluate a paper in which a student has expressed an opinion that seems wrong-headed, what criteria would you apply in evaluating it? Regardless of your own views, you would, of course, include in your answer the fact that he has the right to free expression and, therefore, your grading of his paper would be based on other criteria.

Suggestions for Further Reading

If you have time to read only one book for understanding the high school environment . . .

Powell, A., Farrar, E., & Cohen, D. (1985). *The shopping mall high school.* Boston: Houghton Mifflin.

Or

Sizer, T. (1996). *Horace's hope: What works for the American high school.* Boston: Houghton Mifflin.

For understanding middle schools . . .

Jackson, A., & Davis, G. (2000). *Turning points 2000: Educating adolescents in the 21st century.* New York: Teachers College Press.

For understanding the governance, funding, and legal framework of schools . . .

Webb, L. D., Metha, A., & Jordan, K. F. (1999). *Foundations of American education* (3rd ed., chaps 11, 12, 13). Upper Saddle River, NJ: Merrill/Prentice Hall.

Other excellent resources . . .

Gutek, G. L. (1991). *An historical introduction to American education* (2nd ed.). Prospect Heights, IL: Waveland Press.

Kozol, J. (1991). *Savage inequalities: Children in America's schools.* New York: HarperCollins.

Spring, J. (1991). *American education: An introduction to social and political aspects.* (5th ed.). New York: Longman.

References

Bauman, P. C. (1996). *Governing education: Public sector reform and privatization.* Needham Heights, MA: Allyn & Bacon.

Berliner, D. C., & Biddle, B. J. (1997). *The manufactured crisis: Myths, fraud, and the attack on America's public schools.* White Plains, NY: Longman.

Carroll, J. M. (1990). The Copernican Plan: Restructuring the American high school. *Phi Delta Kappan, 50,* 358–365. .

Cooper, J. M., Leighton, M. S., Martorella, P. H., Morine-Dershimer, G. G., Sadker, D., Sadker, M., Shostak, R., Tenbrink, T. D., & Weber, W. A. (1999). *Classroom teaching skills.* (6th ed.). Boston: Houghton Mifflin.

Counts, G. S. (1922). *The selective character of American secondary education.* Chicago: The University of Chicago Press.

Earley, P. M. (1994). *AACTE Briefs. 15*(7), 1–3.

French, W. M. (1957). *American secondary education* (pp. 101–102). New York: Odyssey Press.

George, P. S., & McEwin, C. K. (1999). "High schools for a new century: Why is the high school changing?" *NASSP Bulletin, 83*(606), 10–24.

Gutek, G. L. (1991). *An historical introduction to American education* (2nd ed.). Prospect Heights, IL: Waveland Press.

Jones, R. (1995). "Wake up!" *The Executive Educator, 17*(8), 15–18.

Hanson, E. M. (1991). *Educational administration and organizational behavior.* Boston: Allyn & Bacon.

Hardy, L. (1999). "A cold climate." *The American School Board Journal, 186*(3), 31–34.

Kadel, S. (1996). *Reengineering high schools for student success: Hot topics and usable research.* Washington, DC: Office of Educational Research and Improvement. (ERIC Document No. ED366076)

Kozol, J. (1991). *Savage inequalities.* New York: HarperCollins.

McNergney, R. F., & Herbert, J. M. (1995). *Foundations of education.* Needham Heights, MA: Allyn & Bacon.

Myers, C. B., & Myers, L. K. (1995). *The professional educator: A new introduction to teaching and schools.* Belmont, CA: Wadsworth.

National Association for Secondary School Principals. (1996). *Breaking ranks: Changing of an American institution.* Commission on restructuring of the American High School. Reston, VA: NASSP.

Powell, A., Farrar, E., & Cohen, D. (1985). *The shopping mall high school.* Boston: Houghton Mifflin.

Report of the National Commission on Governing America's Schools. (1999). *Governing America's schools: Changing the rules.* Denver, CO: Education Commission of the States.

Resnick, M. A. (1999). *Effective school governance: A look at today's practice and tomorrow's promise.* Denver, CO: Education Commission of the States.

Rettig, M. D., & Canady, R. L. (1996). "All around the block: The benefits and challenges of a nontraditional school schedule." *The School Administrator, 53*(8), 8–14.

Rich, J. M. (1992). *Foundations of education.* Upper Saddle River, NJ: Merrill/Prentice Hall.

Sizer, T. (1996). *Horace's hope: What works for the American high school.* Boston: Houghton Mifflin.

U.S. Department of Education. (1997). National Center for Education Statistics, Common Core of Data. *National public education survey*. Washington, DC.

U.S. Department of Education. (1999). National Center for Education Statistics. *Early estimates of public elementary and secondary education statistics: School year 1998–1999*. Washington, DC. p. 9.

Webb, L. D., Metha, A., & Jordan, K. F. (1999). *Foundations of American education* (3rd ed.). Upper Saddle River, NJ: Merrill/Prentice Hall.

Ziebarth, T. (1999). *The changing landscape of education governance*. Denver, CO: Education Commission of the States.

PART 2

Your Students: Understanding and Working with Adolescents

3

Understanding the Nature and Diversity of Adolescents

Why is it that at the very times when my students need acceptance and understanding the most, they are the hardest to accept and understand?

Secondary French teacher

Fasten your seatbelts. You are about to board a roller coaster. At least that's how you will feel as you experience the daily ups and downs and unexpected turns that come with teaching adolescents. It's important that you know what you're getting into. But you're ready. After all, you wouldn't have bought a ticket for this ride if you didn't expect a thrill, right?

Secondary teachers today work with the most diverse student population in our history, young people who are also in the most chaotic time of their personal development. They face myriad psychological, emotional, and social pressures that wreak havoc with their struggle to become adults. Add to this raging hormones and you have students who are in flux and who feel 10 feet tall and bulletproof one day and self-conscious and insecure the next. Fortunately, if you understand some of the basics of where they are developmentally and the cultural influences that are present, your interactions will seem more like "predictable unpredictability."

This chapter focuses on adolescents themselves, both their nature and the increasing diversity they represent. You will review a few of the most common theories about their development and how you can apply this knowledge to your teaching. The chapter then provides important facts about our multicultural nation as well as terms that cause people problems. After a brief discussion of cultural factors that shape your and your students' perspectives, the central concepts of multicultural education are summarized. It concludes with some suggestions regarding your own preparation as you incorporate these principles in your classroom.

The Nature of Adolescents

Influences on Secondary Students: What Makes Them Tick?

Do you remember how it felt to be a student in secondary school? What did you think about every day? What things in your life represented pressure or pushed your buttons? More than likely, you were more concerned with yourself, your friends, and your family (in that order) than with anything that went on in class. These priorities are natural—students at this age are doing what they are supposed to do as they grow up. Many experts believe that what teenagers learn about themselves during this volatile time is key to how they will handle the rest of their lives. Don't be fooled by the nonchalant exterior of that student sleeping in the first row. More than likely and on any given day, he is in some turmoil over something that has nothing to do with your lesson.

You will want to learn as much as you can about your students as soon as possible. Many teachers gain valuable insights by using a questionnaire such as the type described in Activity 3.1 during the first few days of the school year. The responses provide immediate feedback regarding what is important to the students.

External Influences: Peers and Family

While the order will vary with each student, research confirms that the most important external influences on students are their peers and family. Many teachers would argue that the media is an equally strong influence. True or not, this means that you (and any other adults) come in third. Does this mean your influence is limited? Not at all. You can still have an amazing impact if you are constantly aware of what their real priorities are.

The Bad News for You

Students believe that most adults don't have a clue about what teenagers want or what they are about. Therefore, often very little of what you say about many, especially personal, topics will get much of a response. Despite this, they want to be accepted and value most those teachers who work to understand them.

Students will probably be critical of most everything you do and say. (Ask any parent.) You'll see the telltale rolling of the eyes, sighing, and general body language that will feel like disrespect. It's usually nothing personal—this annoying habit is actually developmentally appropriate. They are just busy trying to figure out who they are, and you represent something from which to deviate as they find their way.

ACTIVITY 3.1

Getting to Know Your Students

There are many good ways to find out about your students. Two are the following:

1. Create an information sheet for your students to complete the first day. You may want to ask them about their families, hobbies, their favorite music, extracurricular activities, and so forth.
2. Have students participate in an activity that helps them to get to know each other as well as providing you with an opportunity to get to know them. Distribute a sheet (such as Figure 3.1) and ask them to follow the directions. The questions can be varied to reflect the interests and grade level of the students you are teaching. At the end of the exercise, collect the sheets for your own information.

Both of these activities can be turned into a class activity where students share the information with the group.

____

Name of Person Being Interviewed

Background

Age ______________ Birth date ______________

Number of brothers ______________ Number of sisters ______________

Where are you in your family (youngest, oldest, only child)? ______________

Where were you born? ______________

Do you speak a language other than English? If so, which one? ______________

Personality

	What is your favorite?	**What is your least favorite?**
TV program	______	______
Food	______	______
Animal	______	______
Sport	______	______
Hobby	______	______
Subject	______	______

What is one thing you look for in a friend? ______________

____

What is one thing you would not like a friend to do? ______________

____

**(Students are paired up to interview each other. Then students introduce their partners to the class.)*

FIGURE 3.1 I'd Like to Get to Know You Better
An Interview Sheet for Student Use
Courtesy Joy Van Zandt

Secondary school students value the opinion of their friends much more than anything you offer. This is why parents get so concerned about who their children are spending time with. They want to be part of a group and are willing to conform for this to happen. In fact, most secondary school students (approximately 80%) belong to two basic kinds of groups: the clique and the crowd (a collection of cliques; Dunphy, 1963; Duseck, 1991;

Grinder, 1969). Cliques are usually small groups of six to eight students who are good friends and talk about and plan activities for the crowd. The advantages are the sense of belonging and security the students crave. On the other hand, if the clique requires too much conformity, it can suppress individuality. Cliques also can foster snobbish behavior that makes other students feel rejected.

The crowd is the center of weekend social activities. Crowds promote opportunities for all types of interactions and are less intimate than cliques (Duseck, 1991).

Students may exhibit a sense of entitlement, especially in schools with a more economically privileged population. Generally, students today have been given more attention and material possessions than ever before. Some would even argue they have been given too much. Additionally, often with parent encouragement, they have become savvy about their "rights" and what you and the school "owe" them.

While students want to get good grades, this doesn't necessarily translate into being committed to learning. They need good grades for college and sports eligibility and have learned how to get them. Usually it means that during a stimulating discussion, someone will interrupt by asking, "Is this going to be on the test?"

The Good News for You

While teenagers are drawn to their peers during these years, parents and other significant adults tend to have long-term, and thus more enduring, influence. This fact is reinforced as teenagers often pick friends who have values and backgrounds similar to their own.

Secondary students are interesting! You will not be bored teaching them. They are clever, insightful, fun, and stimulating (see Activity 3.2).

In many ways, your students represent a clean slate in terms of your potential ability to mold and influence them. They are searching for answers to everything, and this makes them veritable sponges for information, modeling, and any other messages that they will consider as they define who they are.

Regardless of how they may act, they want your approval and will go a long way to get it.

Most students love school. Yes. This closely guarded secret is a fact. And why wouldn't they? It's their world. This is *not* to say that they love studying or doing homework, but they do love seeing their friends, participating in activities and sports, and going to the prom. Sadly, for many from unstable homes, it's also the only place they get meals, have a routine that provides some structure in their lives, and encounter adults who show concern for them on a daily basis.

Unfortunately, for some students, however, school can be a place of humiliation and persecution by their peers. You will feel their constant, warm appreciation when you serve as a consistent source of understanding, guidance, and support during these difficult years. You are important to them.

REALITY CHECK 3.1

Your ability to deal effectively with your students often has a lot to do with your age. This factor can cut both ways. For example, younger teachers usually have the most to learn about the best ways to work with adolescents simply because they are not much older than the students themselves. Teachers who are somewhat older tend to command a certain respect that comes with age. On the other hand, there are students who may respond better to younger teachers—ones who are "with it" and attractive.

Internal Influences: Their Personal Pressures

1. Many students today are stressed. They are doing too much—participating in too many activities, taking too many courses, assuming too many responsibilities at home, and somehow trying to have a social life. The result is that you may be teaching young people who are sleep deprived and overly anxious.

2. They worry that they will not succeed—at school, at home, in activities, in life. To them, not succeeding means they are losers, and they would rather be anything but a loser.

3. They want to be popular. This usually means they want others to see them as "cool," which translates into being attractive, fun, outgoing, clever, and fashionable in their friends' eyes. For many, being popular is the ultimate achievement in high school. Popular students

Knowing Your Students as Individuals

As the year progresses, you should be seeking opportunities to know your students better. You have questionnaires from the first few days so you know some things about them. Now make a concerted effort to know them better as individuals by showing a sincere interest in them.

Make a point to have one sustained conversation with at least two students a week in each class until you have chatted with everyone. Ask about their lives and school activities, staying away from the topic of your class (unless they want to discuss it). After a few of these talks, see if you can detect a pattern in their life priorities. Create at least 10 resolutions for yourself relative to your teaching and personal interactions that will enhance their self-esteem and positive attitudes toward you and your class.

are perceived as self-confident and smart, and they are usually from the socially dominant class (Clark & Ayers, 1988).

4. Secondary students believe everyone is always watching them and paying attention to their every move. This naturally results in their being self-conscious most of the time.

5. They need affirmation and praise. They will agonize for days over a negative comment made carelessly by you or any other significant person they are trying to please. Be careful. These are fragile emerging egos you are grooming.

If you remember these few things, you will avoid doing damage to your personal relationships with your students, assist them in their growth path, and engage them in what you are trying to teach. For example, if you know they need to succeed, provide opportunities for that to happen in your class. Because you also know they are stressed, organize your syllabus so that they know well in advance what to expect and when things are due.

"All-Time Greatest Hits" Theories: What Developmental Patterns Are Present?

If you are going to work with adolescents, it will help to understand where they are developmentally. You could spend a lifetime reading and studying the many theories regarding the intellectual, social, moral, cultural, and other aspects of human development. To simplify, consider the following, which represent some of the most respected views regarding the biggies: the cognitive, social, and moral development of secondary students.

Cognitive Development

Swiss psychologist Jean Piaget's theory of cognitive development describes how people learn. He claimed that there are three basic concepts related to intellectual development. The first is *content* (or behavior), either as action or verbal explanation of thought processes. The next is *structure,* or cognitive operations for behaving in particular ways. The third is *function,* or adaptation and organization. Adaptation consists of assimilation and accommodation. *Assimilation* is when a person incorporates new information into what she already knows. *Accommodation* is when a person changes how they think to receive the new information, thus learning something new (Dusek, 1991). *Equilibrium* is when students organize new information in their minds, making sense out of things based on what they already know. When they try to figure out things that don't make sense, it is referred to as *disequilibrium*.

What does that mean? All of this is to say that students learn because they are given information (content) and then they process it (structure). They then assimilate the new material into what they currently know and make intellectual adjustments to internalize new knowledge (accommodation).

Piaget identified four stages of intellectual development that occur at certain ages.

Sensorimotor Stage—From Birth to 2 Years Old

Goal-Directed Learning

- Children learn that something exists even if they cannot see it (object permanence).
- Learning is goal directed. Children realize that certain actions will get desired responses.

Preoperations Stage—From 2–7 Years Old

Increasing Language Ability

- Children acquire skill in the use of language and mental imagery.
- Children are egocentric. All their learning revolves around them.

Concrete Operations Stage—From 7–11 Years Old

Working Logically

- Children can understand concrete but not abstract problems.
- They begin to understand the point of view of others.

Formal Operations Stage—From 11 Years Old to Adult (Your Students)

Solving Abstract Problems

- Students can reason theoretically.
- Students can think logically and abstractly.

Clearly, most of your students will be functioning at this stage.

REALITY CHECK 3.2

Stages of any developmental theory are not written in stone. Naturally, individuals vary. Therefore, it is good to be aware of the stages directly before and after the one that most generally applies to your students, to accommodate the needs of students who are less or more advanced than the norm. For example, while you should be able to expect your students to reason theoretically (Formal Operations), you may have some who can still only understand concrete problems (Concrete Operations). Your goal is always to move them to the next stage.

Personal and Social Development

Erik Erikson provides a theory for understanding the emotional and psychosocial development of people. This refers to how humans relate to each other and feel about themselves. Like Piaget, he views development as occurring in stages that emerge within a series of psychosocial "crises." Each crisis has two possible outcomes, which are polar opposites. As people develop, they work out the outcome, bouncing between the two opposites as the ego develops (Dusek, 1991). The crises are as follows:

1. Trust versus Mistrust (0–1 years old)
   Infants develop a sense of trust when basic needs are met. For example, one may have learned to trust Mom but is fearful of strangers.
2. Autonomy versus Shame (1–3 years old)
   Toddlers develop autonomy as they experiment. Consider the terrible twos, who exhibit autonomy as they explore the house but deal with shame when they break something.
3. Initiative versus Guilt (3–6 years old)
   Preschoolers learn to take the initiative within the confines of restrictions. They will initiate activity but feel guilt when they make a mistake or don't please an adult.

4. Industry versus Inferiority (6–12 years old)
   Elementary school years provide chances to develop competence at tasks. Children also experience feelings of inferiority when they aren't chosen for the team or are not invited to a party.

5. Your Students: Identity versus Confusion (12–18 years old)
   Adolescents struggle with who they are. Erikson believes that students must develop a personal philosophy of life and a vocational identity during these years. They must face their abilities and limitations (maybe they won't really make it to the NBA). They must also explore their religious and political beliefs. This is a tall order. In effect, they are developing a way to deal with life and their own behavior (Erikson, 1963).

6. Intimacy versus Isolation (young adult)
   Young adults ask themselves such questions as "Should I live at home or in an apartment after graduation?" and "Should I get married?"

7. Generativity versus Stagnation (middle adult)
   Middle adults wonder if they should look for new ways to grow and develop or if their best years are over.

8. Integrity versus Despair (older adult)
   Older adults review their lives and determine whether they should have lived the way they wanted to or not.

Moral Development of Kohlberg

Like Piaget and Erikson, Lawrence Kohlberg (1976) believed that the moral development of people parallels intellectual stages—in this case, levels. His goal was to describe the thought structures that inform moral judgments and an individual's sense of right or wrong. There are three basic levels. While each level actually has two components, the discussion here will summarize them into broader categories.

1. Preconventional Level—Children's concept of right and wrong depends on whether they were punished for some action. If they were rewarded, it must be the right thing to do. If they were punished, it must be the wrong thing to do. No wonder there are so many students who are confused about what cheating really is when their parents support their taking term papers off the Web.

2. Conventional Level—The priority is to conform to the laws of society and live up to the expectations of others. In other words, students consciously choose to follow the rules—or not.

3. Postconventional Level—Moral values are determined based on what the person believes is right.

Your students are probably between the Conventional and Postconventional levels. There will be a struggle to develop their own principles based on what they have been taught and what has been modeled for them. Ultimately, they must develop their own judgment about what is morally correct.

Brain Research: How Do Students Think?

As anyone who has spent much time around teenagers will tell you, comprehending how the mind of an adolescent thinks, let alone learns, is a challenge. For years, educators have assumed that organizing material into logical patterns will make transfer of information easier for students. Yet this approach, which seems so obvious to teachers, often does not work for most high school students.

New research indicates that adolescents are not unique in this regard. Most *useful* learning is random. "Individuals learn in different multipath sequences, not by depending solely on well-ordered lesson plans. While these plans can serve as a base, students' previous individual experience serves as the only meaningful foundation to which more learning is added. Therefore, much of the logical group instruction you will be oriented to deliver, will inevitably produce a large degree of failure," unless you incorporate students' personal experiences into your teaching (Hart, 1999, pp. 101–112). You will need to focus on meeting the students where they are—viewing content from their perspective.

The following represent some key points in a growing body of research about how the brain of a high school student works. The implications for teaching your class should be clear.

1. If students are relaxed, feel safe, and are motivated, they learn better (Caine & Caine, 1991).

2. The left hemisphere of the brain is associated with verbal learning and logical thinking; the emotional and affective elements are located in the right brain. Most teaching at the high school level is geared to the left brain. Effective teaching should be to the whole brain, incorporating methods that relate to both processes.

3. There is a difference between *knowing* and *verbalism*. Repeating information without really understanding it is verbalism. High school students are, for the most part, taught isolated bits of information and generalizations and have been rewarded for their ability to verbalize. When asked to explain in their own words something they have memorized for a test, they often haven't a clue how to do so. To really understand a new concept, they must "examine information, establishing relationships among the facts, and draw conclusions" (Clark & Starr, 1996, p. 30).

4. The human brain takes learning cues from its environment. Today's teenagers live in a fast-paced world. Their brains respond to short, unusual, and novel stimuli. Therefore, teachers need to have an exciting environment where students can make appropriate interconnections. In other words, faster learning takes place with greater meaning (Sousa, 1998).

5. How students *feel* about school determines how much they will pay attention to it. Emotions and reason interact to encourage or inhibit learning. Daniel Goleman (1995) indicated that we need to teach young people how to use their emotions intelligently. He identified the following five areas of emotional competency necessary to succeed in life: self-awareness/impulse control, persistence, zeal, self-motivation/empathy, and social skills. These emotional skills are key for effective learning in school (Shelton, 2000).

6. Secondary students learn best when they see a relation between what they are studying and their own lives. Students make more meaningful mental connections when activities are designed with this in mind (Sousa, 1998).

7. The shorter the concentrated learning situation, the better the learning. Students tend to remember best the things that came first in a lesson, and remember second best the information that came last (Sousa, 1998).

Learning Theory: How Does Learning Theory Help You to Teach Secondary Students?

Contrary to the belief of many, there is nothing more practical than good theory. Effective teachers understand the developmental nature of students and that their actions are symptomatic of their age and stage (see Activity 3.3). What can you take from the theories about the developmental nature of your students that will make you more effective?

Applying Piaget, Erikson, and Kohlberg to Learning Situations

There are several implications of Piaget's work for you. Remember that most of your students should be at the Formal Operations stage and thus should be able to think logically and abstractly. They will need just the right disequilibrium to keep them stimulated (hard

ACTIVITY 3.3

Incorporating Learning Theory into Lessons

Look at the last two lessons you prepared. (If you have not prepared any lessons yet, observe a lesson being taught by a veteran teacher.) Now look at the seven findings on brain research listed above. Identify how many ways you have incorporated the findings into each of your lesson plans. Remember that you are expected to reflect all of them in every lesson when possible. Note how often you (or the teacher you are observing) have done this.

Create a new version of one of the lessons, making a concerted effort to reflect as many of the findings in the new lesson as possible.

enough to challenge them, but easy enough to succeed). Interestingly, even secondary school students like an occasional assignment that lets them drop back a stage. A computer science teacher asked her students to create Mother's Day cards to demonstrate skills in the previous lesson. She was afraid the students might think it was too babyish, but to her surprise, they seemed more engaged and interested than they had been in weeks.

Erikson's work suggests that since students will be in the stage of Identity versus Confusion, socially and emotionally they are trying to learn about themselves. They are primarily concerned with *me, me, me*! Therefore, you will need to look for activities that ensure their engagement in the learning process—activities that require them to use their own experiences and perspectives. These would include cooperative learning, discussion, problem solving, and anything that involves peer interaction. Assignments that reinforce the development of their own self-concepts will be the most productive and meaningful.

Kohlberg's theory suggests that these students are somewhere between the conventional and postconventional levels. They will be trying to formulate their own definition of right and wrong based on what they have been taught at home and school as well as any other influential sources in their lives. Focus on discussion and problem-solving activities that require their reflection regarding moral dilemmas. For example, one English teacher always looks for opportunities to discuss moral decisions faced by characters in novels she assigns. Not only does it further their understanding of the novel, but it provides students with a chance to wrestle with such questions for their own consideration. (See also Activity 3.4.)

The Sociocultural Approach

Lev Vygotsky provides a sociocultural perspective, suggesting that students learn primarily through interaction with others. It is the give-and-take of the communication process as the students are presented with new information that results in meaningful learning. With this in mind, several key terms will be helpful as you teach.

ACTIVITY 3.4

Applying Theory to Practice

1. Try to identify students in your classes who represent one or more of the developmental stages.
2. Practice applying what you know about the developmental stages of these theorists and how they affect what you do with your students. Begin by adapting your next lesson. Create at least one activity that addresses the learning needs these stages of Piaget, Erikson, and Kohlberg represent.

1. Self Talk guides students' thinking and actions. You model how to do a problem in math, speaking each step out loud as you give students the vocabulary and framework to ask themselves the same questions when they are on their own. Students talk to themselves as they learn a process. Gradually, these statements become part of the automatic actions they take. For example, a student reading about a battle in social studies hears the teacher ask the class "Who is fighting?" Why are they fighting?" and "What are the consequences of their actions?" He internalizes these questions and asks the same ones of himself when he is alone.

2. Assisted Learning and Scaffolding is when teachers guide learning by providing assistance when needed and then weaning students to independence. The teacher or peers provide examples, clues, and other suggestions to help them discover answers on their own.

3. Zone of Proximal Development (ZPD) is when the student is stuck at a certain point but can move ahead with support from the teacher. This movement can be facilitated when students are asked leading questions or are prompted by reminders of previously learned material. Teachers need to recognize this zone so that they offer assistance before the student gets frustrated and gives up (Burke, Brown, Jones, Spragley, & Petroskey, 2002).

Constructivist Learning Theory

Constructivism is a theory about knowledge and learning rooted in the notion that students construct knowledge based on previous knowledge and their personal perspectives. The theory reflects some of the basic principles of such educators as Piaget, who suggests that discovery is more important than expository teaching. It also reflects the views of Vygotsky, who recommends guided exploration and coaching combined with the student's prior knowledge and beliefs. Learning is self-regulated and becomes apparent through concrete experience, conversation, and reflection. This view emphasizes the active role of learners as they make sense of the universe. Thus, constructivist classrooms are planned by both teachers and students and include such methods as open-ended discussions, problem solving, and cooperative learning activities.

REALITY CHECK 3.3

Notice how many of the theories of these experts suggest methods such as discussion, problem solving, group work, and other student-oriented activities? They reflect the students' developmental preoccupation with themselves as a normal pattern. No wonder the teachers who limit their instruction to lectures are referred to as boring. After all, if the topic isn't about the students themselves, how interesting can it be?

The Diversity of Adolescents

"I'm not that concerned about issues like diversity in my classroom. People think about it too much. I'm a math teacher—I teach math and I treat all my kids alike. I'm not going to get bogged down by worrying that everything I say or the way I teach is going to offend someone. I do the best I can to teach everybody. Some students do well—others don't. Can I help it if my white kids are simply smarter than my blacks or Hispanics?"

Third-year teacher

Does the opinion of this teacher sound familiar to you? Worse yet, does that opinion *feel* familiar to you? If so, get a mirror and take a long look at a teacher who needs a serious wake-up call about some issues related to diversity. After all, our country is clearly a nation of diverse populations racially, culturally, economically, religiously, and in many other ways. Your students are not all the same, and more so than ever in our history, their differences *must* be acknowledged and taken into account as you deal with them each day. You don't have the luxury of indulging a cavalier attitude of insensitivity such as the one above. You are dealing with vulnerable adolescents whose overall development is your professional responsibility.

Diversity: How Do the Facts Affect Your Perception?

How do you react when you hear the word *diversity?* Experts have found that how teachers view the issue of diversity is a direct indicator of the extent to which they will pay attention to it at all in their classrooms. There are usually three attitudes. First, some see diversity as a *problem*. To them, it is an annoyance that is affecting them only because it is an item on someone's political agenda. Some feel that it is an inconvenient add-on to the countless other things they must be aware of as they teach. Others see diversity as a *right* and equate it with the civil and minority rights of students in schools. They believe the schools have an obligation to address these issues. Another group sees it as a *resource,* an opportunity to enhance the curriculum and enrich the lives of their students. These teachers agree with the following comment from Vivian Paley (1989, p. 56):

> It is often hard to learn from people who are just like you. Too much is taken for granted. Homogeneity is fine in a bottle of milk, but in a classroom it diminishes the curiosity that ignites discovery.

So how about you? Is diversity a problem, a right, or a resource?

Baggage

Do you think you can focus solely on the teaching of the content of your course and ignore the factors related to diversity? Take note of the facts. Nationally, students of color represent over one third of the school-age population today. By the year 2020, this will increase to one half. Depending on where you teach, you may or may not encounter a teaching situation that mirrors your own background. Demographic data indicate that, based on birthrates and immigration patterns, there will be more Asian American, Latino, and African American students filling classrooms in the coming years, but fewer students of European descent. However, the gender and race of their teachers follow a very different pattern: 86.5% of today's teachers are White, and 75% are female (Gollnick & Chinn, 2002). In other important ways, fewer than 6% of American children belong to families where the father works and the mother stays at home, and one third of all high school students are identified as "at risk" (Guillaume, 2000, p. 161).

When you and your students meet on the first day, all of you bring your own individual perspectives and experiences relating to issues of diversity. In addition to the positive aspects of this reality, some of what everyone brings is baggage—some of it heavy. This baggage is often based on misconceptions regarding other cultures.

If you are like most humans, you have prejudices. Yes, you. And there are many prejudices you may harbor unknowingly and unintentionally that can do damage to the students you deal with every day. You may think you are just trying to teach art. But the lessons your students will remember most are the subtle messages they get from you about their value as human beings. Perhaps you are turned off by students who are overweight or have a strange accent. Maybe you just don't like redheads. Are these the students least likely to be called on? A study in 1992 reported that teachers favor boys and encourage their assertion and achievement whereas they encourage girls to be compliant (Wellesley College Center for Research on Women, 1992). Do you think there's been much change in the last decade? Does this study describe your behavior?

While you are consciously or unconsciously indulging your judgments, remember that your students come to you having had 12–17 years to develop prejudices of their own. If you happen to be the object of such prejudice, your job is automatically made more difficult. A fundamentalist protestant student may decide immediately that you, a Jewish teacher, have little of value to teach him. This will make your job harder, won't it? Will some of your attitudes make learning more problematic for your students?

Reality Check 3.4

Obviously, you can't control the baggage your students bring into your classroom any more than they can control what prejudices you have. The difference is that it is your job to control your attitudes and assumptions. You must pay attention to your students' attitudes and provide an environment of openness, one where at least the students *feel* valued and accepted by you, even if you don't feel accepted by some of them. If you sense that a student has a prejudice toward you, be patient. Try to get the student to focus on your role as the instructor rather than on you as a person. Don't take their attitudes personally.

Diversity: Coming to Terms with Terms

As you prepare to work with secondary students, get ready to negotiate a field of terminology landmines. In this day and age, it seems that people are more sensitive than ever about certain words, labels, or terms. This sensitivity is the result of decades of damage caused by thoughtless as well as intentionally hurtful use. As a result, many people try to avoid the use of some terms altogether. Others use (or abuse) terms to get a desired effect. For example, few words can incense a well-meaning White teacher as much as being called a "racist." Teachers, especially conscientious males, work hard to avoid being called "sexist." Regardless, people have become careless in their use of terms, misusing them too often or saying them to the wrong people.

Unless you pay attention, you will surely offend someone at some point about something and thus potentially sabotage your ability to work effectively. You are in the age of political correctness, whether you see that as a positive or negative state of affairs. Consider the case of a social studies teacher who always calls his female colleagues "girls," much to the irritation of several. He doesn't intend to demean them, but several are offended anyway. Interestingly, some of them don't mind at all. Often, White, and especially older, teachers are unsure whether to refer to students as Black, African American, or even Afro-American. Does it matter? To some, yes. To others, no. The problem is that you don't always know till you have made a mistake.

More has been written and discussed about terms and words associated with issues of diversity than space here allows. Understanding exactly what some of the most common terms mean may help you to avoid inadvertently insulting others.

There are several terms that are often used interchangeably, but are basically different.

Diversity simply refers to the quality of being different in any way. In effect, every person is different from everyone else. This general term covers differences of any type.

Multicultural, on the other hand, refers to differences in multiple cultures.

Prejudice is a judgment or opinion that one has before the facts about a person or situation are known. Essentially, the term represents preconceived ideas.

Bias, on the other hand, is a predisposition toward something, a partiality or leaning toward a certain way of thinking.

There are also several common terms that are generally negative and can be inflammatory, depending on context.

Racism is feeling antagonistic toward another race based on the feeling that your own race is superior.

Sexism is feeling superior about one's own gender.

Homophobia is the unreasonable fear of same-sex attractions or of people who have same-sex attractions.

Able-body-ism is seeing a physical disability as imperfection (Robinson & Howard-Hamilton, 2000).

Class-elitism is the belief that one's social status is superior to that of others.

The five "isms" described above are based on the Robinson Model on Discourses (see Figure 3.2).

Robinson believes that all identities are socially constructed and have overt and subtle meanings. The people who are members of groups on the top of the line are valued more than those below the line. All of these "isms" are based on a need to be "better than" someone else (Myers et al., 1991). Being on the receiving end of any of these isms is harmful. But at the fragile developmental stage of teenagers, in particular, the impact can be devastating.

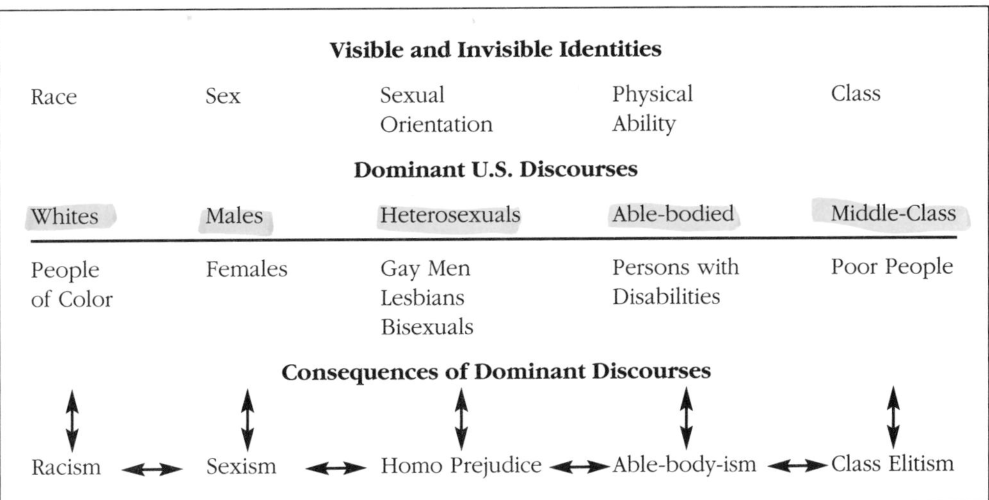

FIGURE 3.2 Robinson Model on Discourses

Reprinted From "The Intersections of Dominant Discourses Across Race, Gender, and Other Identities," *Journal of Counseling and Development* 77, 1999 pp. 73–79. © ACA. Reprinted with permission. No further reproduction authorized without written permission of the American Counseling Association.

Terms That Are Often Used Interchangeably

While these terms have different definitions, popular usage has often resulted in describing them based on sociological distinctions. Only the most rabid of the terminology police will be upset by your misusing these.

1. Race—Race is a social perception. It is not a scientific concept. Anthropologists and medical scientists have shown that human gene pools are extraordinarily mixed and that there is more diversity within any "race" than there is between the "races." Nevertheless, even though teachers increasingly avoid using the term, this word remains a part of daily thought and action. When you refer to a student's race, you are describing one of only three perceived groupings of mankind based on such features as color and texture of hair, color of skin, and so forth. These three are Caucasian (loosely, the White race), Negroid (loosely, the Black race), and Mongoloid (loosely, the Oriental race; *Webster's New World College Dictionary,* 2000, p. 1180). Race is different from, but is often confused with, culture. You are born with race. You learn culture.

2. Ethnicity—This term indicates an affiliation with a group distinguished by customs, characteristics, language, and so forth. It suggests attributes that may be peculiar to a race or nation, people who share a distinctive historical tradition (*Webster's New World College Dictionary,* 2000, p. 488).

3. Culture—This term refers to the "habits, skills, art, institutions of a given people in a given period in time" (*Webster's New World College Dictionary,* 2000, p. 353). Culture provides guidelines that affect the way people think, feel, and behave in society. One's culture is "in us, and all around us, just as the air we breathe" (Erickson, 1997, p. 33).

Understanding More About Culture

What else should you know about culture as it relates to secondary students? Gollnick and Chinn (2002) described two processes to explain how one learns the culture he is born into: enculturation and socialization. *Enculturation* is the process of acquiring the characteristics of a culture and function in accord with its ways of behaving. For example, American teenagers wear jeans and T-shirts. *Socialization* is the process of learning the social norms of a culture, internalizing its social expectations. These teenagers learn to think of themselves as individuals with rights and ambitions. It is important to remember that culture is shared by people and that it changes constantly as well (Gollnick & Chinn, 2002). Your students are actively involved in these processes, which coincide with their developmental tasks.

Traditionally, the dominant culture in our society has evolved from a Western tradition—the biggest influence being a White, Anglo-Saxon, and Protestant (WASP) perspective. But this is changing. Other cultural influences are clearly evident. This is happening as a result of assimilation, when cultural groups adopt or change the dominant culture, or through a pattern of cultural pluralism, which allows two or more distinct groups to function together without requiring any assimilation (Gollnick & Chinn, 2002). Our nation is truly multicultural.

Diverse Perspectives: Where Are You and Your Students Coming From?

Your Perspective

How comfortable are you with diversity in the first place? Do you find yourself uneasy if you encounter people from a different culture or those who have a different lifestyle? Are you tolerant and understanding of differences?

Fortunately, like most people who choose the teaching profession, you probably at least *think* of yourself as tolerant and understanding of others—especially teenagers. This is good. It means that you know on some level this is the right way to feel if you are going to teach. It isn't always easy, however. But it is crucial for you to *behave* in a manner that models tolerance and understanding regardless of how you feel. Like almost everyone, you do have blind spots—areas of prejudice that you may or may not have identified as such. What are they? Reflect on what they might be as you complete Activity 3.5. Remember that your blind spots can result in your being both overly positive to one group of students and negative to another.

Activity 3.5

Identifying Your Blind Spots

Directions: List one or more examples of people or groups that you might tend to favor more than others and those that you might tend to discount or ignore. (You may not have anyone in some of these categories and you should feel free to add categories not listed.)

Caution: Consider that you may not be objective enough to identify all of your blind spots as well as someone else can who knows you well could. As you do the exercise, talk with a close friend or colleague about his or her perceptions of you in this regard.

	Groups you might favor	Groups you might discount
1. Race		
2. Gender		
3. Culture		
4. Physical appearance		
5. Other?		

There are several things you will want to keep in mind about yourself and your own blind spots. You have already taken the biggest first step: becoming aware of what some of them are. Actively face your own prejudices. Sit down and think about them. Then consider strategies that you can use to counter these tendencies. Consider the following traps many teachers fall into as they face issues of diversity.

First, more than likely, you take for granted your own frame of reference. If you are African American, it may be very natural to refer to the "White girls" who always talk in your class while you refer to the "girls" (African American) who talk. Since the individual differences within your own race are a given, you might inadvertently use a group label when referring to students outside your immediate experience. One teacher was reminded by a colleague that she never said "Jewish boys," yet did not hesitate to refer to the "Black boys." She realized that because she was Jewish, she was always aware of the individual differences among Jews and was probably unable to come up with generalizations about Jews that would be meaningful to her. Interestingly, however, when she heard non-Jews make such remarks, she thought of them as either ignorant, indifferent, or prejudiced (Paley, 1989, pp. 135–137).

Second, you will probably be more interested in issues that reflect your own experience. In fact, studies prove that teachers usually approach dealing with their students based on their own perspective instead of considering the students' needs first (Guillaume, Zuniga, & Yee, 1998). If some rich, popular cheerleaders rejected you in high school and made you feel unattractive or inferior, you may tend to be less sympathetic to them now. Likewise, if your experiences with people from a different race were positive, you may find that you favor those students over others in your class. In other words, you will be prone to connect with certain groups of students and not connect with others based on your personal history. You may find that you are drawn to the students on the honor roll, because you were that type of student yourself, and less patient with the class clown because you remember one who teased you relentlessly in algebra class. Or vice versa.

Third, you may tend to view students who are different from you as being deficient in some way. How do you respond to students who use poor grammar, have a foreign dialect, or don't observe Halloween because they believe it is satanic? Are these differences that you take in stride as examples of predictable and acceptable diversity, or do you secretly think, "What an ignorant belief" or "This student is stupid." Your attitude is everything. *You* are the creator of your classroom environment, the teacher of the hidden curriculum of racism, sexism, or any of the other isms that mold your students' take on the world in a permanent way.

REALITY CHECK 3.5

You can't fake how you really feel—at least not for long. The students can see who you really are and what you truly believe. Your ability to affirm them is everything! Identify your prejudices, accept that they exist, and work on adjusting your attitude. It's a challenge, but you are the teacher. This is not an option. Besides, as difficult as it will be for you, it may be more possible for you to adjust your thinking and behavior than it is for some of them to adjust at this stage in their lives. On the other hand, many of your students may be more open to new ideas and cultures than you are. Be receptive to learning from *them*.

The Student Perspective

Think back to when you were a secondary school student. What baggage did you carry around with you in thinking about other individual students, groups, or teachers? Did you have stereotypical images of those who were of a different race or religion? Probably you did, and like you, your students have them, too.

By the time your students reach secondary school, they have received 12 or 13 years of conflicting messages about cultural ways of being. The school environment, in fact, contributes to this confusion. This is because culturally diverse students must function in settings that are designed to promote the values and goals of the dominant culture. How minority students see themselves and how those of the dominant culture see them may vary significantly. Thus, in many situations, how can minorities possibly be comfortable and see school as a welcoming place? Because they often have difficulty adapting, they can find themselves in a no-win situation. This results in poorer academic performance and higher drop-out rates (Yeh & Drost, 2002). Therefore, a solid multicultural academic program is the best remedy. Not only can it offer students a better balance in terms of subject content, but it also can help them to understand the nature and gifts of diversity as well as promote better relationships among all students.

You will have students who simply don't like you because you are White or Black or male or female or any number of things with which they have negative associations. Their words or mannerisms will send you a clear message: "Don't talk to me. I don't have to listen to no white lady" (Paley, 1989, p. 13). Unfortunately, these students often have grounds to feel this way. For example, research suggests that African American students and students with disabilities face unequal academic opportunities and are underrepresented in science (Moore, Jensen & Hatch, 2002). But one other thing is also true. They would love nothing better than for you to prove them wrong.

REALITY CHECK 3.6

This genuine unease can be a tough thing to manage, especially if you really do have some pretty serious hang-ups about a group or issue. A secondary health teacher candidly admitted that he has a "real problem" with the issue of homosexuality and with anyone who is gay. It makes certain topics difficult to teach with objectivity. If you find yourself in this situation, find a way to address it. Seek advice from colleagues and curriculum specialists who may provide valuable guidance.

It is not uncommon for teachers either to avoid talking about a topic that makes them uneasy or to overcompensate for their discomfort by trying to show how unprejudiced they are. One Muslim student complained that whenever anything remotely relates to the Middle East in his social studies class, the teacher asks for the student to provide a comment, as if he were the resident expert. Likewise, the teacher would ignore him completely, not even making eye contact, if a discussion of the war on terrorism emerged.

Teaching with Diversity in Mind: How Will You Create Meaningful Learning Experiences?

Now you know that you need to know about diversity. How will that awareness translate into better lessons? First, take into account your students—their differences, frames of reference, and so forth. Make a commitment to be fair. See your students as people—all having their own unique combination of inherent and learned influences that makes them who they are. You won't be able to streamline what you teach so thoroughly that each student will have an individualized curriculum, but you can become more sensitive to ways your instruction can be enhanced if you are more aware of your students' culture and its influences.

Multicultural Education

Multicultural education is an educational strategy by which students' cultural backgrounds inform the development of effective classroom instruction. Its purpose is to support and expand the concepts of culture, diversity, equality, social justice, and democracy in formal school settings (Gollnick & Chinn, 2002). An important result would be to help culturally diverse students experience less isolation and intolerance. Experts believe that policies supporting multicultural education must come from within the school rather than be imposed from outside and should include social resources to blend old and new ideas with practices. The concept is an ongoing process as well as a reform movement to offer equal opportunities for all students. Cultural pluralism as a national goal can be achieved through multicultural education (Vaughan, 2001).

Multicultural education is not a new idea, although it has been modified over time. Educators in the 1920s were interested in making intercultural studies a priority. The goal was to make the dominant population more tolerant toward first- and second-generation immigrants (Montalto, 1978). In the 1960s, with the desegregation movement, differences in students were considered deficits. In the 1970s, disadvantaged groups were described as "different." This attitude acknowledged that their culture existed, but that it was different from that of the dominant group. It was followed by influences from the civil rights movement and the simultaneous growth of ethnic studies. The objectives were to promote understanding between groups and eliminate stereotypes. This included working with teachers to encourage them to have positive attitudes toward others (Sleeter, 1999).

It became clear that these programs alone would not guarantee a positive affirmation of cultural diversity. It was obvious that students from the dominant culture needed to learn about the history and contribution of other cultures. The curriculum in schools began to reflect more focused efforts to represent the multicultural nature of the nation, expanding the concept to the current approach of multicultural education.

Today, multicultural education is based on the following basic beliefs (Gollnick & Chinn, 2002):

1. Cultural differences are important and have value.
2. Schools should model respect for cultural differences.
3. Social justice and equality for everyone should have the highest priority in the design and implementation of curricula.
4. Schools are in a position in society to promote democratic attitudes.
5. Education can provide knowledge and skills for democratically decided redistribution of power among diverse groups.
6. Educators can create an environment supportive of multiculturalism.

Incorporating Multicultural Education in Your Classroom

So what can you do? There are components of the multicultural approach to education that include such courses as ethnic studies, global studies, and women's studies. Aspects of these also are present in units of study within courses. Assuming you are not actually teaching a class that focuses directly on these topics and have no special background yourself in these areas, you will need to make a special effort to incorporate appropriate concepts into your teaching. How will you determine the appropriate concepts?

First, make notes about your students as you consider this task so that you can focus on areas that will enhance their sense of value, regardless of what you teach.

Second, ask yourself which additional aspects of diversity require attention?

Third, look at your curriculum and the accompanying texts or other reading materials to determine the degree to which they reflect the diversity in your school and community. Make notes for yourself regarding which areas need more emphasis so that you can supplement them.

Fourth, create a master list of the areas you want to incorporate into your teaching during the course of the year. Approximately where in the curriculum should they appear? Which reading materials and other resources (human and other) will you need to compile as you create your syllabus and lesson plans? What special arrangements will you need to make to enrich your course?

Fifth, especially if this is new to you, discuss your thinking and concerns with someone who is more knowledgeable to get ideas and suggestions for refinement.

To Expand Your Preparation

If you are not an expert in the area of multicultural education or have limited background with issues related to diversity, the learning curve might seem steep. Perhaps it's enough of a challenge just to teach your own content, let alone try to superimpose another instructional dimension that will take valuable time to prepare. The question you really need to ask yourself is, "How important do I think helping students in this way really is?" If your answer is "very important," then resolve to make some efforts to help yourself become more knowledgeable. You must become culturally proficient yourself. This means you must recognize how you, because of your ethnicity and other life experiences, may offend someone (Robins, Lindsey, Lindsey, & Terrell, 2002). How will you do this? Study! Teach yourself about other cultures. There are several basic ways to begin—all doable and accessible on your own schedule.

1. Read about the topic. Find resources, articles, books, and anything else that may provide you with insight about your students.
2. Attend workshops and lectures that are provided through your school system or through other means.

3. Talk to people about these issues, especially those who represent diverse groups with whom you have little real contact or about whose cultures you have little understanding.

The important thing is for you to be proactive and work to become a person for whom thinking about diversity is second nature.

Becoming a Model of Diverse Thinking

Ideally, if serious change is to occur in schools, *everyone* in the school must buy into the need for multicultural education. This attitude begins at the top with those in leadership positions. Conversations about these issues must be commonplace—a part of faculty and departmental meetings. These discussions should result in proactive measures to create a school climate that exemplifies acceptance of all students (Shields, Larocque, & Oberg, 2002). Regardless of whether this attitude is a priority in your school, you can still foster this approach in your classroom.

Granted, some teachers embrace opportunities to promote diversity awareness more than others. Research (Levine-Rasky, 2001) suggests that there are three indications that you might be a teacher who will be an effective multicultural educator. Do you qualify?

1. Some want to see change because they identify with educational inequality. They may have been victims themselves of some form of discrimination.
2. Some agree with the idea that multicultural education can not only empower students, but that it can also change society for the better.
3. Some are simply curious about how the phenomenon of educational inequality has come about and want to study the topic. By knowing more, they inevitably implement teaching strategies that reflect multicultural education.

The key to being an effective teacher is treating your students as individuals. Like the teacher at the beginning of this section, many proudly claim that they treat all their students the same. On the surface, this sounds fair. But is this really a fair attitude? Doesn't treating them the same imply an inherent discounting of their differences—differences that define who they are? One African American teacher, Rose, described an exchange with her White colleague and friend, Alice. Alice told Rose that she felt comfortable talking with her about anything and regarded her as a close friend. She then said, "I don't even think of you as African American. I think of you the same way I think of my White friends." Alice meant the comment as the supreme compliment, but Rose told her that she was going to seize this teachable moment to enlighten her friend about relating to those from other cultures. She explained to Alice that she didn't want her *not* to think of her as African American. "In fact, I insist that you do. It's not a disability that you have found a way to overlook," she said. "It's a part of who I am—a part I'm proud of. Don't ever forget it."

TIPS from the TRENCHES

The following are suggestions about the *nature of adolescents* that beginning teachers wished they had followed when they began teaching.

1. Keep an open mind and expect anything.

2. Accept their style, music, and dress. Regardless of how outrageous you think some of their preferences are, show an interest and don't judge them.

3. Remember that they are not your equals. You are the adult, which means that you are hopefully further along on the maturity scale. It won't always be easy, but avoid being drawn into their confusion.

4. Things you said in class that you think are a big deal, students may not even remember, and vice versa. Try not to spend too much energy worrying

(Continued)

about an incident unless you have reason to think it should be followed up.

5. Likewise, the things that bother you may not bother them at all. Even if it's your personal goal to return tests right away, it may not matter to them if it takes you three days to return tests rather than one day. Or the other way around!

6. It will be safer to avoid talking about family unless they bring it up. Until you know their situations better, make vague references to "the person you live with" rather than to a dad.

7. Avoid touching them unless you are absolutely sure of how it will be received.

8. If you are young, try not to work too hard to be "cool." It can backfire.

9. Remember that there is a big difference between dealing with sixth graders and eighth graders in middle schools and freshmen and seniors in high schools.

10. Read a good novel about adolescents—one that will help you get into their heads. Text/theory books will also help you to understand them as well. Ask your school librarian for suggestions.

11. Never forget that they want to be treated like they are adults but cared for like they are children.

The following are suggestions about the *diversity of adolescents* beginning teachers wish they had followed when they began teaching.

1. Spend time with students from other cultures. Listen to them and learn from them.

2. Pay attention to what you say and how you treat all students, especially those from other cultures.

3. Do your homework. Find out all you can about the cultures of the students you teach.

4. Ask yourself each time you plan a unit if you are paying enough attention to issues around diversity. Adjust your lessons where necessary.

5. Use human resources to enhance your students' exposure to other cultures.

6. Be patient with students when they show ignorance of another culture. Use these opportunities as teachable moments.

7. To help students who do not speak English well or at all, include them daily in as many activities with other students as possible.

PRAXIS™

Praxis Competencies Related to the Nature and Diversity of Adolescents

Several tests in the Praxis Series address issues related to the nature and diversity of adolescents. For example, the Principles of Learning and Teaching: Grades 7–12 (0524) test indicates that you may see questions on topics related to the needs and characteristics of students from diverse populations and appropriate teacher responses to individual and cultural diversity (ETS, 2001, *Test-at-a-Glance,* Principles of Learning and Teaching [PLT] pp. 34–35).

Sample Question

Directions: The following question asks you to analyze teacher goals and actions that will result in the teacher meeting that goal. You must decide whether the action makes it LIKELY or UNLIKELY that the goal will be achieved and select the best reason that the action is likely or unlikely to lead to the achievement of the goal.

GOAL: To prevent ethnic tension from disrupting a tenth-grade class that includes a number of students who have expressed hostility toward students from other ethnic groups in the class

ACTION: The teacher plans projects based on factual data that the students are likely to find interesting. The projects require the students to work in small groups that are structured so that each group is composed of students from different ethnic backgrounds.

(A) LIKELY, because students are required to work with students they would otherwise not associate with, and these interactions often lead to altered perceptions about those individuals.

(B) LIKELY, because the teacher limits the projects that the groups are to work on to those that do not require opinions or nonfactual interpretation.

(C) UNLIKELY, because one or two students usually dominate a group, and other students in the group may feel resentment, thus leading to increased tension in the classroom.

(D) UNLIKELY, because the teacher should maintain control in situations where ethnic tensions are a factor, and teacher-centered teaching methods, such as lectures and direct questioning, are safer.

(ETS, 2001, *Test-at-a-Glance,* PLT, p. 41)

The correct answer is **A**. Cooperative, small-group work is frequently cited as an important method for dealing with tension of many sorts in the classroom.

Other tests in the Praxis II Series may also ask you about these issues. For example, the Introduction to the Teaching of Reading test (0200) and the Reading Across the Curriculum: Secondary test (0202) address environmental and sociocultural factors. You will be asked to respond to questions that demonstrate your ability to "recognize the influence of ethnic, socioeconomic, regional, and cultural linguistic differences and to select appropriate instructional strategies and materials to address these factors as well as to recognize and support cultural and ethnic diversity" (ETS, 2002, *Test-at-a-Glance,* English, Reading and Communication, pp. 43, 49).

Suggestions for Further Reading

If you have time to read only one book related to issues in this chapter, choose either. . .

Kohl, H. (1994). *I won't learn from you: And other thoughts on creative maladjustment.* New York: New Press.

Or

Tatum, B. (1997). *Why are the black kids sitting together in the cafeteria? And other conversations on race.* New York: Basic Books.

References

Agnes, M. (Ed.). (2000). *Webster's New World Collegiate Dictionary* (4th ed.). Cleveland: IDG Books.

Burke, M., Brown, M., Jones, H., Spragley, K., & Petroskey, M. (2002). *Instructor's notebook: Understanding the learner* (3rd ed.). Chapel Hill, NC: NCTEach.

Caine, R. N., & Caine, G. (1991). *Teaching and the human brain.* Alexandria, VA: ASCD.

Clark, L., & Starr, I. S. (1996). *Secondary and middle school teaching methods* (7th ed.). Upper Saddle River, NJ: Merrill/Prentice Hall.

Clark, M. L., & Ayers, M. (1988). The role of reciprocity and proximity in junior high school friendships. *Journal of Youth and Adolescence,* 17, 403–411.

Dunphy, D. C. (1963). The social structure of urban adolescent peer groups. *Sociometry,* 26, 230–246.

Dusek, J. B. (1991). *Adolescent development and behavior.* Upper Saddle River, NJ: Prentice Hall.

Educational Testing Service (ETS). (2001). Test-at-a-glance: Principles of Learning and Teaching; Introduction to the Teaching of Reading (0200); Reading Across the Curriculum: Secondary (0202); English, Reading and Communication. Princeton, NJ: ETS.

Erickson, F. (1997). Culture in society and in educational practices. In J. A. Banks & C. A. M. Banks (Eds.), *Multicultural education: Issues and perspectives* (3rd ed., pp. 32–60). Needham Heights, MA: Allyn & Bacon.

Erikson, E. (1963). *Childhood and society* (2nd ed.). New York: Norton.

Goleman, D. (1995). *Emotional intelligence*. New York: Bantam.

Gollnick, D. M., & Chinn, P. (2002). *Multicultural education in a pluralistic society* (6th ed.). Upper Saddle River, NJ: Merrill/Prentice Hall.

Grinder, R. E. (1969). Distinctiveness and thrust in the American youth culture. *Journal of Social Issues, 25,* 7–20.

Guillaume, A. M. (2000). *Classroom teaching: A primer for new professionals*. Upper Saddle River, NJ: Prentice Hall.

Guillaume, A. M., Zuniga, C., & Yee, I. (1998). What difference does preparation make? Educating preservice teachers for learner diversity. In M. E. Dilworth (Ed.), *Being responsive to cultural differences: How teachers learn* (pp. 143–159). Thousand Oaks, CA: Corwin.

Hart, L. A. (1999). *Human brain and human learning*. Kent, WA: Books for Educators.

Kohlberg, L. (1976). Moral stages and moralization. In T. Lickona (Ed.), *Moral development and behavior: Theory, research and social issues*. New York: Holt, Rinehart & Winston.

Levine-Rasky, C. (2001). Identifying the prospective multicultural educator: Three sign posts, three portraits. *Urban Review, 33*(4), 291–319.

Moore, R., Jensen, M., & Hatch, J. (2002). Our apartheid. *American biology teacher, 64*(2), 87–88, 90–91.

Montalto, N. V. (1978). *The forgotten dream: A history of the intercultural education movement 1924–1941*. Dissertation Abstracts International. 39A 1061. (UMI No. 7813436)

Myers, L. J., Speight, S. L., Highen, P. S., Cox, C. I., Reynolds, A. L., Adams, E. M., & Hanley, P. (1991). Identity development and world view: Toward an optimal conceptualization. *Journal of Counseling and Development, 70,* 54–63.

Paley, V. G. (1989). *White teacher*. Cambridge, MA: Harvard University Press.

Robins, K. N., Lindsey, R. B., Lindsey, D. B., & Terrell, R. D. (2002). *Culturally proficient instruction: A guide for people who teach*. Thousand Oaks, CA: Corwin.

Robinson, T. L., & Howard-Hamilton, M. L. (2000). *The convergence of race, ethnicity and gender*. Upper Saddle River, NJ: Merrill/Prentice Hall.

Robinson, T. L. (1999). The intersection of dominant discourses across race, gender and other identities. *Journal of Counseling and Development, 77,* 73–79.

Shelton, C. (2000). Portraits of Emotional Awareness. *Educational Leadership, 58*(1), 30–32.

Shields, C. M., Larocque, L. J., & Oberg, S. L. (2002). A dialogue about race and ethnicity in education: Struggling to understand issues in cross-cultural leadership. *Journal of School Leadership, 12*(2), 116–137.

Sleeter, C. E. (1999). *Making choices for multicultural education: Five approaches to race, class and gender* (3rd ed.). New York: Wiley and Sons.

Sousa, D. (1998). The ramifications of brain research. *Educational Leadership, 1*(55).

Vaughan, A. C. (2001, November). *Cultural pluralism: Implications for educational practices and comprehensive school reform.* Paper presented at the Biennial Convocation of Kappa Delta Pi, 43rd, Orlando, Florida.

Wellesley College Center for Research on Women. (1992). *The AAUW report: How schools shortchange girls.* Washington, DC: American Association of University Women Education Foundation.

Yeh, C. J., & Drost, C. (2002). *Bridging identities among ethnic minority youth in schools.* New York: ERIC Clearinghouse on Urban education.

4

Classroom Management

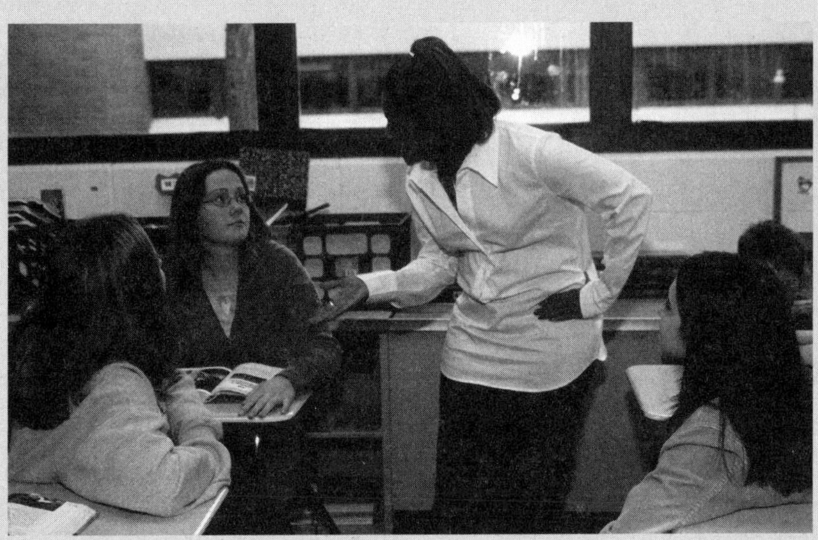

Teaching five classes of teenagers is going to be a challenge for me. After all, I'm not that much older than they are. And if they are unmotivated students, I know that means they will be tough to deal with. I'm also not sure about how to handle any discipline problems that come up. I never have liked a bunch of rules and I'm sure my students don't want that either. I want them to like my class. I think that the best thing to do the first day is to tell them that we will only have one rule: We will respect each other. That should be enough.

Mr. Lenardi, a first-year teacher

The comments above are typical of inexperienced, especially young, teachers who want to make their classroom an inviting place to be. They are also an indication of the concern Mr. Lenardi has about his ability to manage his students' behavior—a concern shared by most new secondary school teachers as they begin their careers. By the end of the first week, perhaps sooner, he will learn that some of his assumptions, and ultimately his approach, need adjusting (see Activity 4.1).

This chapter addresses one of your biggest challenges: how you will manage your classroom and gain the cooperation and compliance of your students. If you are unable to achieve this, all the hard work you have done to teach your subject will be lost. After all, teaching in secondary schools is rarely about instructing individual students; it's more about managing groups.

Teachers use the terms *classroom management, classroom control,* and *discipline* interchangeably to refer to basically the same thing. Generally, effective classroom management includes control and discipline. The dictionary defines discipline as "training that develops self-control, character, or orderliness and efficiency" (Agnes, 2000). Since this is what secondary school teachers aim for, you will hear fellow teachers, administrators, parents, and local citizens use the term *discipline* when they refer either to the control teachers have over their classes or to general classroom management.

This chapter addresses two major components of managing your classroom, reflecting two ways of thinking about the word *discipline*. The first part of the chapter, "Effective Management of Your Classroom," relates to the procedures and rules you should consider for it to be a disciplined, well-managed environment that is conducive for learning. What things can you do at the beginning of the school year and continue in the months that follow to ensure an orderly classroom with few disruptions? The second part, "Maintaining Order and Control," focuses on how you should address disruptions that will inevitably occur, regardless of how thoroughly you have tried to prevent them. What kind of a discipline plan will you have? Which annoying behaviors of your students can you ignore and which ones require action? In other words, good discipline is something you want to *have* so that you don't have to *use* it.

Discipline: Effective Management of Your Classroom

On the first day of a class on teaching methods, without any explanation, the professor asked all of the students to stand up, walk around, and cluck like chickens. At first reluctant, they began to do so, one by one, until the entire class sounded like a barnyard. After a few minutes, he asked them to sit down. He then announced that he had just demonstrated how much power he, as a teacher, has over his students. "I have just taken a group of bright, educated young adults and, because you want to please me, you clucked like chickens. Do you see how much power you have?" This somewhat dramatic illustration makes a vitally important point.

Activity 4.1

Considering Mr. Lenardi's Approach

When you have read this chapter, reread the introductory vignette, Mr. Lenardi's approach to managing discipline in his class as he begins the school year. List several assumptions he is making about his students that may or may not be accurate and what will be effective with them. Perhaps you already have a response.

How Does Your Personal Style Affect the Creation of a Well-Managed Classroom?

Your classroom is a blank slate and *you* have the power to create a climate and set a tone that will either encourage your students to cooperate with you or create problems. *You* are the teacher, the one who is in charge. And guess what? Teenagers *want* you to be in charge, no matter what they say—and they will say a lot. You can blame the students ("I have unmotivated students") or you can blame other factors ("The room is too small and is very hot"). But the bottom line is that you—your style and your demeanor—have more to do with the smooth or bumpy interactions within your classroom than anything else does.

It's the students' developmental task at this age to test you. As young adults struggling to grow up, they are full of contradictions. They want direction but don't want you to boss them; they want you to be nice, but not too nice. The truth is, they are not sure what they want day to day. They are so busy trying to discover who *they* are that they have to challenge who *you* are to find their way. It will be natural for you to want them to like you. But if being liked is your guiding principle, you're in for a rough emotional ride. Not only will you be ultimately disappointed, but you cannot possibly have a well-managed classroom. In trying to be one of them, you are giving your control as teacher to the students.

REALITY CHECK 4.1

Most everyone has had a teacher who proudly claimed, "I'm not here to win a popularity contest. I don't care if the students like me or not." Such individuals are not being completely truthful. With rare exceptions, every teacher wants to be liked. But being liked can't be the motivation that drives your actions as a teacher. What you really want is your students' respect. Don't worry, the students will like you if they respect you.

Authority or Power?

Developing and maintaining control of your classroom requires both *authority* and *power*. Authority can be described as the right to determine the choices you make available for your students. You, as the teacher, can decide what is acceptable to help your students meet the goals you have set for them. The state board of education and your local school district delegate this responsibility and grant you the authority to act in accordance with that responsibility. Therefore, students must respect your authority (Froyen, 1988).

On the other hand, while authority can be conferred, power must be earned. Although you have the authority to assign work to your students, you must have power to get them to do it. Authority is of little consequence without power (Froyen, 1988; Raven, 1974; Shrigley, 1986). Teachers who are perceived as being in charge of their classrooms have fewer behavior problems than teachers who are not seen as being in charge. "The critical distinction is that the teacher must act as an authority and not as an authoritarian" (Grossman, 1995, p. 17). In other words, teachers must exercise power effectively to fulfill their obligations as authorities.

Teachers exercise five forms of power (Froyen, 1988):

1. Attractive power is essentially relationship power. The students do things for you because they like you. This power requires two things to be effective. First, the students must actually like you, and second, you must communicate that you like the students (Levine & Nolan, 1996).

2. Expert power is knowledge power. The teacher is recognized as being the expert in one or more fields and the students are both drawn in by the opportunity to work with this knowledgeable teacher and motivated by his or her enthusiasm for the subject taught.

3. Reward power is praise power, when students are motivated by praise and positive feedback from the teacher. The reward may be in the form of good grades or sustained personal encouragement from the teacher.

4. Coercive power is punishment power, where the teacher imposes an array of negative consequences if students do not comply. While it should be a last resort, coercive power is used too extensively.

Forms of Power	*Management Functions*		
	Content	Conduct	Context
Expert	Teacher inspires and challenges students to excel.	Teacher monitors pupil progress and provides corrective feedback.	Teacher uses activities that foster high levels of pupil involvement.
Legitimate	Teacher offers reasons for rules.	Teacher consistently enforces rules.	Teacher permits students to participate in rule setting.
Attractive	Teacher is a model of decorum.	Teacher helps students acquire academic and social engagement skills.	Teacher promotes a sense of belonging and group cohesiveness.
Reward	Teacher offers verbal commendations for academic accomplishment.	Teacher provides tangible recognition for appropriate behavior.	Teacher expresses satisfaction with pupils as persons.
Coercive	Teacher takes away a privilege.	Teacher imposes a penalty.	Teacher withdraws approval.

FIGURE 4.1 Management Style Power Choices for Classroom Control

Froyen, Len A. (1988). *Classroom Management: Empowering Teacher Leaders* (39). Upper Saddle River, NJ: Merrill/Prentice Hall.

5. Legitimate power is role power. This comes from the students' belief that teachers have the right to prescribe the standards and expectations because of their role in schools. They respect the teacher's position as the one who is functioning in this role (Froyen, 1988; Levine & Nolan, 1996).

Teachers make power choices based on their particular personal and management styles. Figure 4.1 illustrates how the forms of power are reflected as you approach the task of managing your classroom.

Your Presence

Your students will size you up in the first 5 minutes they are in your class. You have only one chance to make a first impression, and first impressions are often everything to students, who sometimes decide quickly how they feel about a teacher and change their minds slowly. In the beginning, students will watch your every move, evaluate your reactions, and assess your attitudes toward them, looking for clues about what kind of teacher you are. By the end of the first few days, they will have drawn conclusions that will determine how they conduct themselves in your classroom. As much as adolescents don't like to be judged, they can be quick to judge others, especially their teachers.

How do they see you? As teenagers, they first notice how you carry yourself, what you wear, how comfortable you seem with them and with your classroom, and how businesslike you are. Depending on what they want or like in a teacher, naturally their views will vary from one student to another. Obviously, you won't be able to please everyone. The goal is to exude confidence and a comfort with yourself and what you are doing. Sounds simple, but it's not always easy to do when you are under constant critical scrutiny. They will notice how you handle yourself in every setting they see you in—with other teachers, in the cafeteria, and even after school, when you are in the mall. All of these random impressions inform their overall assessment of you. Granted, theirs may not necessarily always be an accurate or fair system, but it's the one they use.

For example, what is their first impression when they enter a classroom in which the teacher is wearing jeans and a flannel shirt and is sitting on the desk, joking with students, not ready for class to begin? One student sees an approachable, laid-back teacher who will be comfortable to work with this year. Another student sees a sloppy, unprofessional teacher who will probably be easy and will try to be one of the students. Likewise, how might they perceive another teacher whose handouts are already on the desks, who has an opening assignment on the board, who is professionally groomed, and who begins class as soon as the bell rings? One student sees an organized teacher who will expect a serious attitude toward the class. Another student sees a strict, no-nonsense disciplinarian who will be no fun. Being human, some students respond better to one style than to another, but the impression of what will take place in your class—good or bad—is set. You must make your choices, ones you think will work.

Mr. Lenardi's approach failed. The first day, he explained to the students that he planned to run a relaxed class and had only one rule: that they all show respect for everyone. This seemed great to most of the students, who liked the idea of more freedom and responded initially by describing him as a cool teacher. This reaction convinced him that he had the right idea. As days went by, he allowed them to come and go to the restroom at will, observed more and more off-task conversation while he was teaching, and found that many were turning in assignments late. His honeymoon lasted only a short time. He was becoming more frustrated and getting less done each day. Being a cool teacher meant that many days he didn't feel like a teacher at all. But the pattern was set, and he spent the rest of the year trying to gain control of the class.

Of course, you could choose the opposite approach, providing a clearer statement of what is and is not acceptable behavior in your class—and sticking to it. This requires focused attention to developing a system of procedures and rules and persistent effort to maintain your system. It's hard work, especially in the beginning, but it will result in an easier year for you in the long run. If students perceive you to be strict ("mean"), they first will test you constantly to see if you stand by what you say. If you do, more than likely, they will accept and ultimately respect your expectations, assuming they are reasonable and consistently enforced. One teacher noted that it's usually the teachers the students love the first day who are the ones with little respect or popularity at the end of the year. This may not be true in every case, but it will be important that you give some thought to how you come across to students and where you are on the *easy–strict* continuum.

Withitness

From the 1950s into the 1970s, Jacob Kounin studied the influence of certain behaviors on the tendencies of students to be cooperative and concluded that teachers who are perceived as "with it" by the students have a positive impact on their behavior. He used the term *withitness* to refer to a teacher's awareness of what is happening in the classroom. He found that student engagement and on-task behaviors depend on how well the momentum is maintained and how smoothly teachers transition from one activity to another. He found that students decide a teacher is "with it" if:

- The teacher takes action to address discipline problems and suppresses misbehaviors of the people who caused the problem (blaming the wrong person is a sign that the teacher is *not* "with it").
- When two problems arise simultaneously, the teacher handles the more serious one first.
- The teacher nips off-task behavior in the bud (Kounin, 1977; Kounin & Sherman, 1979).

"With it" teachers usually have a businesslike, no-nonsense atmosphere in their classrooms. A businesslike atmosphere is a "learning environment in which students and the teacher conduct themselves in ways implying that achieving specified learning goals takes priority over other concerns" (Cangelosi, 1997, p. 89). Students sense this by the way teachers handle themselves and use eye contact and facial expressions. They need to see that you are calm and in charge of the class and that you expect to be taken seriously. Every part of class time together has a purpose.

Part of being a "with it" teacher is anticipating as many problems as possible and deciding in advance how you will respond. Often, beginning teachers start by thinking about their own behavior in secondary school. But many beginning teachers who experience discipline problems were well-behaved students in secondary school. They don't understand the motivation of an uncooperative student or why anyone would want to be a problem. "With it" teachers try to understand how their students think—especially the ones who are most likely to cause problems. Knowing how the class clown thinks is a very useful skill.

One second-year teacher who proudly claims that he has few discipline problems put it this way:

> My worst fear when I began teaching was that I would run into myself as a student. I was horrible! I never did anything really bad—nothing they could really send me to the office for. I just kept talking, getting up, doing little things that would drive teachers nuts. I never knew why they put up with it. I guess it was because I was smart and in the advanced classes. But the more they let me misbehave, the more I did. It was a game to me and I was getting loads of attention from my buddies. It was fun seeing what I could come up with each day. I'm not exactly sure what they should have done with me, but I sure gave it a lot of thought before my first day as a teacher, and I was ready. I guarantee you no one acts that way in my room!

First Impressions: Attitudes That Will Serve You Well

Begin with what you want your classroom to feel like to the students. More than likely, you want one thing: a cooperative atmosphere where the students are respectful and are willing to comply with your requests for engagement with your subject. It would be easy if there were a specific formula for what exactly you should do to manage your classroom effectively and make things happen. There is none. Countless variables affect your success as a good classroom manager. Some things you can't control, but others you can. Focus on those. Ultimately, you have to do what works for you, and finding out what that is may take some time. But as you develop your own approach, internalize these four attitudes:

1. Adopt a no-nonsense attitude toward your subject and the tasks at hand. No matter what subject you teach, it is important or it wouldn't be in the curriculum.

REALITY CHECK 4.2

Some beginning teachers, most often young teachers, think that it is fine to let their students call them by their first names. One explained, "My father is Mr. Buxton. It feels weird to me for my students to call me that. Besides I think it is more comfortable for the students and me to be on a first-name basis." Get over it. This is *never* appropriate. It is important that students recognize that you are an adult who has been hired to supervise them and their instruction. You deserve the respect that comes from being in that role.

2. Remember that the students are not your equals. They are your students. Yes, we are all equal under the constitution, equal as human beings deserving respect. But in your role as a teacher, *you* are the one in charge in this setting. This will be a challenge in some situations. Teenagers today have been raised by their baby-boom parents to think that they, in fact, *are* your equals and should have equal say in all kinds of matters, such as what they should study, what grades they should get, and how much work is appropriate. Not so!

3. Don't make the mistake of trying to be their friend. This is not to say that you shouldn't be friend*ly*. But putting yourself on the same level with your students can compromise your ability to do your job as their teacher.

4. Dress professionally and appropriately. Respect what you do by dressing as the professional that you are. *No jeans!* Ignore the examples you have seen on *Boston Public*. This doesn't mean you have to dress up—just dress professionally.

How Will You Manage Your Classroom Effectively?

What Do Secondary School Students Want?

You have a pretty good idea of what *you* want to go on in your classroom. But do you know what *your students* want? You must understand what they want, or you will have trouble reaching your goals. Like most people, secondary school students want five things (Chernow & Chernow, 1984). First, they want to be heard. They are sure that they have important things to say about how they should be treated, and insist on their "rights." Nothing turns a student off faster than when he or she thinks you aren't listening. Second, they want a piece of the action and want to be included in the decisions that affect them, to the extent possible. Third, they want choices. They are used to being able to pick from 50 flavors at the ice cream shop and 100 channels on television. Therefore, their generation likes to have options in assignments as well as options in terms of penalties you impose. Fourth, they want to have the opportunity to be themselves. They need opportunities for expression. Unfortunately, this can mean that a student might continually break rules if it's his only way to "be somebody." You will want to look for activities in which your students can express themselves in positive ways. Finally, and possibly most important, they want to be accepted, if not loved. Remember that during these adolescent years, their actions are often hard to accept, which sometimes will make loving them next to impossible. That's OK, it's not written anywhere that you need to love your students (although it sure helps if you do). But you must accept them as they are.

It won't take you long to become very familiar with those of your students who are continually disruptive. Often, the ones you dread seeing come into your room, because you know the negative effect their presence has on the entire class, are rarely absent. What do *these* students want in addition to the five things already mentioned?

They need first and foremost to feel that someone is in charge. Not someone who will boss them around, but someone who is consistently in control. The structure that is missing in their lives is what they seek at school. They look to you to provide this and desperately need to feel that you will set and enforce some limits for them.

They want you to be a strong and fair person who will serve as the elusive role model they can find nowhere else. They want to be shown that their behavior is separate from the person they are. They crave constant and repeated guidance in how to deal with their problems and how to control their feelings. They want recognition and rewards for the progress they make.

No matter how unpleasant some of their behavior is, you must remember to respect the dignity and value of *all* of your students. You owe this to them as individuals whose personal as well as academic development is part of your responsibility. Knowing what they want is the first step in developing an approach to managing your students individually and collectively.

Consistency

Perhaps in a perfect world, people would be absolutely consistent. This is an impossibility because in any situation with human beings, there are always extenuating circumstances that will require modifications. But as a teacher, you need to strive for this goal, at least in your classroom. Few things frustrate secondary school students more than a teacher who is inconsistent and, therefore, unfair. ("I thought you said no one could turn anything in late. You let Lakeisha have two extra days.")

Consistency means that you have the same expectations for everyone's behavior at all times. It also means that you have the same penalties for everyone. This presents an interesting dilemma for teachers when they try to deal with students as individuals. After all, treating everyone fairly is not the same thing as treating everyone the same. For example, if Nicole is having personal problems at home, you may feel that it is appropriate to allow her two extra days to complete a certain assignment. In your mind, you are not being inconsistent; you are making a modification appropriate to her circumstances. Regardless, the students will see you as inconsistent. In some cases, explaining the situation will help them to see things with better understanding—both for the other student and for you. Other times, this will not be a good idea. They will simply have to trust that you have your reasons. Each situation will be different and each requires a judgment call by you.

Surprisingly, you will be able to be more consistent than you think, if being consistent is a priority. When consistency is a problem for teachers, it's usually for one of several reasons. Sometimes they have unworkable expectations to begin with. For example, a rule that no student is allowed to leave class for any reason will prove unworkable. As exceptions occur, the rule becomes meaningless and your enforcement of it seems arbitrary and inconsistent to the students.

Another thing that causes teachers to appear inconsistent is not monitoring the class well. As a result, the teacher won't see the misbehavior of one student but will catch and punish another. Also, teachers are rarely consistent about rules they don't want to enforce. If any of these are the case, there are several things to do to get back on track. Either remind the class of the rule or procedure and follow it more diligently or consider changing the rule altogether (Emmer, Evertson, Sanford, Clements, & Worsham, 1984).

What Are Your Students Doing During Your Class?

While they are in your classroom, students are engaged in one of three behaviors at all times: (a) They are on-task and engaged, which means they are attempting to follow your directions and are involved in the classroom activity; (b) they are off-task, which means they are doing something else, but not really causing trouble (e.g., the daydreamer and the student who is doing homework for someone else's class are off-task); or (c) they are being disruptive and either distracting students or encouraging them to be disruptive. Disruptive behaviors are usually the source of teachers' greatest concerns. Nondisruptive off-task behaviors, if not addressed, can quickly turn into disruptive behaviors (Cangelosi, 1997).

Your number one goal each day should be to get your students on-task as quickly as possible and keep them actively involved for the entire period. *On-task* does not have to mean pen-to-paper work every minute. It means there is some purposeful activity under way. As the teacher, you get to define what *purposeful* is. For example, at the beginning of the period, have the students working on some aspect of your activity or an assignment while you take care of "housekeeping" chores. Similarly, don't stop class about 5 or 6 minutes early so the students can get ready to go. Do the math. If you lose 6 minutes each day, multiplied by 180 days a year, you have lost 1,080 minutes a year. This is the equivalent to almost 20 teaching periods, assuming your classes are 55 minutes each. Amazing, isn't it?

What Rules and Procedures Will You Implement?

The number one cause of most of the problems new teachers face is a lack of effective procedures, rules, and routines (Wong & Wong, 1998). To eliminate most of your problems, you need to determine exactly what your expectations are and make them clear to the students. More than anything else, they want to know what they can and cannot do in your classroom.

Rules: Two Kinds

Yes, you need rules. Think about your own life. How fast would you really drive to work if there was no rule about speed? Don't you find that you are more productive in most situations if you know what the rules are? It's the same with your students. Of course, no one likes too many rules, so there should be very few of them, ones that the students and you can remember—*experts suggest no more than five.* The rules should be written, posted, and preferably signed by the students (and their parents) at the beginning of the school year. In effect, they constitute a contract of sorts, an agreement that this is how things will proceed in your classroom.

There are two kinds of rules (Wong & Wong, 1998). The first kind are the *general* rules such as "Show respect." These rules cover a broad spectrum of behaviors and offer the teacher flexibility. The problem is that they may be too flexible and require explanation. Exactly what does "show respect" mean? Usually more experienced teachers are successful with general rules because they have learned how to use authority and power.

The other kind are *specific* rules, a checklist of what students can and cannot do. These tell the students exactly what is acceptable and what is not. But since you want to limit your list of rules to 5, it will be hard to cover every conceivable potential problem. One third-year teacher of ninth-grade science dutifully posted a long list of rules to cover every possible problem. When one student spit at another and was reprimanded, the student replied, "But it's not on your list." The teacher had to rethink his approach. Rather than drawing up dozens

ENVIRONMENTAL SCIENCE

1. Do not talk when someone else is talking.
2. Paper throwing, horseplay, or other inappropriate behavior will not be tolerated.
3. Be in your seat when the bell rings.
4. Follow laboratory safety rules.
5. Students are responsible for knowing important dates.

FIGURE 4.2 Mr. DeMarco's Classroom Rules

of rules on physical contact, he substituted just one: "No physical contact with another student will be tolerated." He learned that specific rules had to be global enough to cover a range of misbehaviors. As a new teacher, you will also find that specific rules may help you more than general rules. But word them carefully, making them "specifically broad."

Bottom line, it's up to you to determine how specific or loose you want to be with different groups of students. Your approach must be something you and your students can live with. In Figure 4.2 are sample rules that one first-year teacher found helpful as he began the school year. Note that he has tried to have both specific rules (#1 and #3) and "specifically broad" ones (#2, #4, and #5).

Procedures

Procedures are different from rules. They are the ways you are going to do things. When you are in your own home, a *procedure* might be that whoever gets the mail puts it on the telephone table. A *rule* might be never to leave the mail in the den.

REALITY CHECK 4.3

Rules versus procedures. Semantics? No, not really. It's more a fine-tuning of how you are going to think about managing your class. Vocabulary can be everything. How you describe what's going to happen in your class reflects your attitude toward what you want done and how you regard students' ability to do it. Both rules and procedures are helpful, and you would be well advised to have some of both in place the first day. Your decisions may also vary by class. Some groups may need more rules, and others will respond just as well with procedures.

Everyone follows procedures. They are important in your lives and they are especially important in your classroom. Many educators even feel that thinking in terms of procedures rather than rules is a more positive way of working with students. In other words, if you have effective, clear procedures, you may not need rules. For example, if you have a procedure that describes how students deal with each other when someone else is talking ("Listen respectfully to the views of others"), then you don't need a rule that states "No talking while someone else is speaking." Classroom procedures might address how you will collect papers, file them, and store them. How do you handle tardies or students who have no materials to work with? Sample procedures might also include the following guidelines for your students:

Missing assignments

Make-up work

Heading papers

Using pens or pencils

Writing on the back of papers

Neatness and legibility

Incomplete assignments

Turning in late work

Due dates

Preventing Problems

Clearly the best way to avoid problems is to prevent them in the first place. There are several basic things that will help you prevent problems regardless of the subject you teach or the type of students you have in your class.

1. Get to know your students as people as well as possible as soon as possible. Use a seating chart to learn their names immediately. Find out about their interests. Talk to them outside of class. Observe them in extracurricular activities.

2. Constantly move around the class both as you are teaching and as they are working in group activities. Some of the worst classroom managers are teachers who teach from their desks or from one place in the room. Often you can prevent inappropriate behavior just by being nearby. Watching the students as they work also keeps them on-task.

3. Keep them busy. Remember the old adage "Idle hands are the devil's workshop?" Still true. Most of the time when your students are causing you problems, it is because they don't have enough to do. While you are collecting papers and engaging in a one-on-one conversation with a student, many will choose some disruptive behavior. From their perspective, why not?

4. Have well-planned, interesting lessons that are organized and understandable for your students. Directions should be clear. There shouldn't be lots of questions like "I don't understand what to do with number three." This will inevitably lead to several behaviors you don't want—calling out their questions, asking a friend in the next seat what it means, or giving up on the assignment altogether. Often these behaviors happen simultaneously, causing the class to dissolve into chaos. If several students are having trouble with number 3, perhaps it wasn't clear enough and needs to be explained to everyone.

5. Develop a plan for smooth transitions between activities. Transitions are the minutes between activities and are often one of the most difficult skills for beginning teachers to master. The goal is to have students productively occupied at all times. For example, when a test is given and some students are still working while others have finished, teachers should have something for the other students to do; for example, "If you finish before time is called, go ahead and begin reading the introduction to the next chapter." It helps to write it on the board as well. Then, if a student begins talking, you can simply point to the board.

Several common mistakes teachers make with transitions are the following (Grossman, 1995):

- Thrusts—suddenly interrupting an activity without warning.
- Dangles—leaving them hanging while you take too long to set up.
- Flip Flops—switching back to an old activity once you have started a new one.
- Fragmentations—moving a group piecemeal, part of the class at a time.

6. Follow the rules and procedures you have outlined for your students.

7. Educate yourself about school- and systemwide policies. Make sure your expectations are compatible with systemwide regulations and that you understand what can and cannot be done in disciplining students.

Discipline: Maintaining Order and Control

I have never had any discipline problem I couldn't handle pretty easily. Then along came Rupert. He was big, belligerent, rude, and insulting to me. "Are you sure you are qualified to teach school?" he would ask, soliciting snickers from the rest of the class. His ability to undermine everything I was doing was scary. Determined to handle this by myself, I tried every suggestion I could come up with, talking to other teachers, the guidance counselors, and administrators for suggestions. His attitude was contagious, and I was losing control of this group. One day, he tossed something out the window, and all the students began to laugh and run to the window. It was the last straw. I was so frustrated that I punished the whole class by taking away a movie they were supposed to see. I sent for the assistant principal, who immediately took Rupert out of my class and, because he had been a serious problem for other teachers as well, sent him to an alternative school. I wondered why I had waited so long to ask for help.

Fourth-year special education teacher

How Will You Handle Student Misbehavior?

Most teachers, especially if they are inexperienced, worry about their ability to control a group of secondary school students. They have grounds. Adolescents are a developmental mixture of adult and child, with the endearing and irritating attributes of both. One thing is certain: you need to expect the unexpected. Being prepared will ensure your success.

Discipline Plans

The first step in managing the behavior of your students is to create a discipline plan, one that reflects your consideration of as many potential problems as possible. Use Activity 4.2, Activity 4.3, and Activity 4.4 to help you develop your discipline plan. You will never create a perfect system, effective with every student in every situation, but you can come close. Know up front that the one you create won't be etched in stone; it will be a fluid document that you will constantly review and refine. In fact, you will probably have to modify it from year to year, from class to class, and, possibly in some cases, from individual to individual. The important thing is to have one and to follow it. It also must be a plan that suits your personality and your style of dealing with conflict. It will do you no good to decide that you will simply counsel a student when he misbehaves if you know that you are not skilled as a counselor or that the student will not respond to counseling from you.

There are all kinds of discipline plans. Harry Wong and Rosemary Wong (1998) said that most are on a continuum, with the student in control at one end and the teacher in control at the other end. They identified three points on the continuum, each representing an approach. *Plan 1* (Student in Charge) is when the teacher is primarily a listener, silently looks on, uses nondirective statements, and accepts excuses. *Plan 2* (Collaborative Model) is when both the teacher and student are involved. The teacher questions the student about the misbehavior, uses directive statements, and models appropriate behavior. Agreements between them are then reached. *Plan 3* (Teacher in Charge) is when the teacher accepts no excuses, uses interventions, and provides reinforcement. Ultimately, the teacher decides what is to be done (Wong & Wong, 1998). For students of any age, there are times when all three should be implemented, depending on the situation. But for the most part, secondary school students respond best to Plan 2 (when the student and teacher work together on solutions) and Plan 3 (when the teacher is in charge).

Plan 3 (Teacher in Charge) is also supported by the *assertive discipline model* (Canter & Canter, 1976). This approach is based on the belief that you must assert your right to teach in an orderly and disruption-free classroom. For this to happen, teachers must have rules that govern the behavior of students, and they must enforce them with clearly defined consequences. Accept this fact: Someone is always in control of the class—it will be either you or the students. Decide now that it will be you.

Developing Your Discipline Plan

Of course, you hope for a cooperative, well-mannered group of teenagers to teach. And you may get such a group if you are lucky. But just as you take an umbrella to work and hope you won't need it, you should have a discipline plan in place for those cloudy days that arise in classrooms. Before you actually develop a discipline plan, ask yourself some key questions.

- Exactly what do you want from your students in terms of their behavior?
- What 3–5 things *must* they do to help your class go smoothly?
- What behaviors are you willing to let go and what do you feel compelled to address?
- How will you reward good behavior?
- How will you punish inappropriate behavior?
- What will secondary school students most likely respond well to?
- What secondary school teachers have you observed who were good classroom managers and disciplinarians? What did they do that made them effective?

Activity 4.2

Interviewing Good Classroom Managers

Interview two teachers who are considered good managers of student behavior. Ask them:

1. To describe their philosophy and approach to good classroom management.
2. If they have discipline plans. If so, what do they look like?
3. What behaviors they never tolerate.
4. What behaviors they suggest you ignore.
5. What suggestions they have for you as you begin your career.

Activity 4.3

Observation of an Effective Disciplinarian

Observe a teacher who has a reputation for being a good disciplinarian. Note the following misbehaviors and indicate on a 1–10 scale (10 = *most effective*) how effective the teacher is in managing the students. (*Effective* is defined as the degree to which the students are complying with teacher expectations.)

Kind of misbehavior	Teacher response	Effectiveness 1–10
Talking		
Daydreaming		
Sleeping		
Disrupting class		
Throwing things		
Out of seat		
Off-task behavior		
Playing		
Other		

There are many approaches to developing a classroom discipline plan, and you may want either to adopt one as it is or to create a composite plan of your own, one that combines aspects of several to accommodate your personal style and preferences. Consider the work of Glasser (1986) and Kounin (1977), whose findings are still acknowledged as particularly effective for secondary school students. Glasser's approach recognizes students as rational beings who can control their own behavior. He recommends that the teacher accept no excuses for misconduct and make sure that reasonable consequences follow. Kounin's "withitness" theory (already mentioned) encourages teachers to develop an awareness of what's going on in all parts of the room at all times. His approach reflects an understanding that the teacher has the ability to influence the behavior of all the students by dealing with those who are misbehaving (ripple effect).

Perhaps the most-used approach is the assertive discipline model of Canter and Canter (1976), which recognizes that the student has the opportunity to *choose* how to behave in your class and must accept the consequences of his or her choices. The teacher is expected to follow through with promises and the reasonable, previously stated consequences that have been determined.

The Assertive Discipline Model

The following steps for developing an "assertive discipline" plan, as suggested by Canter and Canter (1984) and used with any number of variations, are very effective with secondary school students.

Step 1

Determine the behaviors you will require of your students. Translate them into the rules for your classroom (maximum of 5). Be sure they are observable rules (e.g., "Raise your hand to be recognized before you speak"). *Caution:* rules such as "Work efficiently" are vague and not observable. Most secondary school teachers combine observable rules with management rules that reflect the subject taught.

Examples of observable rules:

- Be in class and seated when the bell rings.
- Bring books, notebooks, and pens to class.
- Keep hands, feet, and objects to yourself.

Examples of subject-specific rules:

- Clean up lab stations before leaving class.
- Be dressed in gym clothes 5 minutes after the bell rings.
- All safety rules must be followed while using the lab equipment.

Step 2

Prepare for the worst: the students don't follow your rules. Determine your disciplinary consequences, keeping in mind the following:

1. Choose consequences you are comfortable with (e.g., don't keep students after school if you are not comfortable staying yourself).
2. Make sure the consequence is something the students will not like. It should not be physically or psychologically harmful, however.
3. Limit your consequences to five, and list them in order of severity. The number of times the student breaks a rule determines the consequence. Canter and Canter refer to these consequences as your "disciplinary hierarchy." Figure 4.3 provides a sample.

1st time student breaks rule:	Name on board	= Warning
2nd time student breaks rule:	Name +	= One detention
3rd time student breaks rule:	Name ++	= Two detentions
4th time student breaks rule:	Name +++	= Two detentions, call parents
5th time student breaks rule:	Name ++++	= Two detentions, call parents, send to office

FIGURE 4.3 Sample Disciplinary Hierarchy

To implement the hierarchy, be sure to do the following:

1. Every time a student breaks a rule, apply the consequence as soon after the misbehavior occurs as possible.
2. Follow due process (students should already know the rules).
3. Involve parents, and especially administrators, toward the end of the hierarchy.
4. Start the list over every day.

REALITY CHECK 4.4

Sooner or later, it's going to happen to you. You will send a student to the office who has, in your opinion, been very disruptive and deserves to be suspended from school. You discover that the assistant principal has merely assigned him cafeteria duty for a week.

You are furious. But remember: *once you send a student to the office, it is out of your hands.* You have, in effect, said, "I cannot deal with this, help me." You are obliged to accept whatever decision is made. This does not mean that you shouldn't discuss the situation and your concerns with the administrator, and it might be helpful to do so. Perhaps he didn't have all the details. Or perhaps he thinks you are overreacting. Regardless, it was ultimately his call. Live with it.

The disciplinary hierarchy doesn't apply in severe situations, and the students should be aware of that. This would include such misbehavior as fighting, vandalism, defying you, stopping the class from functioning, and so forth. They don't get a warning if they strike another student. In these cases, you would want to consider sending the student directly to the office.

What kinds of consequences are appropriate for secondary school students? The following are some of the most common ones that secondary school teachers routinely impose and have found effective:

- After-school detention
- Lunch detention
- Last one to leave the classroom
- Letter to parents
- Send to office
- Campus cleanup
- In-school suspension
- Supervised lunch
- Send to another room
- Assigned to a designated seat
- Room cleanup

If your consequences are not working, you will need stronger measures. Don't just give up. Secondary school students need to understand that you mean what you say. It may be hard on you early in the year to stay on top of your discipline plan and all of its consequences while you are trying to learn the ropes in every other area. But as the year progresses, you will find that your persistence has paid off and that things get easier.

Reward the Good Students

What about the students who do behave? You will want to reinforce positive behavior, both for the whole class and for individuals. After all, if all the extra attention goes to the trouble-makers, some students may wonder why they are bothering to cooperate. To reward individuals, use a positive note discreetly given to a student on his or her desk or on the last page of an assignment, a positive note or call to parents, a positive note mailed home, free admission to a school function, an excuse from one pop quiz, and so forth. Group reinforcers might include no homework one night, free time in class, having class outside, popcorn while watching a film, a class trip, and so forth.

Reality Check 4.5

One thing that should *not* be on your list of possible consequences is corporal punishment. Don't even think about it. True, it is legal in some states. The Supreme Court ruled in 1977 that it is not cruel and unusual punishment, and it could be authorized without the permission of the parents. Thus, wide latitude exists in decision making regarding its use (Kauchak, Eggen, & Carter, 2002, pp. 298–299). But legal or not, it is never appropriate.

Communicating Your Discipline Plan

Now you are ready to let everyone know what you're going to do. The person whose support you will need the most is the administrator in charge of discipline at your school, your first audience. Take your discipline plan, which contains both negative and positive

Activity 4.4

Developing Your Discipline Plan

Most secondary school teachers use a combination of *procedures* that will govern the routines of the class and specific *rules* that will need to be observed.

To avoid problems . . .

1. Decide first what your *procedures* are and whether you want to explain them verbally, post them, explain them and post them, or if you just want to refer to procedures as they are needed. (Think twice about the last one.)

To respond to problems . . .

2. List the *rules* for your classroom (maximum of 5).
3. List the consequences for breaking each rule:
   First offense:
   Second offense:
   Third offense:
   Fourth offense:
   Fifth offense:

To reward positive behavior . . .

4. Develop a system for recording positive group and individual behavior (such as a point system).
5. List the rewards you will use:
   Individual rewards:
   Group rewards:

Adapted from Canter, L., & Canter, M. (1984). *How to develop a classroom assertive discipline plan.* Los Angeles: Canter & Associates.

Mrs. Gilbert's Classroom Rules and Procedures

Procedures

1.
2.
3.
4.
5.

Rules

1.
2.
3.
4.
5.

Rewards

1.
2.
3.
4.
5.

Consequences

1.
2.
3.
4.
5.

FIGURE 4.4 Sample Format for Classroom Rules

consequences, and get his or her approval *before* you put the plan into effect. Be sure to put it in writing, leaving a copy with this person, and ask if you can discuss the plan. Ask what the administrative role will be in implementing it and what this person will do once the student is sent from your class. Be prepared to modify your plan if needed.

The second audience is your students. Most teachers find that posting the rules, with consequences, in some prominent place in the room and on a large poster, is helpful as a constant reminder of what is expected (see Figure 4.4).

The messages you want to send to the students from the first minute they enter your room are (Canter & Canter, 1984):

- No student will stop me from teaching or other students from learning.
- I will not accept inappropriate behavior.
- You have a choice: Follow the rules and reap the benefits or don't follow them and accept the consequences.

The third audience is the parents. You will want to send a letter home to your students' parents that includes your rules and the consequences for noncompliance as well as a request for their support (see Figure 4.5). Ask them to sign your letter and return it to you. Follow up with phone calls to parents who have not returned their letters.

Your students' parents can be valuable allies as you work with their sons and daughters each day. This letter is important. However, don't be shocked if some of the parents whose support you may need the most could care less about helping you deal with the discipline problems of their sons and daughters. Some of them have the same issues (or worse) at home with them. It doesn't mean they don't care; they just feel powerless to help you. In fact, they may be looking to you for solutions. Regardless, they need you to inform them of your expectations.

Morgan Middle School

14 Valley Road
Columbus, Ohio 43113

Dear Parent(s):

I will be your eighth grader's science teacher this year and am looking forward to working with this group of students. In order to make sure that your son or daughter and all of the students in my class enjoy the excellent educational environment they deserve, I have created a Discipline Plan that will be in effect at all times.

When in my classroom, students must comply with the following rules:

1. Follow my directions as soon as they are given.
2. Complete all assignments and turn them in on time.
3. Keep hands, feet, and any objects to yourselves.
4. Raise your hand and wait to be called on before speaking.
5. Be on time to class and in your seat when the bell rings.

If a student breaks a rule, the following consequences will occur:

1. First time student breaks a rule:	Warning
2. Second time student breaks a rule:	One detention
3. Third time student breaks a rule	Two detentions
4. Fourth time student breaks a rule	Two detentions, call parents
5. Fifth time student breaks a rule	Call parents, send to principal (possible in-school suspension)

If a student is very disruptive, he or she will be sent immediately to an administrator.

There are some rewards for students who behave well. I may choose to provide students with such incentives as no homework or special class activities.

I need your support in order for this plan to be effective. I have discussed the plan with the class already but am requesting that you do so with your son or daughter as well. Then please return it to me signed.

Thank you for your support in this matter.

Sincerely,

Parent/Guardian Signature Date

Student's Signature Class

FIGURE 4.5 Sample Letter to Parents

Many beginning teachers skip this very important step of sending home the letter and asking that it be signed by a parent and returned. Some claim, "It's not even going to get home, let alone be returned." Maybe so—especially for the type of student whose behavior you most want to correct. Do it anyway. This letter gives you a baseline for conversation with parents who will appreciate the gesture, one that will serve you well when situations arise. Besides, if the letter never gets home, doesn't that demonstrate another example of how the student has not been responsible as you pursue the problem at hand? Use the fact that the letter was not returned as a reason to contact a parent by phone, thus laying the foundation for future dialogue.

How Will You Monitor Student Behavior and Misbehavior?

Everything's in place—the discipline plan and the communication of that plan. Everyone understands how to behave and what happens if he or she doesn't behave. There shouldn't be any problems, right? Wrong.

Your Conflict Style

Many high school students naturally resist the idea that someone is telling them what to do. (Ask any parent.) How comfortable are you telling people what to do? If you are not comfortable, you will be in for some real struggles with some of your students. Your effectiveness as a teacher is largely dependent on your understanding that you must be in control of your classroom, and this inevitably means that you will be in control of your students' behavior. This can result in conflict, and how you handle conflict is key to successful resolution of problematic situations.

How well do you handle conflict? Activity 4.5, based on the research of Thomas and Killman (1974), provides some valuable clues about your natural tendencies as you work in situations of conflict. Complete Part I of the activity and determine your location on the grid in Part II.

Notice that there are five conflict–style descriptors. Beginning with the left side of the grid, the top box represents the "teddy bears," who tend toward high cooperation (HC) and low assertiveness (LA). These people usually want to get along at all costs and dislike discord. They want everyone to be happy and will go a long way to make that happen. Below the teddy bears, in the bottom left quadrant, are the turtles, with low cooperation (LC) tendencies and LA scores. Like the animals they represent, these people are not aggressive in trying to solve crises that arise, nor are they willing to go very far to press for a solution. They are most comfortable hiding in their shell till things blow over.

On the right side of the grid at the bottom, there are the sharks, who are comfortable forcefully pushing their views (high assertiveness [HA] scores) but who aren't willing to compromise very much to gain peace (LC). The top right represents the owls, who are willing to express their views forcefully but are also willing to work hard to cooperate so that satisfactory solutions can be found. There are several things you need to remember about this exercise. First, it's not gospel; it's just an indicator, something for you to think about. Second, there are no "good" or "bad" types. In fact, the more comfortable you are moving around the grid depending on the situation, the better a classroom manager you will be. In conflicts with secondary school students, you should be prepared to be an owl in one situation and a turtle in another. Third, where you are on the grid (how close you are to another type, how far up a scale you are) also should give you some idea about how much of a teddy bear or a shark you are.

Finally, and most important, notice that in the middle are foxes, which represent a relative comfort level with all of the styles. Being a fox is your goal.

General Management Techniques for Secondary School Classrooms

What actions can you make part of your regular classroom routine to support your discipline plan and to ensure that you rarely have to use it? What follows are some of the most common and most effective (Epanchin, Townsend, & Stoddard, 1994; Grossman, 1995; Levine & Nolan, 1996).

Planned Ignoring

Your high school students will do many things during class that are of such short duration or are so insignificant that they simply should be ignored. It won't be that you don't see it, but that you have chosen to ignore it. If a behavior is not a violation of one of your rules, or if reacting to it would interrupt a lesson or call unwanted attention to it, leave it alone (Emmer, Evertson, Sanford, Clements, & Worsham, 1984). For example, Tina had a student in her fourth-period French class who sat in the back of the room putting on makeup every day. This student had many problems and could become volatile and disruptive if provoked. Interestingly, she was always able to answer questions and disturbed no one. Tina decided to choose her battles—she ignored the behavior. "I never would

ACTIVITY 4.5

Your Conflict Style

Part I

Directions: Generally speaking, on a 1–10 scale (10 being *most assertive*), how assertive are you in most situations? Think of the term *assertive* as referring to how far you will go to get your way or to make yourself heard and understood. How proactive are you in difficult situations? It's true that you may be more assertive in some situations than in others, but try to consider how you are most of the time.

Assertiveness score 8

Likewise, on a 1–10 scale (10 being *most cooperative*), how cooperative are you in most situations? Exactly how far will you go to keep the peace?

Cooperation score 9

Part II

Directions: Use Figure 4.6 to find the number across the bottom of the scale that corresponds to your assertiveness score. Then move your pencil directly up until you get to the number that corresponds to the cooperation score on the left. Mark this location and notice which of the style descriptors best fits you in most circumstances.

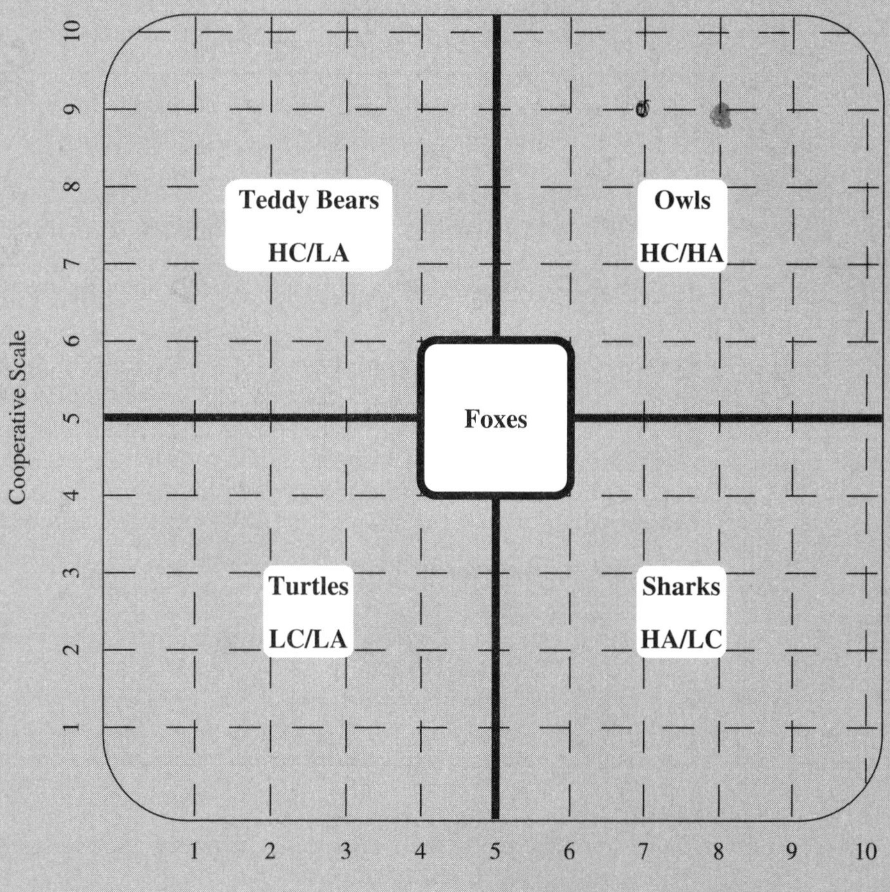

FIGURE 4.6 Your Conflict Style
The Thomas-Kilmann Conflict Mode Instrument
Thomas, Kenneth W., & Kilmann, Ralph H. (1974). Developing a forced choice measure of conflict handling behavior: The mode instrument. XICOM.

have believed that I would have allowed someone to do this in my class," she explained. "But this is a unique situation and seems to work."

Proximity Control
Standing beside the desk of a student who is talking as you move around the room continuing to give directions will usually cause the student to stop the disruption. As a rule, people, especially secondary school students, don't want you in their personal space. They'll stop the misbehavior just to get you to move on.

Interest Boosting
Nothing keeps students from getting into trouble like keeping them more interested in something you are doing. Creating lessons and activities that will stimulate them and engage their interest will be much better than spending your energy calling them down.

Humor
You don't have to be Jay Leno, but teenagers respond well to humor. You need to be able to laugh at amusing things during the day. Help them to see and appreciate the lighter moments that give everyone a healthy perspective on what's happening.

Sticking with Your Routines
Your routines are the basics of the way your class functions. When students know what to expect and follow a pattern each day, they tend to comply with what you want them to do more of the time. They know what's coming and do it out of habit. This means that for some activities and portions of the class time, they are on automatic pilot.

Removing Distracting Objects
Anything that seems to capture the attention of your students while they are supposed to be engaged in your lesson is a distraction. If Morty is fascinated by the prom pictures that Lucille is passing around, then he can't be fascinated with anything you are trying to teach him. Store the pictures in your desk for Lucille till class is over.

Signal Interference
Sometimes a signal the teacher uses to indicate that a student should stop some behavior works well. It might be a gentle tap on a student's desk, pointing at the trash basket to indicate something should be thrown away, or putting a finger to your lips to indicate that a student should stop talking.

Removing the Problem Student
Separating students who are causing problems from the rest of the group is not only an effective technique but may be your only option in some cases. If a student refuses to respond to any of your attempts to get him or her to cease the disruptive activity, then you may need to ask the student to move to another location in the room or leave the class altogether.

Imposing Restrictions
Following the guidelines you have indicated on your discipline plan should result in your students' knowing and having repeatedly confirmed what your expectations are.

You will find that some of these techniques are more comfortable for you to implement than others. For example, there's nothing more pitiful than someone who is not able to be funny trying to be a comedian. Experiment with the ones that work, add your own techniques to the list, and come up with your own style. Many different styles, if developed thoughtfully and applied consistently, can be effective.

Four Critical Relationships That Impact the Behavior of Secondary School Students

Warren began the year as an excellent student in Jim's physical education class. Jim had always given Warren special attention, asking him to take roll and to lead the class with its opening calisthenics. But as the first semester progressed, Warren was becoming increasingly disrespectful and hostile to Jim. He began refusing to do the tasks that Jim asked him to do and even undermined Jim's efforts with the rest of the class, making faces to his classmates and rolling his eyes at certain exercises. To Jim, it seemed that the problem was a growing one just between the two of them.

The reason adolescents do the things they do is never as simple as it seems. While they are in your classroom, they are actively involved in *four* relationships at the same time, each influencing their behavior in some way. The four relationships are (a) student and self, (b) student and peers, (c) student and class or activity, and (d) student and teacher (DeBruyn, 1991).

Based on the type of impudent comments Warren was making, Jim had concluded that he was asking too much of him: "He's just a kid—maybe he isn't ready for that much responsibility. I'll lay off." The facts of this situation were quite different, however. The misbehavior arose because the popular students in that class rarely participated (student and peers relationship), making fun of Warren as he dutifully did his squat thrusts. Wanting to be liked by his classmates much more than he wanted to be liked by Jim, Warren felt humiliated (student and self relationship). He also became increasingly resentful of Jim for putting him into this situation each day (student and teacher relationship). Eventually, he not only refused to lead the class, some days he didn't participate at all. His grade dropped from an A to a C (student and class relationship).

Dealing with issues that arise means that you must always be aware of all four of these relationships at all times. Even if you don't know exactly what dynamics are at work with each of your students (you couldn't possibly), knowing this phenomenon exists will inform your own actions. Because you know that the student's relationship with his peers is one of the strongest influences, you will avoid humiliating students in front of the class. Likewise, because you know that your relationship with students is an important factor in their success in your classroom, you will work to get along with them.

REALITY CHECK 4.6

There will be times when you feel so desperate to get a student to cooperate that you will be tempted to use sarcasm, put-downs, or any other leverage that seems to work at the time. Avoid this. Remember that you have the authority, but it must be used carefully. Even if you win the battle at hand, you could lose the war with a student. It's a tricky dilemma you will face many times. Tread lightly. And never lose your temper.

Land Mines: Words and Gestures That Make Students Explode

It's hard enough to figure out how to turn kids on, let alone what turns them off. But it's important that you try. You must attempt to identify which words, gestures, or other habits *you* have that contribute to problems with your students. Most communication between all people is nonverbal and unconscious, which means that, more than likely, you have no clue how annoying you may be to certain students. What personal habits of yours could get on a student's last nerve? Some of the most common are the following:

Gestures to Avoid

- Pointing your finger at them.
- Turning your back on them while they are talking (unless you are going to the board to write down what they are saying).
- Rolling your eyes, sighing, or giving a look of disgust. Students can handle anger; they cannot tolerate disgust. Verbal communication can tell students we disapprove of what they have done; nonverbal communication may be misinterpreted as disgust for them as persons (DeBruyn, 1992).
- Staring at them—especially if they don't know why.

Things to Avoid Saying

- Comparisons to siblings ("You look just like your sister," or worse, "I hope you are not like your brother!")
- Beginning sentences with, "You always . . . " or "You never . . . "
- "Because I said so."

- Threatening to punish the whole class for the actions of one or a few.
- Answering "because it's my job" when students ask why you are doing something. They want you to do things with them because you *want* to, not just because you have to.

Remember these additional principles as you attempt to avoid words and gestures that are hurtful and demoralizing. First, secondary school students are sensitive about everything that could remotely have to do with them. Teenagers assume that everyone is watching them—the "imaginary audience" that they believe is judging them every minute of the day. Thus, they are extremely self-conscious about how they look and how they appear to others. You can be sure that anything you do or say that can in any way be construed as negative will be viewed as criticism and a judgment (DeBruyn, 1992).

Feel like you're walking on eggshells? To a certain extent, you are. And it's inevitable that you will say or do something at some time to irritate somebody. A gesture that one student responds well to will drive another student nuts. Just try to be aware of the most common irritants and avoid them. You can usually tell by students' expressions or responses. Be consistently on the lookout for how *your* students react to certain things you do and say and modify your own behavior accordingly when possible.

How Will You Address Problems?

The crux of the problem with most teachers and secondary school students is the issue of control. You've got it; they want it. How do you use it and not abuse it? Don't forget that you have the authority to make things happen or not happen in your classroom. But being teenagers, your students want to feel that they have power, too. You will want to help them feel that they have some control over their circumstances. Getting hooked into power struggles with your students will only create an atmosphere of conflict.

Confronting Misbehavior: Power Struggles in Your Classroom

Teachers do several things that result in power struggles. First and foremost is the habit of overreacting—instantly, automatically, and negatively—to anything students do or say that you might perceive as a threat. You don't always have to be right—you just have to be in charge. And even if you are right, *be right gently and quietly*.

Also, taking certain things students do personally and too seriously is a mistake. After all, your students are adolescents. They are growing up and will say and do things today that they may not even believe tomorrow. It will help if you don't try to change or control them—accept them for who they are.

You can prevent power struggles by doing some of the following things.

1. Take yourself less seriously and look for the humor in things.
2. Stop blaming the students and work for solutions to problems.
3. Listen with an open mind to what students say.
4. Confront privately and give the student a chance to respond.
5. Hold students accountable for appropriate behavior and for their work.
6. Present yourself as someone worthy of respect.
7. Be honest and straightforward in your dealings with students.
8. Use noninflammatory language even if the student is being disrespectful.
9. Maintain your dignity to keep your personal power intact, no matter what the student says.

The Classic Power Struggle

A typical situation that you will probably encounter at some point is the student who is openly defiant toward you. Often this occurs in front of the other students, and your immediate reaction will probably be to feel that your authority is being threatened. It is—especially if you don't handle the situation well. What's more, if the student is allowed to get away with it, he will likely do it again, and the other students will think they can, too. Because the student has provoked the confrontation, he will not want to back down and lose face in front of his peers. Shouting him down is a mistake. It will not only *not* diffuse the situation, but it will cause you to lose your dignity.

So, what should you do? First of all, usually you can avoid the potential power struggle altogether if you are able to discuss the situation with the student alone, away from the curious eyes of other students. It also helps if you can depersonalize the event: "We are losing valuable time with the lesson. I will talk to you about this in a few minutes." This kind of comment will give the student a few minutes to calm down and redirect the class's attention to the task at hand. If the student wants to continue the confrontation, your best bet is to ask him to leave the room and wait in the hall. Give the other students something to do so that you can talk with him privately. If the student refuses to calm down or leave the room, send another student to the office for assistance.

Now it's just you and the student. Your first step is to handle *yourself*. Enter this encounter prepared to *underreact*, to be calm and to stay objective, refusing to be drawn into an argument. Remember that you are usually not the real target anyway, even though you are on the receiving end of his anger. You're just the available object. As often as not, the student will have had a fight with her boyfriend or parent that morning; another may have learned that he did not make the football team. Regardless of the reason, it's still your problem to face now.

Begin by letting the student speak first if possible, asking him to explain why he is doing what he is doing. Play back what you heard the student say: "If I understood you correctly, you think that . . . " Then it's your turn. Focus on the misbehavior (not the student), reminding him why the rule exists at all. Maintain eye contact and insist that the student do the same. Take the action you feel is best for the situation. If you are unclear about how to respond, say that you will think about it and will discuss it with him later (Emmer, Evertson, Sanford, Clements, & Worsham, 1984, pp. 105–106).

The same basic approach is helpful when you have two students involved, usually in some sort of a dispute or fight. Depending on the situation, you may want to attempt some basic mediation strategies (Slaikeu, 1996). Again, allow each student to be heard about his or her perceptions of what happened, and then tell them how you see the problem and why it concerns you. Finally, the emphasis should be on the question of how to solve the dilemma and prevent future repeats of the misbehavior.

Severe Behavior Problems

While most of your behavior issues will be mild, occasionally, some are severe. Severe consequences should be used only as a last resort. The following sample techniques have been very effective for secondary school teachers (Canter & Canter, 1984):

- Assertive Confrontation—This is where you let the student know you will not tolerate the misbehavior. "I care too much about you to allow you to disrupt my classroom."
- Behavioral Contracts—These are agreements between the teacher, student, parent, and administrator. They include what you want the student to do, what will happen if he or she doesn't comply, and how long the contract will be in effect.
- Tape-Recording the Behavior—The teacher places a tape recorder next to the disruptive student. This can be played back in several situations that may be helpful (with a parent, with an administrator, or just with the student).
- Sending the Student to Another Class—This involves the cooperation of another teacher.
- Parent Attending Class—The parent observes the misbehavior.
- Assigning Discipline Cards—These are signed by more than one teacher each period (especially effective with middle school students).

Documentation

Always document each incident of misbehavior, especially if it appears to be becoming a pattern. Keep a file card of student misbehavior with time, date, description of the incident, and what action you took. These records will be helpful in conversations with the student's parents or administrators who will surely ask how long this has been a problem and will want to know what you have already tried. There is nothing more impressive or persuasive than a teacher who can present a record of incidents and produce a list of strategies and interventions that have been tried.

Classes of Offenses—Which Misbehaviors Matter Most?

Fortunately, most behaviors that we can categorize as inappropriate are *Class 1 Offenses*—better known as goofing off. While teachers worry that students will be openly defiant and that some violent incident might occur, research (Cangelosi, 1997; Jones, 1979) indicates that 99% of off-task behaviors are minor issues—talking out of turn, clowning, daydreaming, or getting out of seats. These are usually the "sand in your swimsuit" type of irritations that can really annoy you if you let them. These mild offenses might also include chewing gum, wearing hats, making noises, passing notes, tardiness, and so forth. Plan for some way to react (or not react) to these before they occur. These situations affect only the smooth operation of your classroom and should be handled by you rather than an administrator.

Class 2 Offenses are those of immorality such as cheating, lying, and stealing and could result in in-school suspension, individual or group counseling, or any number of other interventions. They might also include deliberate disruption on a school bus, the use of profanity or obscene gestures, cutting class, littering on school property, and leaving class without permission. Depending on the situation and the policy in effect in your school, either you or an administrator might handle them.

Class 3 Offenses would include any defiance of you or your authority, such as refusing to cooperate with you. These also include major things such as the use of drugs and alcohol, fighting, threatening to attack another student, sexual harassment, stealing, defacing school property, and throwing things or in any way endangering other students. These may result in in-school or out-of-school suspension and definitely require action by an administrator. This kind of measure is usually taken for the protection of the student and others and to help the student deal with his or her problems. Principals are required to follow due process before action can be taken, including investigating the situation, talking to the parents of the student, and providing written notice of suspension.

Class 4 Offenses are the most serious and might result in the student's being subject to exclusion from the school system. These usually include threatening physical harm to or attacking a school system employee; attacking another student to gain money from that student; creating or encouraging students to join in a disturbance; and possession of a gun, rifle, explosives, or any sharp instrument that might cause injury; arson; sexual assault; and so forth.

Each school and school system identifies which offenses fall into which category. Class 1 Offenses are the only ones that you have total control over, and even then, some of your rules may be part of a schoolwide or systemwide set of disciplinary directives.

Violence in Secondary Schools

So much is in the news about violence and students carrying guns to their schools, especially since the incident at Columbine, Colorado, when two students killed 13 others before killing themselves. When polled, teachers as well as parents rated "school safety and discipline" highest on a list of concerns about school quality (Elam, Rose, & Gallup, 1994; Olson, 1999).

Feeling safe is a basic need for everyone. But 1 of every 4 students reports some sort of violence-related issue in their schools, and 40 violent school-related deaths occurred during the 1997–1998 school year (Portner, 1999a). Student concerns about violence and safety are actually highest at the eighth-grade level and tend to decline as they attend high school. Students in urban areas (33%) tend to report more serious problems with violence than do suburban students (22%) or rural students (18%). Most concerns about violence are in high-poverty areas (Kauchak, Eggen, & Carter, 2002).

The possibility of violence may be a concern for you, but you need to keep this concern in perspective. Incidences of this magnitude are rare, and when you consider how many students and other people pass through the halls of secondary schools every day, the number is very small. Overall, violence has been down despite well-publicized incidents. Most of your problems will not be nearly this dramatic. They will be predictable minor discipline issues that arise because adolescents are being adolescents. Their behavior problems can be easily and quickly handled if you are a "withit" teacher who is paying attention, is addressing small problems before they become bigger ones, and is being consistent in your reactions.

Are You *the Discipline Problem in Your Classroom?*

You could be part of the problems in your classroom. Kellough and Kellough (1999) identified several teacher behaviors that inevitably cause problems in secondary school classrooms. Make sure you avoid these habits. They are:

- Giving extra assignments for misbehavior that could result in students' associating a class with drudgery
- Embarrassing students
- Giving group punishments
- Favoring harsh and humiliating punishments
- Being inconsistent
- Loud talking (your own voice talking over the students')
- Lowering grades for misbehavior
- Nagging students
- Using negative touch control (grabbing a student who is grabbing someone else teaches the student that it's OK if you are doing it)
- Using physical punishment (running laps for punishment)
- Making premature judgments and actions
- Issuing threats and ultimatums
- Being too hesitant to take action
- Giving writing punishments

You are just starting out. Be patient with yourself as you learn about managing your classroom and your students' behavior. According to Glasser (1986), many parents and teachers believe that, regardless of how motivated a student is, a good teacher can teach all students. This is based on the assumption that students want to learn what is taught. But although some teachers are more skilled than others, Glasser believes that there is no teacher who can teach a student who does not want to learn.

Likewise, many believe that a good teacher can handle every discipline situation that arises. Not so. While some teachers are certainly better than others are at managing their classrooms and controlling their students, no teacher, no matter how skilled, can handle *every* discipline problem with total success. With time and experience, things do get easier. And as the master teacher you will become, you will find that your issues related to discipline and classroom management have decreased dramatically. This thought should give you comfort.

TIPS from the TRENCHES

The following are suggestions beginning teachers wish they had followed when they began teaching.

1. Develop a discipline plan, stick to it, and communicate it clearly to your students, parents, and administrators.

2. Take to heart what you learned about yourself from the "Conflict Style" activity. Actively practice to become more comfortable in all four quadrants and focus on becoming a fox.

3. Be consistent in what you expect and in how you apply penalties. Some days it will be the hardest thing you do. Be ready to be challenged by your students if they think you are inconsistent.

4. Dress comfortably, but professionally. Your appearance does contribute to the students' perceptions of how seriously you take your job and them.

5. Talk to other teachers about students who are persistent problems in your class. If they are familiar with the students, they can often provide excellent insight into the students' background and what strategies for working with them have been effective.

6. Take time to examine student files for information that will help you work with the discipline problems in your classroom.

7. Be tough at the beginning of the year. It is easier to lighten up than it is to try to regain control after it has been lost.

8. Understand the "wild pack" theory. While the comparison isn't necessarily flattering, it has some merit when applied to your students. Adolescents, like packs of animals, can sense vulnerability or weakness. When packs of wolves sense vulnerability or weakness in another animal, they go in for the kill. Likewise, when adolescents sense that you are weak, one student may attack and the rest will pile on.

9. It will be easy to spend too much time with one student or one group. Monitor the whole class at all times.

10. Never talk over student noise. Wait to get their attention.

PRAXIS™

Praxis Competencies Related to Classroom Management

There are various ways that several of the Praxis examinations might address issues related to classroom management. For example, the Principals of Learning and Teaching (PLT) test (0524) will cover such topics as:

- Establishing and maintaining consistent standards of classroom behavior
- Structuring a climate for learning (such as classroom and school expectations, rules, routines, and procedures)
- Strategies to maintain discipline and to promote student learning
- Behavior management, including methods to encourage desirable and discourage undesirable student behavior

Sample Question

Directions: Analyze the teacher's goal and actions intended to lead to the achievement of the goal. Decide whether the action makes it likely or unlikely that the goal will be achieved and select the best statement of a reason that the action is likely or unlikely to lead to the achievement of the goal.

GOAL: To prevent tensions between two groups from disrupting a tenth-grade class that includes a number of students from each group who have expressed hostility toward each other.

ACTION: The teacher plans projects that are based on factual data that the students are likely to find interesting. The projects require the students to work in small groups that are structured so that each group is composed of students from each of the two hostile groups.

(A) LIKELY, because students are required to work with students they would not otherwise associate with, and these interactions often lead to different perceptions about those individuals.

(B) LIKELY, because the teacher limits the projects that the groups are to work on to those that do not require opinions or nonfactual interpretation.

(C) UNLIKELY, because one or two students usually dominate the group, and the other students in the group may feel resentment, thus leading to increased tension in the classroom.

(D) UNLIKELY, because the teacher should maintain control in situations where such tensions are an issue, and teacher-centered teaching methods, such as lectures and direct questioning, are safer. (Adapted from ETS, 2002, *Test-at-a-Glance,* Principles of Learning and Teaching, p. 41)

Notice that the question is asking you to demonstrate your understanding of the social dynamics of your students and how you can manage tensions between them to maintain control of your classroom. As the teacher, you are looking for a response that offers students a chance to work through their problems, something more than just keeping a lid on potential trouble. Thus, the best answer is **A**. Cooperative and small group work is frequently cited as an effective way to deal with tension of all sorts within the classroom. The other responses suggest that the teacher's top priority should be to avoid anything that will increase tension, and of course, the teacher will want to keep this in mind. But these responses may or may not have this result and the teacher will have missed an opportunity to assist the students in their dealing with each other more productively.

Likewise, other Specialty Area Tests in the Praxis Series will address themes of classroom management. Most address the subject-specific themes related to procedures. For example, the General Science Test (0435) covers laboratory procedures and safety: techniques of safe preparation, storage, use, and disposal of laboratory and field materials and selection of appropriate laboratory equipment (ETS, 2002, *Test-at-a-Glance,* Biology and General Science, p. 63). Teaching Students with Emotional Disturbance (0370) specially targets classroom management issues as well with topics such as data-gathering procedures for certain misbehaviors and choosing consequences for behavior, such as reinforcement and punishment (ETS, 2002, *Test-at-a-Glance,* Education of Students with Disabilities, p. 76). See the *Test-at-a-Glance* for the Praxis II test you will be taking and look for areas related to classroom management that are identified for you.

Suggestions for Further Reading

If you have time to read only one book related to classroom management . . .

Levin, J., & Nolan, J. F. (1996). *Principles of classroom management* (2nd ed.). Needham Heights, MA: Allyn & Bacon.

Other excellent resources . . .

Cangelosi, J. S. (1997). *Classroom management strategies: Gaining and maintaining students' cooperation.* White Plains, NY: Longman.

Grossman, H. (1995). *Classroom behavior management in a diverse society* (2nd ed.). Mountain View, CA: Mayfield.

References

Agnes, M. (Ed.). (2000). *Webster's New World College Dictionary* (4th ed.). Cleveland: IDG Books.

Cangelosi, J. S. (1997). *Classroom management strategies: Gaining and maintaining students' cooperation* (2nd ed.). White Plains, NY: Longman.

Canter, L., & Canter, M. (1976). *Assertive discipline.* Los Angeles: Canter & Associates.

Canter, L., & Canter, M. (1984). *How to develop a classroom assertive discipline plan.* Los Angeles: Canter & Associates.

Chernow, F. B., & Chernow, C. (1984). *Classroom discipline and control: 101 practical techniques.* West Nyack, NY: Parker.

DeBruyn, R. L. (1991). Always consider 4 factors when disciplining students. *Master Teacher, 23,* (10).

DeBruyn, R. L. (1992). Words and gestures that turn students off. *Master Teacher, 24* (3).

Educational Testing Service (ETS). (2002). *Tests-at-a-Glance* (Principles of Learning and Teaching, Education of Students with Disabilities, Biology and General Science). Princeton, New Jersey.

Elam, S. M., Rose, L. C., & Gallup, A. M. (1994). The 26th annual Phi Delta Kappan Gallup poll: Attitudes towards public schools. *Phi Delta Kappan, 76,* 41–56.

Emmer, E. T., Evertson, C., Sanford, J., Clements, B., & Worsham, M. (1984). *Classroom management for secondary teachers.* Upper Saddle River, NJ: Prentice Hall.

Epanchin, B. C., Townsend, B., & Stoddard, K. (1994). *Constructive classroom management: Strategies for creating positive learning environments.* Pacific Grove, CA: Brooks/Cole.

Froyen, L. A. (1988). *Classroom management: Empowering teacher leaders.* Upper Saddle River, NJ: Merrill/Prentice Hall.

Glasser, W. (1986). *Control theory in the classroom.* New York: Harper & Row.

Grossman, H. (1995). *Classroom behavior management in a diverse society* (2nd ed.). Mountain View, CA: Mayfield.

Jones, F. (1979). The gentle art of classroom discipline. *National Elementary Principal, 58,* 26–32.

Kauchak, D., Eggen, P., & Carter, C. (2002). *Introduction to education: Becoming a professional.* Upper Saddle River, NJ: Merrill/Prentice Hall.

Kellough, R. D., & Kellough, N. G. (1999). *Middle school teaching: A guide to methods and resources.* Upper Saddle River, NJ: Merrill/Prentice Hall.

Kounin, J. (1977). *Discipline and group management in classrooms.* New York: Holt, Rinehart, & Winston.

Kounin, J., & Sherman, L. (1979). School environments and behavior settings. *Theory and Practice, 18,* 145–151.

Levine, J., & Nolan, J. (1996). *Principles of classroom management,* (2nd ed.). Needham Heights, MA: Allyn & Bacon.

Olson, L. (1999). Report cards for schools. *Education Week, 18* (17), 28–36.

Portner, J. (1999). Schools ratchet up the rules on student clothing and threats. *Education Week, 18* (35), 6–70.

Raven, B. H. (1974). A comprehensive analysis of power and power preference. In J. T. Tedeshi (Ed.), *Perspectives on social power* (pp. 172–198). Chicago: Aldine.

Shrigley, R. L. (1986). Teacher authority in the classroom: A plan of action. *National Association of Secondary School Principals Bulletin, 70* (490), 65–71.

Slaikeu, K. A. (1996). *When push comes to shove: A practical guide to mediating disputes.* San Francisco: Jossey-Bass.

Thomas, K. W., & Kilmann, R. H. (1974). *Thomas-Kilmann conflict mode instrument.* Tuxedo, NY: XICOM.

Wong, H. K., & Wong, R. T. (1998). *The first days of school.* Mountain View, CA: Harry E. Wong.

5

Students with Special Needs

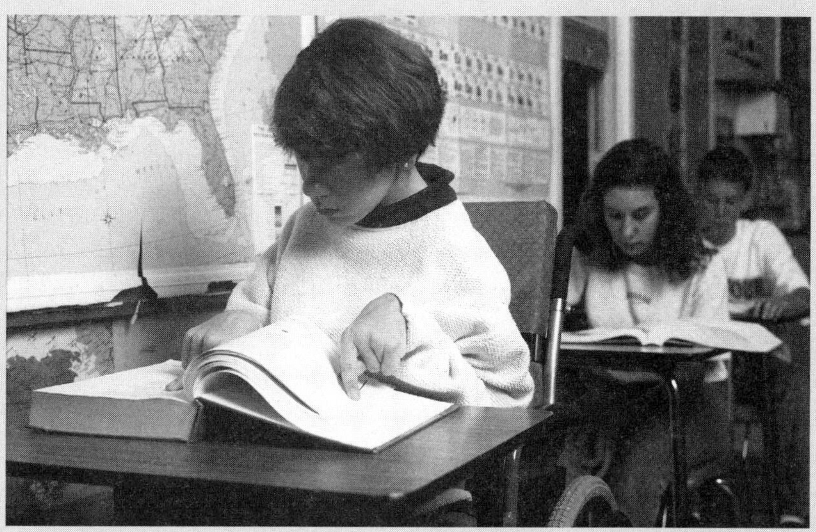

My principal describes my fourth-period biology class as "average." Yeah, right. I have 28 students; 5 are learning disabled and two are EMD (educable mentally disabled)—all with IEPs. I'm sure that at least two more need to be tested and one new transfer is bound to be gifted and was just scheduled in this class by mistake. I don't have a clue as to how to teach this crew!

First-year teacher

Does the situation above sound familiar? If it doesn't, it will. Most assuredly, you will have students with special needs in your classes—many of them—and you will need to know how to identify these individuals and adapt your instruction for them. Approximately 11% of the school-age population is identified as disabled (U.S. Department of Education, 1997), and more than 40% of those students are ages 12–17 (U.S. Department of Education, 1999). Among these students are 10 categories of disabilities. Since this is the case, you should expect 2 or 3 students with some disability in a typical class of 25 students. Unfortunately, while the situation described by the first-year teacher above should not happen often, many beginning teachers will tell you that it does, especially in "average-" or "regular-" level classrooms. Be prepared!

This chapter will provide some basic guidelines to help you identify the students with special needs in your classes. Some of these students—such as those with learning disabilities, mild mental retardation, and physical handicaps—will be formally designated as "exceptional" and have individual education plans (IEPs) to guide your work with them. Others, such as culturally and linguistically diverse students, may not be formally considered "exceptional" students and do not have IEPs but are still considered to have special needs. Still others, such as students who are gifted and talented, *may* be designated as "exceptional" students and have IEPs, depending on the state where they live. You will also learn about some of the most important laws that govern the education of students with special needs. Finally, this chapter will help you to understand how you will identify and refer these students for special services as well as teach them successfully in your own classroom.

Special Students: Who Are the Students with Special Needs in Your Classes?

Each day, Mr. Jenkins, a first-year teacher, dreaded facing a particularly difficult, already overcrowded environmental science class. By the end of November, he noted that seven of the students were routinely frustrated, unruly, or just unresponsive, despite his best efforts to give them more attention. One day, in conversation with one of these students, who repeatedly handed in illegible work, Mr. Jenkins threatened to lower his grade if he didn't improve. "You can't do that!" the student screamed. "My IEP says I'm allowed to turn it in like this."

After class, Mr. Jenkins asked his mentor, "What's an IEP?" She explained that each student with a disability had an individual education plan. He immediately went to the guidance office, where he learned that six of those seven students had some disability. All needed modifications in their instruction. At the same time, Mr. Jenkins discovered that he had 12 students in his other classes who also had disabilities. "I'm amazed! They all seem so 'normal,'" he said. He was furious that someone hadn't told him about their disabilities earlier. True, based on the outlined procedures in his school, it was someone else's job to let him know. But he learned the hard way that he couldn't depend on that. Ultimately, it was *his* responsibility to ask questions sooner and to find out as much as possible about students who seemed to have problems. And, it's yours.

Students with special needs (sometimes referred to as exceptional students) are a diverse group, and like Mr. Jenkins, you will rarely be able to identify who they are by their appearance. Some have trouble learning whereas others learn with ease. Some have trouble behaving. Some have physical disabilities, and others have trouble with their speech or hearing. But most of the time, they look like typical students. They try to. After all, they are secondary school students who want to fit in.

The majority of the students who receive special education have mild disabilities and approximately 75% of those students receive at least part of their education in regular classrooms. More than two thirds of all students who receive special education services are male.

Most students with disabilities (90%) represent the following categories (Turnbull, Turnbull, Shank, Smith, & Leal, 2002):

- Learning disabilities (51%)
- Speech and language impairments (19.8%)
- Mental retardation (11.2%)
- Emotional disturbance (8.4%)

Students who have disabilities make up one part of special education students. The other part is made up of students who are academically gifted and have unusual talents. They are not served under federal law as are students with disabilities. According to Landrum, Katsiyannis, and Dewaard (1998), 33 states have legislation related to gifted education. While two thirds of those states require that gifted students be identified, only one half require special programming.

The most recent description of students with disabilities (Public Law 105–17, the Individuals with Disabilities Education Act Amendments of 1997) states that students with disabilities include those with

> mental retardation, hearing impairments (including deafness), speech or language impairments, visual impairments (including blindness), serious emotional disturbance, orthopedic impairments, autism, traumatic brain injury, other health impairments, or specific learning disability. [Sec. 602(3)(A)(i)]

Attention deficit disorder (ADD) is covered under other federal legislation.

Educators generally group students with special needs in four ways:

1. Students with exceptionally severe learning difficulties, including those with multisensory impairment
2. Students with other mild, moderate, or specific learning problems, including emotional and behavioral difficulties
3. Students with physical impairments
4. Gifted students

Teachers in general education classrooms probably will not encounter students in Group 1 in their classes. However, it will not be unusual for you to teach students in Groups 2, 3, and 4. To be more specific, expect to see the following students with special needs on a regular basis:

Students with an IEP

- Students with learning disabilities
- Students with mild mental retardation (educable mentally disabled [EMD])
- Students with physical impairments

Students Who May Have an IEP (depending on the state)

- Students who are gifted and talented

Students Without an IEP (unless they also have a disability)

- Students who are culturally and linguistically diverse
- Students who are at-risk for school failure

All of these students with special needs will require adaptations in your planning and instruction if you are to teach them effectively (see Activity 5.1).

Activity 5.1

Meeting and Monitoring Your Students with Special Needs

Meet with each student with special needs for an "orientation to your class" session at the beginning of the year to determine the best way for the two of you to work together. After the meeting, select checkpoints on your yearly calendar when you will follow up with respect to each student. For example, mark one day each quarter on which you will be sure to have a personal conversation with each one. These don't have to be many or time-consuming activities—just consistent efforts to monitor progress regularly.

Your Exceptional Students with an IEP

Students with Learning Disabilities

Exactly what is a learning disability? Students with learning disabilities are a heterogeneous population with many learning, behavioral, and social characteristics. Educators use the term so freely when referring to almost any learning concerns that often the exact nature of a student's problems is unclear. The confusion lies in how the term is defined (McNamara, 1998).

There is no universally agreed-on definition of learning disabilities. This is a result of the concept of learning disabilities being influenced heavily by the fields of medicine, psychology, and education. Each field has proposed its own definition. However, several attempts have been made to develop a good definition of learning disabilities that will be useful in guiding professionals as they develop policy and approaches for working with students who are in this category. Despite some differences in these definitions, most states require that three criteria be met: (a) a severe discrepancy between potential or ability and actual achievement; (b) difficulty with academic tasks that cannot be attributed to other disabilities; and (c) the need for special education services to succeed in school.

Most students with learning disabilities show one or more of the following characteristics:

- Reading problems
- Deficits in written language
- Underachievement in math
- Social skills deficits
- Problems with attention and hyperactivity
- Behavioral problems

Basically, these students demonstrate a specific and significant achievement deficiency in the presence of adequate or above-average overall intelligence. In fact, many of these students have at least one area of academic strength. Given the vague definitions of learning disabilities, it is no surprise that determining their existence can be a problem for you. Naturally you should pay careful attention to these individual characteristics should they be present in your students who are having difficulty learning. The nature of the particular problem will determine how you should modify your instruction.

Students with Mild Mental Retardation (Educable Mentally Disabled [EMD])

The term *mentally retarded* has been a rather common and often misused term in society. Educators know that labels have an important impact, both in the way people are viewed and in the way they are treated. Actually, only about half the states use the term *mentally retarded*. Other terms include *developmental disabilities, developmental handicaps,* or *mental disabilities*. More frequently, these students have been referred to as *educable mentally retarded* (EMR) or, more recently, as *educable mentally disabled* (EMD). There are four degrees of mental retardation based on IQ scores: mild, moderate, severe, and profound. Most teachers in general classrooms will face the need to adapt instruction for the mildly mentally retarded.

The American Association on Mental Retardation (AAMR) defines mental retardation as follows (Luckasson et al., 1992, p. 5):

> Mental retardation refers to substantial limitations in present functioning. It is characterized by significantly subaverage intellectual functioning, existing concurrently with related limitations in two or more of the following applicable adaptive skill areas: communication, self-care, home-living, social skills, community use, self-direction, health and safety, functional academics, leisure and work. Mental retardation manifests before age 18.

The 1992 definition connects a student's intellectual abilities and skill limitations to the level and type of support a person needs to function in society. It suggests that a person should be evaluated in four areas:

- Intellectual functioning and adaptive skills
- Psychological and emotional health
- Physical health
- Environmental support

Instead of labeling students as being mildly, moderately, severely, or profoundly mentally retarded, the definition designated students as needing intermittent, limited, extensive, or pervasive levels of support within the categories listed above (Meyen, 1996). Based on testing, the AAMR divides these levels by IQ:

Category of mental retardation	Level of support	IQ
Mild	Intermittent	69–55
Moderate	Limited	54–40
Severe	Extensive	39–25
Profound	Pervasive	Below 25

In general classrooms it is sometimes not easy to determine exactly who the mildly mentally retarded students are. In most cases, the diagnosis of mental retardation requires an IQ score of 70–75 or below. For many years, once identified, these students were placed in special education classes where, educators believed, the material presented to them in these settings would be better (easier) for them to learn. The attitude of educators was that they could better protect the students from rejection by their peers and continual failure in the academic program. Studies, however, concluded that children with mild retardation who were assigned to the regular classes generally performed better academically than those in special classes.

Three major characteristics of mental retardation are limitations in intellectual functioning, limitations in adaptive skill areas, and the need for support (Turnbull, Turnbull, Shank, Smith, & Leal, 2002).

Characteristics Related to Intellectual Functioning

1. Attention—The ability to pay attention and to focus on relevant information while ignoring the irrelevant, to search for new information and to maintain focus (Iarocci & Burack, 1998, p. 350).

2. Memory—The ability of students with mental retardation to remember things learned. For example, researchers believe that these students have slower developmental growth for tasks such as remembering a number of sequential items (Bray, Fletcher, & Turner, 1997, p. 213).

3. Generalization—The ability to transfer knowledge or behavior learned from one task to another and to do so in different settings (Horner, 1988). For example, they may have trouble applying skills they have learned in school to their home setting (Bebko & Luhaorg, 1998).

4. Motivation—The desire to learn, often lacking in students who have experienced frequent failure, as many of these have.

Students with Physical Impairments

Students with physical impairments can usually participate in all regular instructional activities, depending on the physical impairment and the nature of the activities. Of course, those with limited physical mobility, such as those in a wheelchair or those with visual or hearing impairment, may not be able to participate fully. For most of these students, however, their physical problems have little effect on their ability to learn. If this is their only disability, you will not need to modify your instruction in significant ways, but you may have to modify how an activity is carried out for these students. Make sure you understand what specific limitations they might face in terms of participating in your class, and make the appropriate accommodations before any activity begins.

Your Exceptional Students Who May Have an IEP (Depending on the State)

Students Who Are Gifted and Talented

You'll recognize the academically gifted students. They are the ones who finish early, who are the first to raise their hands, and who always know the answer. But how should we define this category? Are these students gifted or just very motivated?

For years the needs of our most capable students have been neglected while teachers focused their attention on students with other types of needs. One reason, according to Susan Winebrenner (2000), is that the academically gifted student does well on assessments, which leads teachers to assume he or she is learning. This may not be the case. "Most gifted students' natural learning abilities place them as far from average as their classmates who struggle to learn" (p. 53). They need special attention as well.

As in the case of students with learning disabilities and those with mild mental retardation, there is not universal agreement concerning a definition of gifted and talented. However, the description included in the Gifted and Talented Children's Act of 1978 (PL 95–561, Section 902) and reaffirmed in 1988 (Elementary and Secondary Education Conference Report, 1988, p. 114) is still often cited:

> The term *gifted and talented children* means youth who are identified at the preschool, elementary, or secondary level as possessing demonstrated or potential abilities that give evidence of high performance capabilities in areas such as intellectual, creative, specific academic or leadership ability, or in the performing and visual arts, and who by reason thereof require services or activities not ordinarily provided by the school.
>
> (Lewis & Doorlag, 1999)

This definition differs from earlier versions because it includes not only those who are intellectually gifted but also those with special talents in the arts or leadership. Basically, *giftedness* is characterized by above-average intellectual ability. *Talented* students, on the other hand, usually excel in one more particular area such as art, music, drama, or the like. Giftedness and talent may occur in combination or separately (Lewis & Doorlag,

1999). Of course, it will be important that you recognize the talents of your students and provide opportunities to develop them. However, often your biggest challenges usually come when you must adapt your instruction for the academically gifted students.

According to Meyen (1996), the following are characteristics of academically gifted students. They:

- Learn and retain basic information easily
- Understand complex, abstract concepts
- Are developmentally advanced in language and reading
- Have an advanced sense of right and wrong and are concerned with ethical issues
- Are willing to take risks to achieve a goal or find answers
- Possess unusual insight
- Have high energy levels
- Have a long attention span and have superior ability to focus on a topic
- Possess an advanced, mature sense of humor
- Are independent and autonomous
- Are unusually sensitive and empathetic
- Are curious
- Pursue logical answers and solutions
- Are able to generate original ideas and solutions
- Have a variety of specialized interests

The way states deal with gifted students varies. In some states, gifted education is mandated and services are a matter of local policy. In most, though not all of these states, IEPs are required just as they are for other exceptional students and specific guidelines are followed to refer, evaluate, and place students in gifted programs. Likewise, special resources are provided and the students are routinely evaluated and their progress monitored on an annual basis. Some states, on the other hand, may not even provide resource teachers (Meyen, 1996).

Teaching gifted students will represent some challenge and hard work for you, if you do it right. Far too many teachers neglect these students, leaving them to fend for themselves because they are able to do the basic class assignments without help. Likewise, while it can be a useful strategy in some cases, many teachers also overuse them as tutors for less able students instead of focusing on their particular academic needs. Instead of focusing all of your attention on fixing learning problems of students who are experiencing some difficulty, you must find a way to concentrate on the strengths of these students as well. It is important that you keep them intellectually excited and curious. For years, programming for gifted students was designed either to accelerate or to enrich. Educators now suggest a more comprehensive program that still includes opportunities for enrichment and acceleration, but that extends learning beyond the classroom (Renzulli & Reis, 1986).

As is the case for all exceptional students, most gifted students spend the majority of their school time in general education classrooms. According to Meyen (1996), teachers can serve these students best by:

1. Accurately determining the instructional level for each student
2. Creating flexible ability groups for academic projects and subjects
3. Individualizing assignments and activities
4. Making modifications in the standard curriculum

Your Exceptional Students Without an IEP (Unless They Also Have a Disability)

Students Who Are Culturally and Linguistically Diverse

Culturally and linguistically diverse students represent a more complicated situation for you. While they may not have trouble cognitively understanding concepts and mastering the educational objectives you have for them, they may need special assistance with respect to the language. Communication problems will invariably result in learning difficulties. Thus, to the extent possible, it is your job to make sure that language isn't a problem. Likewise, the customs, traditions, and values of their culture may create barriers to their being accepted by their peers.

It is important that you do your homework before you begin working with these students. Find out what level of comprehension students who are not native speakers of English have. Are they fluent in English? Are they bilingual, or are they just beginning to learn English? Seek the help of other professionals in your school or other students in determining how to modify your instruction, if you need to at all. One of the best ways to help students become more proficient in English is to make sure they are included in all activities and have opportunities to interact with the other students.

Likewise, when you design lessons, you need to be mindful of the customs and traditions of other cultures represented in your class. Look for opportunities to incorporate their culture and traditions into your lessons not only so these students will be validated as members of the class, but also so the other students may learn from them. Be sensitive to special holidays. Scheduling an important review for a major biology test on Yom Kippur when you have two Jewish students absent that day would be unfair and would demonstrate a lack of regard for them.

Students Who Are At-Risk for School Failure

Students who are at-risk for school failure present unique challenges for you as well. These are the students who are "potential drop-outs, potential or actual delinquents, runaways, teen-age parents and suicide risks" (Lewis & Doorlag, 1999, p. 7). Depending on where you teach, you are likely to have many of these students. They are faced with numerous social problems such as poverty; homelessness; and physical, sexual, and drug and alcohol abuse. Although some may also be disabled in some way, many are not, and often you will not need to alter your instruction. Their success in your class is in jeopardy, however, because of these other potentially debilitating conditions. You will need to combine your skills as a teacher with your skills as a social worker. These students are likely to be distracted, to lack follow-through on assignments, or to be absent often. Find out as much as you can about their circumstances and demonstrate a sincere concern for their welfare as both students and people. Consult appropriate resource personnel for assistance, and stay aware of any changes in their lives outside of school that affect their performance in class or their overall potential for success.

Legal Considerations: What Laws Govern the Education of Special Needs Students?

Few areas of your professional responsibilities require you to be aware of legalities more than areas dealing with special needs students. Terminology and legal compliance requirements change rapidly. Too busy to find out about all of this? Find the time. It is your job and your professional responsibility to know. As a professional, you are expected to be aware of these changes. Not being aware of your role in working with special needs students means that you will not be serving your students appropriately. There's a lot to learn about this aspect of your responsibilities—probably more than you have time to master as you begin teaching. The good news, however, is that you do not have to know *everything* to do a good job—just the basics of legal expectations and where to go for assistance within your school. The following is a quick overview of the current laws that are in effect and the procedures you must follow.

Recent Background

Prior to the 1970s, many states had laws permitting public schools to deny enrollment to children with disabilities. When students were served, they were often labeled inaccurately. Thus, schools practiced both exclusion and misclassification. In the early 1970s, federal courts ruled those practices unconstitutional.

As local schools began to accept some responsibility for educating certain exceptional students, a philosophy of segregation prevailed. Special education was strongly influenced by the case of *Brown v. Board of Education* in 1954, in which the Supreme Court declared that education must be made available to all children on equal terms. In a class-action suit in 1972, the court ruled that all children with mental retardation are entitled to a free, appropriate education, and placement in a regular classroom is preferable to placement in a segregated setting.

In 1975, Congress passed PL 94-142, The Education for Handicapped Children Act, which mandated a free and appropriate public education (FAPE) for all handicapped children and youth. An IEP was required and was to be developed in conference with parents. An important feature of this law is the principle of "least restrictive environment" (LRE), which suggests that, to the extent possible, children should be educated in a regular classroom situation.

Individuals with Disabilities Education Act (IDEA)

In 1990, Congress amended PL 94-142 and renamed it Individuals with Disabilities Education Act (IDEA). Congress reauthorized IDEA in 1997 (PL 105-17). Although this law did not change the spirit of PL 94-142, it gave further assurances that the needs of students with disabilities would be met. It also substituted the term *disability* for the term *handicapped* and included "people first" language (rather then saying "learning disabled students," people are to say "students with learning disabilities"). This marked the culmination of the efforts of many educators, parents, and legislators to bring together in one comprehensive bill the laws regarding students with disabilities. It also eliminated some of the stigma associated with the word *handicapped.* A student must have a disability and need special education and related services to be eligible for rights under IDEA, and age factors further determine those rights. IDEA encompasses the following six major principles:

1. Zero Reject—Schools must educate all children with disabilities regardless of the nature of the disability.

2. Nondiscriminatory Identification and Evaluation—Schools must use nonbiased, multifactored methods of evaluation to determine whether a child has a disability and, if so, whether special education is needed.

3. Free Appropriate Education—All children with disabilities shall receive a free, appropriate education at public expense.

4. Least Restrictive Environment (LRE)—Students with disabilities must be educated with students without disabilities to the maximum extent possible and should be removed to separate classes or schools only when the nature of their disabilities is such that they cannot receive an appropriate education in the regular classroom.

5. Procedural Due Process—Schools must provide due process safeguards to protect the rights of children with disabilities and their parents.

6. Parent Participation—Schools must collaborate with parents and with students with disabilities in the design and implementation of special education services.

Inclusion or Mainstream Classes?

pp1 1st thing

Terminology has a great impact on practice. This is especially true when considering how we work with students with disabilities. From the late 1970s until the mid-1980s, the process of educating students with disabilities in regular classes was referred to as *mainstreaming*. It meant placing students with disabilities in classes with students who were not disabled (Turnbull & Schultz, 1979). This usually translated into the students with disabilities participating in the nonacademic portions of the general education program, such as art, music, and physical education (Idol, 1997). In effect, they were in general education classes for a very small part of their day. Most teachers were uncomfortable with their ability to teach these students well, even if they were generally supportive of efforts to help these students, and some were even vocal against mainstreaming altogether (Turnbull, Shank, Smith, & Leal, 2002).

Over time, many began to challenge the very nature of schools that separated general and special education. Advocates of the *inclusion* movement began to support the placement of students with disabilities, with support and services, into general education classrooms from the very start. Therefore, they are "included" in the general education classroom as much as possible, for as many subjects as possible. Inclusion simply means that students with disabilities are being authentic members of general education programs (Turnbull, Shank, Smith, & Leal, 2002).

The following are key components of inclusion (Sailor, 1991):

- All students receive education in the school they would attend if they had no disability.
- School and general education placements are age and grade appropriate.
- Special education supports exist within the general education classes.
- All students with special needs have access to the general curriculum.

We now have more students with disabilities than ever before receiving their education with students without disabilities. Most teachers now understand that students with disabilities are an integral part of their classes. "Inclusion is not only legal, it's the right thing to do" (Ruder, 2000).

Procedures: How Will You Identify and Refer Special Needs Students?

The Referral Process

The initial referral is the first step in the process of getting the student with a disability an appropriate education. Although not always the case, most students with special needs have already been identified by the time they reach secondary school. However, if you are concerned that a student might need to be referred for evaluation, you should immediately discuss the situation with the special education teacher or the chairperson of the school-based special services team as soon as possible. Most students at the secondary school level have already been identified by resource professionals in elementary school. However, your role is to be aware of the fact that there still might be a student who needs special services. You are key to his or her success when you make this observation, when you initiate the process, and when you serve as a member of the service team to provide support throughout the year.

Identifying Students for Nondiscriminatory Evaluation

The first step of the referral process is screening, which is a schoolwide process that occurs at the elementary level. All students take tests that begin to identify students' abilities and needs. These might include intelligence, achievement, vision, and hearing tests.

Students identified as possibly needing special services will continue to the next step, *prereferral,* which is most likely where you will begin the process if you suspect that a student at the secondary school level may have a special need. This step has two purposes: (a) It provides immediate and necessary help to you as you experience challenges in teaching the student, and (b) it guards against misidentifying students as having disabilities when they don't.

At the prereferral stage, you will not yet be seeking a formal evaluation. Instead, you are requesting help from colleagues on the school's evaluation team who provide suggestions for appropriate interventions with the student. Basically, this stage is usually a problem-solving process, identifying the nature of the concern and trying different ways to solve it. Sometimes, prereferral is enough to assist you in dealing with learning challenges with some students. If not, you will need to move to the next stage: submitting a formal written request (a *referral*) for a student to receive formal nondiscriminatory evaluation (see Figure 5.1).

Most of the time, the special services team determines the criteria that teachers must follow in making referrals to it and will assume responsibility for the entire referral and evaluation process. The team uses a referral form that usually asks for specific and comprehensive information about the student, including:

- Basic screening information
- Areas of educational concerns that prompted the prereferral process
- Descriptions of the nature of the prereferral interventions and the results achieved
- Any concerns expressed by the student or the student's family (loneliness, etc.)

The special services team reviews the referral form and any other information provided and makes a decision about how best to address the concerns (Turnbull, Turnbull, Shank, Smith, & Leal, 2002).

School Service Team

At the secondary school level, a team of resource people will conduct the evaluation process and serve as a support if the student is declared eligible for services. These team members must include:

- At least one general education teacher
- The school psychologist
- An administrator (or other representative of the school who is qualified to oversee the specially designed instruction and is knowledgeable about general education curriculum and available resources)
- At least one special education teacher
- The student's parents
- The student (when appropriate before 18 and almost always after 18)
- Any other key people (including one who can interpret instructional implications of evaluation results)

The team must make sure that forms and pertinent additional information are submitted to the proper resource people in a timely manner. They must also help the student understand the process and work with the parents, whose permission is required before the evaluation can proceed. Good communication between the home and school are essential if the process and any subsequent interventions are to be successful.

FOCUS OF CONCERN/SCREENING

Student: ____________________ School: ____________________

Sex: ______ Race: ______ Grade: ______ Parent/Guardian: ____________________

Date of Birth: ____/____/____ Age: ______ Address: ____________________

____

I.D. Number: (optional): ____________________ Telephone: ____________________

I. Parent Conference / Contact Record

A. First Contact / Attempt Date: ____/____/____

School Person Making Contact: ____________________

Type of Contact: ____ School Conference ____ Letter/Note ____ Home Visit ____ Phone Call

____ Other: ____________________

Purpose: ____________________

Comments on Conference: ____________________

B. Second Contact / Attempt Date: ____/____/____

School Person Making Contact: ____________________

Type of Contact: ____ School Conference ____ Letter/Note ____ Home Visit ____ Phone Call

Purpose: ____________________

Comments on Conference: ____________________

II. Parental Notification of Screening Procedures Form (RE2) Sent

Notice Sent by: ____________________ Date: ____/____/____

III. Classroom Observation

Observer: ____________________ Position: ____________ Date: ____/____/____

A. Subject Observed

- ____ Language Arts
- ____ Music
- ____ Free Time
- ____ Art
- ____ Other: ____________________
- ____ Social Studies
- ____ Science
- ____ Physical Educ.
- ____ Math

B. Learning Situation

- ____ One-to-One
- ____ Class
- ____ Small Group
- ____ Independent

C. Student Behavior

- ____ Attentive
- ____ Sits quietly
- ____ Talks out of turn
- ____ Easily distracted
- ____ Overactive, restless
- ____ Talks excessively
- ____ Immature behavior
- ____ Withdrawn
- ____ Works well independently
- ____ Disruptive
- ____ Trouble finding place
- ____ Disorganized work habits
- ____ Avoids eye contact
- ____ Difficulty copying from board
- ____ Careless, doesn't complete tasks
- ____ Constantly out of seat
- ____ Contributes to class discussion
- ____ Short attention span
- ____ Friendly
- ____ Displays leadership ability
- ____ Easily frustrated
- ____ Aggressive toward children
- ____ Obscene language
- ____ Neat appearance
- ____ Demands excessive attention
- ____ Perseverates (repeats behavior)
- ____ Daydreams
- ____ Tries to control others
- ____ Avoids groups
- ____ Cooperative
- ____ Doesn't follow directions
- ____ Unusual language
- ____ Speech problem
- ____ Other: ____________________

Additional Comments (if any): ____________________

RE 1(a) / HCA

Student: ____________________ School: ____________________ Grade: ____________

FIGURE 5.1 Sample Referral Form

Source: Exceptional Children State Forms (RE and DEC). Raleigh, NC: Division of Exceptional Children, North Carolina Department of Public Instruction. http://www.dpi.state.nc.us/ec/ecforms.html

IV. Screening Committee Data Collection

A. Records Review - School History

1. Attendance Pattern (indicate where problems occurred):

Grade				
Days Enrolled				
Absences				
Tardies				

2. Past and Current Subject Marks (three most recent, if appropriate):

School Year	Grade				
		Subject/Mark	Subject/Mark	Subject/Mark	Subject/Mark

3. Review of Previous Testing:

a. Instrument Used: ______________
Date: ______________
Results: ______________
____
____

b. Instrument Used: ______________
Date: ______________
Results: ______________
____
____

c. Group Standardized Test Scores (record percentile scores)
Name of Test: ______________

Subtest	Year/_____	Year/_____	Year/_____
Reading			
Language			
Math			
Total Battery			
Other			

B. General Medical–Health Screening

1. Describe any serious illness or accident since birth:
______________ Date: ____/____/____ Hospitalized ( ) Yes ( ) No
______________ Date: ____/____/____ Hospitalized ( ) Yes ( ) No

2. Other Relevant Health Information:
____
____

3. Visual Acuity
Far Pass/Fail (Circle one) Date: ____/____/____

4. Hearing Pass/Fail (Circle one) Date: ____/____/____

C. Social Functioning, Environmental and Cultural Status

Information concerning the social, environmental, and cultural status of this student has been reviewed.
( ) Yes ( ) No
Comments: ______________
____
____
____

RE 1(b) / HCA

Student: ______________ School: ______________ Grade: ______________

FIGURE 5.1 Sample Referral Form *(Continued)*

V. Intervention Strategies

Area of Concern: ____________________

Interventions Utilized	Dates (Month/Day/Year)		Results (Check)			
	Beginning	Ending	No Change	Erratic	Improvement Noted	Success Noted
1. Praise/Attention						
2. Modified Instruction						
3. Modified Environment						
4. Counseling, Support Group						
5. Behavioral Contact, Point System, Charting						
6. Parent Follow-Up						
7. Time-Out						
8. Detention						
9. Specialized Instructional						
Equipment						
10. Peer Tutor						
11. Chapter 1						
12. Other Supports (Volunteer)						
13. Public/Private Agency						
14. Community Resources						
15. Change in Schedule						
16. Change in Teacher(s)						
17. Other (Specify)						
18. Other (Specify)						
19. Other (Specify)						
20. Other (Specify)						

Signature of Person(s) Using Strategies: ____________________ **Date:** ____/____/____

____________________ **Date:** ____/____/____

____________________ **Date:** ____/____/____

RE 1(c)/HCA

Student: ____________________ School: ____________________ Grade: ____________

FIGURE 5.1 Sample Referral Form *(Continued)*

VI. Based on information gathered during the screening process, it is the decision of this committee to:

A. First Meeting

(Check One)

1. _______ Refer for evaluation.
2. _______ Continue regular education program with new strategies for _____ weeks.
3. _______ Continue regular education program with strategies proved effective during screening process.

Explanation of the above checked action: ____

____

____

____

____

____

____

____

____

Committee Members' Signatures	**Position**	**Date**

B. Second Meeting (Only needed if A(2) is checked above)

(Check One)

1. _______ Refer for evaluation.
2. _______ Continue regular education program with strategies proved effective during screening.

Explanation of the above checked action: ____

____

____

____

____

____

____

____

____

Committee Members' Signatures	**Position**	**Date**

Revised 6/01

FIGURE 5.1 Sample Referral Form *(Continued)*

After the evaluation process is completed, three important steps must be taken to determine the best situation for the student:

1. Determination of the eligibility for special services
2. Placement
3. Development of an IEP

After the resource professionals complete steps 1 and 2, major responsibility returns to you as the classroom teacher to implement instruction that reflects the intent of the IEP.

REALITY CHECK 5.1

Based on the requirements outlined in IDEA, the school support teams are to perform their duties following very specific guidelines. When they work, they are an invaluable part of the process of helping a student. However, many beginning teachers report that it often doesn't happen that way in their schools. Instead, you may find that some people who should be serving on the committee (such as a general education classroom teacher) may never have been asked to serve. In other cases, individuals may be listed on the committee roster but do not participate in meetings or in the process at all. Ask if you can serve on behalf of a student if you have concerns that the classroom teacher's point of view is not being heard.

Meetings of the committees to monitor the progress of the students with special needs are supposed to be held regularly. In reality, however, these may be held rarely or not at all in some schools. When they are held, they are quite helpful in terms of getting the perspective of several people who all have expertise in different areas and who are focusing on the needs of one student. Ask to attend one meeting to gain some insight into the various perspectives regarding a student and his or her disability.

Committee members and/or school staff who are responsible for following the process are supposed to work with parents as well as students to make sure they understand the process. True, at the secondary school level, both parents and students have been aware of the basic process and have been signing IEPs for years. But the specifics of an IEP may be simply recopied onto new forms and business goes on as usual. This should be an annual procedure, taken seriously and with careful thought. Everyone involved should know how things will work for the current year. How will the IEP guidelines affecting a particular student change, if at all? How has progress made during the last school year altered expectations for this year, if at all? These questions are not often asked.

Individual Education Plan (IEP)

An important component of the reauthorization of IDEA in 1997 is the requirement that an IEP be developed for every student with a disability. Some states expand the requirement for an IEP for gifted students as well, defining these special needs students as "exceptional." This instrument serves as an accountability measure to determine the extent to which needs of exceptional students are being met. The IEP does not prescribe teaching strategies, but it does require that the teacher make specific instructional decisions for a student. Teachers make these decisions with the input of others on the student's support team and have a major role in decisions related to what is included in the IEP. Conferences are planning sessions in which everyone who is working with the student is involved. Everyone should leave the conference understanding what needs to be done, who is to do it, and how it is to be assessed.

The federal government is very precise in terms of what should be included in the IEP and how decisions about this should be made. The basic requirements include:

1. A statement of the student's present level of educational performance
2. Measurable annual goals, including short-term educational objectives
3. A statement of the specific special education services that will be provided
4. The extent to which the student will not participate with students who do not have disabilities
5. Any individual modifications in the administration of statewide or districtwide assessments of student achievement
6. The projected date for beginning the services and program modifications and the anticipated frequency, location, and duration of each
7. Transition plans, including
   - Beginning at age 14 and each year thereafter, a statement of the student's needs related to transition services, including those that focus on the student's course of study

ACTIVITY 5.2

Writing an IEP

For practice in understanding the process of writing an IEP, write one for one of your students by yourself. Discuss the finished product with the resource teacher. Even though it may not be used by the school support team, it will give you valuable practice in thinking through the process and defining goals for working with a student with special needs.

- Beginning at age 16 (or sooner if the IEP decides it is appropriate), a statement of needed transition services
- Beginning at least 1 year before the student reaches majority under state law, a statement that the student has been informed of those rights under IDEA that will transfer to the student from the parents when the student becomes of age

8. How the student's progress toward annual goals will be measured and how the student's parents will be informed of the student's progress toward annual goals and the extent to which the progress is sufficient to enable the student to achieve the goals by the end of the school year (Turnbull, Turnbull, Shank, Smith, & Leal, 2002).

REALITY CHECK 5.2

The expectation is that teachers will have a major role in the decisions about the student's program that affect instruction. This simply does not happen except in rare instances. The IEPs at the high school level are often a rewrite, with few if any adjustments, from the middle school IEPs. Likewise, middle school IEPs replicate those from elementary schools. Because classroom teachers in many cases are not consulted or invited to participate on support teams, they usually inherit a document that gives them little information about actually working with the student. New teachers often describe IEPs as useless. They don't have to be. Usually inexperienced teachers do not understand how to use what information is there. Experienced teachers learn to interpret available information and use it productively. If your IEPs do seem useless, you will need to go beyond the IEP to gather what you need to know. You may also want to take the initiative in asking to participate on the support committee on behalf of a student. These meetings can be very informative.

Use Activity 5.2 to practice writing an IEP. Ongoing monitoring of student progress toward IEP goals and objectives is critical. Figure 5.2 is a sample IEP.

Continuum of Services and Placement Options

There are four basic options you will likely encounter in working with secondary school students with special needs. The first (Level 1) represents students who are in regular classes for the entire day. This includes disabled students who are able to get along with regular class accommodations with or without medical or other assistance. This level represents approximately 75% of the students with special needs.

Level 2 consists of students who spend most of their day in general education classes but also receive supplementary instructional services. For example, they may meet with the special education teacher for resource assistance related to study skills or specific help with assignments.

Level 3 includes students who spend part of their day in special classes and part of their day in general education. For example, certain students may need to work with the special education teacher for the basic academic classes but are in general education classes for their electives. Or perhaps they can manage math classes but need to work with the resource teacher for English and social studies since they have trouble reading.

Level 4 includes students who are in special education for the full day.

An understanding of all the levels of service for students with special needs will help you to see in context where your students are on a continuum of support (Turnbull, Turnbull, Shank, Smith, & Leal, 2002).

DEC 4 (1 of 4)

Check Purpose: ( ) Initial
( ) Annual Review

Review

( ) Reevaluation
( ) Addendum

INDIVIDUALIZED EDUCATION PROGRAM (IEP)

Duration of Special Education and Related Services: From: ______/ ______/ ______ To: ______/ ______/ ______

Student: ____________________ DOB: ______/ ______/ ______

School: ____________________ Grade: __________

I. Area of Eligibility

( ) Autistic
( ) Behaviorally-Emotionally Disabled
( ) Deaf-Blind
( ) Hearing Impaired
( ) Multihandicapped
( ) Mentally Disabled
( ) EMD ( ) S/PMD ( ) TMD
( ) Orthopedically Impaired
( ) Other Health Impaired
( ) Specific Learning Disabled
( ) Speech-Language Impaired
( ) Traumatic Brain Injured
( ) Developmentally Delayed
( ) Visually Impaired

A. Additional Area(s) of Disability:

II. Consideration of Special Factors

A. Student's overall strengths:

B. Parent's concerns, if any, for enhancing the student's education:

C. Special factors to be considered:

Does the student have behavior(s) that impede his/her learning or that of others?
( ) Yes ( ) No

Does the student have Limited English Proficiency?
( ) Yes ( ) No

If the student is blind or partially sighted will the instruction in or use of Braille be needed?
( ) Yes ( ) No

Does the student have any special communication needs? (If the student is deaf or hard of hearing, see directions.)
( ) Yes ( ) No

Does the student require assistive technology devices and / or services?
( ) Yes ( ) No

D. Other factors to be addressed:

___ Does the student require adapted physical education?
( ) Yes ( ) No

___ Is the student's age 14 or older, or will the student turn 14 during the duration of the IEP?
( ) Yes ( ) No

If *yes*, transition services:
____ component attached ___ stated in the IEP

____ Has the student been informed of his/her own rights, if age 17 and older?
( ) Yes ( ) No

FIGURE 5.2 Sample IEP

Source: Exceptional Children State Forms (RE and DEC). Raleigh, NC: Division of Exceptional Children, North Carolina Department of Public Instruction. http://www.dpi.state.nc.us/ec/ecforms.html

DEC 4 (2 of 4)

INDIVIDUALIZED EDUCATION PROGRAM (IEP)

Duration of Special Education and Related Services: From: _____/ _____/ _____ To: _____/ _____/ _____

Student: ______________________________ DOB: _____/ _____/ _____

School: ______________________________ Grade: __________

III. **Present Level(s) of Educational Performance:** Include specific descriptions of strengths and needs that apply to current academic performance, behaviors, social/emotional development, other relevant information, and how the student's disability affects his/her involvement and progress in the general curriculum.

____

____

____

____

IV. **A. Annual Goal**

____

____

____

____

B. Benchmarks or Short-Term Objectives

C. How Progress Toward the Annual Goal Will Be Measured

FIGURE 5.2 Sample IEP *(Continued)*

DEC 4 (3 of 4)

INDIVIDUALIZED EDUCATION PROGRAM (IEP)

Duration of Special Education and Related Services: From: ______/ ______/ ______ To: ______/ ______/ ______
Student: ______________________________ DOB: ______/ ______/ ______
School: ______________________________ Grade: ______________

V. Least Restrictive Environment (Placement)

A. Appropriate supplementary aids, services, and modification(s)/accommodations for instruction and testing and/or supports for school personnel, if any:

a. grading	f. read aloud*	k. Braille/braillewriter*	p. magnification devices	u. student marks in book*
b. modified assignments	g. extended time*	l. preferential seating	q. interpreting/transliterating*	v. study guides
c. alternative materials	h. portfolio	m. video cassette	r. demonstration teaching	w. multiple test sessions*
d. graphic organizers	i. large print*	n. Cranmer-Abacus*	s. assistive devices*	x. testing-separate room*
e. tech. assist./inservice	j. audio tapes	o. dictation to a scribe*	t. computer/typewriter word processor*	y. one test item per page*
				z. other ______________

NOTE: Only the accommodations with an (*) are approved by the N.C. Testing Program for test validity. **Exception**-Use of the read aloud accommodation on the EOG and EOC Reading Tests invalidates the score. When adding accommodations that are not listed above, consult the testing manual for test validity.
NAEP: Participation in the NAEP is voluntary. If it is anticipated that the student will be included in the NAEP administration and will take it with accommodations, review and select the appropriate accommodations from the list in the testing manual.

1. Regular Program Participation: Circle the regular class(es) and activities in which the student is enrolled and list the letters for any modifications in the blank provided.

____ Reading	____ Library	____ History	____ Foreign Language	____ Recess
____ English	____ Music/Art	____ Science	____ Physical Education	____ Homeroom
____ Spelling	____ Economics	____ Health	____ Chapter 1	____ Vocational
____ Math	____ Social Studies	____ Writing	____ Remediation	____ Other
____ Lunch	____ Assemblies	____ Language Arts	____ Extracurricular Activities	

2. North Carolina Testing Program: List the letter(s) of any accommodations on the line provided.
( ) Regular Test Administration ( ) Test Administration with Accommodations ______________
( ) N.C. Alternate Assessment Academic Inventory ______________
( ) N.C. Alternate Assessment Portfolio ______________
( ) Computer Skills Test ______________
( ) Computer Skills Portfolio ______________
( ) National Assessment of Educational Progress (NAEP) ______________
If a student is taking an alternate assessment, why is the regular testing not appropriate? ______________
____
Comments (if needed): ______________
For preschool children, describe how the child is involved a regular program. ______________
____

B. Anticipated Frequency and Location of Services:

Type of Service Location	Sessions Per: Week	or Month	or Reporting Period	Per Session	Amount of Time
Special Education	_____	_____	_____	________	________
	_____	_____	_____	________	________
Related Services					
( ) Counseling Services	_____	_____	_____	________	________
( ) Occupational Therapy	_____	_____	_____	________	________
( ) Physical Therapy	_____	_____	_____	________	________
( ) Speech-Language	_____	_____	_____	________	________
( ) Other	_____	_____	_____	________	________
( ) Transportation					
( ) None					

FIGURE 5.2 Sample IEP *(Continued)*

DEC 4 (4 of 4)

INDIVIDUALIZED EDUCATION PROGRAM (IEP)

Duration of Special Education and Related Services: From: ______/ ______/ ______ To: ______/ ______/ ______
Student: ____ DOB: ______/ ______/ ______
School: ____ Grade: ________________

C. Continuum of Alternative Placements: Check the alternative placements considered by the committee, and circle the decision reached.

School Age

( ) Regular-80% or more of the day with non-disabled peers
( ) Resource-40% - 79% of the day with non-disabled peers
( ) Separate-39% or less of the day with non-disabled peers
( ) Public Separate School
( ) Private Separate School
( ) Public Residential
( ) Private Residential
( ) Home/Hospital

Preschool

( ) Early Childhood Setting
( ) Part-Time Early Childhood/Part-Time Early Childhood Special Education
( ) Early Childhood Special Education Setting
( ) Separate Setting
( ) Residential Setting
( ) Home
( ) Itinerant Service Outside Home
( ) Reverse Mainstream Setting

D. If the student will be removed from his/her non-disabled peers for any part of the day (regular class, extracurricular activities, non-academic activities), explain why.

VI. Explain how and when parents will be informed of the student's progress toward annual goals:

VII. Extended School Year Status

( ) Is not eligible for extended school year
( ) Is eligible for extended school year
( ) Eligibility is under consideration and will be determined by ______/ ______/ ______

VIII. IEP Team. The following were present and participated in the development and writing of the IEP.

Signature	Position	Date
	LEA Representative	
	Regular Education Teacher	
	Special Education Teacher	
	Parent	
	Student	

IX. IEP Addendum Team. The following were present and participated in the development and writing of the IEP.

Signature	Position	Date
	LEA Representative	
	Regular Teacher	
	Special Education Teacher	
	Parent	
	Student	

X. Reevaluation. The IEP was reviewed at reevaluation and was found to be appropriate. An annual review of this IEP will be conducted on or before ______/ ______/ ______.

Signature	Position	Date
	LEA Representative	
	Regular Education Teacher	
	Special Education Teacher	
	Parent	
	Student	

Copy to: Parent(s) / EC File

Revised 7/03

FIGURE 5.2 Sample IEP *(Continued)*

The Case for Inclusion: How Will You Teach Students with Special Needs?

Because most of the students with special needs that you will have in your classes will be mildly mentally retarded, learning disabled, or gifted students, the discussion will focus on these three categories of students.

Collaboration with Resource Teachers

You are not alone when you determine the best way to work with and adapt instruction for the students with disabilities who are in your classes. It is crucial that you seek the expertise of other professionals—especially the special education resource teacher, who can provide you with the information and expertise you need. When considering IDEA's strong provisions for inclusion, you will be expected to teach these students as effectively as you do the students without disabilities. Depending on your background, this can be a tall order.

Most schools have incorporated processes for general education teachers to collaborate with special education (resource) teachers and other specialized personnel to ensure that each student with a disability will be getting the support he or she needs to succeed. Secondary school resource teachers have a wealth of information and expertise that is often not tapped. They have a variety of important responsibilities. Most of their time is spent providing direct support to students with mild disabilities. Often this is done in a "consultative" capacity as the resource teacher checks in with all students with an IEP periodically to be sure they are making progress and have someone to talk to comfortably about their disability (see Activity 5.3). They also teach classes with a range of disabilities and maintain a mountain of paperwork for each student that must be updated periodically to meet legal requirements.

Unlike their elementary school counterparts, they must also be knowledgeable about all aspects of the curriculum in order to serve effectively as a resource for both the students in inclusion classes and their teachers. They have the expertise to help adapt lessons, activities, and assessment and evaluation procedures for your students in the general education classrooms. Make friends with these people.

To get the most out of working with the resource teachers, keep the following in mind as you begin the school year (Lewis & Doorlag, 1999; Turnbull, Turnbull, Shank, Smith, & Leal, 2002):

- Effective collaboration builds on the expertise and strengths of a variety of people involved in the student's education. Use your resource people.
- Regular meetings with the appropriate resource people are essential.
- Routine assessments and accountability are an integral part of the collaboration process.
- Identify the students with disabilities in your classes.

ACTIVITY 5.3

Collaborating with a Resource Teacher

Plan at least one unit with the help of the resource teacher to learn the best ways to adapt your instruction for particular disabilities.

- Consult with the resource teacher in your school to determine the best way for you to work with him or her regarding your students with special needs.
- Discuss the goals of last year's IEP with the resource teacher and determine new priorities for this year.
- Consult with the resource teacher before you plan each unit of study to determine the best ways for adapting instruction and assessing student progress.

Don't have time to do all that for each student with a disability and consider the needs of the other students, too? Yes, you do. You must make time as you are legally and professionally obliged to do. It won't be easy, but it will be much more manageable with the help and input of others.

REALITY CHECK 5.3

When a school is fortunate enough to have good special education resource teachers, it is often the case that they may be the most untapped professionals in the building. Many new teachers say that they have never asked any of them for information about their students or for help in adapting instruction. Some of them claim that they don't even know who they are. You may think that you just don't have time to talk to them, but you will be surprised at how helpful they can be.

It is also true that some schools have resource teachers who are overloaded with their own class loads, are not skilled enough in adapting the curriculum for the general education teacher, or don't know the curriculum well enough to offer significant help. If this is the case, clearly you won't get much help or advice here. You must find out about the situation in your school.

Categories of Interventions for Mildly Retarded, Learning Disabled, and Gifted Students

According to Edward Meyen (1996), there are important categories of interventions that a classroom teacher might implement when working with students with disabilities. Three of these are self-managed interventions, peer-mediated interventions, and teacher-managed interventions.

Self-Managed Interventions

Self-managed interventions are designed to foster students' management of learning activities on their own. In most cases, by the time they are in secondary school, they are often quite independent. Teachers ultimately want their students to be independent learners, and self-managed interventions are very effective in meeting this goal. Not only are they helpful for the students themselves, enabling them to work on assignments alone, but they free the teacher to work with other students. For example, self-correcting activities are effective forms of self-monitoring for a student with a disability. Often students can learn more by checking their own work than by looking at corrections identified by the teacher. The self-corrected vocabulary test or the math homework problem set will work well. In some situations, students may be encouraged to assign their own grades and to determine a method for further practice.

ACTIVITY 5.4

Creating an Instructional Adaptation Chart

Create an instructional adaptation chart that will list what strategies are effective with which students. You will then be able to incorporate what you have learned from trial and error with what you read about working with certain disabilities and modify your planning over time.

Keep it simple! Creating a complicated chart that is more trouble than it's worth will be a waste of time because you will never use it.

You will want to provide all of your students, including special needs students, as much control as possible in decisions about how they will be taught. For example, contracts between you and the students are useful and can specify tasks you will perform and ones they will perform. At first, you may ask a student for input on some of the components of the contract, and in time, he or she might be able to develop the entire contract alone. Other instructional decisions might include allowing students to decide how they will learn certain material and to choose a topic for research within a unit of instruction.

Teachers who have students with special needs in their classrooms can also teach them how to learn on their own. Techniques such as using mnemonic devices, repeating verbally over and over things they need to remember, and questioning themselves as they read content are particularly helpful for secondary school students. You can also help students to understand material when you ask them to summarize in their own words information they have read (Reid, 1988).

Peer-Mediated Interventions

Many classroom teachers find that one of the most effective approaches to helping exceptional students is to use peer-mediated interventions. The most common strategy is peer tutoring, which is effective for both the tutor and the tutee. It is important to note that the tutor must be very clear about what specific task is to be accomplished and how. Selecting the tutor also requires that the teacher take into account the needs and learning styles of the students and the benefits to both.

The most common peer-mediated method is cooperative learning, in which a teacher creates groups of mixed ability and gives each group a common task (Johnson & Johnson, 1987). The members of the group can reach their goal only if everyone completes his or her particular task. In effect, the students teach each other the material. Students have the opportunity to learn from the other students, to lead the group, and to develop interpersonal skills. Everyone wins, and most of all, everyone learns. But the method is successful only if you carefully construct the groups paying close attention to students' strengths and weaknesses and to related learning and personal needs of the students.

Teacher-Managed Interventions

There are times when you must deal directly with learning situations to meet educational goals of students with special needs. For example, if you want to control the extent to which your students have mastered a concept, the problem may not be with the students' abilities to *understand* but to *do* as many tasks as the other students in the class. Thus, if the objective for a science class is to perform two experiments following the scientific method, perhaps the student with the special need could be asked to do only one.

Likewise, you may need to use various methods to assess the way a student learns material. Some students may be more comfortable answering questions orally, whereas others may want to create a model or compose a rap song; and still others may want to take a written test.

At times, you may need to teach content in different ways. A social studies teacher may choose to have most of the class read a document while two students with reading problems listen to a tape-recorded version. Most teachers find that using a variety of teaching approaches with their students is effective. Some students can understand exactly what to do with one set of verbal directions; others need to see the words to know what to do. Still others need a process demonstrated for them.

Adapting Instruction for Students Who Are Mildly Mentally Retarded

It is important to remember that your students with mild mental retardation may experience substantial deficits only in school and are most likely to be independent adults. There are five main things to keep in mind as you teach them in your classroom. You must continuously look for ways to modify the curriculum appropriately, adapt instructional techniques, place emphasis on vocational skills, and show a major concern for their social development. Then assess your success efforts.

Modifying the Curriculum

First, you will need to modify or adjust the curriculum in some way to focus on functional skills that will help the student succeed independently. It is also important to the students' success to analyze the curriculum carefully and break large tasks into manageable parts. But your biggest enemy is time. This is where it will be important for you to work with the special education resource teacher or an "inclusion facilitator," one who can provide assistance in determining how much of the standard curriculum a student can manage. Adapting instruction for the mildly mentally retarded is a team effort. For example, the following format has been successful in many situations:

1. At the beginning of the unit, meet with the resource teacher to discuss key concepts that will be addressed in a unit of study. You know what you want the student to know, and the resource teacher brings an understanding of the student's capabilities.

2. The resource teacher will suggest appropriate modifications to the curriculum, ones that will be appropriate for both meeting your class goals and for accommodating the student's unique needs.

3. The resource teacher will then create a summary of the curricular adaptations that will be made and review them with you.

4. The resource teacher will also recommend appropriate assessment strategies (Ruder, 2000).

REALITY CHECK 5.4

Many new teachers claim not to have time to deal with modifying the curriculum. Some even say they think they are doing students a disservice in making adaptations for students with special needs. One said, "I teach them all the same—it's unfair to them if I don't." If you are one of those teachers, at least be honest with yourself. You either don't know how to do it or are overwhelmed with preparing the "one size fits all" lesson for the entire class. You must find the time to explore ways to modify the curriculum for students with mild retardation when appropriate and possible. It is unfair to them *not* to do so.

Adapt Instructional Techniques

Now that you have some idea of what you want this student to know, you must look for ways to adapt instruction (see Activity 5.4 on page 135). Again, the resource teacher is key in helping you do this. He or she can help you choose types of materials according to the student's needs, whether they be visual, oral, kinesthetic, or in language clarification. Suzy Ruder, an inclusion facilitator in Illinois, describes an example of the process. In a world cultures class, ninth graders were assigned research projects to finish at home. Every student received a packet of examples and instructions. One student who read at the second-grade level did not have the ability to complete the assignment at home. The classroom teacher and the resource teacher determined the appropriate ways to adapt the instructional techniques that would both meet the class goal and accommodate her needs. This included time for her to work at school under the direction of a support person, modifying each portion of the assignment to her level. An important component of her disability was a desire by the student, as stated in her IEP, to keep her disability from her peers. She does not give formal speeches or read aloud in class. Therefore, on presentation day, she used a poster she had designed to depict what she had learned from the unit (Ruder, 2000).

As is true for all students, disabled or not, adapting strategies for the mildly mentally retarded is often a matter of remembering the essentials from research on how students learn.

1. Students learn best when they are actively involved, so you will design activities that require them to be personally engaged.

2. They develop deeper understanding when they are encouraged to construct their own knowledge. Therefore, you must be aware of what prior knowledge they have and what you have to build on.

3. They benefit from choice. So, you must provide options from which they can select types of learning methods and materials when appropriate.

4. They need time to reflect on and communicate their understanding. Therefore, you will need to give them assignments that encourage them to share what they have learned (Goleman, 1995; Sheldon, 2000; Sousa, 1998).

There are many ways to adapt instruction that are effective for students with mild mental disabilities and have benefits for the rest of the class as well. For example, one excellent technique is to use stations where students can work independently. This approach allows students to work at their own pace in relative privacy while they are doing essentially the same activity as the rest of the class. It also helps them to save face when they need to ask a question or get assistance and want to do so without an audience. Likewise, providing them with multiple options for how the learning can take place gives them a sense of control and empowerment in the learning process.

Emphasize Vocational Skills

You will need to emphasize vocational skills as much as possible for students with mild mental retardation. Remember that the ultimate goal is for all of your students to become self-sufficient and independent members of society after they graduate from high school. There are certain skills that can be incorporated into your assignments and routines that will help them to become more independent. The skills might include a variety of activities that could require students to have their materials ready, organize themselves for the day, make lists, and learn how to make good decisions and choices. Making sure that these types of tasks are part of daily expectations will provide lifelong skill mastery and will be very helpful to the student now and in the long run.

For example, a high school teacher once assigned a research unit on local community agencies. The goal for all students was to determine the nature of effectiveness in the community agencies. Roy, a mildly mentally retarded student, selected the police department. The resource teacher and the classroom teacher arranged for him to interview a policeman about his job and perceptions regarding the effectiveness of his department. They outlined questions with Roy and allowed him to tape-record the responses so that he could concentrate on the conversation. Later, they helped him to take the information and organize it into a brief report.

Roy responded well to the assignment and really gained much awareness of the role and responsibilities of the police. This type of information and the process for gathering it will be helpful for him as a citizen. The targeted organizational and reporting skills will also be of benefit to him, not only in school, but in any job he has in the future.

Social Development

As with all secondary school students, students with mild mental retardation especially need a focused concern for their social development. Teenagers naturally feel vulnerable socially, and students with a disability must face the additional burden of academic vulnerability. Instructional strategies that require a significant degree of social involvement will be of most benefit. One of the best strategies is the use of cooperative learning groups, the social benefits of which have been well documented. As is true for the class as a whole, it is critical that you pay careful attention to where the student is placed. Putting a special needs student who is extremely insecure with a group of overbearing students who tend to bully others would be a mistake. When organizing your groups, consider the unique social as well as learning needs of these students. Create situations where their academic needs can be addressed and social growth can be fostered as well.

Assessment

After considering modifications in the curriculum and ways to adapt your teaching strategies, you must assess how well the instruction has actually helped the students to perform the particular task or skills you designed for them. Whatever assessment tool you use, it should provide information about the student's level of retardation and the degree to which he or she mastered the tasks assigned, and it should give an indication of the best ways to present new material in the future. (Refer to Chapter 10 for a summary of assessment strategies.) The next steps in the instructional process should be to examine your own effectiveness. Use what you have learned from the successes and mistakes of each experience to make the next lessons better.

Adapting Instruction for Students Who Are Learning Disabled

As with all students with special needs, the process of determining appropriate interventions for students who are learning disabled begins with a valid and complete assessment of the learning problems. You already know how difficult this can be. Next comes planning, implementation of the plan, evaluation of the effectiveness of the plan, and then modification where necessary. This entire process is ongoing throughout the year and involves the classroom teacher in conversation with the resource teacher.

There are some basic guidelines for considering the types of adaptations you may want to make for students who are learning disabled. According to McNamara (1998):

1. There is no single correct method to be used with students who are learning disabled. Strategies are chosen based on what the students need to learn and how they learn.
2. The methods newest to the student should always be used. This is true because students often have experienced failure with the same techniques if they have been used over and over.
3. You should positively reinforce the students throughout the learning process.
4. You should keep in mind the nebulous nature of learning disabilities. It can be frustrating to you not to be able to define clearly the cause of a problem, but persevere.
5. It is critical to maintain an accurate and complete record of the students' strengths and weaknesses as well as the progress made and an evaluation of methods that are effective.
6. It is important for students with learning disabilities to have as much time with you as possible.

Reading

One of the most common problems for students with learning disabilities at the secondary level is the inability to read well. This fundamental skill affects so many of the subjects a student is taking. Wendy Towle (2000) discovered that one way to help students who are learning disabled in reading is through the workshop approach. This enabled her to deal with the particular needs of each student and to provide both direct reading instruction and practice. Reading workshops consist of several components:

1. Overview by the Teacher—You spend a few minutes motivating all of the students.

2. Lesson Focus—Address a specific topic and speak to small groups or the whole class. This is a good time to direct the instruction for a student who is learning disabled. Certain skills might be emphasized, such as distinguishing fact from opinion or summarizing main ideas.

3. State-of-the-Class Conference—This is an opportunity to determine with the students how the remainder of the period will be spent. At this point, you might meet briefly with a learning-disabled student to provide direct instruction and provide variations in the procedure that will accommodate his or her needs.

4. Self-Selected Reading and Responding Time—This provides students time for discussion. In addition, several activities might take place, such as writing exercises, projects, or individual conferences. The individualized nature of some of the portions of the

workshop are ideal times to work with students with special needs. The format also provides time for you to work with the group and for the students to work with each other. The workshop format works well for science, mathematics, and other subjects and offers opportunities for regular and individual assessment of student progress.

Note Taking

Breaking learning tasks down into their various components is important when teaching all students. This is especially true when working with students who are learning disabled. Siegal and Gold (1982) suggested that it is very important for teachers to select an appropriate task, create a specific sequence of steps based on the level of the competencies necessary to performing the task, and make the appropriate modifications when necessary. One important skill that impacts most subject areas is taking notes from an oral presentation. Listening and good note taking are necessary for success in most secondary classrooms as well as for many work-related situations after graduation. Many students who are learning disabled are overwhelmed by the demands of lectures that seem to drone on without meaning, and dismiss them as "boring." The truth is that they are frustrated by their inability to follow the lecture, to identify the pertinent points as they struggle to take notes, and to recall the information later. You can help them with this.

The following is one example of a method that might help a student learn to take notes from an oral presentation.

Behavioral Objective: When given an oral presentation of 30-minute duration, on any topic within the student's vocabulary knowledge, the student will be able to write appropriate notes in outlined form without help.

Entering Behavior: The student has adequate hearing, vision, and motor coordination. He tries to take notes word for word and has trouble listening and writing at the same time.

1. Begin with a brief reading selection (two paragraphs) below grade level on a portion of the content being studied. The student is given an outline that requires fill-ins. The tutor alternates with the students in completing the fill-ins. Verbal cues such as "abbreviate" are used.
2. Same as Step 1, but the selections from the content are gradually increased to 3–4 pages.
3. Same as Step 2, but eliminate the outline handout.
4. Same as Step 3, but eliminate the help of the tutor and verbal cues.
5. Record a portion of the content into a brief oral lecture (instead of reading). The presentation should be perfectly organized, spoken very slowly. The student should attempt to follow Steps 1–4 taking notes. The student may use the tape recorder for verification.
6. Same as Step 5, but in normal tempo.
7. Same as Step 6, but increase the length of the presentation.
8. Same as Step 7, but add unrelated points (still use tape recorder).
9. Same as Step 8, but without the tape recorder (Siegal & Gold, 1982, pp. 106–107; see also Deshler, Ellis, & Lenz, 1996, chap. 6, pp. 267–309, "Note-taking Strategy Instruction.").

One of the most difficult problems you will face as the teacher of a student with a learning disability is the lack of motivation. Students who have trouble mastering the basic reading skills are often the same ones who are reluctant to participate in class. You can improve motivation by providing constant reinforcement for the efforts these students make and providing visual displays of their progress in your classroom. They need to see that they are doing well, and also need for others to see it. Look for ways to show that they excel, and create opportunities for them to be recognized for special skills and abilities they do have.

Adapting Instruction for Students Who Are Gifted and Talented

There are several ways that you can adapt instruction for your gifted students. Compacting the curriculum enables the students to demonstrate what they already know and spend their time with more challenging activities. This can be achieved through self-testing or self-paced work and will create time for projects and activities that extend the curriculum during class time. You can routinely design alternative learning experiences that will "differentiate" (adapt) instruction (Tomlinson, 2000).

Many experts urge teachers to begin with the gifted students when they differentiate instruction for all the students. This starting point encourages you to identify the most challenging criteria for students and then to develop appropriate expectations for those doing lower level work. This means that you can accommodate the needs of your students who are gifted and talented while you teach the other students—all during the same class period. But it does take planning.

Sandra Page, Coordinator for Gifted Programs in Chapel Hill, North Carolina, describes examples of efforts to differentiate the curriculum for gifted students. Using Harvey Daniels's *Literature Circles* (2002), teachers expanded student roles such as discussion director and character creator. The gifted students took the lead for the most challenging roles, and the differentiation continued with the other levels so that everyone could participate as well as the others. In another example, she describes differentiating the curriculum for a statistics unit. Students were asked to gather world population figures from a variety of sources, including the Internet. The gifted students interpreted and evaluated their findings with significant attention to detail. The remedial math groups had more structured instructions for completing their research, fewer choices, and simpler steps to take to complete their assignment (Page, 2000). All of the students, however, knew what the expectations were for completion of a class project that led to the defined understandings that were identified by the teacher.

It's usually much easier for classroom teachers to adapt instruction for gifted students. Once the basic content goals have been identified, the teacher must again consider the unique qualities of the students. Most schools have a coordinator for gifted programs or at least teachers who have licensure in gifted education. These people are the best resource to help one refine teaching methods and instructional strategies for the gifted.

TIPS from the TRENCHES

The following are suggestions that reflect what beginning teachers wish they had been told before they started to teach students with special needs.

Before the students arrive . . .

1. If no one has given you a list of students with special needs who are on your class rosters, ask for one.

2. Read their IEPs and student files thoroughly, making notes about them that will help you learn what to expect and how best to teach them.

3. Find out about the process for working with special needs students in your school and identify the resource people who can assist you.

Once the students arrive . . .

4. Talk to each student who has an IEP individually about the best way to work with him or her in your class. How does he or she learn best?

5. Beware of students who play the IEP card. Occasionally a student takes advantage of a special

(Continued)

circumstance listed on the IEP even when it is no longer needed.

6. It is also true that some students may not want to take advantage of specific accommodations (e.g., extra time on tests) even when they would be better off with them.

7. Let students know that you trust their judgment as young adults and will depend on them to initiate contact to make special requests regarding their disability. This is especially important at the high school level.

As you teach students with special needs . . .

8. Look for ways to adapt your instruction, even if it is only in small ways at the beginning.

9. Give these students as much personal attention as you can whenever possible, without singling them out.

10. Follow up on their progress, both in and out of your class.

11. Show them respect and demonstrate a personal interest in their lives.

12. Teach them differently as students when warranted without treating them differently as people.

13. If you have assistants assigned to help you with students who have special needs, focus their work with the students so that the assistants can help you meet your instructional goals. In other words, they should not be viewed as disciplinarians, nor are they the teachers.

Remember . . .

14. You must understand where you fit in with respect to the "services loop." Are you on the school support team? Should you be?

15. Always be an advocate for the student.

16. These are secondary students just as all your other students are, with the same needs, wants, and developmental challenges as other teenagers. They have a disability that complicates their progress in school. Your job is to help.

PRAXIS™

Praxis Competencies Related to Students with Special Needs

The Praxis Tests ask questions that assess your knowledge of how to work best with students with special needs. In most cases, you will be asked to apply very basic information about such things as how to modify teaching strategies for students, how to define goals for these students, and how to assess their progress. Such questions (presented here from the most general to the most specific) may appear on the following tests:

Principles of Learning and Teaching Test

This is the most general application of your knowledge. Topics covered on this test that deal with students with special needs might include (ETS, 2001, *Test-at-Glance*, Principles of Learning and Teaching):

- Planning curriculum
- Modifying objectives to accommodate particular students' needs
- Legal responsibilities and rights related to special populations
- Regulations based on federal law
- Needs and characteristics of special populations
- Diagnosis of student achievement
- Appropriate teacher responses to students with special needs
- Accurate record-keeping for students with special needs
- Roles and functions of professional personnel (e.g., school psychologist)

Praxis II: The Specialty Area Tests for Specific Content

These tests cover mathematics, social studies, languages, biology, and so forth. They focus mostly on the actual teaching of your content area and are designed to determine if you know the basic content you are teaching and how to teach it. However, they will also require that you have enough general knowledge about working with students with disabilities that you can apply basic concepts to your particular teaching situations.

Praxis II: Education of Students with Disabilities

This is the most specific application of your knowledge. Clearly those of you taking this specialty-area test must be very knowledgeable about students with special needs, including such topics as (ETS, 2001, *Test-at-a-Glance,* Education of Students with Disabilities):

- Understanding exceptionalities, including characteristics of students with special needs, and basic concepts relating to them
- Legal and societal issues such as federal laws and legal issues, relationship with families, and historical movements
- Delivery of services to students with disabilities, including implementing curriculum and instruction in all classes, assessments, structuring and managing the learning environment, and professional role

Sample Question

Which of the following is an accurate statement about what IDEA '97 requires for any IEP?

A. It must include a multiyear outline of instructional objectives

B. It must include a section on assistive devices, regardless of the nature or degree of the student's disability

C. It must be in effect before special education services are provided

D. It must not be made available to any school personnel except special education teachers

The correct answer is **C**. According to IDEA '97, an IEP must be in effect before special education and related services are provided to an eligible student. None of the other choices is required (p. 42).

Praxis II: Guidance, Administration and School Services

Many of these tests deal with areas of specialization that require you to have specific knowledge about students with special needs and how to apply it. They include Audiology (0340), School Guidance and Counseling (0420), School Psychologist (0400), School Social Worker (0210), and Speech-Language Pathology (0330). The topics they emphasize vary somewhat by test and the area of specialization you are pursuing, but they all basically require that you understand such topics as (ETS, 2001, *Test-at-a-Glance,* Guidance, Administration and School Services):

- Understanding students with special needs
- Due process and legislation governing working with students with special needs
- Ethical and legal considerations
- Diagnosis and assessment procedures
- Methods of collaboration with other school personnel and families

Suggestions for Further Reading

If you have time to read only one book . . .

Turnbull, R., Turnbull, A., Shank, M., Smith, S., & Leal, D. (2002). *Exceptional lives: Special education in today's schools* (3rd ed.). Upper Saddle River, NJ: Merrill/Prentice Hall.

Other excellent resources . . .

Heward, W. L. (2000). *Exceptional children: An introduction to special education* (6th ed.). Upper Saddle River, NJ: Merrill/Prentice Hall.

Lewis, R. B., & Doorlag, D. (1999). *Teaching special students in general education classrooms* (5th ed.). Upper Saddle River, NJ: Merrill/Prentice Hall.

Mastropieri, M. A., & Scruggs, T. E. (2000). *The inclusive classroom: Strategies for effective instruction*. Upper Saddle River, NJ: Merrill/Prentice Hall.

Meyen, E. L. (1996). *Exceptional children in today's schools* (3rd ed.). Denver: Love.

References

Bebko, J. M. & Luhaorg, H. (1998). The development of strategy use and metacognitive processing in mental retardation: some sources of difficulty. In J. A. Burack, R. M. Hodapp, & E. Zigler (Eds.), *Handbook of mental retardation and development* (pp. 382–409). Cambridge: Cambridge University Press.

Bray, N. W., Fletcher, K. L., & Turner, L. A. (1997). Cognitive competencies and strategy use in individuals with mental retardation. In W. E. MacLean Jr. (Ed.), *Ellis handbook of mental deficiencies, psychological theory and research* (3rd ed., pp. 197–217). Mahwah, NJ: Lawrence Erlbaum.

Daniels, H. (2002). *Literature circles: Voice and choice in book clubs and reading groups*. Portland, ME: Stenhouse.

Deshler, D., Ellis, E., & Lenz, B. (1996). *Teaching adolescents with learning disabilities* (2nd ed.). Denver: Love.

Educational Testing Service (ETS). Tests-at-a-Glance for Principles of Learning and Teaching (2001); Social Studies: Pedagogy (2002); Education of Students with Disabilities (2001), and Guidance, Administration and School Services (2000).

Goleman, D. (1995). *Emotional intelligence*. New York: Bantam.

Horner, R. H. (1988). *Generalization and lifestyle changes in applied settings*. Baltimore: Brooks.

Iarocci, G., & Burack, J. A. (1998). Understanding the development of attention in persons with mental retardation: Challenging the myths. In J. A. Burack, R. M. Hoddap, & E. Zigler (Eds.), *Handbook of mental retardation and development* (pp. 349, 381). New York: Cambridge University Press.

Idol, L. (1997). Key questions related to building collaborative and inclusive schools. *Journal of Learning Disabilities*. *30*(4), 384–394.

Johnson, D. W., & Johnson, R. T. (1987). *Learning together and alone: Cooperation, competition and individualization*. Upper Saddle River, NJ: Prentice Hall.

Landrum, M. S., Katsiyannis, A., & Dewaard, J. (1998). A national survey of current legislation and policy trends in gifted education: life after the national excellence report. *Journal for the Education of the Gifted. 21*(3), 352–371.

Lewis, R., & Doorlag, D. (1999). *Teaching special students in general education classrooms* (5th ed.). Upper Saddle River, NJ: Merrill/Prentice Hall.

Luckasson, R., Coulter, D. L., Polloway, E. A., Reiss, S., Schalock, R. L., Snell, M. E., Spitalnik, D. M., & Stark, J. A. (1992). *Mental retardation: Definitions, classifications and systems of support.* Washington, DC: American Association on Mental Retardation.

McNamara, B. E. (1998). *Learning disabilities: Appropriate practices for a diverse population.* Albany, NY: SUNY Press.

Meyen, E. (1996). *Exceptional children.* Denver: Love.

Page, S. (2000, September). When changes for the gifted spur differentiation for all. *Educational Leadership.* Alexandria, VA: ASCD.

Reid, D. K. (1988). *Teaching the learning disabled.* Boston: Allyn & Bacon.

Renzulli, J. S., & Reis, S. M. (1986). The enrichment triad/revolving door model: A school-wide plan for the development of creative productivity. In J. S. Renzulli (Ed.), *Systems and models for developing programs for the gifted and talented* (pp. 216–266). Mansfield Center, CT: Creative Learning Press.

Ruder, S. (2000, September). We teach all. *Educational Leadership.* Alexandria, VA: ASCD.

Sailor, W. (1991). Special education in restructured schools. *Remedial and Special Education, 12*(6), 8–22.

Sheldon, C. M. (2000, September). Portraits of emotional awareness. *Educational Leadership.* Alexandria, VA: ASCD.

Siegal, E., & Gold, R. (1982). *Educating the learning disabled.* New York: Macmillan.

Sousa, D. (1998). The ramifications of brain research. *Educational Leadership.* Alexandria, VA: ASCD.

Tomlinson, C. (2000). *Differentiated classrooms: Responding to the needs of learners.* Alexandria, VA: ASCD.

Towle, W. (2000). The art of the reading workshop. *Educational Leadership.* Alexandria, VA: ASCD.

Turnbull, A. P., & Schultz, J. B. (1979). *Mainstreaming handicapped students: A guide for the classroom teacher.* Boston: Allyn & Bacon.

Turnbull, R., Turnbull, A., Shank, M., Smith, S., & Leal, D. (2002). *Exceptional lives: Special education in today's schools* (3rd ed.). Upper Saddle River, NJ: Merrill/Prentice Hall.

U.S. Department of Education. (1997). *Nineteenth annual report to Congress on the implementation of the Individuals with Disabilities Education Act.* Washington, DC: Author.

U.S. Department of Education. (1999). *To assure the free appropriate education of all children with disabilities: Twenty-first annual report to Congress on the implementation of the Individuals with Disabilities Act.* Washington, DC: Author.

Winebrenner, S. (2000). The trials and tribulations of being gifted: Has gifted education changed over the years? *Understanding Our Gifted, 12*(4), 10–12.

Part 3

Your Challenge: Effectively Teaching Secondary Students

6

Planning for Instruction

My mentor teacher stopped by after school yesterday and offered to spend some time helping me to plan my year since we teach the same subject. She told me that she knew how hard it was to be a brand-new teacher, and while it was still early in September, she had some ideas for organizing the course that would make both semesters go more smoothly. It was a nice gesture, but I told her I was too busy trying to find something to do with my students tomorrow to take time to talk about planning.

First-year teacher

There are things in life that don't require a plan. Other things won't even happen unless someone has done some planning. Effective teaching is in the second category. You simply cannot have focused, purposeful learning experiences for your students unless you plan. Planning means that you have given considerable thought to (a) exactly what your students need to know and (b) how you are going to get them to know it. These two things don't come to you in a dream or while you sit at a stoplight on the way to school. They happen because you make long-term plans about the entire course *before* students arrive. Then you make short-term plans about what you want to accomplish each semester, each grading period, and each day.

Think for a minute about the best course you had when you were in high school. What made it so? More than likely, you learned a lot and your lessons seemed to have a purpose. This did not happen by accident. It happened because the teacher spent time determining specific outcomes for instruction and creating interesting learning activities that would meet that end. Now it's your turn.

Teachers who teach great courses (a) understand the connection between the curriculum and instruction, (b) are knowledgeable about their subject matter, (c) take time to select and organize content carefully, (d) determine goals and objectives for the course, (e) make effective long-range and short-range plans and modify them as needed, and (f) select and use appropriate resources and materials.

This chapter will address these elements of instructional planning.

Designing a Great Course: What Are the Essentials?

The Connection Between Curriculum and Instruction

The terms *curriculum* and *instruction* are often used together in the field of education. Basically, *curriculum* refers to *what* is being taught, and *instruction* refers to *how* it is being taught. As you consider the *what*, it is critical that you have an overall understanding of the entire range of topics that make up your field of study and how your course represents a microcosm of the whole picture. You will need to have a thorough knowledge of your subject and of the content that is fundamental to your particular course as you develop your instructional plans.

Once the *what* is determined, you can then focus on the *how*. Teaching world history is very different from teaching art, although most methods for teaching one subject are adaptable for most others. Both an art teacher and history teacher may use lecture and discussion as well as many hands-on activities. The main question for you to answer is "What is the best way to teach this lesson?"

Knowing Your Subject Matter

To guide your students' development, you must know your subject and understand why certain fundamental topics have been included in the state curriculum handbooks you are given and are expected to follow. You should also be knowledgeable enough to make judgments about which content should be stressed, which can be incorporated into other portions of your course, and which can be reviewed briefly or deleted altogether because your students already know the material. You can do this only if you know your content well.

Teachers who have little depth in their understanding of the subject usually rely totally on the textbook. (If you are teaching out of your field, you may see yourself here.) They stay a chapter ahead of the students, depending solely on this source for both information that is to be addressed and suggestions for how to teach it. In effect, they are students themselves. One of their biggest fears is that a student will ask a question that requires an answer that is not in the teacher's edition. They may have one or two instructional strategies that they use almost every day—more than likely lecture or worksheets. The reason is obvious: these methods will keep the students busy and focused on the textbook. Most important, unlike methods that involve discussion and the potential for questions, these methods won't expose the teacher's limitations with respect to the content. Decide now that this will not be your situation.

REALITY CHECK 6.1

You may not think you have time to do this, but you must *study*. Knowing your content is the first step to planning appropriately. Even teachers who have a solid background in the field in college find that they must spend time refreshing themselves about the subject they are teaching.

The implications for instruction are clear. Knowledgeable teachers are secure and flexible enough to vary teaching strategies comfortably. Because they know the subject, they can concentrate on the process of teaching students. It's like driving a car. Once you are not so consumed with the actual mechanics of shifting gears, you can pay attention to what's going on in traffic.

Selecting and Organizing Content

There is more to learn in any one subject than you have time to teach in a school year. So where do you begin? How will you make choices in terms of content? First, you must *put your entire course in context* in three very important ways. In other words, you must see the role of the course in the total program. As you study the contexts, make notes for yourself.

The School-Level Context

Where does the course fit into the curriculum of your school? Find the answers to questions about its role and importance. Is it a new course? A requirement? Why does it exist at all as a registration option? Is the class part of a mathematics sequence? If so, what courses are prerequisites for this one? Who is it designed for, advanced or low-ability students?

The State and Local Level Context

Look at the state and local curriculum guides (see Activity 6.1). As a state agency, your school must include certain academic topics that have been determined important for students to master. Likewise, your local school system may have modified in some way or added to the basic state-mandated curriculum. In this age of accountability, it is also possible that your students will be tested on their mastery of these concepts. *It is your responsibility to understand the goals and objectives for your subject and to incorporate them into your instructional planning.*

As you read these goals and objectives, you, in effect, are also getting an overview of national standards for your subject. While there is no national curriculum as such for any one discipline, there are national organizations for most content areas that determine the standards for a field of study. State and local goals and objectives reflect the priorities of national organizations. For example, most state standards for social studies courses represent the goals of the National Council for the Social Studies as well. These goals and standards represent extensive research for the teaching of your discipline. There are increasing efforts to link standards-based goals and objectives of the national organizations to those of local systems. This is a welcome change that will make your job easier. These efforts represent some needed continuity and ensure that the curriculum reflects one overall belief system (Matlock, Fielder, & Walsh, 2001).

Your Classroom Context

These contexts come together in your classroom. Look at the textbook that has been adopted for this course by your school system as well as any other available resources and supplementary materials. At this point, you can begin to see a pattern in terms of what the state, your school system, and your school think is important to address in your class.

Next, *determine what you will be teaching for the year.* Now it's time to put your personal signature on your notes. Identify the content areas that *you* think should be added, emphasized, or minimized, based on what you know about the field and about your students. You should also have a nice long list of topics that will be impossible to cover. Begin making two master lists of topics in order of importance that you should include in your course. The "A list" will be the mandatory topics; the "B list" will be whatever you think will be possible to add for enrichment. For example, Mr. Hanson is fascinated by the Trail of Tears, a sad story of the plight of the Cherokee Indians in the early 19th century.

Comparing State Standards and Textbook Content

Examine the state standards for your course. They will be available in your school or online. Look for places in the textbook you will be using that address each standard. Make a list of standards that are not addressed and determine how and where in your course you will cover this material.

Having spent a summer working on a Cherokee reservation, he has a special interest in the topic and much to share with his students. It is only minimally addressed in the text for his U.S. history class, but he feels strongly that the students can gain some valuable information and insights from his experience. Therefore, he would add the Trail of Tears to his "B list" and plan to extend his "A list" unit on Andrew Jackson and his presidential powers to include more discussion on this.

Finally, *determine how much time you will spend on each topic*. If you decide to spend an entire grading period on poetry, will you have time for the other units you must cover during the rest of the year? Determining what to teach and how much time to spend with each topic, factoring in your personal expertise, are key to the planning process.

Looking at the Big Picture: How Will You Stay on Track?

If you are ever going to master the art of effective teaching, you must somehow become a long-range planner. How often have you heard of U.S. history teachers who never get past World War II? This could happen to Mr. Hanson if he spends too much time on the Trail of Tears at the expense of other important content. He must have a vision of what should be taught for the entire year, develop a preliminary time line for accomplishing this, and make a serious effort to stick to it. He will need to look at the big picture.

The ability to do thorough long-term planning in advance is, of course, directly related to how much lead time you have before the school year begins. If you are hired on Friday and begin teaching Monday, the very idea of long-range planning will seem like a fantasy. You will feel immediately that you are thrust into urgent short-range thinking to be ready for the first day. You don't want to feel that way till the last day of school. Even if you don't think you have time, do a yearly plan anyway. Your plan doesn't have to be extensive—just a tentative outline of how you want to proceed. You can sketch it out in as little as 15 minutes, depending on how familiar you are with your course. Make preliminary decisions about the amount of time you will allot to each section. Enhance and modify it over time. Figure 6.1 illustrates one way to think about a yearly plan. Activity 6.2 (page 154) helps create topical organization for your yearly plan.

Creating a Syllabus

Just as a syllabus was helpful to you as a college student, it is also helpful for your students, especially at the high school level. In very brief form (perhaps no longer than two pages), it should include basic information about the course and your expectations, such as the following:

- General information about the course (the teacher's name, room number, course title, class period, meeting times, etc.)
- Textbook and any other required books
- Goals and objectives of the course (limit to five or fewer)
- Materials required (notebook, graphing calculator, etc.)

Course: American Government

Text: McClenaghan, William A., *Magruder's American Government*

Unit 1 Foundations of Government
- Modern Systems
- Amer. heritage
- Basic Principles
- Division of Powers

Unit 2 Rights of Americans
- Freedom: Expression
- Freedom: Religion
- Due Process
- Fair Trial
- Civil Rights

1st Quarter

Unit 3 Politics of Democracy
- Two party system
- Voting behavior
- Elections
- Public Opinion

Unit 4 Congress (Legislative Branch)
- House of Reps.
- Senate
- Org. of Congress
- Bills become laws
- Expressed/Supplied powers

Semester

Unit 5 Executive Branch
- Presidency/Selection
- Powers
- Executives depts.
- Foreign affairs

Unit 6 Federal Branch
- Nat'l judiciary
- Inferior courts
- Supreme Court
- Special courts
- Judges

3rd Quarter

Unit 7 State/Local Government
- State constitutions
- State Legislatures
- Governors
- State court systems

Unit 8 World Politics
- Gt. Britain
- France
- Japan
- Capitalism
- Socialism/Communism

FIGURE 6.1 Sample Tentative Yearly Plan

ACTIVITY 6.2

Your Tentative Yearly Plan

Using Figure 6.2, create a tentative organization for the topics you plan to teach for the year.

1st Quarter

Semester

3rd Quarter

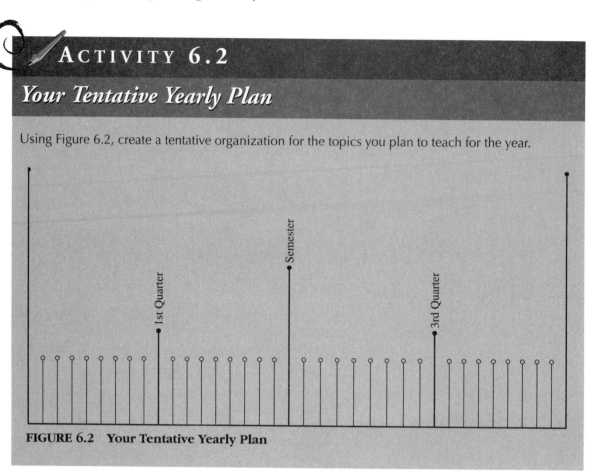

FIGURE 6.2 Your Tentative Yearly Plan

- The schedule of readings and assignments (the nature of each assignment, when each is due, and any guidelines you want the students to follow)
- Policies or procedures (attendance, tardies, make-up or extra-credit work)
- Grading procedures
- Anything else you consider important for the students to know

Planning Daily Instruction: How Will You Organize Your Lessons?

Now you have a road map. You know where you are going and approximately how long each leg (topic) of the trip should take. Will things go exactly according to your plan? Of course not. But if you gave your yearly plan serious thought, it could come close. At the very least, you now have something from which to deviate.

Examine the topics you've selected. Do you have a justification for why each is included and the amount of time you will be allocating to it? What are the goals and objectives for each?

Writing Goals and Objectives

As students were leaving an advanced U.S. history class, the principal stopped one of them and asked a bright student to tell him what they had done that period. The student replied, "We talked about World War I." The principal asked, "What did you learn?" The student said he wasn't sure. Later that day, the principal asked Mr. Belton, the teacher, what his objective was for that class. Mr. Belton replied, "To talk about World War I." The principal asked, "What specifically about it?" The teacher said, "You know, just what happened—what's in the chapter."

In effect, that's exactly what Mr. Belton did—talked *about* World War I, that is, all around the topic. He had no specific objectives in mind. What do the students actually know after his class? That there was a war? Why was it fought?

An objective is described as a learning outcome—the destination, not the journey. A clear objective will help you to clarify exactly what you want your students to learn. It will provide focus and direction and guide the choice of activities (Price & Nelson, 1999). Many teachers, even experienced ones, do not realize the importance of defining precise direction for their students each day. So they don't do it. If you want clear, effective lessons, you *must* always ask yourself, "Why am I teaching this lesson, and what do I want the students to know?" If you can't answer these questions concisely, you shouldn't be teaching this content. ("Because the text has a chapter on it" doesn't qualify as a legitimate response.) To focus specifically, you must identify and *write* goals and objectives for each lesson.

Yes, *write* the goals and objectives (see Activity 6.3). Often, teachers say they have reasons to be teaching something, and those reasons are in their heads. "I never write that down," claim many. In truth, they may never have given a thought to objectives at all. Getting into the habit of writing them even briefly ensures that you understand why you are doing something—you can't be clear about something you can't express in writing. This practice will eliminate fuzzy thinking on your part. It will give you a definite, tangible goal and a standard by which to evaluate your students' learning (Clark & Starr, 1996). Post your list of goals and objectives over your desk as you teach each lesson.

There is a difference between a goal and an objective. A *goal* is a broad statement of the direction you want to go and is described in general terms. For example, "Senior literature students will understand the impact of personal experience on an author's work."

The goal is written simply and addresses the learner and the learning task (Jacobsen, Eggen, & Kauchak, 1989). Basically, it is a statement of desired instructional outcomes that can be broken down into a variety of more specific behaviors. Goals should always be expressed in terms of what students (not teachers) are expected to do. They are usually associated with long-term planning.

Objectives, on the other hand, are "explicit descriptions of what students will be able to do as a result of the instruction they receive" (Reiser & Dick, 1996, p. 23). They have four components (Price & Nelson, 1999):

1. Content (the subject matter the students will learn)
2. Behavior (how students will demonstrate what they have learned)
3. Condition (circumstances under which they will exhibit the behavior)
4. Standard (criterion that represents acceptable performance)

For example, Mr. Belton would have had more focused instruction if he had identified a specific objective for the class, such as:

> The students will be able to list [behavior] the causes of World War I [content] on a review quiz at the end of the class [condition] with 90% accuracy [standard].

ACTIVITY 6.3

Writing Goals and Objectives

Choose a lesson or a unit that you will be teaching. Write three goals and three objectives. Do all of yours meet the criteria for each? Ask a veteran teacher to look at your list and provide suggestions.

Don't misunderstand. Not every objective has to be measured with a test or some written criterion—there are many ways to do this. Think of an objective as a mark you aim for. Consider the farmer who took his grandson with him on a tractor to plow a field. "Do you think you can plow a straight line all the way up that little hill?" he asked. "No problem," his grandson replied, as he began to drive the tractor. When they were at the top of the hill, looking back, they saw that the row the grandson had plowed was a zigzag line covering a wide portion of the field. The grandson was amazed, saying, "I really thought I was going straight the whole time." The grandfather replied, "Let's go back and try again. This time keep your eye on that tree as you plow and do not take your eyes off of it till you get to the top of the hill." When the boy arrived at the top, he looked down to see he had plowed a perfectly straight row. This is what having an objective can do for your instruction.

Using Taxonomies to Determine Objectives

Benjamin Bloom and a group of college and university researchers determined that objectives fall into three domains:

1. The *cognitive domain,* stressing recall and involving some intellectual task. These cognitive objectives vary from simple recall to creating ways of synthesizing material.
2. The *affective domain,* emphasizing feeling, tone, and emotion as well as interests, attitudes, and appreciations.
3. The *psychomotor domain,* emphasizing muscular or motor control and the manipulation of materials.

These objectives are arranged into hierarchies or taxonomies. See Figure 6.3 for a brief summary of each, and note the implications for activities you may plan to address the levels of each.

There are two basic implications of these taxonomies for teachers. First, these skills go from the simple to the more complex. For example, consider Bloom's Taxonomy of Cognitive Development. Before one can analyze something, one must be able to comprehend it. Before playing golf, one must be able to hold the club correctly. Second, teachers should always be trying to assist their students to reach for the highest level they are able to achieve. Too often, teachers assume that the lower ability students should only be taught at the knowledge and comprehension levels of Bloom's taxonomy and the advanced students should be guided to synthesize and evaluate. In fact, *all* students should be instructed with *all* the levels of objectives. Most low-ability students can understand complex concepts if they are presented effectively. Then they will be able to create interesting plays, poems, and songs (synthesis level) to demonstrate their understanding.

In other words, when determining your objectives, consider what you want them to know (cognitive domain), how you want them to feel about it (affective domain), and if there are any concerns about their physically being able to do the tasks you assign (psychomotor domain). Think of the objectives you have for your class as the middle of a giant wheel (see Figure 6.4 on page 158). Your instructional activities—all of the spokes of the wheel—are outgrowths of the middle. Each is directly connected with the center (your objective). Keeping this image in mind will keep you focused.

Long-Range Planning: Units

Given the importance of long-range planning, it will be helpful if you think of your subject in terms of chunks or units of content. Units of study are broad concepts that represent the big picture. Each is made up of subsections that will be the substance of daily lessons. Units vary in many ways, but most have the following components (Myers & Myers, 1995, p. 462):

- Objectives to be achieved
- Content to be learned

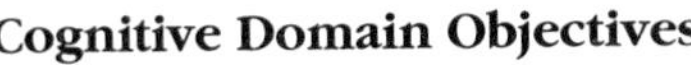

Cognitive Domain Objectives

Benjamin Bloom

What do you want the student to know?

Educational objectives in the cognitive domain range from the simple (remembering) to the more complex (evaluation). They are as follows:

Level	Sample Verbs
1. *Knowledge* Emphasis: Recall	Choose, define, name
2. *Comprehension* Emphasis: Understand	Describe, explain, rewrite
3. *Application* Emphasis: Apply material to new situations	Apply, demonstrate, predict
4. *Analysis* Emphasis: Break down material into component parts	Compare and contrast, debate
5. *Synthesis* Emphasis: Put parts together to create a new whole	Compose, design, produce
6. *Evaluation* Emphasis: Judge the value of material	Justify, evaluate, decide

Affective Domain Objectives

Benjamin Bloom and David Krathwohl

What do you want the student to value or appreciate about what he is learning?

A taxonomy of objectives in the affective domain represents the degree to which the stimulation (new material) has been internalized by the student. The affective domain reflects attitudes, interests, appreciations, and values. The categories range from simply being aware of a stimulus to accepting it, incorporating it into one's personality.

1. *Receiving* The student is aware that there is some stimulation present but has no reaction to it.
2. *Responding* The student responds to the stimulation at first by taking an interest in it and later by enjoying it.
3. *Valuing* The student gradually becomes committed to the stimulation.
4. *Organizing* The student begins to organize personal values into a value system.
5. *Becoming characterized by a value* The student's new values are becoming a part of who he is.

The Psychomotor Domain

Can the student physically do what you want him to as he learns new material?

For most subjects at the high school level, objectives in this domain are not as much of a consideration as those of the other domains. Since the goal is skill development, the stages range from the unskilled to the skilled.

1. *Familiarization* The student becomes familiar with the new skill.
2. *Fundamentals* The student develops the basic skills.
3. *Development* The skill is developed through practice.
4. *Adjusting and adapting* The skill is adapted and adjusted for new situations.
5. *Perfection and maintenance* The skill is maintained through continuous practice.

FIGURE 6.3 Taxonomies of Cognitive, Affective, and Psychomotor Domain Objectives

Secondary and Middle School Teaching Methods by Clark-Starr,

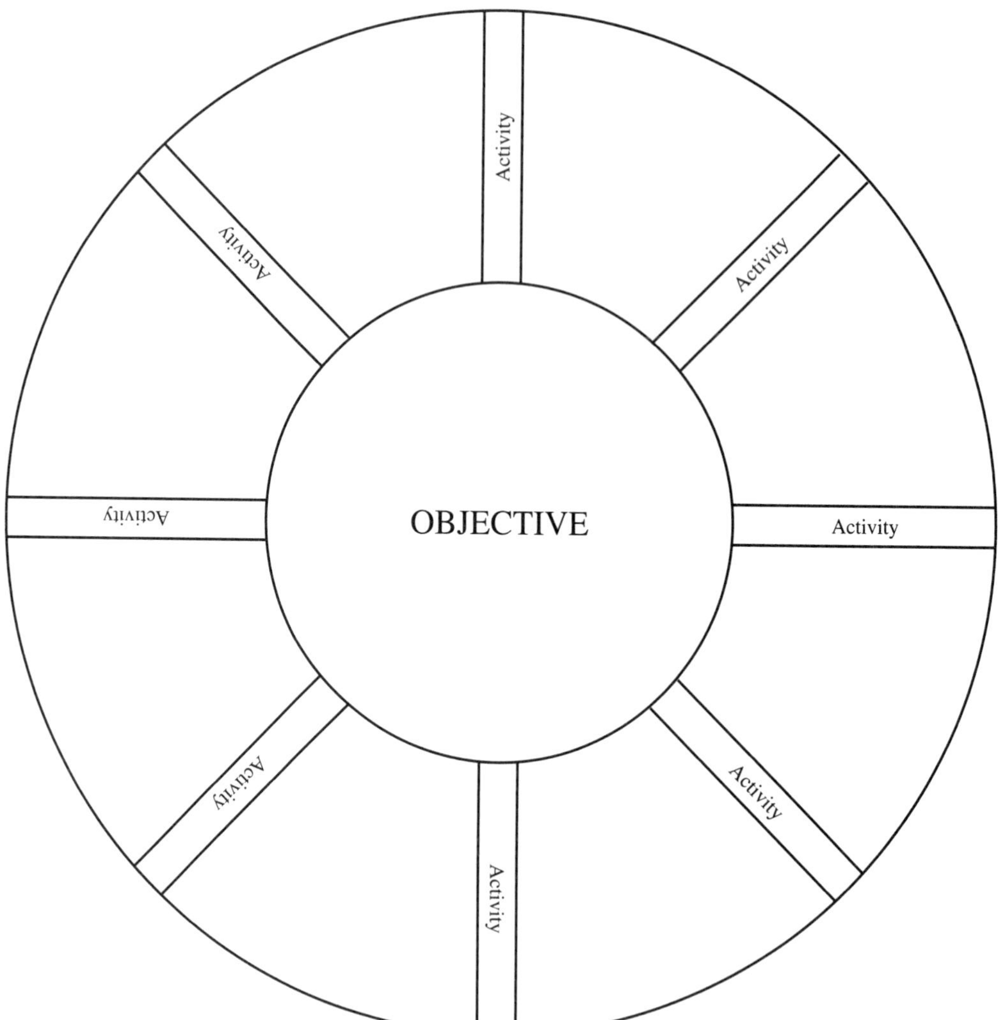

FIGURE 6.4 Objectives: The Center of Your Lesson

- Teaching strategies
- Resources and materials
- Plans for assessment

Textbooks identify and organize the content into units of instruction, listing appropriate subsections that lend themselves to daily lessons. The unit itself usually takes an extended amount of time—maybe days, maybe weeks, or longer. For example, a unit in an economics textbook might be called "Supply in the Marketplace" and may look something like the following (O'Connor, 1988):

Unit 3: Supply in the Marketplace

1. The forces affecting supply play major roles in the free enterprise system.
   - The law of supply
   - The supply curve
   - The profit motive
2. Price does not affect the supply of all products to the same degree.
   - Elastic supply
   - Inelastic supply

3. In addition to price, 5 nonprice factors affect supply.
   - Technological improvement
   - Resource prices
   - Taxes and subsidies
   - Price changes and expectations
   - Market competition

As you can see, the major topic (the unit title) could take a few days or a few weeks to cover, depending on your students and your judgment regarding the amount of time it requires. Perhaps the subsection on the law of supply will take 3 days, but the one on market competition might take a week.

Your textbook is a valuable resource, especially if you are a new teacher. Why reinvent the wheel if the concepts have already been outlined for you? You will want to begin developing your own units of study, however, using not just the text, but many other components as well, including your own experience and expertise as well as related materials. Your ultimate goal should be to have a comprehensive unit for each of the topics covered during the year for your course.

Unit thinking is broad, not specific. It is not just a compilation of separate lesson plans filed together after you have taught them. It's your opportunity to brainstorm in advance as many ways as you can to teach something without limiting yourself to the specific needs of one group. Think of the completed unit ultimately as a smorgasbord of every possible thing you might ever want to do with this topic. It is a resource that you will use and add to each year, pulling out appropriate lessons, activities, and materials to use in particular situations.

There are many ways to develop a unit, and you can be as brief or as comprehensive as you like. The following is a suggested overview to guide your thinking as you develop a unit. While you should address all of the parts of the overview to some degree, you can determine how much elaboration or detail will serve your purpose.

Unit Planning Guide

Brief Format

Concept: A brief description of the concept to be studied

The goals of the unit

Information to be reviewed, extended, or learned

Skills to be strengthened or gained

Attitudes and appreciations

Activities, projects, or assignments

- Introductory (to stimulate interest)
- Developmental (to teach new material)
- Culminating (to bring the concept taught together)

Evaluation activities, projects, or assignments

Resources

Appendix 6A (at the end of the chapter) provides a guide for a more comprehensive format.

Developing a unit seems like an awesome task, especially if you follow the comprehensive format. It can be, but the value to you as you teach and for years to come is unlimited. Eventually, your entire course will be organized as units of study you have spent time preparing. Then with each new year and each new situation, you can easily go to your file and choose very quickly which of your activities and resources will help you teach the information most effectively. See Appendix 6B for a sample of Miss Wineberg's first unit plan (comprehensive format).

ACTIVITY 6.4

Developing a Unit Plan

Directions: Using the Unit Planning Guide in Appendix 6A, develop your own unit. Discuss your completed unit with a veteran teacher. Ask for specific input and advice about refining and elaborating.

Now try to do one yourself. Even if you don't do every step of the suggested format, the process of thinking through your teaching of a unit of study will serve you well. (See Activities 6.4 and 6.5.)

Short-Range Planning: Daily Lesson Plans

In a meeting of three veteran high school teachers who were receiving awards as outstanding instructors, the subject of lesson planning arose. When asked if she had a lesson plan for the day's lesson, Mrs. Everett smiled and held up a 2-inch square Post-it note. "Yes, here it is! I'm starting a unit on the environment today." Mr. Glenn was shocked. "How do you do that? I always write out every part of every lesson I'm going to do. That way I have something solid to follow. I go back and make notes on each one so I can make it better for the next class." Mr. Gates held up his plan book and showed the group that he planned in some detail 2 weeks in advance. He also has a more comprehensive lesson plan for each day on a separate sheet of paper. "I always sketch everything out in pencil in my plan book to think ahead and put the next day's lesson in pen. Then I write out more details for the next day on a separate sheet of paper. This way I have a direction I'm heading but I can change it according to how things go."

Typical responses? Absolutely. Teachers vary widely in both their attitudes and practice when it comes to planning, especially daily planning. But most teachers, especially those who have had formal preparation, admit that learning to write formal lesson plans was essential in helping them think through the process of teaching an effective lesson. This is true even if they no longer engage in the entire process each day. Regardless of what you are hearing from teachers who do not do this or how much of an effort it seems to be to you now, as a beginning teacher, *learning to write formal lesson plans is critical.* Experts claim that, in general, those teachers who have written plans are the most organized and effective.

> **REALITY CHECK 6.2**
>
> You can expect that other, especially veteran, teachers will proudly say that they don't need lesson plans. And maybe they don't. It may even make you feel that you are somehow less competent because you do need them as you begin teaching. You will be wise not to listen to them. Many of those teachers would be better off if they did take the time to write a plan. Regardless, accept that until you are more experienced, you definitely need to have them. You might even find that the habit serves you so well that you continue the practice throughout your career.

The following are two of the most important reasons for writing lesson plans: (a) They will provide a sense of security for each class period you teach, and (b) you will have a written record of the lesson that you can revise and improve for future use. You will also be able to remember what things worked and, more important, what things didn't.

As a new teacher, you will find that written lesson plans serve as your foundation of what's supposed to happen that day. The process of performing in the classroom, much like an actor, is hard enough. Do you want the responsibility of making up the script at the same time? With your content already outlined, you can focus on your role as the instructor. Once the students arrive and you find yourself bombarded with numerous distractions, you will be glad you have the lesson plan in front of you. It will jog your memory, keep you on track, and free you to focus your attention on the students.

There are numerous formats for lesson plans. Some are more detailed than others but all include common elements. Note the similarity in the following examples.

Sample Format A

Kellough and Kellough (1999) suggested that a written lesson plan should contain the following: (a) descriptive course data—information about the course and unit of study; (b) goals and objectives—what you are trying to accomplish; (c) rationale—why you are teaching this lesson; (d) procedure—how you are going to teach it; (e) assignments—what the students will be doing to master the content; (f) materials and resources—what you will use to help you teach this lesson; and (g) a place for assessment, reflection, and revision—how you will evaluate your lesson. They also suggest that you consider how much time each portion of the lesson should take.

Sample Format B

Another approach has five steps: *preparation, beginning, moving on, ending,* and *evaluation* (Capel, Leask, & Turner, 1995, pp. 61–65). The *preparation* step suggests that you plan the lesson and gather materials and resources needed. The *beginning* is essentially the statement of objective and preparing the class for what will take place. The *moving on* stage refers to the teacher-input phase where teachers determine the activities and the transitions that will lead one to the other. The *ending* is closure. *Evaluation* is determining the effectiveness of the lesson and what modifications should be made for the next class.

Sample Format C

Clark and Starr (1996) suggested still another format that includes six slightly different steps.

1. Objective
2. Subject matter or content (outline form)
3. Procedure (introductory, developmental, and culminating activities)
4. Materials
5. Special notes
6. New assignment

Are these formats starting to form a pattern? Clearly, there are many lesson plan formats and it really doesn't matter which one you choose. Some schools provide their own format for teachers to use. As you can see from these samples, they all include in some way the same steps. They all suggest you (a) prepare for the lesson, (b) tell the students what you are going to do, (c) do it, (d) tell them what you did, and (e) reflect on how the lesson worked. See Appendix 6C for a sample lesson from Miss Wineberg's mathematics unit on probability.

If you are like most inexperienced teachers, you will find that you spend quite a bit of time planning your first lessons. Mr. Henderson, a veteran teacher, tells about his first day as a student teacher, when he had prepared over 30 pages of notes for his class. He was sure he had more than enough and that what he had prepared might possibly take 2 days. After 15 minutes, he was finished. Not knowing what else to do, he just sat down and let his cooperating teacher take over.

To keep this from happening to you, after you have completed your plan, ask for some advice about it from veteran teachers. Use these mentors as sounding boards regularly. *Overplan.* Make sure that you have several additional activities in case they are needed. Your students should stay busy and learning for every minute of the class.

Look at planning as a creative endeavor. You must master the basic principles first before you put your personal touch on the process, just as you must know how to work with clay before you can throw a beautiful pot. This means that you must make the effort to understand thoroughly the mechanics of developing a good course, unit, and lesson plan. Once you have mastered and internalized some of the thinking, you may not need to repeat every step on every plan you write. In fact, there is evidence that continuing to write comprehensive lesson plans *after you have learned the process* may not be any more useful to you than developing more streamlined ones in the first place (Maroney & Searcy, 1996).

Prepare detailed written lesson plans if:

- _____ You are unfamiliar with the state/district goals and objectives, as well as test objectives you are assigned to teach.
- _____ Your students are exhibiting poor classroom behavior.
- _____ You are an inexperienced teacher.
- _____ You are unfamiliar with the content you are assigned to teach.
- _____ You are assigned to teach subject area content that demands it.
- _____ You are using a new teaching approach, instructional program, or teaching strategy.

Prepare less detailed written lesson plans if:

- _____ You have an excellent overall understanding of what students need to learn (district goals/objectives) and student outcomes (test objectives).
- _____ You are an experienced teacher whose students consistently experience academic success.
- _____ You are very familiar with the content you are assigned to teach.
- _____ The content you are presenting is less complicated.
- _____ Your students spend the majority of time in class engaged in activities directly related to the district goals/objectives.
- _____ You are very familiar with the teaching approaches, instructional programs, and teaching strategies being used.

FIGURE 6.5 Lesson Plan Level of Detail
Used with permission from Leslie McCarley.

So how detailed should your lesson plans be? See Figure 6.5 for some helpful guidelines.

Young, Reiser, and Dick (1998) found in a recent study that the superior teachers they interviewed didn't employ a systematic planning process at all. In other words, they didn't necessarily follow the guidelines in the order suggested in most traditionally accepted formats. These teachers did, however, plan. The bottom line: As a beginning teacher, *you should learn to employ some systematic instructional planning procedure* even if you develop your own approach as you become more experienced.

Good lessons are like good movies. They include a plot and a theme (the objective and purpose of the lesson), a rhythm and flow (the activities), and a sense of ending (the conclusion; Thornbury, 1999). What you are after is a lesson your students will remember. Make your course interesting, active, and meaty. Plan other touches such as technology and good resources to make the content come alive once class has begun.

As you plan, relate the content to the students' lives and interests as you address the priorities of the curriculum you must teach (Dever & Hobbs, 2000; Wyngaard & Martin, 1998). Try to give them choices as you plan, if possible. Keep in mind that you are teaching students biology—not biology to students. *Note the order of* students *and* biology *in that sentence—students always come first.* This subtle difference should be key to your thinking as you prepare lessons.

Instructional Resources: What Is Available to Help You Plan?

Using National and State Goals to Focus Your Planning

As you begin planning your lessons, the very first resource you should consult is the list of national and state standards that you are expected to address. They are most likely available in your school media center, curriculum coordinator's office, or at some central location in your school system. They are also readily available on the Internet. These standards with their goals and objectives are clearly organized by grade level and may even be accompanied by

ACTIVITY 6.5

Writing a Lesson Plan

Using the following format, design a lesson from the unit you developed in Activity 6.4.

Objective:

Text reference:

Activity	Description	Materials	Time
Focus and review			
Direct instruction			
Guided practice			
Independent practice			
Closure			

- Go over your plans with a veteran teacher or someone else who can provide you with helpful feedback.
- Refine your lesson.
- After you teach the lesson, make notes regarding what worked, what didn't, and how you can make the plan better.

suggested activities and sample lesson plans that can serve as guides. For example, The National Council for the Teachers of Mathematics (NCTM) has identified goals by grade level in their *Principles and Standards for School Mathematics document.* Goal 1 for P-12 students relates to number sense, numeration, and numerical operations. "The learner will understand and compute with real numbers." The standard goes on to say that *all* P-12 students should be able to "understand numbers, relationships among numbers and number systems." For middle grades, this goal is refined to suggest that students should be able to "work flexibly with decimals and percents to solve problems, to compare and order fractions, decimals and percents efficiently and find their approximate locations on a number line." The same broad goal is refined differently for students in Grades 9–12. They should be able to "develop a deeper understanding of very large and very small numbers and various representations of them." High school students should also "understand vectors as systems that have some of the properties of the real number system" (NCTM, 2002, chap. 7, pp. 291–292). There are other indicators for this goal but this should give you some idea about how the standards have been designed. Your challenge will then be to create lessons to meet those objectives.

Using Resources

Theoretically, you should know so much about your subject that you could create a stand-alone lesson based strictly on what's in your head. The text and any other resources would simply be extras. But, in reality, it is impossible to know everything about a topic you want to teach, and you will need to rely on resources to help you plan an effective lesson. These resources will deepen your own knowledge base and make your lesson more meaningful for your students.

Teachers have never before had so many resources available to help them plan. Many are readily available in your school. Librarians and other personnel who work in the media center will be happy to help you find equipment, materials, references, supplementary materials, and other appropriate resources. Even if your school has relatively few resources on-site, there are many easy ways to supplement your instruction. Look for resources that

1. Help you meet the objective(s) you have identified for the lesson.
2. Will enable the students to understand more fully what you are teaching. (If your students are studying the stock market, perhaps a stock broker could visit your class.)
3. Help students learn in a variety of ways. (Are there visual aids, such as films, or tape recordings that will make your lesson on Watergate more real to the students?)
4. Are up-to-date and provide most current perspectives.
5. Are student-friendly and easy to understand.
6. Are available.

Most Common Resources

The following are the most common, readily available resources that teachers find easy to access and use.

The Textbook

A text is "good" if it addresses the most important aspects of your course and reflects the guidelines and standards of your state and school district. The text usually organizes the material sequentially with appropriate topics.

Many texts also offer supplemental materials that will enhance your lessons. Because these were designed to go with the chapters in the text, they will provide enrichment as well as continuity. Most schools are happy to order these supplementary materials for your department. If you don't need all of the materials in a packet, you might decide to purchase parts of these for your own use.

REALITY CHECK 6.3

Many teachers are overdependent on the text. In one episode of *The Simpsons,* the teacher's editions were stolen and Springfield had to close its school. That was supposed to be funny, but some teachers weren't laughing, because they saw themselves in that situation. For them, not having a textbook is a real fear. They are also the ones who claim that there's nothing else they can teach when the assistant principal has collected the texts with two weeks left in the school year.

The text is only a resource to your course. Never make the mistake of thinking that it *is* your course.

Printed Materials and Media Resources

Periodicals, newspapers, videotapes, films, documents, and so forth will help you elaborate on and add depth to your lessons. When you select reading materials, be aware of the reading level of the material. If you suspect that the reading level is too difficult, one quick way to determine this is to have individual students read selections from the book aloud. This should be done with you privately and one-on-one. You will know immediately if they can read without struggling with words and comprehend what they are reading.

Begin a "Resource and Idea File" of printed materials and other resources as soon as possible. This file should include any resources for teaching and should be something to update throughout your teaching career. You can begin by noting things on file cards or keeping a list on your computer. You should include such information as (a) The name of the resource, (b) The unit/lesson the resource will enhance, (c) The location of the resource, (d) How to get the resource, and (e) Best use(s) of the resource.

Resources could include almost anything that will help you to teach your class more effectively. They might be books, articles, newspapers, games, videocassettes, the Internet, software programs, people, pictures, and so forth. Your own list could be very long.

Be aware of copyright laws that prohibit the unlawful use of copyrighted materials. This includes those sources on the Internet. You may find that you need to get written permission from the author or publisher to use some materials.

The Internet

The Internet provides countless possibilities to explore. You can surf the World Wide Web and discover numerous sources and a lot of information about a subject you are teaching. Many teachers also find free and inexpensive teaching materials through connections with electronic bulletin boards on the Internet. But scrutinize the Web site and evaluate its quality—*anyone* can create a Web page.

Research in Education

There are two places you will want to look to find the most current teaching ideas and state-of-the-art research about teaching. First, professional journals and periodicals for your content area are readily available in your school library, or a library nearby, and online. Many include detailed lesson plans. Such journals also provide helpful ideas for teaching your content and provide information about resource materials. Professional journals and periodicals for secondary teachers might include such publications as *The English Journal, The Middle School Journal, The School Musician, Social Education, The Mathematics Teacher, The American Biology Teacher,* and *Voices from the Middle*. These and many others represent the most current ideas for each respective field.

Second, the Educational Resources Information Center (ERIC) provides access to a wide range of information and research in the field of education. You can access ERIC at any library. Your media specialist can assist you.

Human Resources

Don't forget the numerous ways you can include human resources in your planning. Students love to hear firsthand about certain topics they are studying from guest speakers. Often these individuals can be informative, and they are always a novelty for students. However, keep in mind that speakers can also be boring or ineffective. If so, you have wasted valuable class time. Therefore, take the time to plan their involvement carefully. Consider the following two suggestions:

1. Prepare your guest for the students. Actually talk to the guest speaker first and discuss exactly what you would like for your students to gain from the presentation. Tell the person what the students have been studying thus far about the issue at hand. What other things should the presenter know about the class before coming?

2. Prepare your students for the guest. Provide them with some background about the person and why he or she has been invited. Encourage them to ask questions and listen for specific information.

PLAN: What Should You Remember About Planning?

You will have a lot on your mind as you begin the planning process. Therefore, make it easy on yourself by developing some habits that will ensure that you routinely incorporate effective planning. Before you prepare every lesson, think of the acronym *PLAN.* The letters stand for the following:

Point—What is your *point* for the lesson? In other words, what is your objective?

Lesson—How will you approach the *lesson?*

Activities—What *activities* will you use to teach the lesson? Lecture and discussion? Perhaps a group activity? An independent research project?

Needs—Consider the *needs* of your students. Have you paid attention to the diversity represented in your classes and created a lesson with their frame of reference in mind? What are the other *needs* that you have to make the lesson complete and effective? What resources and materials will you need?

Remembering these few points will help you to focus on the most critical elements of good planning.

TIPS from the TRENCHES

The following are suggestions beginning teachers said they wish they had when they started their careers. Consider them as you begin planning.

1. Do it! Yes, *plan*! Try to get ahead of the year by thinking long term and ahead of each day by planning a few days in advance.

2. Write your plans. Don't depend on your memory and wing it during class.

3. Reflect on and revise your plans, making notes after each lesson.

4. Organize and keep your plans for future reference. Why reinvent the wheel next year?

5. Get everything ready the day before. Murphy's Law reminds you that "anything that can go wrong, will go wrong." Waiting till a few minutes before class to decide which handout to use and then facing a line at the copy machine will cause unnecessary stress.

6. Be flexible as you plan. Try to consider more than one way to teach a class in case there is a problem.

7. Have some activity ready to buy some time in emergency situations. For example, if the bulb in the overhead goes out and you need 10 minutes to get and install a new one, have something the students can be working on.

8. Expect that the plans you prepared for fourth period may not work for sixth period. Build in potential modifications as you plan.

9. Talk to other teachers as you plan. Use their expertise to get ideas for ways to prepare lessons. This doesn't have to take extra time. It can occur in a conversation at lunch.

10. Check your media center for catalogues that sell materials and resources. Often these will give you ideas for planning your lessons, even if you don't order anything.

PRAXIS™

Praxis Competencies Related to Planning for Instruction

The topic of planning for instruction is addressed in several ways on some of the tests in the Praxis Series. Questions usually appear in sections of the test referred to as "Pedagogy" and focus on your ability to explain how you would create a lesson or design activities. For example, the secondary section of the Principles of Learning and Teaching Test (PLT)(0524) suggests that you may be asked to structure lessons based on instructional objectives and select appropriate resources and materials (ETS, 2001, *Test-at-a-Glance*, Principles of Learning and Teaching).

While there may be few, if any, multiple-choice questions that relate directly to this topic, most tests address the issue with constructed-response or essay questions. The following are examples.

Music: Concepts and Processes (0111)

Sample Question

Design a step-by-step plan for a lesson focusing on texture that would be appropriate for a general music class for Grades 9–12.

- Begin your response by indicating the length of the lesson that would be appropriate for the grade-level range you have chosen.
- Your plan should follow a logical sequence and include at least one specific musical selection and one participatory experience to demonstrate texture.

- Conclude your response with suggestions for reinforcing this concept through additional learning experiences and appropriate literature (ETS, 2001, *Test-at-a-Glance,* Art, Music, and Theatre).

This one question, with its additional parts, asks you to describe several things in a constructed-response format. As you can see, they are looking for some indication of your ability to create a good lesson. As you plan the lesson, the test makers want to know that you understand what elements should be present if the lesson is designed effectively and how well you understand the developmental nature of your students in these grades. Your response to this comprehensive question will also reflect your knowledge of methodology for your discipline as well as your ability to understand scope and sequence of the curriculum (follow-up lessons). You are also asked to demonstrate your knowledge of literature and how it can be incorporated into the lesson. Remember always to outline briefly (just a few words) your response before you begin writing in the test booklet.

Mathematics: Pedagogy (0065)

Sample Question

Describe how you would present a lesson introducing the concept of absolute value to a ninth-grade class with below-average ability. The goal of the lesson is for students to develop a conceptual understanding of what absolute value is, how it can be used to represent the distance between two points on a number line, and how it is represented notationally.

Your description should include

- How you would motivate the students' interest in the concept of absolute value
- An outline of what you would do to achieve the goals of the lesson
- Sample exercises that could be used to reinforce student understanding of the material presented in the lesson (ETS, 2001, *Test-at-a-Glance,* Mathematics).

As in the other examples, regardless of the content area, the emphasis is on your ability to design a lesson and activities based on a specific objective. This question also asks you to demonstrate your knowledge of how to adapt lesson content for below-average students. They want you to include motivational strategies, an outline of your lesson, and actual sample exercises that might comprise the essence of your activities.

Suggestions for Further Reading

If you have time to read only one book to understand instructional planning . . .

Reiser, R., & Dick, W. (1996). *Instructional planning: A guide for teachers.* Needham Heights, MA: Allyn & Bacon.

Another excellent resource . . .

Price, K. M., & Nelson, K. (1999). *Daily planning for today's classroom: A guide for writing lesson and activity plans.* Belmont, CA: Wadsworth.

References

Capel, S., Leask, M., & Turner, T. (1995). *Learning and teaching in the secondary school.* London: Routledge.

Clark, L. H., & Starr, I. (1996). *Secondary and middle school teaching methods* (7th ed.). Upper Saddle River, NJ: Prentice Hall.

Dever, M. T., & Hobbs, D. E. (2000). Curriculum connections: The learning spiral—toward authentic instruction. *Kappa Delta Pi Record, 36*(3), 131–133.

Educational Testing Service (ETS). (2001). *Test-at-a-Glance—Art, Music and Theatre*. Princeton, NJ: Author.

Educational Testing Service (ETS). (2001). *Test-at-a-Glance—Mathematics*. Princeton, NJ: Author.

Educational Testing Service (ETS). (2001). *Test-at-a-Glance—Principles of Learning and Teaching*. Princeton, NJ: Author.

Jacobsen, D., Eggen, P., & Kauchak, D. (1989). *Methods for teaching: A skills approach* (3rd ed.). Upper Saddle River, NJ: Merrill/Prentice Hall.

Kellough, R. D., & Kellough, N. G. (1999). *Secondary school teaching: A guide to methods and resources*. Upper Saddle River, NJ: Prentice Hall.

Maroney, S., & Searcy, S. (1996). Real teachers don't plan that way. *Exceptionality, 6*(3), 197–200.

Matlock, L., Fielder, K., & Walsh, D. (2001). Building the foundation for standards-based instruction for all students. *Teaching Exceptional Children, 33*(5), 68–72.

Myers, C. B., & Myers, L. K. (1995). *The professional educator: A new introduction to teaching and schools*. Belmont, CA: Wadsworth.

National Council for the Teachers of Mathematics (NCTM). (2002). *Principles and Standards for School Mathematics*. Chapter 7. (http://standards.nctm.org/document/chapter7/reas.htm)

O'Connor, D. E. (1988). *Economics: Free enterprise in action*. Orlando, FL: Harcourt, Brace & Jovanovich.

Price, K. M., & Nelson, K. L. (1999). *Daily planning for today's classroom: A guide for writing lesson and activity plans*. Belmont, CA: Wadsworth.

Reiser, R. A., & Dick, W. (1996). *Instructional planning: A guide for teachers*. Needham Heights, MA: Allyn & Bacon.

Thornbury, S. (1999). Lesson art and design. *ELT Journal, 53*(1), 4–11.

Wyngaard, S., & Martin, S. M. (1998). Starting with the students (teaching ideas). *English Journal, 87*(3), 79–83.

Young, A., Reiser, R., & Dick, W. (1998). Do superior teachers employ systematic instructional planning procedures? A descriptive study. *Educational Technology Research and Development, 46*(2), 65–78.

Appendix 6A Unit Planning Guide

The Comprehensive Format

Concept: A Brief Description of the Concept to Be Studied

This could be a paragraph or two explaining the concept itself, its importance, and where it fits into the overall instructional picture.

The Goals of the Unit

These need to be broad, general goals that describe the purpose of the unit—perhaps no more than five.

Information to Be Reviewed, Extended, or Gained

Reviewed: What specific information (perhaps from previous units of study) will be reviewed? Be brief.

Extended: What specific information the students learned previously will be broadened in this unit? Be brief.

Gained: What *new* information will be learned? An outline of the new information will be helpful and can be as detailed as you find useful.

Skills to Be Strengthened or Gained

Strengthened: List previously gained skills that will be incorporated in this study.

Gained: List new skills that will be introduced during this unit.

Attitudes and Appreciations

List specific attitudes and appreciations the unit is intended to develop.

Activities

Here is your chance to dream. Regardless of what is possible in every situation, begin thinking of every type of activity that, under some conditions, would be effective with the following group sizes. For example, if your social studies class is studying the legal system and you think it would be great to have the class visit a prison but are aware that your current teaching situation would not allow it, put it down anyway. There may be another situation where this activity would be workable.

Introductory Activities

These activities are intended to set the stage for the new unit of study. Their primary purpose is to get the students' attention and motivate them to learn new information, skills, and attitudes. Write a minimum of 10 activities, projects, or assignments for each of three groups: *large group, small group,* and *individual students.*

Developmental Activities

These activities are the heart of the unit. It is during this part of the unit that your students will review previously learned material and encounter new information and skills. This is the most time-consuming and critical part of the unit plan. Write a minimum of 15 activities, projects, or assignments for each group: large, small, and individual students.

Culminating Activities

The purpose of culminating activities is to bring everything together. They represent a summary of the content learned and bring closure to the unit. They also often serve as a link to the next unit. Write a minimum of 10 activities, projects, or assignments for each of the following groups that you might use to integrate information and develop appropriate attitudes and appreciations of the concept studied: *large group, small group,* and *individual students.*

Evaluation Activities

List activities, questions, and exercises that you can use to evaluate the effectiveness of student learning and your effectiveness as the instructor. Write a minimum of 10.

Resources

Create a master list of all the resources you can find related to the information you are teaching in this unit. Add to the list every time you teach the unit.

List bibliographic and other resources to enrich your own knowledge and understanding of the concepts you are teaching.

List any resources you can find that will help you teach the information to the students. This list may include visual aids, computer programs, books and other printed material, and any other resources you think will be helpful.

List any materials you have made for the unit and indicate where you have stored them.

APPENDIX 6B Miss Wineberg's Unit

Topic: Introduction to Probability

Unit: Introduction to Probability

Concept: Students will be able to understand simple probability and its applications.

Brief explanation: There are few things in life that occur with certainty. Thus there are a great many things in life that are uncertain. To model these uncertainties, math people, more specifically Fermat and Pascal, developed probability theory. In today's society, people rely on probability more than they realize. For example, the weatherman reports the probability that it will rain tomorrow, the bookie uses probability to gamble his money, and the actuary computes insurance rates using probability. Many probability applications can be solved using simple counting principles, permutations, and combinations. We shall discuss these applications in the upcoming unit.

Information to Be Reviewed, Extended, and Gained

Reviewed: Ratios, union of sets, intersection of sets, disjoint sets, percentages

Extended: Relationship between the inclusive "or" and the exclusive "and"

Gained: Definitions: probability, outcomes, sample space, event, fair/unbiased, probability of an event occurring, mutually exclusive events, complements, with replacement, without replacement, factorials, tree diagrams, independent events, dependent events, permutation, combination, uniform probability models, experimental probability

Properties of Probability

Theorems: Addition Counting Principle
Probability of the Union of Mutually Exclusive Events
Probability of Union
Probability of Complements
Multiplication Principle
Selection With Replacement
Selection Without Replacement
Permutation Theorem (Formula)
Combination Theorem (Formula)

Courtesy of Heather Wineberg.

Skills to Be Strengthened or Gained

Strengthened: Communication skills, writing skills, reading mathematics skills, fraction skills, problem-solving skills, computer skills, calculator skills, experimental skills

Gained: Computation of probabilities using the theorems and concepts we learn, computations of permutations and combinations, applications of probability to real life and math, compute factorials

Attitudes and Appreciations:

1. Foster an appreciation for probability theory.
2. Foster an appreciation for counting theory.
3. Foster an appreciation for applied mathematics.
4. Foster an attitude that math can be applicable to real life.
5. Foster an attitude that math does not always model the certain.

Introductory Experiences

Large group:

1. Bring in the *Charlotte Observer* and have students guess where some examples of probability would be. Show them some examples of probability like weather forecasting.
2. Bring in cards. Find the probability of drawing a spade. An ace. A spade and an ace.
3. Use sports statistics from the school. Based on last week's stats, which I would get from the newspaper, what's the probability (or relative frequency) that Scott Lilly (one of my basketball students) will make his free-throws at the next game?
4. Play "Let's Make a Deal." Determine when you should switch doors. Reference: *Functions, Statistics, and Trigonometry,* teacher's edition, 1992, Scott Foresman.
5. Solve the "Birthday Problem." Reference: *Functions, Statistics, and Trigonometry,* 1992, Scott Foresman.
6. Have people stand up if they're in a certain category. For instance, what's the probability in our classroom that someone has blond hair and blue eyes? Brown hair or brown eyes?
7. Find a ranking of the highest paid, lowest stressed jobs. Actuarial Sciences is high on the list. What is that?
8. Show how insurance companies use probability to make insurance premiums.
9. Play dice games. Figure out the probability of rolling a 6. Figure out probability of rolling a 4 on the first die and a sum of 6.
10. Have a class lottery where the winner receives a homework pass. Determine the probability that a boy will be chosen, a girl will be chosen, someone with blond hair, or someone with brown hair.
11. Have a guest speaker come from the weather station to speak about predicting the uncertain weather.

Small groups:

1. Have students conduct their own experiments to find the probability of getting heads on a coin or of picking an ace from the deck.
2. Give a worksheet that will review/teach ratios and percentages leading up into probability in which the groups all attempt to get the correct responses.

The groups will not be able to move on to the next step until these worksheets are perfect.

3. Have each group research a different aspect of Fermat or Pascal's life. Prepare a skit about the aspect they researched.
4. Have each group develop a game show that has some degree of uncertainty. They may not know how to solve the probability of winning at this stage but hopefully by the end of the unit they will be able to see the probability of winning. We will play the game later in the unit. (Examples may be their own Price Is Right, Wheel of Fortune.)
5. Have each group make up a survey about different aspects of the school and collect data. For example, one group could survey hair color at the high school, and another could survey feet size. We will take predictions about what the probability of an event is, and by the end of the unit, we will compile the data for the real probability.
6. Have each group of students combine to make up an insurance policy for a certain client. Each group will defend why they chose the insurance premiums they charged.
7. Give each group a portion of statistics to compute (a sports summary from last night's basketball game, the president's race). See which group comes the closest to the correct answers without formalized instruction.
8. Give each group the "Let's Make a Deal" problem. Have them reach a decision about whether or not to change doors and support why they made that decision in front of the class.
9. Have each group determine an example of probability in real life they will explore. For example, a group can choose gambling, weather forecasting, insurance, or lotteries. The group will do a presentation on the aspects of the example that they think involve probability. After the presentation, the group will be responsible for finding out particular statistics for the topic they chose, which we will use in class throughout the unit.
10. Have each group come up with a certain situation that would be a harmful effect of trying to model uncertainty. We will then discuss these with the whole class. An example might be we know too much about the weather and we fear things that people before had no reason to fear.

Individuals:

1. Complete a worksheet reviewing/teaching ratios and percentages that will gear one up for probability.
2. Give each student a penny. Have them conduct an experiment about the probability of flipping a head. Then we will compare with the rest of the class.
3. Find a newspaper, magazine, or journal, and look up three different examples of probability. Write a paragraph on each about how they affect the lives we live.
4. Think of 5 different examples of probability in real life today. Write a short essay (1–2 pages) about why you think it's important for us to study probability theories.
5. Research one specific aspect of Fermat or Pascal's lives, and design a poster to symbolize what you have learned.
6. Have individuals pretend they are actuaries and give them clients with different situations. Have them decide on an insurance premium for the client and write a paragraph about why the student charged them as she did.
7. Talk to an older friend (as in a grandparent, parent, guardian, etc.) and ask them how people knew what the weather was going to be like for the next

week when he was little. Ask if he knew what tools were used to predict the weather. Students may tape the interview (on video or cassette) or write the questions and answers down to show me.

8. Give each student a prequiz to determine their prior knowledge of probability and probability theory.
9. Have each student write a paragraph about how statistics are used in everyday life. They can write about probability but it is not necessary, just make sure to use statistics in the journal.
10. Give each student a superball that you get out of the vending machine. Have each person come up with one experiment that could use uncertainty and modeling mathematics for that superball. For example, what is the likelihood that every superball that the teacher gave out will be red?

Developmental Experiences

Large group:

1. Have people in the class demonstrate the theorems of probability. For instance, to demonstrate the Addition Counting Principle Theorem, have all the people with brown hair stand. Then have all the people with size 8 shoe stand. Finally, have all the people with brown hair *and* size 8 shoes stand.
2. For the visual learners, use Venn diagrams to show why the Addition and Multiplication principles relate to each other and probability.
3. Give the class a word, like PROBABILITY, and have them compute the number of words that can be formed.
4. To show the multiplication principle, have students decorate cookies. Show the total possible types of cookies with toppings of sprinkles, red icing, and green icing.
5. Bring in a bag of marbles or cards to show how different it is to compute selection with replacement and selection without replacement.
6. Have a guest speaker from the weather station come in to talk about predicting the uncertain weather.
7. Compile, as a class, a set of statistics that each person brought in. For example, have every student find out the favorite colors of ten different people and find the probability that blue is people's (at least in our sample space) favorite color.
8. To show that uniform probability does not necessarily look uniform. Present the following problem to the class. Which number is the spinner most likely to land on?

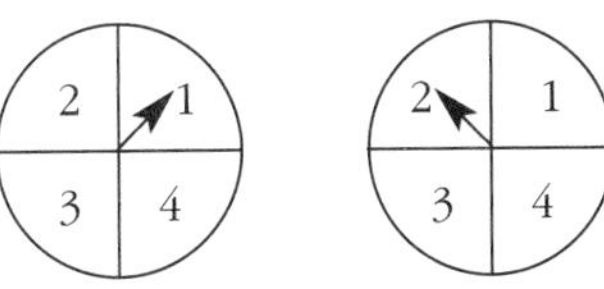

9. To show that probability must be between (0,1) have students write names on a piece of paper and put it into a hat on the table when they walk into the classroom. Ask students to find probability that their name will be chosen out of the hat.
10. Give students a situation in which the possible outcomes is fairly high (like 27). Tell students to find every possible outcome. Hopefully, some of the students will miss a few, so that they will see a need for the Tree Diagram. (Reference: 1.)
11. Show students a few tree diagrams. Have the students try to see the pattern that each one has with the total number of outcomes. This is the multiplication principle.

12. Bring in a guest speaker from a local insurance company to speak on the use of permutations and combinations in the insurance business.
13. Divide class into half. Give half the class two bags that contain 1 red and 1 green marble in each. One marble is chosen from the first bag and one from the second. Give the other half of the class a bag that contains 2 red and 2 green marbles. Two marbles are drawn at random. The first marble is not replaced before the second one is drawn. Show the difference between independent and dependent events.
14. To show difference between combination and permutations: Stress that in a permutation, the order in which the elements are arranged does matter. In a combination, the order doesn't matter. Write the letters *A, B, C* on the board. Have students list all 2-letter permutations on the board, then list all 2-letter combinations on the board. Discuss the reasons that these are different.
15. Plan a field trip to the weather station to see how probability is used there. Look for computer applications.

Small groups:

1. Divide the class into small groups and assign each group an experiment such as the following: roll a number cube; flip a coin; pick a card at random numbered 1–10. Have the groups repeat the experiment 60 times, tally the results, and compare the actual results to the expected results. Reference: 1 (see reference section).
2. Divide the class into small groups, give each group two coins of different denominations, and have each group perform the following experiment.
   A. Toss the coins 50 times and complete the table.

	HH	HT	TH	TT
Penny				
Nickel				

   B. Make a bar graph to display the results.
   C. Were the results expected? Explain.
   D. If you tossed the coins 100 times, would the results be closer to what you expected? Explain. Reference: 1.
3. Divide the class into small groups and give half of the groups two bags that each contain 1 red and 1 green marble. One marble is chosen at random from the first bag and one from the second. Give the other half of the groups one bag that contains 2 red and 2 green marbles. Two marbles are drawn at random. The first marble is not replaced before the second one is drawn. Have groups compute the probability of drawing a red marble, then a green marble. Have each group explain why the probabilities are different in a presentation to the class. Reference: 1.
4. Divide the class into small groups and have each group perform the paper cup experiment and complete exercises 9–12. Discuss exercises 13 and 14. Reference: 1.
5. Divide the class into small groups and have them cooperatively complete the Group Project Worksheet given in the Teacher's Resource Book from Reference 1. The group project emphasizes the importance of experimental probability.
6. To help students understand the concept of experimental probability, give each student a page from an old phone book. Have students determine the experimental probability that 9 is the last digit of a telephone number is 1/10 using the following steps.

A. Let a be the number of telephone numbers in 1 column. Let b be the number of telephone digits in the column that have 9 as the last digit. What is the value of the ratio b/a?
B. Find the value of the ratio b/a using all the telephone numbers on one side of the page.
C. Find the value of the ratio b/a using all the telephone numbers on both sides of the page.
D. Compare the values of the b/a in steps 1, 2, 3 above to the theoretical probability (1/10). Reference: 2.

7. Divide the class into small groups and have them calculate the probability that n people have n different birthdays for $n = 2, 3, 4$, and k. What is the smallest value of k for which this probability is less than .5? Have each group test their result on a group of people. Tell the whole class their findings in a class presentation. Reference: 3.
8. Divide the class into small groups and give each group a set of 5 books that are each a different color. Arrange them in as many ways as possible. Try to think of a possible pattern/formula for the number of unique arrangements there are.
9. Obtain the rules, entry sheets, and an information sheet for different lotteries. Divide the class into small groups and give each group information about one lottery. Using this information have each group find the probability that you will win first prize with a single entry, and the probability of winning any prize with a single entry. Would you advise someone to buy those lottery tickets? Then have groups trade information. How does the other lottery's probability of winning compare to the original? Have the student groups prepare an assignment that shows the data of their work and a summary about their conclusions. Reference: 3.
10. To help students learn to read mathematics as well as learn probability, break class into small groups. Give each group a topic to research on probability. Each group will give a classroom presentation on their section, including visual aids.
11. Divide the class into small groups and have each group develop a game show that is dependent upon uniform probability. They will tape an initial episode on video-camera (during class) and write up a summary of the mathematical concepts they used.
12. Divide the class into groups and give them the "Let's Make a Deal" problem. Have them reach a decision about whether or not they would change doors. Show the probability theory behind their decision in a class presentation.
13. Divide the class into small groups and give them a list of ten different events. Have them confer to see if the groups are independent or dependent events (on each other). In either condition, find the probability of both of them occurring at the same time. Each member will be responsible for reporting for the group on each probability they determine.
14. Have each group look up the terms *independent, dependent, uniform*, and *probability* in the dictionary. Have them write a paragraph about how the definitions in the dictionary relate to the mathematical definition.
15. Give each group a situation in which the sample space needed to compute the probability is fairly large. See if they can find a pattern to computing a large sample space. (Multiplication Principle)

Individuals:

1. Calculator Activity from the Teacher's Resource Book. Reference: 1. This focuses on factorials.
2. Problem Solving Activity from the Teacher's Resource Book. Reference: 1. This focuses on making an organization list.

3. Estimation Activity, "Using Probability to Estimate," from the Teacher's Resource Book. Reference: 1.
4. Alternate Quizzes from the Teacher's Resource Book. Reference: 1.
5. Practice Masters Worksheets from the Teacher's Resource Book. Reference: 1.
6. Give each individual a newspaper article with a statistic contained in it. They are to find out who conducted the research, what the sample space was, and what type of counting principle did the research use?
7. Have each student make an organized list to solve this problem. How many positive odd whole numbers less than 1,000 can be formed using the digits 0, 1, 2, 3, if no repetitions are allowed?
8. Have each student perform an experiment using coins, cards, or dice. Have them perform the experiment 25 times. What is the experimental probability? What is the real probability? Explain why there is (or may be) a discrepancy between the two in a short 1/2-page paragraph.
9. Have each student complete an Enrichment Activity Worksheet in Resource book of Reference 2. This activity focuses on permutations and combinations.
10. Problem Solving Activity in Resource book of Reference 2. This activity focuses on Tree Diagrams.
11. Computer Activity in Resource book of Reference 2. This activity focuses on computerized probability.
12. Have each student interview a person whose career includes using probability. The student will submit their questions and responses to the teacher.
13. Have the student make a poster that represents an application of probability in the real world and present it to the class or to a small group.
14. Have each student read the next section in the text and do the exercises that I assign. If they don't understand the section, they must write what questions they have over the reading to address in class.
15. Have each student look up the terms *independent* and *dependent* in the dictionary. Have them write a paragraph about how the definitions in the dictionary relate to the mathematical definition.

Integrating Experiences

Large group:

1. Bring in a guest speaker from the weather station to tell students about how he uses probability in weather forecasting.
2. Bring in a guest speaker from Adidas who is a market researcher to show students how probability can be used in the work force.
3. Bring in an actuary from a local insurance company. Let her speak to the students about her job and how probability relates to it.
4. Compare the predictions that we made from our introductory experience about the sports to what actually happened. How far are the predictions off? Why do you think this is so?
5. Discuss with the class the dangers of trying to predict what will happen in the future. Does this affect why we should or shouldn't study probability?
6. As a class, make a outline of the topics that were covered in the unit. This will serve as the review for the test.
7. Play Jeopardy with problems, definitions, and theorems in the unit.
8. Have board races to try to figure out different probabilities the quickest and the most accurately.

9. Discuss the upcoming uses that probability will have in their mathematics careers such as in the Binomial Theorem.
10. Have them decorate cookies. They can each decorate one if they, as a class, can find the probability of each situation.

Small groups:

1. Divide the class into small groups and have each group develop a test over the unit on probability. Each group will take the other group's tests to help prepare for the unit test.
2. Each small group will think of and research a career that deals with probability. Each group will prepare a class presentation about how the career-person uses probability that we have covered, what some interesting aspects about the career is in general, and why they chose that career. Each individual should be involved. Visual aids are a must.
3. Each small group will develop a crossword puzzle with directions that uses the vocab that we have learned throughout the unit.
4. Give each group of students a section of the newspaper that has some sort of statistics in it. Have them research those statistics to see if they are accurate. They will present their findings to the class in a presentation.
5. Have each group use the games that they made up during the introductory experiences to compute the actual probability of winning. Compare this actual probability with what they thought it was when they made up the game. Were the two close? Explain the reasons.
6. Have each group compile a list of 10 different applications for probability. Find an example of each of these applications and prepare a short presentation to perform in front of the class.
7. Have each group investigate the following situation: If r and s are numbers between 0 and 9 inclusive, what is the probability P that the function $f(x) = x^2 + rx + s$ has real roots? See Reference 3.
8. Have each group pick a type of insurance. Find out all the variables that affect the premiums you would have to pay if you wanted this type of insurance and what it would cost you to obtain such insurance. Have each group do a presentation on what they find out about insurance. Show how probability and statistics have a lot do with what these premiums are.
9. Have each group develop an outline of the unit highlighting the most important terms, theorems, and problems. This will serve as a review for the final test.
10. Give each group an application of probability that deals with algebra. For example, give them a worksheet where they are shown how combinations are used to find coefficients of binomial expansions. Each group will explain how this relates to what we have been studying and present it to the class.
11. Problem Solving Application for small groups: Space Message Error Codes. Reference: 4.

Individuals:

1. Have a student interview a person whose career has something to do with probability or modeling uncertainty. Demonstrate how the concepts that we learned in class affect them each day.
2. Have a student call an insurance agency and find out all of the variables that affect the premiums. Have the student write a summary of how the information that they learned in the last unit can help them understand the insurance business.
3. Have each individual outline the unit highlighting the most important terms, theorems, and problems. This will serve as a review for the final test.

4. Have students put their knowledge of computers and collection of data to use and learn to use a database. Reference: 1.
5. Have each individual make up a test that will serve as a review sheet for them.
6. Complete the Chapter Review in Reference: 1.
7. Have each individual write an essay that summarizes the most important elements of the unit. This will help the student learn to write mathematics as well as compute.
8. Give each student a worksheet on expanding binomials. The next unit will include the Binomial Theorem, which includes combinations and binomials.
9. Have each student write a story that includes real statistics, some probability, and a plot that helps them put everything together.
10. Have each student make up a puzzle using the definitions, theorems, and problems from this unit.

Evaluation

1. Did the students perform up to the prescribed expectations that I set for them in my objectives?
2. Have the students fill out an evaluation form that evaluates how well they enjoyed the unit in comparison to others.
3. Have the students fill out a form that asks them to tell which activities were the best, the worst, the most informative, and the least informative.
4. Have an observer come in to observe lessons.
5. Look to see which lessons went really well and what examples went well and mark it down. Write down as well things that didn't go over really well for that class.
6. Look at the competency scores of the students at the end of the year.
7. Look at the test scores to see if the tests reflected the amount of knowledge the student wanted to convey.
8. Review the test to see if there were any questions that could have been better worded and see if the test achieved its goal of emphasizing the objectives.

References

1. Cohen, M. P. (1992). *Applications of high school mathematics* (teacher's ed.). Boston: Houghton Mifflin.
2. Dolcani, M. P., Sorgenfrey, R. H., & Graham, J. A. (1992). *Mathematics structure and method* (teacher's ed.). Boston: Houghton Mifflin.
3. Rubenstein, R. N. (1992). *Functions, statistics, and trigonometry*. Glenview, IL: Scott Foresman.
4. Smith, S. A. (1992). *Algebra and trigonometry* (teacher's ed.). Menlo Park, CA: Addison-Wesley.

APPENDIX 6C Lesson Plan

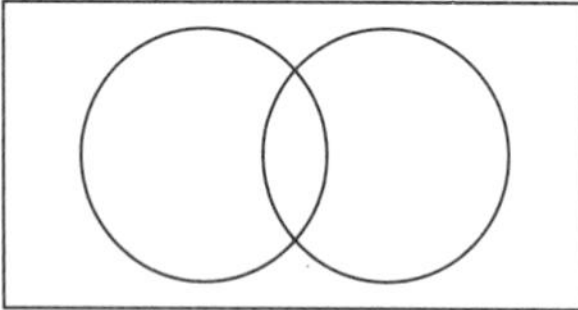

§7.2 Unit: Probability

Focus and Review:

F: Definition of probability of an event

R: Unions and intersections: Unions (A ∪ B); contain elements of A *or* B, not both. (A ∪ B) = (A or B) Intersections (A ∩ B); contain elements of A *and* B. Have a student come up and show each.

Courtesy of Heather Wineberg.

Objective:

Each student will be able to identify mutually exclusive events. Each student will know and be able to apply the addition counting principle and the Theorem of Probability of Union.

Teacher Instruction

- Mutually exclusive: tell them it means *disjoint*.
- Can someone come up and show 2 mutually exclusive sets?
- How about mutually exclusive probability events?
- How do you think we join two mutually exclusive sets together? We want all the elements in one new set (Union).
- Therefore, the Addition Counting Principle: $N(A \cup B) = N(A) + N(B)$
- What about $P(A \cup B)$? $P(A \cup B) = P(A) + P(B)$ for mutually exclusive events.
- Now what about events that are not mutually exclusive?
- Do you think that it would be the same as before?
- Let's do an experiment in our class. Stand up if something I say pertains to you:

  P (Girl) =
  P (Boy) =
  P (Girl or Boy) = P (G) + P (B)

  P (Girl) =
  P (Brown Hair) =
  P (Girl or Brown Hair) = $P(G) + P(Br) - P(G \cap Br)$

General form of Probability of Union: $P(A \cup B) = P(A) + P(B) - P(A \cap B)$
Why do you think we call this general?
What do you think is the Probability of Intersection?

Guided Practice

A pair of dice is thrown. What is P (double or sum over 7)?

P (doubles) = 6/36

P (sum over 7) = 15/36

P (double and sum over 7) = 3/36

$P(D \cup S7) = 6/36 + 15/36 - 3/36$

§7.2 10–20 even, 24 challenge

Closure

Ask students for what we did—Mutually exclusive terms, Addition Counting Principle, Probability of Union

Test #1 on §7.2 Name:____________________

1. State the Theorem of Probability of Union given mutually exclusive events C and D.

2. **Forecast for Tomorrow**

	Wind speed (MPH)		
	Less than 10	*10–30*	*≥30*
Sunny	.30	.16	.08
Partly cloudy	.14	.08	.06
Overcast	.09	.06	.03

   a. What is the Probability that opening day will be sunny?

   b. What is the Probability that wind speed will be 30 MPH or greater?

   c. What is the Probability that the weather will be overcast *or* the wind speed will be over 30 MPH?

   d. What is the Probability that the weather will be overcast and partly cloudy?

3. In math, when we use *or,* we call it the "inclusive" or. In the realm of what we learned in the previous section, how do you think that P (overcast or wind speed <30 MPH) is inclusive? (*Hint:* Think of the Venn diagrams.)

Courtesy of Heather Wineberg.

7

The Art of Effective Teaching

I used to hate math. I've never made good grades and just don't seem to get it. But this year I have Mr. Howard. He's great! I don't know exactly what he does, but he has a way of helping me to understand everything. My grades are up and I can't wait to get to his class every day. He's fun to talk to and always has really neat things for us. Everyone I know wants him for their teacher.

High school junior

Teachers are artists and their medium is the most precious of all. They work with human beings. The master potter pays careful attention to details as he throws a pot, blending his skills with patience and care to shape a masterpiece. Each creation is unique. Similarly, teachers pay attention to the details of their craft, using all of their artistic talent with patience and care to shape their students.

Effective teaching has a mysterious quality. A student learns and becomes enthusiastic when several factors combine at the right time and in the right way. These factors vary from person to person. For one student, it may be a genuine regard for the teacher; for another, a desire for grades for college admission. The master teacher understands the science of learning but is sensitive to its art as well. She may sense what is needed, even if she cannot name it. When the student doesn't learn, has the teacher taught or just presented information? As important as a carefully planned lesson is, it is meaningless if other elements aren't present to ensure that real learning takes place. These other elements are what put the magic into your teaching.

Remember that *how* you teach is as important as *what* you teach. Your style speaks volumes to students about how you feel about them, your subject, your job, and yourself. As knowledgeable as you are about content, knowledge alone will not guarantee an instructional experience that is conducive for all of your students to learn. The art of teaching involves sensitivity to many factors that affect how your students will respond to your class. This chapter addresses some of these factors. They include your teaching style and its effect on different students, your ability to motivate individuals, and a positive climate in the classroom.

Your Teaching Style and Your Students' Learning Styles: How Do Differences in These Affect Student Learning?

When you were a teenager, how did you learn to drive a car? Did you take drivers' education in school and study the booklet, take tests, watch videos? Did you listen to a parent describe what to do? Did you practice in a parking lot? More than likely, you did all of these things. Would you have learned to drive anyway just by observing others? Probably not.

Learning and Teaching Styles

Think of the last time you tried to learn something in school. How did you do it? Were you able to understand the information by reading about it? Did you need to see it illustrated? Did you learn best in conversation with other students? Did you have to apply information to real life? Do you need to do all of these things? Your response is an indicator of your *learning style*, that is, how you tend to learn. Likewise, your students have their own personal learning styles. And, at the same time, their learning styles are greatly affected by your teaching style. Research shows that assessing both the learning styles of your students and your teaching style will help you to adapt your instruction to teach *all* of your students more effectively (Doolan & Honigsfeld, 2000).

The Learning Styles of Your Students

Albert A. Canfield's work (1988) is one example of research that can be very helpful as you try to understand the learning styles of your students. He developed an inventory that reveals the particular learning style of each test taker. He identified nine categories of learner types:

1. Social—students who prefer interacting with peers and instructors, having no strong preference for either applied or conceptual approaches. They like instruction involving small groups and teamwork.

2. Independent—students who prefer to work alone, having no strong preference for either applied or conceptual approaches. They respond well to analysis of case studies or self-selected and self-paced programs.

3. Applied—students who like activities directly related to real-world experience, having no strong preference for either social or independent approaches. They like instruction that involves practicums, site visits, team labs, and so forth.

4. Conceptual—students who like to work in highly organized language-oriented materials, having no preference for either social or independent approaches. They respond well to instruction that involves lectures and reading.

5. Social/Applied—students who like to have opportunities to interact with other students and instructors in activities that relate to real-world experiences. They like instruction that involves role playing, group problem solving, and supervised practicums.

6. Social/Conceptual—students who like to interact with students and instructors using highly organized language-oriented materials. Effective instruction involves a balance of lecture and discussion.

7. Independent/Applied—students who prefer to work alone toward individual goals in activities closely related to real-world experiences. They respond well to instruction that involves labs or unsupervised technical practicums.

8. Independent/Conceptual—students who prefer to work alone toward individual goals with highly organized language-oriented materials. They like instruction that allows for independent reading and literature searches.

9. Neutral preference—students who tend to have no clear areas of strong preference. They may be comfortable in any other type but may also find it difficult to become completely involved.

You can see from Figure 7.1 how the learning styles relate to each other. Note how far apart certain types are from one another (Applied and Conceptual), and how close others are (Social and Social/Applied). You will have classes that seem to be made up of different groups. For example, in your second-period class, you might see a predominance of Independent/Conceptual learners at one end of the spectrum and a group of Social/Applied on the other. Just what you need—planning one lesson for social butterflies who want hands-on activities on one side of the room and bookworms who want to work alone on projects on the other. Then, in third period, you have an entirely different dilemma. The students throughout your day represent most, if not all, of the learning styles described by Canfield. You have your work cut out for you (see Activity 7.1).

SA Social/Applied	S Social	SC Social/Conceptual
A Applied	N Neutral Preference	C Conceptual
IA Independent/Applied	I Independent	IC Independent/Conceptual

FIGURE 7.1 Learner Typology

Material from the Learning Styles Inventory, by Albert A. Canfield, Ph.D., copyright © 1988 by Western Psychological Services. Reprinted by Prentice Hall by permission of the publisher, Western Psychological Services, 12031 Wilshire Boulevard, Los Angeles, California, 90025, U.S.A.

Determining the Learning Styles of Your Students

Select one of your classes. Administer the Canfield Learning Styles Inventory (LSI) to them. Chart their profiles and consider activities for your next unit that will be most beneficial for your class. List an alternate activity for students who might require a different activity. The LSI is available from:

Western Psychological Services
12031 Wilshire Boulevard
Los Angeles, California 90025

Even if you don't want to administer the complete inventory, you can get a sense of which of the learner types your students represent in two ways. First, watch them. Observe how they respond and perform in certain types of activities. The brief descriptions should give you some ideas. For example, if you are teaching your geometry students to do proofs, try three or four methods. Perhaps some of your students will respond well to verbal explanation (Conceptual). Others may benefit from working the proofs in small groups (Social). Still others may like an explanation by the teacher and a discussion of the proof (Social/Conceptual).

Your Teaching Style: How Does Your Manner Affect Student Learning?

You suffered from them—teachers who know their subject but can't get it across to their students. There may be many reasons for this but often it is because their teaching style simply didn't work. It wasn't compatible with the learning styles of their students. You come to your classroom with a personality, a temperament, and attitudes about what good teaching is, based on your own experience as a student. Teachers usually teach as they were taught. If taking pages of notes from a daily lecture was the predominant method that you were exposed to as a student, more than likely you will think that is the way you should teach also.

Determining Your Teaching Style

As in the case of determining a preferred learning style for students, Albert Canfield and Judith Canfield (1988) developed an Instructional Styles Inventory (ISI) for teachers. They proposed the same typologies as those for learners (see Activity 7.2).

1. Social—teachers who like to see students interacting with each other and teachers interacting with the students. They are less likely to use learning methods that require solitary or self-directed activity and tend to use group discussions and teamwork in their lesson planning.

2. Independent—teachers who prefer for students to work alone toward individual goals. They tend to be less willing to allow social interaction than most teachers. They like case study analysis and developing self-paced programs that match their own interest.

3. Applied—teachers who like for students to be engaged in activities that relate to the real world and everyday experiences. They have little use for lectures and reading. Instruction usually involves site visits, team labs, practicums.

4. Conceptual—teachers who like highly organized, language-oriented materials. Methods usually include lectures and reading.

5. Social/Applied—teachers who like for students and the instructor to interact in activities related to the real world. They like role playing, group problem solving, and supervised internships.

6. Social/Conceptual—teachers who like activities that involve student interaction and use language-oriented materials. They prefer lessons involving a balance of lecture and discussion.

7. Independent/Applied—teachers who prefer for students to work alone toward individual goals using materials that are closely related to the real-world experience. Activities involve individual labs or less supervised technical practicums.

8. Independent/Conceptual—teachers who create opportunities for students to work alone toward individual goals using organized language-oriented materials. They tend to emphasize independent reading and library work.

9. Neutral preference—teachers who have no strong preference. They may find it easy to shift and adapt instruction to suit the needs of a given set of students or material. On the other hand, no preference may indicate some degree of detachment, making it hard to generate enthusiasm and to motivate students.

You probably already have a good idea of what your style is. But you also should recognize the potential advantages of expanding your approaches to meet the learning needs of students who do not share your style.

The most valuable information for most teachers is the comparison between their instructor types and the learning types of their students. If you were to determine the predominant learning styles for any one group and you knew your instructional style, implications for adjusting your teaching should become clear.

Look at Example A in Figure 7.2, which compares the teacher to one student. You can see that the teacher is Independent/Conceptual (someone who may like to assign individual work that requires much reading), while the student has the completely opposite style (Social/Applied). The student likes activities that include working with others and seeing the connections to the real world. You can see the potential problem. This teacher will be unsuccessful with this student unless he or she modifies the teaching approach.

Example B illustrates how complicated things can become when you examine the learning styles of an entire class. The teacher has an Independent/Conceptual style, the style of only five of the students. Clearly, instructional modifications must be made on a regular basis to accommodate everyone else. There are several things the teacher may want to do. First, he must pay attention to the fact that most of the class is made up of social or applied learners. Therefore, he must plan activities that will appeal to their natural predispositions (group work, discussions, etc.). He might also team with another teacher who is a social or applied instructor type.

As you watch your students, you will see what they respond to and what doesn't work. Consider what teaching style you are most comfortable with. You know right now

Activity 7.2

Determining Your Instructional Style

Take Canfield's ISI to get a clearer picture of your most natural teaching style. Read carefully the descriptions of the instructor types. Make notes based on observations of your students as well as what you may have learned if you administered the LSI to them. It's probably not realistic to think that you can go from one extreme to the other on the Typology Grid (see Figure 7.1). Focus on the types that are close to your style as you begin to expand your comfort with new approaches. List activities you need to include to reach more of your students.

Example A
Example Typology Grid
(Instructor to Individual Learner)

Social/ Applied L	Social	Social/ Conceptual
Applied	Neutral	Conceptual
Independent/ Applied	Independent	Independent/ Conceptual I

Example B
Example Typology Grid
(Instructor to Learner Group)

Social/ Applied 9	Social 8	Social/ Conceptual 3
Applied 4	Neutral 2	Conceptual 2
Independent/ Applied 10	Independent 6	Independent/ Conceptual I 5

FIGURE 7.2 Example Typology Grids

Material from the Instructional Styles Inventory, by Albert A. Canfield, Ph.D. and Judith S. Canfield, Ed.D., copyright © 1976 by Judith S. Canfield and Albert A. Canfield, copyright © 1988 by Western Psychological Services. Reprinted by Prentice Hall by permission of the publisher, Western Psychological Services, 12031 Wilshire Boulevard, Los Angeles, California, 90025, U.S.A. Not to be reprinted in whole or in part for any additional purpose without the expressed, written permission of the publisher. All rights reserved.

REALITY CHECK 7.1

Most, especially beginning, teachers plan the same one-size-fits-all lecture for every class. They then wonder why second period is so good and third period is so uncooperative. "I don't get it. I have the exact same lesson plan and my third-period kids just don't respond," complained Mr. Javettes. It might be that second period as a whole is more responsive to his predictable daily lecture format (Conceptual) and third period tends to have more students who are Social learners. If you're thinking that you don't have time to create five different plans, you don't have to. *Just modify one plan.* Once you've outlined thoroughly and planned the content for one class, it's not difficult to adapt its delivery for other groups. You owe this effort to your students.

REALITY CHECK 7.2

You are not going to be able to have a perfect match of activity type and learner type for many—if any—of your classes. The exception would be if you have a small group and the students happen to have similar styles, but this is rare. The Canfield Inventory is just one guide—there are many others. The point is for you to be aware of the fact that your students actually have different learning styles and to make thoughtful decisions regarding the best instruction for them.

that you are only one person. You can't have the perfect activity for each person in the class at the same time. So you must plan for the majority of the group, knowing that you will provide enough variety during the entire course to match almost everyone's learning style at some point.

Accommodating Different Learning Styles

Obviously, for your students to really learn something, several methods need to be used. If you are like most people, you have tendencies toward more than one of the types yourself. Stretch your own abilities by focusing deliberately on their learning styles on a regular basis. You aren't expected to be proficient with every one. In fact, some research suggests that while universal proficiency might be appealing, it is simply impossible to provide instruction with all of them successfully (Dillon, 1998). *However, remember that using styles other than traditional lecture results in significantly higher recall for many students* (Searson & Dunn, 2001).

One of the most helpful things you will gain from having developed a complete unit (chapter 6) is that you have already considered many types of activities from which you can choose. Now go to the list of activities you have created and select the best ones based on what you discovered about the learning styles of your students. You already know that some are visual learners and must see what you are talking about. Others are auditory learners who can get it from hearing you discuss material. Some need more practice than others. Therefore, it is important that you (a) adjust your teaching strategies for different students, (b) vary your teaching enough so that every student finds a learning situation that is compatible with his or her learning style at least some of the time, and (c) help students expand their comfort level with a variety of learning styles to increase their success in a variety of situations (Clark & Starr, 1996).

Adapting Instruction: How Do You Move from Teaching Subjects to Teaching Students?

Three Approaches to Teaching

Before reading this section, complete Activity 7.3.

So where did you land? In one group? In more than one? Was it hard to decide? If so, you are not alone.

ACTIVITY 7.3

Some Clues About Your Teaching Approach

Directions: Check each of the following statements in the three groups that you believe apply to you. When you have finished, which group appears to best represent your general approach to teaching?

Group 1

______ 1. I make lists of what I want to do each day with my students.
______ 2. I like objective measures of my students' achievement.
______ 3. I stay on top of the content and current methodology of my field and incorporate that content into my coursework.
______ 4. My students do well on end-of-course tests.
______ 5. I feel stressed if I am unable to get the required material covered.

Group 2

______ 1. If forced to choose, I would worry about my students' personal development more than their academic achievement.
______ 2. My students tend to come to me often with their personal problems.
______ 3. I always make time to come to after-school functions that involve my students.
______ 4. I make my assignments relevant to the personal lives of my students.
______ 5. I see my role as a friend as well as a teacher.

Group 3

______ 1. I don't want my students' minds to be locked into too much prescribed content.
______ 2. I see my role as one who should encourage students to "break out of the box" when they are solving problems.
______ 3. I feel a need to raise the consciousness of my students about themselves and the world.
______ 4. I see much of what the content I am expected to cover as irrelevant to their "real" education.
______ 5. I see time in my class as an opportunity to prepare students for life.

In addition to your instructional style, you will want to consider your *approach* to teaching. How you view your role and the process of instruction will strongly influence your teaching style. Fenstermacher and Soltis (1998) identified three basic approaches to teaching that will be useful to review.

The *executive approach* (Group 1) typifies the teacher who wants to get things done. This person feels responsible for making sure certain concepts are learned using the best methods available. Good curriculum materials are critical to this approach because they provide a guide that will result in maximum learning. These teachers make use of every minute, planning as much as possible for each lesson. There is a high premium on student achievement. Critics of the approach describe the teacher as sort of a production-line manager, regulating the content. The approach stresses time-on-task, performance, and results at the expense of other priorities such as the needs and interests of the students. However, its value is that it provides a clear, straightforward way to get students to learn material. It increases the probability that the students will learn more content.

The *therapist approach* (Group 2) sees the teacher as an empathetic person whose primary task is to help students grow. This view is based on psychotherapy, humanist psychology, and existential philosophy. All of these focus on the students' development as authentic people through meaningful educational experiences. To the teacher using this approach, "filling the student's head with specified knowledge that has been packaged, selected and conveyed by others only keeps the student from understanding himself as a human being. It separates the student from himself as a person by forcing him to attend, not with his own feelings, thoughts, and ideas, but to the sterile thoughts, images and attitudes of others" (Fenstermacher & Soltis, 1998, p. 27). Critics think that these teachers concern themselves too much with the touchy-feely aspects of teaching, at the expense of real learning. However, the best use of the approach is to incorporate what you know about students as people into the teaching of content, making a special effort to focus on relevance to their lives.

The *liberationist approach* (Group 3) views the teacher as a liberator, someone who frees the individual's mind and helps to develop a well-rounded, rational, and moral person.

> The "manner" of the teacher is critical to the liberationist approach, for it determines, in large measure, whether the knowledge and skill to be learned will free the mind or simply trap it with dull and irrelevant facts and skills. In addition to studying the appropriate forms of knowledge as determined by the teacher, the liberationist places emphasis on how the forms should be taught. The aim of educational liberationists is to raise critical consciousness. The liberationist approach is rooted in philosophy—not psychology. It reflects the notion of the liberally educated student—study that makes a student well-rounded and prepares a student for life.
>
> (Fenstermacher & Soltis, 1998, pp. 16–50)

REALITY CHECK 7.3

Reviewing instructor types and teaching approaches is not an attempt to get you to box yourself into some astrological sign of teaching. ("What's your sign? Conceptual or Applied?") Hopefully, you will see yourself in some of the descriptions and make note of ones that you don't relate to. Remember that your students as a group will need a bit of all of them. The extent to which you can expand your styles and approaches will ensure your ability to teach more of your students more effectively more of the time.

Combining these approaches in a flexible, creative way is rooted in the science of learning and central to the art of teaching.

There is value in being aware of such approaches. The goal is not to choose one and decide that this is the way to teach. Instead, awareness of all provides an opportunity for you to reflect on a variety of ways to think about your approach, to be more intentional about how you go about the process of teaching, and to look for opportunities to use different approaches as the situation merits.

Multiple Intelligences

Harvard psychologist Howard Gardner has expanded what was traditionally accepted regarding how people learn. For years, educators have placed a disproportionate emphasis on a child's I.Q. and his reading and mathematics abilities. While other subjects were included in the curriculum, they were not viewed as important basic skills. Instead, Gardner proposed the existence of eight intelligences, all having equal value, to broaden how we define human potential (Armstrong, 1994; Gardner, 1993). While learning styles are concerned with differences in the learning process, the concept of multiple intelligences centers on learning content and products (Silver, Strong, & Perini, 1997). The eight intelligences are:

1. Linguistic intelligence—the capacity to use words effectively orally (such as storyteller, politician) or in writing (poet, journalist)
2. Logical-mathematical intelligence—the capacity to use numbers effectively (statistician, scientist)
3. Spatial intelligence—the ability to perceive the visual–spatial world accurately and creatively (architect, artist)
4. Bodily kinesthetic intelligence—expertise in using the whole body to express ideas (actor, athlete, dancer)
5. Musical intelligence—the capacity to perceive and express music (music critic, music performer)
6. Interpersonal intelligence—the capacity to perceive and make sense of the moods and feelings of others
7. Intrapersonal intelligence—the capacity to understand oneself
8. Naturalist intelligence—capacity to understand nature

Gardner stressed that the first point teachers need to remember about his theory is that each person has all eight intelligences and that most people can develop each one to an adequate level of competency. The intelligences also usually work together in complex ways. For example, to plan a vacation, one must read a map (linguistic), determine distances (logical-mathematical), and decide on activities to satisfy members of the family (interpersonal and perhaps bodily kinesthetic or musical). There are also many ways to be intelligent within each category. A student may not be able to read well but he can tell a great story. Understanding the importance of all of the intelligences and being able to identify them in your students will enable you to determine learning activities that will be more effective and engaging. Blending what you know about learning styles with Gardner's theory will result in a more enlightened approach to teaching.

Teaching Diverse Students

The increasingly diverse nature of today's classrooms means that you will need to be a teacher with a multicultural perspective. This means that you must understand that culture, ethnicity, race, gender, religion, socioeconomic status, and exceptionality are powerful variables acting in complex ways in the communication and learning process of your students. Being aware of cultural differences will make you more successful in helping students who are influenced by different cultural norms and rules (Davidman & Davidman, 1997). This does not mean that you celebrate Black History Month in February and ignore the contributions of African Americans the rest of the year. Rather, you must look for ways to infuse cross-cultural studies and experiences into your everyday teaching.

Having and exhibiting a multicultural perspective should become a part of the fabric of who you are as a teacher. As suggested previously, each day make a concerted effort to look for (a) ways to select content that provides opportunities to explore these connections, (b) experiences that will expand the thinking of all of your students in these matters, and (c) activities that will help them to become more culturally sensitive themselves. Over time, this thinking will become a part of who you are as a teacher and who they are as students.

Reality Check 7.4

You are human. More than likely you will enter your classroom with some stereotypes about the various cultures that exist in your classrooms and how they learn. After all, like your students, you are the product of *your* experiences in school and in life. Are there particular learning styles that tend to be present in certain ethnic groups? Perhaps not. Remember that each of your students is unique. Attitudes that you model as a teacher will do more to help or hinder the development of positive attitudes toward everyone in our society than anything you say or plug into your curriculum.

Differentiating Instruction

You already know that it is impossible to individualize instruction for every student for every lesson for the entire school year. But no matter how daunting such an undertaking is, you should look for opportunities to do so anyway. There are ways of thinking about teaching that will help you to do this more often than you thought possible.

You must begin by viewing your class as a collection of unique individuals, each of whom has specific learning needs different from everyone else in your room. There will be days when you have to teach everyone as a group, days when you believe whole group instruction is the best method. You will have decided that this activity will best meet the needs of the most students in the most efficient way. But replacing whole-group methods occasionally with activities that are based on your understanding of how individuals in the group learn will reap amazing results.

Differentiating instruction (making instruction different) is a philosophy that is based on the idea that teachers should adapt instruction to accommodate student differences. You can do this by keeping in mind their abilities, their varying levels of readiness, their different learning styles, and their preferences and interests.

According to Carol Tomlinson (2000), teachers differentiate their curriculum through content, process, and product. *Content* differentiation refers to when students are given different material to learn. If a student is ahead of the others in terms of his own experience, then he could be given another assignment that will be more appropriate. Teachers differentiate through *process* by compacting the curriculum so that students who already understand certain concepts may move faster through the material. This can be done by having the students test out of certain material they already know. They can then move on to more challenging material better suited for their performance and ability level (Reis, Burns, & Renzulli, 1992). *Product* differentiation refers to allowing students to demonstrate what they have learned through different assessment formats (Wehrmann, 2000). For example, students who have poor reading and writing skills might be allowed to take their tests orally.

Differentiated instruction is not new. Teachers have been individualizing instruction for years in some way and for different purposes. It happens whenever they use learning contracts, projects, or any other form of individualized instruction. The extent to which you will be comfortable using this approach is a direct reflection of how knowledgeable you are about your content, how well you understand your students and their needs, and how comfortable you are implementing a variety of methods. Many high school teachers are notoriously committed to traditional strategies such as lecture on a daily basis. According to one principal, however, "traditional schools are designed for organized left-brain learners who are book lovers. But this type of learner only represents one-quarter of the population" (Rasmussen, 2000 p. 14).

Motivating Students: How Will You Keep Their Interest?

Motivation is the biggest question for educators. If there were a simple answer, there would be no unmotivated students. They would all rush to school each day, anxiously anticipating an opportunity to learn. Unfortunately, this is not the case, so motivation remains a challenge.

Teachers often talk about motivating students. This is, in fact, impossible. *You* cannot motivate another person. Motivation must come from within the student. The teacher's job is to create an educational climate and circumstances that will result in *students* being motivated.

Motivating Secondary Students

Each day, you face groups of adolescents going through the most difficult developmental time in their lives as they struggle to figure out who they are and what they want. They have many things on their minds, and for many, your class may not be a big priority. The art of teaching involves finding ways to engage their motivation.

There's no one answer for what motivates high school students. What motivates one person may not motivate another. It's hard enough to understand the intricate motivational patterns of one person, let alone the many you teach each day. Since motivation is a reflection of individual needs, how are you going to address that with so many students at the same time? You can't. You will have one student who is achievement oriented and works hard. The student beside him is driven by a desire to be popular, spending his energy entertaining the class rather than studying. It won't be easy to hook both, not to mention the other 28 students in the room who have their own motivational drives, during the same 55-minute period.

So how will you get your students motivated? One safe bet is to focus on their favorite subject: themselves and anything that directly affects them. Students want to see the relevance of what they study. Be prepared to answer the age-old question "Why do I need to know this?" Mr. DiMarco tries to put his environmental science lessons in a social context, using economic terms that his students can connect to their own lives in some way. They seem to respond better to this approach than when he limits himself to the curriculum as outlined in the text. He also tries to be enthusiastic about the content at all times, trying to sell some topics that don't have an automatic appeal to his students. Does it always work? Of course not. Despite Mr. DiMarco's best efforts, there are many days when he sees the classic bored expression of some of his students. (You will learn to recognize this—it's usually accompanied by an occasional rolling of the eyes.) Don't assume that students who are not interested in your lesson on *Moby Dick* are not motivated individuals, however. Borich (1988) defined motivation as what energizes or directs a learner's attention, emotions, and activities. If this is true, those students who are not interested in your lesson are most certainly motivated by *something*. Find out what it is and use it to help them learn.

Child (1986, p. 95) said that motivation comprises "internal processes which spur us on to satisfy some need." It will be your job to find some way to redirect the attention of those uninterested students to what you are trying to teach. After all, while many students aren't interested in studying, they are usually interested in learning. Focus your content on something they want to learn, rather than something they need to study (Henson, 1993).

Of course, there is no formula that will result in success with all students. Given what you know about the self-absorbed nature of teenagers, center your thinking on them (their needs and abilities)—not on the content. Remember that they are generally motivated by factors such as (Capel, Leask, & Turner, 1995):

- Achievement (finishing a big project)
- Pleasure (getting a compliment from a teacher)
- Preventing or stopping less pleasant activity (avoiding after-school detention)
- Satisfaction (understanding a complex problem)
- Success (doing well on a test)

Fortunately, there are some positive strategies, such as the ones listed below, that successful high school teachers find helpful in most situations.

1. Involve students in as many aspects of the class as possible—For example, student contracts are often good motivators because they involve an agreement between you and the student about what is to be done and how and by when.

2. Use both intrinsic and extrinsic rewards. Intrinsic motivation comes from within the students—such as desire to understand a concept. Mrs. Leary tries to stimulate the students' curiosity about issues she will be studying by posing an intriguing question at the beginning

of every lesson. The students are immediately engaged. Extrinsic motivation comes from outside the student—such as grades or a privilege for completed work. Mr. Cavanaugh gives extra points for completed homework assignments. Is it a lofty strategy? Not necessarily. But bribery often works.

3. Build the self-esteem of the students. They are fragile during these years. Don't be fooled by a student who saunters into your room without any books and an "I hate history—try to impress me" attitude. He's not as confident as he tries to project. Look for ways to make him feel successful and to feel good about himself and your class by first accepting him as he is and then rewarding positive behavior and sincere effort.

4. Make your lessons interesting, using all that you know about where students are developmentally and their learning styles. As you are organizing the content to be covered, consider the attributes of your students as learners. Ask yourself such questions as "What do I know about this group that will help me to decide what activity to use?" Vary your daily format somewhat. Routine and predictability are fine to a point. But students will get less bored with an occasional surprise.

5. Be enthusiastic. Your excitement will be contagious. Avoid starting a unit with a sigh and a comment such as "This topic isn't my favorite, but we have to cover it anyway." Yes, you know it's true. Teachers say things like this all the time and then wonder why their students aren't engaged in the class.

6. Be lighthearted. Teaching and learning are fun. This is not to say that what you teach and what students learn isn't serious and important business. It is. But your class should be an enjoyable experience. Be relaxed with them. Students aren't drawn to people or situations that are constantly heavy or tense. How often have you heard a teenager tell a teacher or parent to "chill out"?

7. Make your classroom a pleasant environment (Clark & Starr, 1996). Give some thought to what your students see each day as they sit in your room. They look around and notice more than you think about their surroundings. One teacher noticed a student who rarely paid attention staring intently at her as she was teaching. The teacher posed a question, and the girl raised her hand for the first time all year. Gratified that this student was finally interested in something she was saying, the teacher called on her for a response. The girl said, "You have chalk on your dress."

Creating Stimulating Assignments and Activities

Nothing will turn your students off like boring, uninteresting assignments—tasks that feel like busywork. Likewise, few things will motivate your students more than a challenging assignment that captures their imagination. Assignments aren't just homework, given quickly as an afterthought at the end of the period. They should always have a purpose that supports what you want your students to learn—not just something to be handed in for a grade. They should (a) be a direct part of your study, (b) hook students' interest in what you are teaching, (c) help students make connections in terms of what you want them to know, (d) provide practice and application of concepts, (e) represent higher order thinking skills, and (f) provide opportunities for feedback.

When possible, novel and unusual assignments that tap into their natural curiosity are best—the more bizarre the better.

How you give assignments is also key to students' desire to do them. They must first know exactly what you want them to do and how you want it done. Nothing is more frustrating when they get home than to discover that they are unclear about directions. It will inevitably result in numerous excuses for not doing the work at all ("I couldn't find my book," or "I didn't know what you meant by 'summarize the important things'"). Giving the directions in writing will also be helpful to them. They will have something tangible to use as a reference.

Motivating them to do the assignment before they ever leave class is also useful. Setting the stage, giving them ideas about how to pursue a topic, and making sure they know that it is worth doing will encourage them to become engaged immediately. Many will actually look forward to finishing it. Getting them started while you are there to answer questions will eliminate any misunderstandings. Make sure students can proceed on their own. Students don't often complain about a good assignment. On the other hand, assignments they don't understand get labeled as "boring," "busywork," or "stupid."

What are "good" assignments? Basically, they:

- Are worthwhile
- Seem reasonable to students (in terms of the nature of the assignment as well as the length and difficulty)
- Capture their interest
- Are clear
- Have definite guidelines
- Allow for the individual differences of your students
- Reflect the students' abilities to complete them (Clark & Starr, 1996).

REALITY CHECK 7.5

OK. Not *every* assignment will be the epitome of stimulation—nor should it be. Some assignments by their very nature may be a necessary part of your instruction and are critical to students' understanding, but are not the most thrilling for some students. That's fine; don't apologize for them. In fact, an assignment that is drudgery for one student may actually be a pleasure for another. To be safe, aim for variety in your assignments, making them as interesting for a majority of students as possible.

Playing the "Socializing" Card

Recent trends in instruction reflect a fact that most people have known for years—high school students are social beings. Use this fact to your (and their) advantage. The influence of the social context of learning cannot be overemphasized. Some even claim that all higher order thinking evolves only through thinking aloud with another person. "Students become socialized into the talk and practices of different disciplines through interaction with more skilled members of the discipline—i.e. their teacher" (Hogan & Pressley, 1998, p. 1). In this context, *instructional scaffolding* occurs as conversations move students from the things they know to new content in an academic discipline. For example, teachers use instructional scaffolding when they talk individually with students and provide hints and suggestions that will help move them along. The purpose is to encourage students to think for themselves, without exercising too much direction in the process. The goal is for the student to be able to proceed on his or her own (Hogan & Pressley, 1998).

Engaging each student in a one-on-one conversation takes time—time high school teachers don't have. It is a labor-intensive process that is often impossible to do with an entire class at once. However, certain activities, such as group work and individualized projects, provide an opportunity for teachers to do this. The approach is very similar to the *social constructivist* model, which is based on the idea of students developing their own knowledge bases through conversations. Generally, it happens as follows (Hogan & Pressley, 1998):

1. Learners accept the opportunity to learn new information.
2. They restructure the information in ways that make sense to them.
3. They connect new content with previously known content.
4. They converse with the teacher and other students about the content as it becomes internalized.

5. They experiment with the new information with other students, engaging in problem-solving idea formation.
6. They become independent problem solvers.

As you can see, there is a progression from a teacher orientation to a student orientation. At the beginning, as the most knowledgeable, teachers control and guide the activities. They then share this role with the students, allowing them more involvement as they progress. Eventually the students take the lead, ideally accepting the responsibility for their own learning and for further learning that will take place on the topic.

Communicating Effectively: What Will Make Your Conferences Valuable Interactions?

Talking one-on-one with another person is the most direct, personal way to communicate. But how often do teachers make communicating in this way a priority? Not often. Be different. Look for opportunities to talk to your students and their parents individually whenever you can. Most high school teachers will tell you that this kind of interaction rarely occurs unless there is a problem. Therefore, most students and parents often dread a conference with the teacher. Your job is to make such experiences as pleasant, productive, helpful, and nonthreatening as possible.

Conversations with Students

Individual student conferences provide you a special opportunity to work with a student on a particular academic or behavioral situation. A private talk with the teacher is attention that students secretly crave, especially if it is characterized by concern, support, and genuine interest in the student's welfare. It is a golden opportunity to find common ground. Secondary teachers say that they have numerous casual conversations with their students after school, during lunch, and even during class. Sometimes these relate to students' work; other times they are of a social nature. For purpose of discussion here, a "conference" is any interaction with a student that is one-on-one, private, and has a planned purpose. Teachers report that they have relatively few of these during the year.

Make a serious effort to plan conferences with students you think are having academic problems (or behavioral problems discussed in chapter 4). When you meet with the student to discuss his academic progress, set the stage by considering the following:

1. Make sure you have enough time to talk for as long as it takes to address the problem as thoroughly as needed. Students hate to feel rushed. Such an encounter might even be between classes if the topic is one that won't take much time.
2. Be specific and clear about the nature of the problem.
3. Ask the student to express how he or she sees the problem. Give him or her a role as an actor in this conference, not just a listener.
4. Agree on a plan of action for improvement.
5. Follow up with the student in some way.

Students usually appreciate the time you will be taking to help them *if* they think that you care about them and are not just reprimanding them for poor performance. Be sincere and patient, but direct about what needs to occur. Remember: the conference should be a conversation, not a lecture.

Conversations with Parents

When parents get a call to come for a conference at school, they know it's probably not good news. This is especially true of the parents of the students who have had a history of problems in school. Most, however, appreciate knowing what's going on. Conferences can be an incredible help or a disaster—depending on how you handle them.

Often seeing the parent and having the parent see you is the best way to come together to determine how to help the student. The parent has more than likely had some rather creative interpretations from the student about what you are like and what's been going on in your class. This is a good chance to let him or her see a different perspective. It is also an opportunity to show the parent examples of the student's work and explain it. Depending on the situation, you may also want to include the student in the conference. There's nothing like a meeting of the minds with everyone included to have the best opportunity for improvement.

Some parents may be resistant to coming to the school for the meeting. If so, often much can be accomplished with a telephone conference. Some will also claim that they can't leave work for conferences. However, many states now have laws in place that require employers to allow their employees to attend such meetings. Find out what the laws are in your state.

Your goal is a successful, positive experience for everyone concerned. You also want the meeting to result in a partnership in which you and the parents are working together for the benefit of the student. This happens when things don't go wrong. To make sure this doesn't happen to you, use the suggestions in Activity 7.4 and avoid the following:

Don't

- Overwhelm parents with too much detailed information.
- Use educational jargon.
- Try to bluff an answer. If you don't know, say so.
- Predict life success from any data. ("He'll never make it to college.")
- Complain about your own problems to the parent. ("How do you expect me to give him that kind of attention when I have 130 students?")
- Use communication cut-offs (ordering, advising, lecturing, judging, shaming).

Do

- Your homework before you schedule the conference. Gather examples of the student's work, and organize what you want to say before parents arrive.
- Be punctual. Don't make the parent wait.
- Begin with positive information. This may not be easy in some situations—but find something! Even a broken clock is right twice a day.
- Be open, pleasant, courteous, and tactful.
- Make sure parents understand what the problem is. Give examples.
- Encourage parents to ask questions if needed, and ask for their cooperation.
- Document everything that occurred in the meeting after parents leave.
- When appropriate, follow up in some way.

Reality Check 7.6

Expect anything and plan to underreact. Most of the conferences you schedule will be with parents of students who are not doing well. They've heard it all before. Many also still feel like they are being summoned to the principal's office themselves when you call. Some may think they are being judged as parents. Others may seize the opportunity to blame you for the problem.

Keep the conference focused on the student and your intent to help him succeed. Be professional and patient in response to any defensiveness and avoid being defensive yourself. This will be easier said than done at times.

Activity 7.4

Refining Your Conferencing Skills

Getting feedback from another professional will help you as you become more proficient in conducting both student and parent conferences. Choose one of the following formats to refine your approach.

Format One

Observe another teacher in conference with a parent or student. After the conference, ask for the teacher to (a) explain his or her thinking and rationale for organizing the conference in that way and (b) respond to what occurred in the meeting. Make notes for yourself from what you saw.

Format Two

Ask another teacher to observe you in a parent or teacher conference. After the conference, ask for feedback. Make notes for yourself.

A Positive Classroom Climate: What Will Make Your Students Feel Welcome?

Inviting Students into Your Classroom

Every classroom has a feel to it. You can almost see on the faces of the students as they enter a room how they respond to it. Like many factors associated with understanding teenagers, that elusive "something" must be present if the students are to be engaged. An atmosphere that is warm and inviting will be one where the students want to go and want to learn.

What can contribute to making your classroom one high school students like? It's often hard to say. However, research indicates that there are usually five conditions present (Clark & Starr, 1996; Riordan, 1982, p. 309). A welcoming classroom has:

1. Open communication that is dialogue rather than monologue
2. Students who like each other
3. Expectations that encourage productive work and allow students to be themselves
4. Students who are stimulated by the teacher and each other
5. Flexibility in terms of how work gets done

Any one of these can be enough to entice some students to be drawn to a learning environment ("All my friends are in third period"). Likewise, the absence of any one might be enough to turn off other students ("Mr. Anderson is too hard").

Your room is also a place where students will spend at least 180 hours a year. What does it look like? Is it pleasant, clean, bright? Add some personal touches to the room (such as plants, pictures) and put up interesting and creative bulletin boards as well as student work. As discussed in chapter 2, these gestures add interest and show that the entire environment supports the learning and that you care enough to not subject them to bare walls.

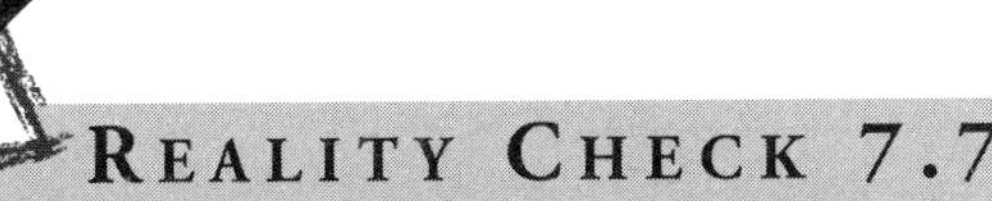

Reality Check 7.7

Granted, you only have so much control over the basic decor, and if you are a traveling teacher, you have even less. But in situations where you do have control, exercise it. Yes, it will take some time to think through what you want your room to look like. But it will make a difference in your students' attitudes, even if it's a subtle one. You may even let some of the students organize stations and create bulletin boards for you. Not only will it be a learning experience for them, but it will also help you; besides, they'd much rather look at their own handiwork than yours.

Arrange your classroom so that your teaching is enhanced. Granted, in some situations, you may have little control over this, such as science labs that must be arranged around equipment. For other situations, arrange your desks to support the kind of instruction you are providing. Group work will require a very different arrangement from a lecture.

The Impact of Your Concern

There is no substitute for being genuinely concerned about the welfare of your students and making sure they know you *want* them to be in your class. This is different from just *accepting* them as individuals on your roster and *allowing* them to attend. To the extent possible, they need to feel that your day is better because they are a part of it. This won't always be easy, but the positive impact on your students of your trying to do this is almost impossible to measure.

You can't fake it—they know how you feel, sometimes despite your best efforts. But your goal is for them to feel comfortable, relaxed, and invited to be part of the group. William Purkey (1992; Purkey & Novak, 1998; Purkey & Strahan, 1995) described the positive effects on students when they feel this way. You may have prepared the best lesson in the world, but if the students don't think you care whether they are there, it will have minimal effect. Purkey's invitational learning theory reflects the importance of trust, respect, optimism, and *intentionality* when dealing with students. This means that you should actively welcome them to be part of your class. This could occur in a variety of ways. It might be as simple as making a point of looking up when students enter the room and giving them a smile, beginning class with a warm greeting or a comment about one of their interests—the game the night before or the prom that's coming up. Dr. Purkey actually greets every student in each of his classes with a handshake as they enter. Think that would make *you* feel invited?

Begin by learning their names and their interests quickly. Mrs. Van Zandt's room is one where students feel good. She combines skills and sensitivity in a way that makes learning pleasurable for her students. She actively looks for ways to let them know that she sees them as people and wants them to be happy and successful in school. She uses questionnaires at the beginning of the year, regular informal conversations with them, and their writing to help her understand them. Mrs. Van Zandt works hard to be approachable and fair with her students. They can see that she likes them and that she likes teaching. This is apparent in the many ways she tries to make them partners in the learning process. For example, Mabel, a student in her class, couldn't write. She began the school year refusing to take any tests. But it was clear to Mrs. Van Zandt that she knew the material by the way she answered verbally. Mabel would just sit there and watch the rest of the class when any writing was required. One day, Mrs. Van Zandt became her "scribe." She took notes for Mabel as she freely responded to every question on the test. As the year progressed, Mabel began to participate more freely and eventually even began asking for help with her writing skills.

The example above is typical of the attention Mrs. Van Zandt pays to her students. She exhibits five qualities of excellent teachers. She incorporates what she observes about her students' personal and academic needs into every class period. She is willing to listen, is respectful toward her students, accepts them, is easy to talk with, and demonstrates warmth and kindness. The students love to come to her class and thrive on her enthusiastic love of teaching. She has mastered the art of teaching.

TIPS from the TRENCHES

Consider the following suggestions beginning teachers said they wish they had heard before they started their careers.

1. Pay attention to how the students are responding to your lesson. If a method you are using with students isn't working, change it.
2. Try to see humor in most situations.
3. Before your conference with either a student or a parent, do your homework. Try to anticipate every question that may come up.
4. In a conference, always consider the views and perceptions of a parent or student.
5. Keep a record of any significant event that relates to either the academic or behavioral progress of your students (both good and bad). You never know when you will need such documentation.
6. In conferences, in addition to the parent and the student, include any other school personnel who may be of assistance (counselor, administrator).
7. Pay special attention to students who are failing. Work with them early in the year, before it's too late.
8. Be proactive in making contact with parents. No matter how busy you are, take the time to make phone calls, send notes, and develop a relationship with them as soon as problems appear.
9. Let parents know about good news—not just the problems—regarding students.
10. If you suspect that a conference with a parent or a student could be dangerous or explosive, have an administrator present.
11. Spend time making your room attractive. Not only will the students enjoy class more, but you will also.

PRAXIS™

Praxis Competencies Related to the Art of Effective Teaching

There may be questions on some of the Praxis Examinations that relate to the science and art of teaching. More than likely, you will be asked to demonstrate an understanding of

1. Motivation
2. Learning styles
3. How you can adapt instruction for individual needs
4. Designing lessons based on the knowledge, experiences, skills, strategies, and interests of the students in relation to the curriculum
5. An appropriate climate for learning, including interpersonal relations
6. Methods for clear communication with students and parents
7. Ways to help students become independent learners (ETS, 2001, *Test-at-a-Glance*, Principles of Learning and Teaching).

Sample Question

A teacher gives his students a list of terms to use in an essay and intends the list to serve as a kind of learning support called a scaffold. If the students use the list effectively, which of the following would be an appropriate next step for the teacher to take when assigning the students their next essay?

(A) Asking the students to come up with their own list of terms to use in the new assignment

(B) Giving the students a longer list of terms to use in the new assignment

(C) Giving the students a list of terms and asking them to write down a definition of each before beginning the new assignment

(D) Asking the student to use the same terms in the new assignment

The correct answer is **A**. Your goal is to help students become more independent. When you ask the students to come up with their own list of terms, you are, in effect withdrawing the scaffold you provided in the beginning. None of the other answers provides this opportunity (ETS, 2001, *Test-at-a-Glance,* Principles of Learning and Teaching).

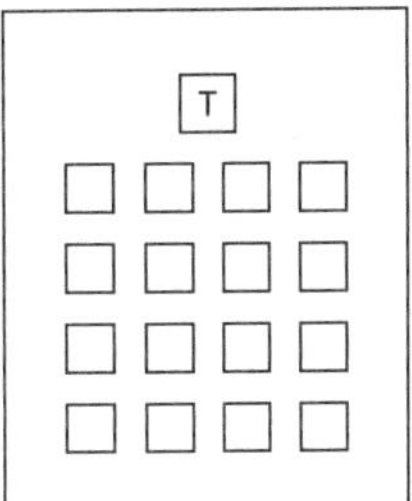

Sample Question

The way the desks in the classroom are arranged in the diagram above is best suited to which of the following activities?

(I) Independent work

(II) Hands-on demonstration

(III) Lecturing by the teacher

(IV) Writing exercises in which small groups of students work together

(A) I and II

(B) I and III

(C) II and III

(D) III and IV

The best answer is **B**. The consensus among researchers in education is that for disseminating information and independent study, the traditional seating arrangement as pictured is most conducive (ETS, 2001, *Test-at-a-Glance,* Principles of Learning and Teaching).

Suggestions for Further Reading

If you have time to read only one book . . .

Armstrong, T. (1994). *Multiple intelligences in the classroom.* Alexandria, VA: ASCD.

or

Tomlinson, C. (1999) *Differentiated classrooms: Responding to the needs of all learners.* Alexandria, VA: ASCD.

References

Armstrong, T. (1994). *Multiple intelligences in the classroom.* Alexandria, VA: ASCD.

Borich, G. D. (1988). *Effective teaching methods.* Upper Saddle River, NJ: Merrill.

Canfield, A. A. (1988). *Learning styles inventory.* Los Angeles: Western Psychological Services.

Canfield, A. A., & Canfield, J. S. (1988). *Instructional styles inventory.* Los Angeles: Western Psychological Services.

Capel, S., Leask, M., & Turner, T. (1995). *Learning and teaching in the secondary school.* London: Routledge.

Child, D. (1986). *Psychology and the teacher* (4th ed.). London: Cassell.

Clark, L. H., & Starr, I. S. (1996). *Secondary and middle school teaching methods* (7th ed.). Upper Saddle River, NJ: Prentice Hall.

Davidman, L., & Davidman, P. T. (1997). *Teaching with a multicultural perspective* (2nd ed.). New York: Longman.

Dillon, J. T. (1998). Using diverse styles of teaching. *Journal of Curriculum Studies, 30*(5), 503–514.

Doolan, L. S., & Honigsfeld, A. (2000). Illuminating the new standards with learning styles: Striking a perfect match. *Clearing House, 73*(5), 274–278.

Educational Testing Service (ETS). (2001). *Test-at-a-Glance—Principles of Learning and Teaching.* Princeton, NJ: Author.

Fenstermacher, G. D., & Soltis, J. S. (1998). *Approaches to teaching.* New York: Teachers College Press.

Gardner, H. (1993). *Multiple intelligences.* New York: Basic Books.

Henson, K. (1993). *Methods and strategies for teaching in secondary and middle schools* (2nd ed.). New York: Longman.

Hogan, K., & Pressley, M. (1998). *Scaffolding student learning.* Cambridge, MA: Brookline Books.

Purkey, W. (1992). An introduction to invitational learning. *Journal of Invitational Theory and Practice, 1*(1), 5–15.

Purkey, W., & Novak, J. (1998). An invitational approach to ethical practice in teaching. *Educational Forum, 63*(1), 37–43.

Purkey, W., & Strahan, D. (1995). School transformation through invitational education. *Research in the Schools, 2*(2), 1–16.

Rasmussen, K. (2000). Differentiating instruction. *Educational Leadership, 58*(1), 9–15.

Reis, S. M., Burns, D. C., & Renzulli, J. S. (1992). *Curriculum compacting: The complete guide to modifying the regular curriculum for high school students.* Mansfield Center, CT: Creative Learning Press.

Riordan, R. J. (1982). *Educational climate: Discussion in improving standards and productivity.* Edited by Herbert J. Walberg. Berkeley, CA: McCutchan.

Searson, R., & Dunn, R. (2001). The learning style teaching model. *Science and Children, 38*(5), 22–26.

Silver, H., Strong, R., & Perini, M. (1997). Integrating learning styles and multiple intelligences. *Educational Leadership, 55*(1), 22–27.

Tomlinson, C. (2000). *Differentiated classrooms: Responding to the needs of all learners.* Alexandria, VA: ASCD.

Wehrmann, K. S. (2000). Baby steps: A beginner's guide. *Educational Leadership, 58*(1), 20–23.

8

Implementing Instruction

Making Each Class Period Count

I've only been teaching three months and it seems that I do the same thing everyday—go over homework, teach the new section in the text, assign more homework. If I'm already bored with class, how must my students feel? I don't even know if they are learning anything. There must be a better way to teach this and I'm going to find it.

First-year teacher

Too often these words are true. At least the teacher quoted above *knows* she's getting into a rut and is looking for better ways to teach. Many teachers don't. They assume because the students are cooperative that their approach must be working. So they continue doing the same thing day after day and year after year. They never reexamine whether it was actually the best or most effective way to help their students learn.

This chapter addresses some of the nuts and bolts of effective teaching. Exactly what will you do with your classes tomorrow and how will you do it? How will you use your precious class time; what activities will you select? This chapter provides sample strategies that will appeal to students with different learning styles, including suggestions for making your lectures and discussions better. Finally, it explores ways to encourage your students to think, both by using appropriate strategies and by refining your questioning skills.

Wake-up Call: What Should You Know About Class Time?

Some Facts About Class Time

Students spend approximately 1,080 hours per year in school, and the individual student spends about 165 of those hours in your classroom. Sounds like a lot? Now subtract the days your students will miss your class because of standardized testing, schoolwide assemblies, early dismissal for inclement weather, as well as the days at the beginning and end of the year that seem to be devoted to organizational concerns. This may leave, in reality, only 145 hours of instruction—so little time to teach all that content. Yet, if you consider the time students and teachers spend in extracurricular activities as well as time spent on school-related projects and homework, school is how secondary students (and you) spend most of their waking hours.

Time is your biggest enemy. Teachers complain constantly that there's too much to do and too little time to get it done. This is because the amount of time actually spent on instruction during the typical class period is 37 minutes, not 55, and only 23 of those minutes represent the amount of time that students are actually working on the task, using resources and engaging in activities that are appropriate for their instructional levels. Surprised?

Uses of Time

What is happening during class in most secondary schools? Unfortunately, most teachers are not engaged actively in the process of teaching. Look at Figure 8.1, which illustrates the typical use of class time.

Clearly, as a whole, very little time is spent in active instruction (15%) and half of a teacher's time (50%) is spent monitoring what was given to students to do. This often translates into time when teachers do other things while students are working on handouts or text assignments. No wonder many students leave class unclear about how to do follow-up assignments or what they have learned that period. Although some of every class needs to be spent organizing activities and dealing with unrelated matters, these should never take 35% of any period.

Figure 8.2 illustrates how time would be better used when 55% of the class time is spent teaching and 25% spent monitoring that instruction.

This emphasis is appropriate and suggests where the priorities of the teacher should be. The elements of effective direct instruction include the need for sufficient time for instruction and adequate coverage of the content. After the students have been given new material, it is essential to monitor the performance, providing immediate feedback to the students on their progress. How can teachers do this unless they start as soon as the bell rings and model a time-on-task attitude? Is it so unreasonable to expect that a clear majority of the class time be spent actually teaching?

Wasting Time

There is a tremendous amount of wasted time in school—precious minutes here and there that add up to hours. Sometimes circumstances will be out of your control, but most of

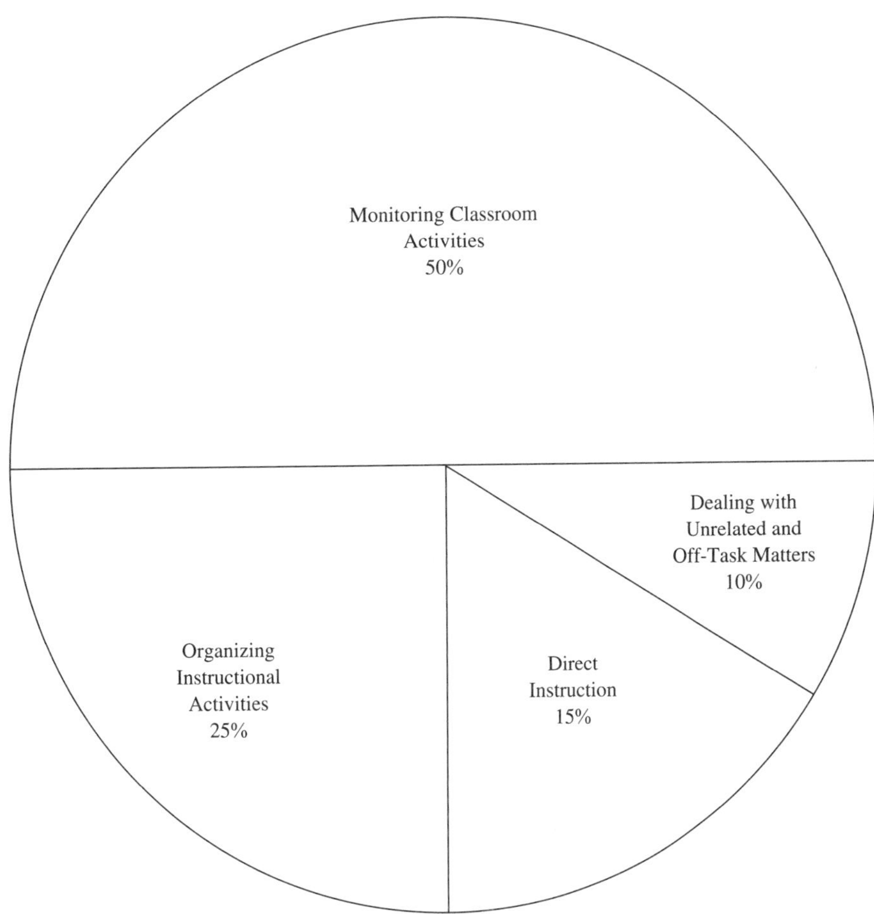

FIGURE 8.1 Typical Use of Class Time

the time, you call the shots in your classroom. Teachers often unwittingly waste time when (a) they have not planned well, (b) they do not have smooth transitions between activities, (c) they are not clear about assignments, (d) their students are not clear about teacher expectations, and (e) their students do not understand class procedures (collection of materials, when to work alone and when to work with others, etc.).

You should always be aware of time as you teach—how best to spend it and how not to waste it.

Rolling Up Your Sleeves: What Are You Going to Do in Class Tomorrow?

Creating a Climate for Learning

The term *classroom climate* means one thing to most teenagers: "Do I like the people in that class?" Ask any guidance counselor how often students add and drop courses or request schedule changes just to be with their friends.

Almost nothing is more important to secondary students than fitting in. They want to be known and liked by others. In your classroom, this need goes beyond their social priorities; it drives how they perform and how much they learn. They want to be with their friends and belong to a group. Contrary to what teachers may assume, students often don't know each other unless they happen to be involved in some extracurricular activity together. To provide an effective learning experience for them, you must make students feel they belong in your classroom.

Therefore, as much as you may want to begin right away with the first topic on your syllabus, consider the overall benefits of addressing the social needs of your students at

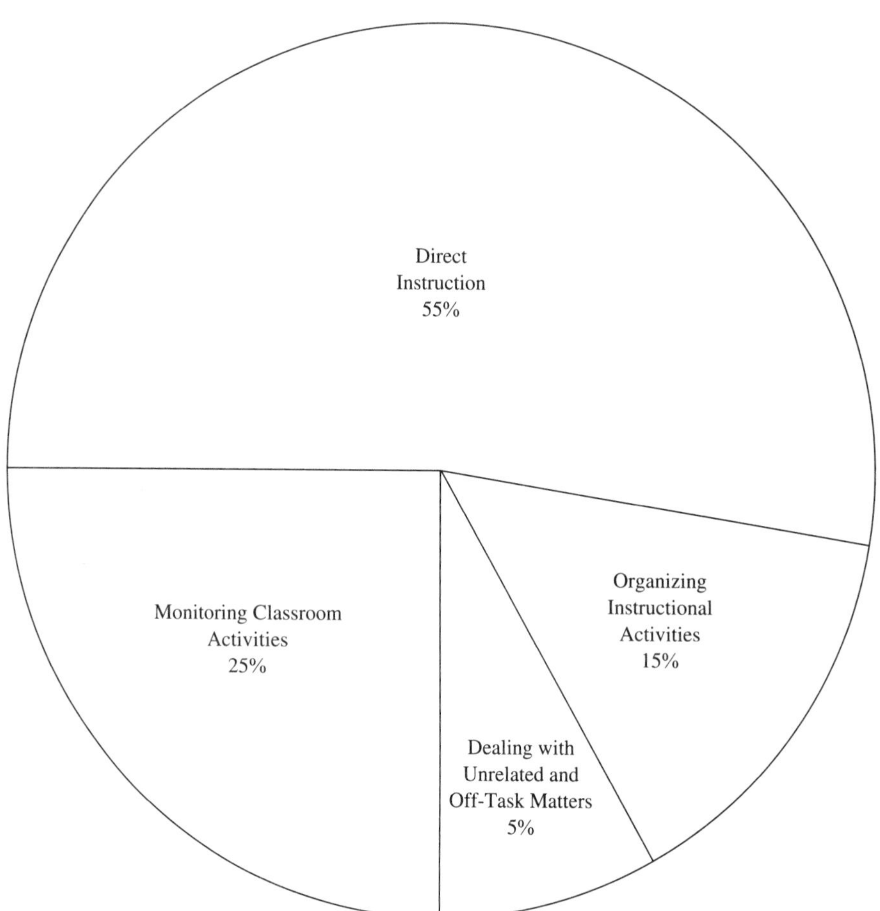

FIGURE 8.2 Productive Use of Class Time

the outset. Doing this may take a variety of forms, depending on your personal style, the characteristics of students themselves, and the nature of your subject. Many teachers have an "introduce your neighbor" exercise or create other activities that require students to get to know each other personally, such as the one Mrs. Van Zandt uses at the beginning of every year (chapter 3). She says they refer to some of the things they learn about each other all year long.

Teacher Expectations

As a teacher, it is natural for you to have certain expectations of your students, and those expectations are an important influence on a student's ability to learn. Try as you might to hide them in some situations, these expectations are often readily apparent to your students. You should always make it clear that you expect students to do their best work but that your expectations are realistic. In other words, don't expect them to do something that they can't do.

Expectations are essentially attitudes and assumptions that teachers have regarding what their students can actually achieve. This means they will have a tendency to expect certain levels of performance from students. These attitudes may or may not be accurate. Thus, you will have to guard against the tendency to have and convey great expectations for your gifted students and lower expectations for your below-average achievers. It won't always be easy to do. But you must. Research indicates that teachers' attitudes toward particular students vary according to their expectations and that these differences create different learner self-concepts and strong or weak motivation (Good & Brophy, 1991).

Starting the Day

Classroom climate is also influenced by the way you start each class period—especially with respect to procedural matters (discussed in chapter 4). Running your classroom each day will require certain "housekeeping" chores that you can't avoid. You will need to take attendance, collect random assignments, follow up on school procedures, handle tardies, and so forth. Your goal should be to limit how much time these tasks take. According to Jere Brophy, the way a teacher starts class sets the tone and pace for the rest of the period (Brophy, 1987).

REALITY CHECK 8.1

Try to avoid the habit of calling the roll each day. It wastes valuable class time and gives the students an opportunity to become distracted. Granted, the first few days you may want to do this to learn names, but after that, find another way.

As soon as possible after the bell rings, you must get and keep the attention of your students. Many teachers say that beginning the lesson may be the most difficult part of the class. They find that getting their students involved as soon as the bell rings sets a productive tone for the rest of the period. Some have "interest centers" around the room with displays, magazines, and newspaper articles that relate to their subject to generate interest and enthusiasm. Students can begin looking at these even before the bell rings. Other teachers have a prompt on the board for students to begin responding to in their journals as soon as they enter. The idea is to focus their attention quickly.

After the housekeeping chores, the next thing you will want to do is to review briefly what you did yesterday. Remember that the students have five or six other classes and a life outside of school. A brief review gets everyone on the same page before you continue. Two very simple, but effective, suggestions for reviewing are to ask a student to summarize what was taught the day before or to give a short quiz (Rosenshire & Stevens, 1986).

The Process of Selecting Activities

Exactly what are you going to do with your students tomorrow? Start identifying your intentions for student learning. Ask yourself, "What do I want them to know and how can I best get them to learn it?"

Aim to select activities that support the concept of *powerful learning* (Levin, 1996, 1997). You want to create situations in which students see meaning in lessons and can make connections between what they learn in your classroom and the real world. Learning experiences have three dimensions: what is learned (content), how the content is learned (instruction), and how these come together (the total learning environment). It is important that these three dimensions be completely integrated (Hopfenberg, Levin, & Associates, 1993). The concept of powerful learning is consistent with constructivism and brain research discussed in chapter 3. Students learn differently and draw on their personal styles, abilities, knowledge, and experiences as they explore new concepts. Teachers should make use of their understanding of students and how they learn best as they determine instructional formats (Webb, Metha, & Jordan, 1999).

So what activities will best help you to accomplish powerful learning? There are four broad activity types.

Whole group lecture—When you want to give students important information, to demonstrate a skill, or to practice listening and note taking.

Whole group discussion—When you want to share ideas, knowledge, or experiences and make applications to the lives of your students. This will also help you to check for understanding and to get a sense of what students' interests are.

Small groups—When you want the students to do specific learning tasks and to develop social skills. This also allows them a chance to develop leadership skills and to be more directly involved in the planning of their learning.

Individual work—When you want the students to work at their own pace and pursue their own interests. Also use this when you want to personalize instruction (McNeil & Wiles, 1990).

There are times when it will not be easy to decide which type of activity is best. Because you have a class of 30 students and limited time to cover material, you will have to determine first the *best* way to teach them. Certain concepts lend themselves to group work, others to individual activities, and still others to whole group activities. Then consider your current circumstances and your students. If time is a factor, it may be most efficient to deliver an overview of the unit to the entire class at once. Other times, the nature of the content or the students will govern your decision. Perhaps you have several students who need to develop social skills or seem to respond best when interacting with others. You will choose a group activity. Other situations may require that students work alone at their own pace.

Patterns of Teaching

How much control over the teaching situation do you want or need? There are three patterns that characterize control teachers exercise in the classroom. The first is *direct teaching,* reflecting a high degree of teacher control over the learning process. This usually includes an emphasis on *mastery learning,* which focuses on specific objectives and acceptable levels of performance by students. Mastery learning is based on several assumptions.

1. All students can learn a concept if the learning units are small enough.
2. For learning to take place, instruction must be varied accordingly.
3. Some students take longer to learn than others.
4. Most learning outcomes are measurable and observable.
5. Most learning concepts are sequential and logical.
6. Students can experience success at each phase of the process (Kellough & Kellough, 1999).

Research indicates that this pattern results in positive achievement, longer retention of information, and students who are more engaged.

Direct teaching also emphasizes the advantage of using certain questioning techniques as a part of instruction. Questions should be short, should provide immediate reinforcement by the teacher, and should focus on answers (pause-prompt-praise). This approach is very effective with both academically disadvantaged students and high-ability students. It is effective with the mastery of basic skills and increases textbook learning and general understanding.

Much of the teaching that goes on in secondary classrooms includes some form of group interaction. This is the *indirect teaching pattern* (also referred to as interactive teaching) and involves shared teacher–student control over the learning process. Here, the teacher is more flexible with the students. Questioning techniques are more open-ended and include extended *wait-time* (more than 3 seconds) for student response. The teacher builds on student responses by asking additional, higher level questions. This approach results in longer and higher level verbal responses by the student and more student involvement in the class. This pattern also includes group work and cooperative learning. One of the biggest advantages of this method is that it meets group goals and provides for individual accountability (Slavin, 1989). When groups include students of mixed ability, there is increased achievement in all content areas as well as in reading comprehension. If students are grouped by ability, research indicates only slight gains at the secondary level.

The third pattern, *independent learning,* includes opportunities for self-pacing and self-monitoring. Contract learning and programmed instruction are among the most common examples of personalized systems of instruction (PSI). Teachers who use this pattern understand that students are not all alike and that, as they mature, they become more and more different in terms of how they learn. Teachers who follow independent learning also believe that students learn best if allowed to do so in their own way and at their own pace (Guskey, 1985).

There are clear advantages and disadvantages to all three patterns. Direct instruction allows you to cover more material but may not provide opportunities for student input. The indirect, self-directed, and independent instructional modes may allow for students to understand the content in more depth but are time-consuming and give the teacher less control over the process. All three patterns are important and there will be circumstances when each is the best approach. Most experts suggest that teachers become comfortable with all three and implement each as necessary.

Suggested Strategies: What Are Some Activities That Work with Secondary Students?

There are many resources with lists of activities a teacher might use in planning a lesson. In fact, you can almost find yourself overwhelmed by too many choices. Some are going to be more appealing to you than others, depending on your own teaching style and what you want to accomplish. The students and their learning needs should be the center of your thinking as you make these decisions. Therefore, one way of thinking about the activities is to consider Canter's learning and instructional styles discussed in chapter 7. The following is a sample list of 33 activities that work well for high school students, described according to Canter's four basic learning types. Clearly, almost all of the methods can be adapted for whole class, small group, or individual learning activities.

Sample Strategies That Appeal to Conceptual Learners

These strategies will appeal to those students who respond best to language-oriented activities.

1. Lecture—This is the old standby. It can be used effectively when the teacher wants to give the class lots of information and facts. Students are usually passive and take notes. This method is also abused by some teachers who operate under the assumption that if they didn't tell the students what they need to know, they couldn't possibly have learned it. Not so. (See the section on "Effective Presentations.")

2. Overhead notes—This method allows the teacher to face the class while he or she "takes notes" for the students on an overhead. It has many of the same advantages of the lecture, but is especially helpful for students who need to develop spelling and note-taking skills.

3. Oral instruction—This method is different from a lecture in that it is a process in which the teacher is going over information piece by piece. In effect, the teacher is walking the students through assignments, allowing time to complete sections piecemeal.

4. Audiovisual aids—Using films, videos, filmstrips, or slides can provide students with information in an entertaining and informative way. This is excellent for visual learners.

5. Question-and-answer periods—Entire lessons can be structured around a series of questions. The content is, in effect, taught using the questions and soliciting answers that engage the students and involve them directly in the discovery of the concepts.

6. Integrated learning—This method involves the teachers of two or more disciplines working together to design lessons that address content in both their areas.

7. Symposium—"Authoritative" speakers give prepared talks on some subject and different points of view are represented. There may be questions and answers at the end.

8. Directed use of resources—Teachers have specific directions for the use of some resources they have provided for the students. They are given specific information to gain from the resource based on carefully specified criteria. For example, the use of an 1898 Sears catalog might serve as a means for students to gather information about clothing styles and their prices at the time, as well as other information related to the 19th century.

9. Students as teachers—This method allows the students to teach material to other students. Based on the old adage that you learn best what you teach, this is an effective (and popular) method both middle and high school students enjoy.

Sample Strategies That Appeal to Social Learners

Students who prefer activities that include interaction with peers and the teacher will respond well to these strategies.

10. Class discussions—This popular method provides students with an opportunity to share ideas and learn from the other students.

11. Role play and reverse role play—This method gives students an opportunity to act out their perceptions of how people in situations related to the content would respond. Because it is done with the participation of the other students, it allows for social development.

12. Cooperative learning groups—The classic method for encouraging students to learn from each other.

13. Listening teams—Students are put into groups and told to pay attention to different aspects of a speech, movie, or presentation. They compile and share their findings with the group. When all groups are finished, the entire class has a better idea of the complexity of the total concept.

14. Games—This offers students a chance to learn or review information.

15. Debates—Students work together in teams to study and argue the finer points of an issue.

16. Problem-solving discussion—Students focus on a problem and brainstorm ways to solve it.

17. Dramatics—Students work together to write, direct, and perform dramatic presentations that illustrate the content they are studying.

18. Think-pair-share—This method gives the student a chance to think first about a problem posed and then discuss it with another student. Both then combine their thoughts and share them with the class.

Sample Strategies That Appeal to Applied Learners

Students who prefer activities related to the real world will be attracted to these strategies.

19. Field trips—By going off-campus, the students can see the application of what they are studying.

20. Laboratory learning—This can be used as part of a class (such as biology) where students experience learning in a hands-on environment. Remember dissecting those frogs?

21. Practicum—Students actually intern in a situation that teaches them content studied. As in field trips and lab situations, they learn by doing. (Usually best suited for high school students.)

22. Demonstrations—Students observe a procedure or concept performed by the teacher.

23. Panels—Students apply what they know as panelists who are discussing different points of view regarding some concept studied. Visiting experts also serve as panelists.

24. Case studies—Concepts studied are described in real-world situations that pose certain questions for resolution.

Sample Strategies That Appeal to Independent Learners

These strategies will be effective with those students who prefer to work alone.

25. Reading—Students work on their own to gather information.

26. Self-paced modules—Students move at a pace that is comfortable for them, under the teacher's guidance.

27. Personalized system of instruction (PSI)—Students are given an instructional plan designed just for them.

28. Computer assisted instruction (CAI) and computer managed instruction (CMI)—CAI is when the teacher provides certain software or programs to help the student learn a new concept or drill an old one on his own. CMI requires little if any teacher involvement since the software program manages the students' learning pace.

29. Research and oral or written reports—Students work alone to gather information, organize it into a formal report, and/or present it to the class.

30. Projects—Students can create and develop their own representation of something they are studying.

31. Learning centers—Teachers have stations in the classroom that allow students to work independently or in small groups with certain materials or resources.

32. Outside school assignments—Students attend presentations, visit sites, or conduct research off-campus as part of the class's study of a concept.

33. Tests and examinations—This can be a wonderful teaching strategy. For example, you may choose to go over a returned test and use it as the basis for a lesson. Because the students are invested in the responses they made, they "hear" the correct information and focus better. Tests can be turned into study sheets as well.

REALITY CHECK 8.2

Secondary students today (especially at the middle school level) have a very short attention span. Therefore, you will need to vary your activities not only from day to day, but within the class period itself. This is especially true if your primary activity is a lecture. Try to have at least two activities per period.

Refining the Basics: What Can You Do to Make Your Lectures and Discussions Better?

Direct Expository Teaching

Talking to your students is what you do for a living. It's the centerpiece of your involvement with them. However, in many cases, teachers simply talk too much. Students will tune you out if this is the case. But it's true that you have a lot to tell them.

There are three types of "telling" approaches that secondary teachers use. These are (a) short talks in which the teacher presents or explains certain concepts or procedures, (b) formal lectures in which the teacher presents content at length, and (c) teacher comments and reactions given while other activities are going on (Clark & Starr, 1996).

Make everything you say worth hearing. Because how you talk to them matters, keep the following points in mind (see also Activity 8.1):

- You must be *clear.* Use proper English and good examples that students will understand to make your points. Use illustrations, demonstrations, pictures—anything that will ensure they comprehend what you are saying.

- Avoid using vague language (such as "sorta," "might be," etc.). The most common speech habit of beginning teachers that interferes with the clarity of your talk is the use of "uhs" or "you know" or similar unnecessary filler words or sounds.
- Make what you say interesting. Do anything necessary to get and keep their attention. What makes something interesting to secondary students? Remember what was stated before: anything that has to do with *them*. This could include making part of your lesson real-life examples, stories, illustrations, and problems. Likewise, some offbeat approach or unusual topic that relates to your content will get their attention.
- Make sure you can be heard. Don't talk over the students. Always wait to get their attention before you speak.
- Avoid talking too fast.

Effective Lectures

There are many ways to teach secondary students. The truth, however, is that most teachers, especially high school teachers, use lecture more than any other method. The fact that it has endured through the ages suggests that it is essentially a good method. Despite the increased and valid criticism that it is overused and misused, lecturing still remains the most direct way to give students information in a short amount of time. Mastering the art of creating an effective lecture will serve you well regardless of the subject you teach. The process itself requires that you (a) identify the pertinent information, (b) organize it for clarity, (c) sprinkle it with interesting anecdotes and stories, and (d) practice it before delivery. Once you get this process down pat, subsequent lectures will take less time to prepare and will be more effective.

Consider carefully when you should use the lecture method. Use it only if you are addressing students who are able to take notes, who are auditory learners, who can follow a variety of ideas delivered orally, or some combination of these. Even in perfect circumstances, research indicates that most students are able to comprehend only 52% of a lecture's important ideas (Henson, 1993; Maddox & Hoole, 1975). King (1990) stated that when students take notes during a lecture, they are more likely to record bits and pieces of the lecture verbatim or simply paraphrase information. They do this rather than organize what they hear into some sort of conceptual framework or relate the new information to what they already know.

Of course, lectures have many weaknesses. Students complain that they are boring and don't allow for them to be involved. Lectures also tend to make students nervous,

ACTIVITY 8.1

Monitoring Your Own Teacher Talk

Either tape one of your classes or have another teacher observe your class. During the lesson, indicate with tally marks how often you make one of the following errors in talking with your students.

1. Being unclear
2. Using vague language
3. Talking over the students
4. Not talking loud enough
5. Talking too fast
6. Engaging in any other annoying or distracting talking habits you might have

more so than any other method, primarily because they can make teachers appear too structured and authoritarian. This is true especially when teachers are showing off their own knowledge or talking too fast.

The lecture works well when it is well planned and is aimed at students who are capable and motivated (Rothstein, 1990). It is an excellent method to introduce a unit, to provide information not readily available any other way, to explain difficult points, and to clarify matters for students. The following are suggestions for improving your lectures:

1. Find some clear and interesting way to introduce the objectives for the lecture at the beginning. This will provide your students with a roadmap for where you are heading, making it easier to take notes and organize what they are hearing.
2. Monitor the pace of your lecture. If it is either too fast or too slow, students will begin to zone out.
3. Spice up the lecture by doing things to keep their attention. Moving around the class as you speak, gesturing, pausing, and varying your voice level all result in more attentive students.
4. Pay attention to the structure of your lecture. Do this by organizing the content into three to five major concepts, ordering them in a natural or logical way. Limit the lecture to 10 to 15 minutes and make sure that you summarize the concepts.
5. Don't talk over the heads of the students. Avoid using too much jargon or unfamiliar language.
6. Use audiovisual aids when possible. Not only is it a more natural way for visual and auditory learners to absorb new information, but it enables all of your students to have several places to focus their attention, keeping them more alert.
7. Include humor when possible.

8. Keep it simple and to the point. Remember the three basic steps: (a) tell them what you are going to tell them, (b) tell them what you want them to know, and then (c) tell them what you told them.

REALITY CHECK 8.3

You may find yourself using a lot of slang and other language patterns that you think students will understand and relate to. Be careful about this. You are possibly the only role model for some students of the correct way to use grammar and to speak appropriate English. This is not to say you sound stuffy. For example, instead of talking as some of your students do by saying, "Hey—you done good!" you can say with the same level of enthusiasm, "I'm so proud of you—you did well on this test!" Now that's not too stuffy, is it?

Above all, make the lecture easy to follow and understand. Consider giving students an outline with the main points accompanied by space for them to write additional notes with each item. Break up the lecture with questions or other stimulating strategies that will keep their attention.

Facilitating Effective Discussions

The second most used method in secondary classrooms is the group discussion. A class or group discussion is a purposeful conversation, not just a bull session that wastes time. It is one of the best ways for students to integrate the new material they are learning with what they already know. It also provides students with an opportunity to share their own experiences with the class and learn from those of others. Students can develop a better understanding of the concept taught, which naturally results in more personal meaning. The major positive effect of a discussion is that it gives students practice in thinking—a chance for them to say out loud what is in their minds. They also examine their own ideas, formulate and apply principles, and receive immediate feedback from their peers.

Your role as the leader is crucial to the success of any discussion. You should begin by introducing the topic for discussion clearly, perhaps by posing a key question to get students talking. It is also your responsibility to keep the discussion going, and tactfully keep some students from dominating. You will also want to pull all of the ideas together and summarize from time to time (especially at the end). As much as you may want to, try to avoid dominating the discussion yourself.

Your biggest challenge will be when the discussion begins to go off on a tangent. It happens all the time. You began by discussing poetry and before you know it, the class is involved in a heated discussion about the football game Friday night. There's nothing wrong with an occasional diversion. Students love to talk about things other than the topic at hand. But the longer you let it go, the more time you waste and the harder it will be to get the students back on track. As a good discussion leader, you will want to demonstrate the following (Clark & Starr, 1996):

- A genuine interest of your own in the topic
- A sense of humor
- A sense of seriousness
- The ability to suppress your own opinions
- An impartial attitude
- An accepting and encouraging manner

Lessons That Encourage Thinking: What Approaches Will Make Them Use Their Heads?

True learning occurs when students are thinking—not just absorbing unrelated facts for a test. Helping students to think about what they are studying is a much more complicated process than just providing them with information and seeing how much of what you said they can remember. You want them to exhibit "intelligent behavior," behavior that represents a student's increased ability to be persistent about completing tasks. You also want students to listen to others and learn from them, be flexible in their thinking, apply knowledge to new situations, and be curious (Kellough & Kellough, 1999, pp. 365–367). There are many teaching behaviors that, by their nature, encourage students to think. The most popular approaches with secondary teachers include problem-solving, inquiry, and discovery strategies.

Problem-Solving Strategies

Solving problems is the way people learn, grow, and develop intellectually all of their lives. The process forces individuals to experiment with solutions to a problem, using everything they already know and applying learned information to new situations. Students can learn much more from engaging in problem solving than from memorizing facts. When done in a group setting, the added dimensions of social interaction and shared input make the experience one of true learning with meaning. The approach creates behavioral changes in students' lives by teaching them to focus on future solutions rather than past failures (Schieffer & Schieffer, 2000). Therefore, you should look for ways to incorporate this crucial component in your lessons.

The basic steps of the problem-solving strategy include the following:

1. Students become aware of the problem. Although under some circumstances, they might identify the problem themselves, often students at the secondary level, especially middle school, need the problem identified for them. The problem is usually posed as a question.
2. Students define the problem. At this point you will need to help them define exactly what it is they want to know. If they don't do this, they will find that discovering a solution to a nebulous idea is quite difficult.
3. Students do research that will help them solve the problem. This means using whatever they can find on their own or whatever you can provide to give them information.

4. Students form a hypothesis of what the problem is—a theory of the solution.
5. Students test the solution as often as needed to solve the problem.

You will need to serve as an active resource throughout the process to keep students from going astray as they investigate their problem. You can do this by asking key questions as they proceed and continually steering them in the right direction. You can also help them draw conclusions and bring in other concepts they have learned that may be challenged or used to confirm findings. What you want is a positive attitude regarding the process of problem solving that will carry over to other subjects and throughout a student's life (Miller, 2000).

Inquiry Teaching and Discovery Learning

Inquiry and discovery are often confused, probably because they both deal with problem solving. However, they are not the same. The differences between discovery and inquiry come from who identifies the problem and how much control the students have over the process. Both have in common the assumption that students profit more from actively seeking knowledge than from having it given to them in a lecture or a similar approach. The difference between the terms *discovery, inquiry,* and *true inquiry* can be described in 3 levels.

Level 1 inquiry is traditional teaching, where both the problem and the way to solve it are defined for the student. The process is usually designed so that results are inevitable. In effect, the student "discovers" what the teacher wants him to find. This has also been referred to as guided inquiry or discovery. While Level 1 is useful in many situations, it is not *true inquiry* because the teaching outcome is predetermined. Students do not have the opportunity to be involved at the highest levels of mental challenge. However, making sure that students are adept with the problem-solving skills that are part of Level 1 inquiry is necessary before teachers advance them to Levels 2 and 3 (Adamovic & Hedden, 1997).

Both Levels 2 and 3 represent *true inquiry.* In Level 2 inquiry, students determine and design processes for inquiry for a problem identified by the teacher. The conclusions are tentative and subject to revision. At Level 3, students recognize and identify the problem as well as decide the way to reach a conclusion. Secondary students should be working at this level. It often appears in project-centered teaching. Unlike the Level 1 inquiry, which is more linear in nature (with steps that result in a conclusion), higher levels of inquiry are cyclical in nature.

In true inquiry, students develop both the ideas and the means to test the ideas. One way to stimulate inquiry is to use resources and springboard ideas that are nonthreatening in nature, so that students feel encouraged to think freely. Obviously, this requires more time both to plan and to implement than Level 1 inquiry, which is based on a more direct teaching model. (Discussion of Inquiry and Discovery Learning adapted from Kellough & Kellough, 1999.)

Questioning Techniques: How Will the Right Questions Guide Student Learning?

Since the beginning of time, most meaningful learning has been a result of effective questioning techniques. Asking students good questions results in their active engagement in class. Constructivist theory recognizes the importance of the student's ability to think, and thinking ability is a function of being able to ask and ponder critical questions. Teachers need question-based problem-solving strategies that are understandable, adaptable to different students, productive, and transferable (Richetti & Sheevin, 1999). Good questions motivate students to stretch their own understanding of what is being addressed.

Types of Questions

There are all kinds of questions, each designed for a different purpose. Sometimes you may ask a question to find out what a student knows, at other times to motivate or provide practice or reinforcement. Some of your questions will be designed to help a student learn to think.

Questions may be described as *cognitive memory questions, convergent questions, divergent questions,* or *evaluative questions.* Cognitive memory questions require simple recall of information ("What were the five most important causes of World War I?"). Convergent questions have only one correct answer ("What is the chemical symbol for oxygen?"). Divergent questions have many possible responses, with no one correct answer ("What are some ways the main character in the novel could escape her fate?"). Evaluative questions ask students to make a judgment ("Which of the economic principles described in the case study is most effective?").

Other types of questions include *cueing questions* (giving students hints), *focusing questions* (focusing their attention), and *probing questions* (getting them to take an answer a step further). You will want to use a variety of questions in the course of your lessons. Good questions are ones that (a) are clear and straightforward, (b) are challenging and thought-provoking, (c) can be adapted for different students, and (d) are appropriate for the lesson's purpose (Clark & Starr, 1996).

Posing Excellent Questions

Teachers ask literally hundreds of questions a day. They range from the procedural ("Does everyone have a review sheet?") to the more thought-provoking ("How do you think the hero in the novel survived the ordeal?"). The ones related to learning vary in terms of quality. There are bad questions and good questions. Bad questions are ones that lack focus or are unclear. In effect, they are almost impossible to answer. (Thus the blank stares from students.) For example, "Who are the four characters in the story, do you like them, and why?" Here there are actually three questions to be answered. Which of the three should the students answer? It would be impossible for a student to provide a concise response. On the other hand, an excellent question might be "Which of the four characters do you consider the most evil and why?" This question addresses higher order thinking skills and is clear.

The best lessons almost always include some good questions. As you plan, make a point of sprinkling some thought-provoking questions throughout your activity or lecture to keep students involved and thinking, rather than sitting as passive recipients. Many of the questions you and they ask, however, will be spontaneous as the lesson progresses, if things are going well.

There are three important things you should remember when posing questions. First, ask interesting questions that will inspire curiosity and stimulate the imagination of your students. For example, when asking a student to define suspension of disbelief (a perfectly acceptable question in Bloom's comprehension category), follow up the question with one at a higher level. It might be "Where in the novel is the reader asked to engage in suspension of disbelief and why?"

Second, when asking questions of the whole class, always ask the question first, *then* call on a student. This ensures that all students will give the question thought because they don't know who will be asked to respond. Third, avoid repeating questions or answers unless absolutely necessary. Students listen more attentively when they know they will hear a question only once.

Research indicates that teachers rarely give students enough time to think after they ask a question. In fact, one study found that the average amount of time teachers allowed students was 1 second! If a student did not respond immediately, the teacher "either repeated or rephrased the question, asked another question, or called on another student" (Rowe, 1974; Wilen, 1982). Obviously, the more time you give students to respond, the better the quality of their responses. They shouldn't need 5 seconds to respond to a question such as "What is your address?" But teachers should give students 3 to 5 seconds for questions that require thought. It will seem like an eternity sometimes, but the result is better and more thoughtful participation by students.

Responding to Student Questions

Before you concern yourself with how to field student questions, you must have a climate in your classroom where questions are welcome in the first place. Look for every opportunity to encourage questions. As you respond, your manner will be the biggest single factor in students' decisions to ask questions again. If you are receptive and respectful, they'll ask again. They should see posing their own questions as a key element in their learning and something that makes participation in class more fun. This will happen if you give credence to every question asked (regardless of how inane you might feel it is) and are not threatened if they ask you something you don't know. When students begin by saying, "I know this is a stupid question, but . . ." Stop them right there to remind them that no question is stupid. Readily acknowledge when you are not sure of an answer yourself. In fact, students love to see this happen, assuming you know most of the answers most of the time. Mr. Henson states that he can actually see the students become more involved when he doesn't know an answer but wants to find out what it is. "It's more fun to be a fellow traveler on the journey than to try to be a never-ending source of information. Besides, I'm human—I don't know everything." Not knowing something and discussing how to find the answer together makes students feel involved in the process of learning. Encourage students to answer each other's questions as well.

REALITY CHECK 8.4

You shouldn't feel the need to be enthusiastic about every response. There is a difference between being an accepting responder to what's being said and saying "Good job!" to everything. Give positive responses only when warranted. This way, when you compliment a response, it means something. On the other hand, validate every attempt to respond by acknowledging the student's effort and probing to help him find the correct answer.

Your Supplementary Curriculum: What Other Factors Will You Need to Incorporate into Your Teaching?

Reading and Writing Skills

It is the responsibility of every teacher, regardless of subject, to promote the basic literacy of students. This includes regular, sustained attention to reading and writing skills. Often teachers say, "I teach social studies—not reading" or "I'm a physics teacher—not a writing teacher." Wrong. *Every* teacher is a reading and writing teacher. With few exceptions, every subject should require students to use and develop their reading and writing skills. It may be as simple as having them maintain a journal in which they write daily reflections related to what you are studying. Perhaps reading supplementary books or articles for your subject as well as the text would enhance their abilities. Look for ways to incorporate these skills.

Increasingly, teachers are using the computer to help students develop better reading and writing skills. Students like working on the computer, especially if they have trouble with schoolwork. It makes them feel as though they are doing the same thing as everyone else and their problems with reading and writing are not so apparent. There are many software programs available, but working one-on-one with a student works just as effectively, either at the computer or at a desk.

Study Skills

An important goal of education is to motivate students to become independent, lifelong learners. High school may be the last opportunity before they enter college or the world of work to help students learn on their own. This means knowing how to study.

This may come as a surprise to you, but many of your students, especially middle school students, have no clue about how to study. Therefore, it should be one of your priorities to teach this important skill with as much intention as you teach your content. After all, there are certain ways to study your discipline, and you are the best person to demonstrate and model this on a daily basis.

Students often think they have studied because they read the material once or paid attention during class. This attitude is encouraged when teachers give the students time in class before the test to study! This can be appropriate in some cases but shouldn't take the place of independent study. Mastering material means taking the time to think about the content, to reread important information, to reflect on what's being studied, and to allow time for it to sink in as they apply the material to new problems or situations.

In effect, you must teach your students how to learn. As discussed in chapter 7, students learn in different ways. It will be important for you to help them discover what their natural learning styles are and apply them when studying. Sometimes this will mean translating what they *hear* in class to something they can *see*, if they are visual learners. Include a variety of approaches to learning content during instruction and then help your students to see how they can focus on the way that works best for them when they are studying on their own. Learning how to study also includes a variety of skills. Three of the most critical and most problematic for high school students to master are (a) setting aside a time and place for quiet study on a regular basis, (b) knowing what resources are available and how to use them, and (c) concentrating on the content at hand.

The extent to which you can help them see the importance of these will greatly enhance their capacity for learning your subject and other subjects on their own.

One method that helps students learn how to learn is the process of self-interrogation (McNeil & Wiles, 1990). In this method, students develop a series of questions to ask themselves as they are reading and reviewing information—such questions as "Exactly what do I have to do?" "What is the main idea in this paragraph?" "What is another way of thinking about this problem?" These questions will vary somewhat by content area, and you will help your students as they study if you can identify the questions they should ask themselves and model the process during class while you are with them. This way, when they alone, asking themselves the questions will come automatically. In fact, self-monitoring during study is critical to effective learning.

Mrs. Martinez works diligently to develop reading comprehension skills in her English class of low-ability ninth graders. She tells them to follow her Four-Step Plan:

1. Read each paragraph carefully.
2. After each paragraph, ask yourself, "What is the main idea?"
3. Ask yourself, "What's going on?"
4. If necessary, reread or go on.

These are basic steps, but she reminds students of them frequently during class and encourages them to write down the responses if necessary. Her students say that this simple process is one they can remember on their own and has helped them in other classes as well.

Take time to consider a way of helping your students study your content area. You may want to begin by asking yourself how you learn it. Formulate some simple strategies that can be easily remembered and reinforce them in class each day. Sounds like common sense, but it's not to many students. Too often, teachers say, "Study chapter four for a quiz tomorrow." It's no wonder they are disappointed with the results. It is unlikely that you will see your students develop good study skills if you do not teach the skills directly and practice them with your students.

Homework

There are few words that elicit more groans in school than *homework*. This is understandable for several reasons, some of them related to students and others related to teachers.

Students' concerns are largely based on two factors. First, they are tired at the end of the day—they are tired of school, that is. They spend between 7 and 8 hours a day in class, listening to and responding to requests from six or seven teachers. It's no surprise that, except for the academically motivated, doing additional work at home doesn't appeal to many. Second, with support and encouragement from their parents, students today participate in record numbers in extracurricular and community activities. They also hold jobs and have home responsibilities. When football or track practice isn't over till 6:00 p.m. or youth activities at church take part of the evening or weekend, students feel that there isn't enough time for additional schoolwork. They may be right.

Teachers also contribute to the negative perception of homework. One reason is that they give more than needed to accomplish the learning goal. If students can master the process of solving equations in algebra by doing 5 examples, why assign 15? The excess becomes time-consuming busywork that turns students off. Second, some teachers are careless about both the nature and clarity of homework assignments. Hastily telling them to answer the 10 questions at the end of the chapter as the bell rings falls on deaf ears for many. This is equally true when teachers don't make sure that all 10 of those questions serve the intended purpose and that the students understand what to do when they get home. Finally, many teachers are guilty of using homework as punishment, thereby ensuring that students will associate homework with a negative activity instead of educational reinforcement.

Despite these facts, homework can be and should be a *good* thing—*if* assignments are carefully and thoughtfully designed with the specific purpose in mind, as well as the students' ability to profit from the exercise. Students simply must also be able to do it on their own. Ask yourself the following questions as you determine whether to assign homework.

1. Is this homework assignment absolutely necessary to help students master the content? If the answer is no, skip it.
2. Is this assignment the best one to help them master the content?
3. Is this an interesting assignment that they will be motivated to complete?
4. Can the students finish the assignment in a reasonable length of time?
5. Can they do this on their own, without help?
6. How will it be evaluated—if at all?

How to grade or evaluate homework is often a dilemma for teachers. Many secondary school students won't do it at all unless they are extrinsically motivated. Thus, the age-old question "Does this count?" Some teachers grade homework. However, beware of this practice. Homework, by definition, is supposed to be an opportunity to practice and get reinforcement. Besides, do *you* want a set of homework papers to grade each night? Wouldn't your time be better spent planning good lessons?

If you choose to grade their practice work, then everything you assign is, in effect, a test. When do they get the opportunity to make mistakes and learn from them if not with homework? (This does not refer to take-home tests.) There are ways to give credit for completed homework without giving it a grade. Some teachers make a notation on homework and/or in their grade books that assignments were completed. Regardless of the system you develop, respect the time your students spent working on each assignment by providing feedback or acknowledgment in some way.

TIPS from the TRENCHES

The following are suggestions beginning teachers wish they had followed when they began teaching.

1. Before you begin every unit, connect what you will be studying to the lives of your students in some way.

2. Always have more than one activity per class period.

3. Even though you want your students to enjoy being in class with their friends, avoid letting them sit together (except for during group activities).

4. If an activity isn't working, change it.

5. Select activities that allow your lower achievers to have leadership roles. Create opportunities for them to showcase their talents.

6. Ask your students how they feel about activities you select. Get their input as often as possible regarding how they will best learn a topic.

7. Try not to be so concerned with teaching the lesson you planned that you fail to notice whether they are learning. In other words, as you teach, pay attention to

(*Continued*)

how it's being received. Look at facial expressions, the level of participation, and the general interest that exists.

8. Avoid getting so comfortable with one or two methods that they are all you do with your students.

9. Videotape yourself teaching an entire lesson. Look for ways to improve. Ask a veteran teacher to look at it with you.

10. In the margins of your lesson plans, write questions you will ask the students.

PRAXIS™

Praxis Competencies Related to Implementing Instruction: Making Each Class Period Count

You will see questions related to topics reviewed in this chapter on most of the Praxis II Series (content-area tests) as well as the Principles of Learning and Teaching (PLT) test. For example, the topic overview section of the PLT Test (0524) for Grades 7–12 specifically refers to structuring a climate for learning and questioning techniques. It also suggests that you should be prepared to respond to questions that demonstrate your "understanding of learning strategies such as teacher-directed instruction, cooperative learning, independent study and laboratory and hands-on approaches" (ETS, 2001, *Test-at-a-Glance,* PLT).

Sample Question

Which of the following is something that should almost always be discussed with students when they are given a type of assignment that may be new to them?

(A) Whether the students will be tested on the material covered in the assignment

(B) Whether the assignment will be graded according to the same criteria as other assignments with which the student is familiar

(C) What the students can expect to learn from doing the assignment

(D) What kind of prior experience the teacher has had with this type of assignment

The answer is **C**. Educators believe that students learn only when motivated, and to be motivated, they must be engaged in meaningful activities to gain knowledge and master skills. Discussing goals with the students helps them to be motivated to learn (ETS, 2001, *Test-at-a-Glance,* PLT).

Specific content-area tests also address these issues. For example, the Physical Science: Pedagogy test (0483) requires test takers to provide "a fully detailed description of instructional strategies and activities that include elements of inquiry based learning and are appropriate for teaching the lesson" (ETS, 2001, *Test-at-a-Glance,* Physical Science, p. 61). Likewise, the Mathematics: Pedagogy test (0065) focuses on teaching strategies and your ability to explain what informs your instructional decisions.

Suggestions for Further Reading

If you have time to read only one book related to the issues in this chapter . . .

Kellough, R. D., & Kellough, N.G. (1999). *Secondary school teaching: A guide to methods and resources* (chap. 6–9). Upper Saddle River, NJ: Prentice Hall.

References

Adamovic, C., & Hedden, C. J. (1997). Problem-solving Skills. *Science Teacher, 64*(6), 20–23.

Brophy, J. (1987). On motivating students. In D. C. Berliner & B. V. Rosenskiner (Eds.), *Talks to teachers* (pp. 201–245). New York: Random House.

Clark, L. H., & Starr, I. S. (1996). *Secondary and middle school teaching methods* (7th ed.). Upper Saddle River, NJ: Prentice Hall.

Educational Testing Service (ETS). (2001). *Test-at-a-Glance—Physical Science.* Princeton, NJ: Author.

Educational Testing Service (ETS). (2001). *Test-at-a-Glance—Principles of Learning and Teaching.* Princeton, NJ.

Good, T. L., & Brophy, J. E. (1991). *Looking into classrooms* (5th ed.). New York: Harper Collins.

Guskey, T. (1985). *Implementing mastery learning.* Belmont, CA: Wadsworth.

Henson, K. T. (1993). *Methods and strategies for teaching in secondary and middle schools* (2nd ed.). New York: Longman.

Hopfenberg, W., Levin, H., & Associates. (1993). *The accelerated schools: Resource guide.* San Francisco: Jossey-Bass.

Kellough, R. D., & Kellough, N. G. (1999). *Secondary school teaching: A guide to methods and resources.* Upper Saddle River, NJ: Prentice Hall.

King, A. (1990). Reciprocal questioning: A strategy for teaching students how to learn from lectures. *Clearing House, 64*(2), 131–135.

Levin, H. (1996). Accelerated schools after eight years. In L. Schauble & R. Glaser (Eds.), *Innovations in learning: New environments for education.* Mahwah, NJ: Lawrence Erlbaum Associates, 329–352.

Levin, H. (1997). Raising schools' production: An x-efficiency approach. *Economics of Education Review, 16*(3), 303–311.

Maddox, H., & Hoole, E. (1975). Performance decrement in the lecture. *Educational Review, 28,* 17–30.

McNeil, J. D., & Wiles, J. (1990). *The essentials of teaching: Decisions, plans, and methods.* New York: Macmillan.

Miller, C. M. (2000). Student researched problem-solving strategies. *Mathematics Teacher, 93* (2), 136–138.

Richetti, C., & Sheevin, J. (1999). Helping students ask the right questions. *Educational Leadership, 57* (3), 58–62.

Rosenshire, B., & Stevens, R. (1986). Teacher functions. In M. C. Wittrock (Ed.), *Handbook on research in teaching* (3rd ed., pp. 376–391). New York: Macmillan.

Rothstein, P. R. (1990). *Educational psychology.* New York: McGraw-Hill.

Rowe, M. B. (1974). Wait time and reward as instructional variables. *Journal of Research on Science Teaching, 11,* 81–94.

Schieffer, J. L., & Schieffer, David J. (2000). Problem-solving skills: Solution-focused strategies for student development. *Journal of School Improvement, 1*(2), 14–19.

Slavin, R. (1989). Research on cooperative learning: Consensus and controversy. *Educational Leadership, 47*(4), 52–54.

Webb, L., Metha, A., & Jordan, K. (1999). *Foundations of American education* (3rd ed.). Upper Saddle River, NJ: Merrill/Prentice Hall.

Wilen, W. W. (1982). *Questioning skills for teachers* (p. 18). Washington, DC: National Education Association.

Wilen, W. W. (1991). *Questioning skills for teachers* (3rd ed.). Washington, DC: National Education Association.

9

Your Content Area

Using Resources and Technology to Become an Expert in Your Field

I can't imagine my life without music. Even as a young kid, I was always part of singing groups and in the band. In high school, I had a great orchestra teacher who encouraged me to major in music in college and pursue a career in the field. I decided then that I wanted to be just like him. If I can inspire just one of my students the way he did me, I will feel like a success.

Middle school music teacher

Your content area—you will be spending most of your professional days as a teacher thinking about and teaching this subject. Does that idea excite you or overwhelm you? Perhaps both. Was it your major in college and therefore something you enjoyed learning about? Or are some of your daily classes assigned merely because they needed someone to teach the course? Hopefully, your situation represents the former, but as you well know, beginning teachers often have at least one class a day that wasn't on their preference list. That's fine. Most of your course load should be in your field anyway. Like most secondary teachers, you think of yourself first and foremost as a teacher of your particular discipline.

This chapter addresses some fundamental things you want to focus on relative to your content area. You will review what every content area teacher must be aware of in terms of the standards, curriculum, and best practice for teaching in your area. There will also be a discussion of resources, reading in your content area, and ways of thinking about integrating your content with other subject areas. The chapter then focuses on some ways to incorporate technology into your teaching.

Your Content Area

The Uniqueness of Your Content Area: What Is the Nature of Your Field?

In secondary schools, academic disciplines become more specialized. By definition and necessity, elementary schools provide an "elementary" overview of a range of *subjects;* teachers focus primarily on the fundamentals of each content area and often teach several subjects each day. When students reach middle school, they experience their first formalized exposure to *courses*. Even if the coursework combines content areas and has teachers team teaching, these content areas are more clearly defined as separate, stand-alone areas of study. High school courses are even more separate and comprehensive, addressing topics with greater depth.

The change from middle to high school is reflected in course titles that become less broad and more specific—from Language Arts to English, from Social Studies to U.S. History, from Science to Biology. Secondary school is where students begin to gain a sense of the nature of each content area and the different ways of thinking about each particular discipline. Secondary teachers, likewise, see themselves as "specialists" in their particular field. Thus, principals often hear comments such as this one from a social studies teacher: "I can't teach a section of World History next year—my area is legal, political, and economic systems!" It's natural for teachers to feel this way, given the compartmentalized nature of secondary schools. It's why it is inevitable that you will be viewed by your students, not as a teacher, but as the Spanish teacher.

As a specialist in your area, you are expected to know all the particulars that make your field unique. What is the current approach to teaching history? What are the state-of-the-art methods and strategies that are most effective? While most elementary teachers are aware of these trends as well, their focus is on a more integrated and broad orientation to subjects. Middle grade teachers begin to focus on specific and separate courses. High school students are ready for and expect more depth in their classes.

The Secondary Curriculum

If you are like most beginning teachers, your tendency will be to grab the text that has been adopted for your course and begin with chapter 1. You may want to think about that. You must first understand how your course fits into the entire curriculum. Every school has a curriculum guide containing all the courses and their descriptions. No course is there by accident. There is a scope and sequence for your subject that spans the entire secondary experience, and you need to understand the overall plan if you are going to be an effective part of this content area continuum. The organization and description of these courses reflect many hours of discussion and decision making by teachers, administrators, and community representatives. In other words, every course you see has a purpose.

Ask whoever at your school is in charge of such materials to give you a list of the courses for your school. It may be in a variety of forms, such as the registration booklet or a course or curriculum selection guide, or the like. Take a few minutes to become aware of the total range of offerings available and then examine more closely all of the offerings for your department. Finally, look carefully at the course description for your class.

National, State, and Local Standards for Your Content Area

As mentioned previously, every content area in the secondary curriculum has a set of *content* standards that guide the development of courses within the discipline and the topics that need to be addressed. These standards exist at the national, state, and local levels and reflect instructional goals and objectives for the field. In addition, most states identify *performance* standards. These define various levels of competence for each grade and subject and gauge the degree to which a student has met the content standards. *It is your responsibility to read and understand these standards and design your courses with them in mind* (see Activity 9.1). Don't depend on the textbook to cover all of the important elements. True, most textbooks reflect the current standards for each discipline, but they may not address everything. As you develop your course, you want to include the priorities identified in the standards for two reasons. First, they reflect the content that numerous experts have deemed of most value for students to know. Second, in this age of accountability, many secondary subjects have an end-of-course test that assesses your students' knowledge of content in the standards. Often, school systems provide copies of state and local standards for new teachers during orientation. But if yours has not and you are not sure how to find a copy, ask one of the following people, who should be able to help you:

- The chairperson of your department
- The curriculum coordinator at your school
- The school system's resource person for your content area
- The school librarian
- Another colleague in your department

National standards are available from the professional organizations for your discipline.

Activity 9.1

Identifying Competencies for Instruction

Using the course descriptions for your classes that your school provides and copies of the national, state, and local standards for your content area, make a chart with two columns. One should be a list of competencies that *must* be addressed because they are emphasized in all of these sources. The other column should list competencies that are not found in all of these places, but are deemed important in one or two. Are there any of these competencies that you will give only minor attention to or will omit altogether? Decide now how you will make these curricular decisions. Be careful and intentional about the decisions you make.

Focusing Your Teaching: How Do You Demonstrate Best Practice in Your Field?

Your Course: Reflecting Current Trends in Your Content Area

It is important to be aware of the current trends in your field, both curricular and pedagogical. What are considered the best and most effective strategies for teaching the content? Things may have changed somewhat since you were a secondary student yourself—especially if you are not a twenty-something. For example, social studies teachers now rarely stress memorizing dates as they did in the good old days; instead, they emphasize time frames, selecting only the most important dates for memorization. Likewise, to the extent possible, the principles of grammar are taught within the context of writing rather than in isolation. Few English teachers spend time teaching their students to diagram sentences and much less time is spent conjugating verbs than in the past.

Are these changes good things? Maybe or maybe not. But they represent current thinking for these disciplines. What are the current trends in your content area? There are several ways to acquaint yourself with them, such as reading the publications of your professional organizations and attending workshops and professional meetings that are provided by your state and school system. These publications and meetings will also give you ideas on how to address cultural diversity and use technology effectively.

Each content area has its own list of professional demands. What are the absolute essentials that beginning teachers need to know about their content areas, according to experienced teachers? The following are sample expectations of certain fields of study.

English is the only subject that students must take every year they are in school. Why? Because the content addressed is considered fundamental to every other subject. It represents reading as well as basic communication skills. English teachers must know how to teach literature, writing, and grammar to *all* students. They must also understand how to manage the large paper load that seems to be part of the written nature of their discipline, more so than in most other subject areas. They are often viewed as resources for other teachers who are having trouble dealing with reluctant readers. Other responsibilities that tend be part of the English teacher's job description in most schools are extracurricular in nature but are part of the secondary school experience. They include sponsoring debate, newspaper, yearbook and drama clubs (Carroll, Alexander, Bell, Chadwick, & Rudkin, 2002).

Mathematics teachers must build on students' knowledge and help them to become more sophisticated in problem-solving techniques. They should be increasing their students' abilities to visualize, describe, and analyze situations in mathematical terms. Ultimately, they work to develop a "deeper understanding of the fundamental mathematical concepts of function and relation, invariance and transformation" (National Council for the Teachers of Mathematics, 2002). Mathematics teachers are expected to stress using manipulative materials and be adept in teaching students how to use calculators, define and graph functions, enter data and display a scatterplot, and investigate mathematical problems in a variety of ways. Their instruction must promote conversation about mathematical issues, including more focused questioning, listening, reading, and writing in the field (Pugalee, Bell, Hardin, Royster, McCoy, & Hernandez, 2002).

Science teachers must understand the nature and processes of science. This includes the knowledge and basic understanding of science concepts and the social implications of science. They must know how to design activities and investigations that will help students to construct their own meanings of science concepts (DiBiase, Boger, Cowan, Veal, & Elliott, 2002).

Social studies teachers are expected to know the fundamental concepts of the various disciplines that comprise the field of social studies. This is a tall order because in addition to history, this includes such fields as economics, political science, and psychology. They must also stress the use of current events as references to help students put social studies in some meaningful context, and they need to be adept at dealing with controversial and sensitive issues that are naturally a part of studying human beings. Because the field is so broad, they must know how to seek out, select, and manage the amount of information that is available to them. The nature of the field means that they must constantly confront personal beliefs and identity, both their own and that of their students, as the subject is so value laden. It is especially important that they embrace the value of diversity and multicultural perspectives in social studies and the importance of preparing their students for effective lives as good citizens (Gulledge, Addo, Goode, Jester, Painter, Smith, & Stapleton, 2002).

Special education teachers must face the complexities of wearing two professional hats. In today's schools, *all* teachers have students with special needs. Therefore, special education teachers have a unique role in that they are expected not only to be competent in carrying out the many duties related to students who are assigned to them, but also to serve as the resources for the teachers of other subjects. They must know and understand the philosophical, historical, and legal foundations of special education; be expert in identifying characteristics of special learners; and be able to demonstrate an extensive range of assessment, diagnostic, and evaluation skills. They also must be able to facilitate appropriate communication and collaborative skills with the many constituencies they serve. As they work with teachers in other content areas, they must clarify their roles as special education resource personnel and help them understand the definitions of exceptional children as well as the procedures to provide appropriate services (Wright, Brown, Cooke, Dickens, Core, & Lillie, 2002).

REALITY CHECK 9.1

As you can see, being "expert" in your field is going to require that you immerse yourself in the ways of thinking that are unique to your content area. Obviously, you must know the basics of teaching any group of students—such essentials as classroom management, lesson planning, and methods for evaluation. But knowing these things is only the beginning—the background on which you will now superimpose the specifics of your content and the expectations of required standards as an English or foreign language teacher.

Becoming an Expert in Your Field

You can probably remember at least one teacher from your secondary school who stood out as the expert in his or her field. You and your classmates thought of such teachers as bright, well informed, and excited about their subjects. It was rare that students asked them questions they couldn't answer. Didn't you find that *you* were more interested in their subject because *they* were so passionate about it themselves? They were true teachers—the best. How did they get to be like that? More important, how can *you* get to be like that? The answer is simple, but it takes time and demands some effort on your part. Are you ready? Here it is.

Constantly pay attention to your content area in and out of school and be receptive to interesting opportunities that inspire you to teach it better.

Yes. That's all there is to it. How? Several suggestions will help you.

1. Read everything you can about the topics that you are teaching. This means going beyond reading the next chapter for tomorrow's lesson. It means reading magazines, professional journals, books, and anything else you come across that might increase your own depth of understanding of your subject. Bring some of these articles to class. Create a resource station for students to read about related topics for their own enrichment.

2. Look for events in the real world that relate to your subject, and make them a part of your teaching. For example, if there is a good movie that explores some topic you are studying in your class and will stimulate discussion, use it. How many students were curious about game theory after seeing the movie *A Beautiful Mind*? Is there a play in your community based on a novel you are reading in English? How many discussions have social studies teachers facilitated about the Middle East since September 11?

3. Attend professional meetings where the most current curricular priorities and methodology are discussed.

4. Do some research on some aspect of your content area that interests you and share your findings with colleagues informally or formally at a workshop or meeting.

5. Talk about your content area—with coworkers or others you know who have some interest in the subject. It's amazing how many ideas bubble up that are not only stimulating for you to ponder but that give you a great idea about what to do in class the next day.

Mrs. Morgan is an art teacher and has won awards for her teaching. She is constantly on the lookout for ideas that relate to her class, whether she is at a movie, a flea market, or the mall. She takes every workshop offered by her school system to enhance her own skills and sets aside some time each academic year to do some artwork herself. She personifies the expert teacher.

REALITY CHECK 9.2

Relax. No one is suggesting that you become so consumed with your content area that it is part of everything you do in life. It is simply a matter of making what you teach a part of your consciousness. If your subject area isn't something that you feel passionate about, that's OK. Just make it a part of your personal job description. Consider making a to-do list while you are at school of things that you can do to become more expert—things that can be done while you are in or out of school. Then do them. Gradually you will find that thinking about teaching your subject no longer is part of your daily checklist. It has become a habit.

Textbooks, Materials, and Resources in Your Content Area

Many states have statewide adoption committees to determine which books they will recommend to local school systems for every content area. School systems then select books from the list that they want to use. More than likely, you will be given a copy of the text and the teacher's edition that accompanies it when you first begin teaching. Textbooks do provide some useful assistance to students in several ways. Not only do they arrange content into some logical order, but they identify by subheadings and in bold type which topics are most important. They are also written at the appropriate level for students, incorporating new vocabulary into their reading. They also provide such features as activities, glossaries, questions for review, and resources for enrichment. Even if the text doesn't appear to be one that's particularly useful to you, remember that there's usually a good reason it has been adopted, so at least look it over. Except in rare cases, you are certainly not obligated to plan your entire course around it.

Instead of relying solely on the textbook, however, many teachers use a variety of other resources, such as articles, supplementary textbooks, and publications from organizations that distribute information related to your field. There are valid reasons not to depend on any one source. For example, a single source will expose students to just one point of view. The source may also not be written in a style or format that is useful for your students. Also, a textbook that was written for a national audience might not address particular areas you want emphasized. Regardless of what additional resources you use, it is important for you to check with your department chairperson, curriculum coordinator, or assistant principal. These individuals will help you to determine whether certain supplementary resources meet your curricular needs and do not advance some group's political agenda or ideology that the school does not support. Because every content area has materials and resources that are unique to the discipline, you need to make sure that you know which resources are most useful.

Teaching Reading in Your Content Area

One of the biggest challenges teachers face is whether their students can read the content they are teaching. Regardless of what you teach, you are a reading teacher. In fact, 47 states and the District of Columbia now require specific coursework or have determined a competency in reading methods for all or some of their middle and high school teachers (Romine, 1996). Each content area requires different reading approaches and has esoteric vocabulary that is particular to the discipline and possibly very different from that of other subject areas. What kinds of reading does your discipline require? Find out.

The problem for students is that they have different kinds of reading skills required for different courses. For example, their math class may require an understanding of how to read graphs, diagrams, and equations. English class with a heavy reading load may mean they must improve their skills in skimming. In science, they may have to interpret data. All of the skills assume that the student can read introductory content, directions, and explanations in the first place. Improving their reading skills in general and their reading skills for your class in particular is absolutely critical to your students' success in their total school experience.

First consideration—can they read your textbook? You must find out by determining the reading level of the textbook. There are several ways to do this, but one of the most effective is the Fry Readability Formula (Fry, 1968; see Figure 9.1 and Activity 9.2).

The Fry Readability Graph will assist you as you estimate the grade level of the text. The procedure is as follows:

1. Determine the average number of syllables in three 100-word selections taken one from the beginning, one from the middle, and one from the ending parts of the book.
2. Determine the average number of sentences in the three 100-word selections.
3. Plot the two values on the Fry readability graph. Their intersection will give you an estimate of the text's reading level at the 50 percent to 75 percent comprehension level.

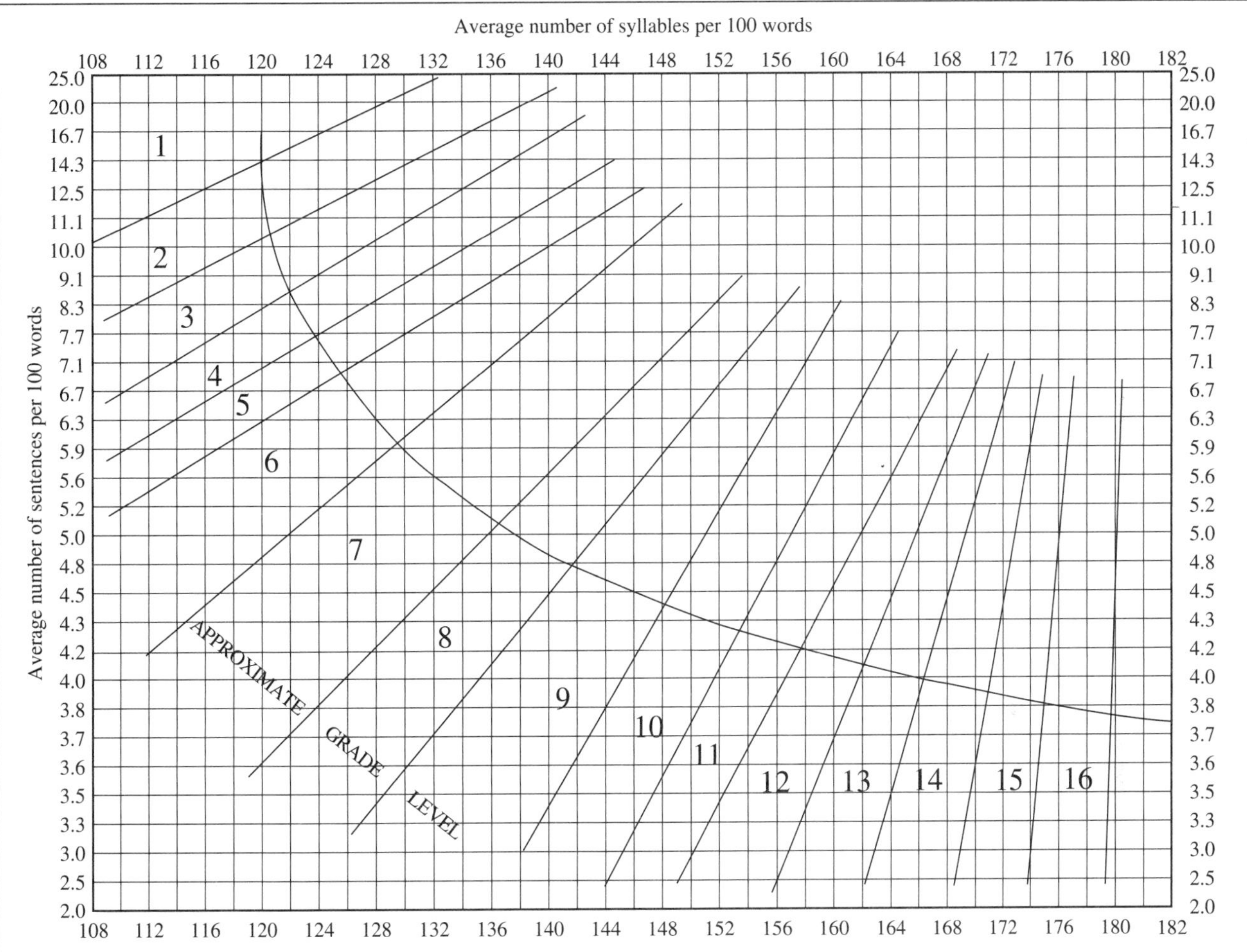

DIRECTIONS:
Randomly select 3 one hundred word passages from a book or an article. Plot average number of syllables and average number of sentences per 100 words on graph to determine the grade level of the material. Choose more passages per book if great variability is observed and conclude that the book has uneven readability. Few books will fall in gray area but when they do grade level scores are invalid.

Count proper nouns, numerals, and initializations as words. Count a syllable for each symbol. For example, "1945" is 1 word and 4 syllables and "IRA" is 1 word and 3 syllables.

EXAMPLE:	SYLLABLES	SENTENCES	
1st Hundred Words	124	6.6	
2nd Hundred Words	141	5.5	
3rd Hundred Words	158	6.8	
AVERAGE	141	6.3	READABILITY 7th GRADE (See dot plotted on graph)

Edward Fry, "A Readability Formula That Saves Time," *Journal of Reading* (April 1968), 11:587

FIGURE 9.1 Fry Readability Graph

ACTIVITY 9.2

Determining Reading Levels

Using the Fry Readability Graph, determine the grade level for the text for the course you teach. Then do the same thing for another course in your discipline but one that is either at a lower or higher level. Can you recognize the difference in level?

Use the Cloze technique with a group of your students to determine their ability to read your text. What did you learn? How will you change any reading assignments, if at all, based on what you have discovered?

Now you need to determine how well your students can read the text. You can do this with the Cloze technique (Bormuth, 1968). The approach is as follows:

Select from the book several typical passages of a total of 400 to 415 words. Delete every eighth word except for those in the first and last sentences, proper names, numbers, and initial words in the sentences. You will probably have deleted about 50 words. Replace the deleted words with blanks, duplicate the passages, and distribute them to students. Ask them to fill in the blanks with the most appropriate words they can supply. Collect the papers. Score them by counting all the student-supplied words that are the same as those in the original text and dividing this number by the total number of blanks. Some educators recommend that you count only the words that are exactly the same; others would allow synonyms. Perhaps you should not count synonyms or verbs of a different tense (McKenna, 1976).

$$\text{Score} = \frac{\text{Number of same words supplied}}{\text{Number of blanks}}$$

You may assume that students who score better than 50% can read well, that students who score between 40% and 50% are able to read on the level of instruction, and that students who score below 40% will have trouble reading the text.

Based on the assumption that your students have mastered to some extent basic reading and language skills in their elementary reading program, they must now be able to locate information and improve their independent study skills. Two of the most important areas you should focus on relative to reading in your content area are (a) vocabulary development and (b) comprehension (see Activity 9.3).

Building vocabulary in the content area is essential, and it can be done several ways:

1. Providing appropriate context for new words
2. Teaching key words

ACTIVITY 9.3

Adapting Lesson Plans to Address Reading Needs

Create two versions of the same lesson—one that specifically focuses on improving students' vocabulary skills and one that is designed to improve comprehension in your content area.

3. Improving word-attack skills
4. Encouraging the use of the dictionary
5. Using vocabulary notebooks

Improving students' vocabulary is vital to helping them become more comfortable with the discipline itself. It is often those unknown words and terms in their reading that turn them off and convince them that the class is too hard. Teach vocabulary upfront. Then, as they read, they won't close the book in frustration when they see a term like *monopolistic competition* in economics class. Instead, with a sense of accomplishment, they will know what it means and will read further.

The other important area to improve is comprehension. To learn in your class, students must understand what they read. Remember to do the following to increase their comprehension skills (Callahan, Clark, & Kellough, 1992):

1. Provide background experience—They need a context in which to relate new information to what they already know and understand.
2. Give complete homework assignments—Make sure that they fully understand what they need to do and how they need to do it.
3. Teach them how to use the textbook—Explain the format and special features that are present so that they will begin to use the book as a resource on their own.
4. Use study guides and worksheets—These written guides will be helpful as students try to determine exactly what they are looking for in their reading.
5. Use directed reading lessons—For example, have the students read certain passages that contain information that is critical to their understanding of a lesson as a class. Give them material that has a particular focus in mind or a couple of questions to answer that will guide their thinking.

The Interdisciplinary Curriculum: Integrating Content

Definition of Integrated Curriculum

Your content is not just a slice of information unconnected to the rest of the world. It has been compartmentalized for a variety of reasons, including the convenience of educators who find it more effective to focus on specific areas of study in isolation. However, this reality requires that students must find some way to make connections between content areas on their own. Wouldn't their learning be more meaningful if teachers helped them to make these connections? Helping them may be as simple as looking for opportunities to connect with what the teacher down the hall is doing.

Mrs. Allen, a U.S. history teacher, always plans several of her units with Mr. Hinson, the English teacher next door. For example, he assigns his students *All Quiet on the Western Front* to coincide with her unit on World War I. Together, they plan activities and classes that pull these two content areas together for the students. Their intention is to have an *integrated curriculum*. Having an integrated curriculum means that two or more separate disciplines are related to each other in such a way that overlapping content becomes more meaningful to students.

Of course, you won't need or even want to use the integrated curriculum approach in every case, but trying to help students make these connections when the opportunities arise will be very valuable and enjoyable for your students (see Activity 9.4).

Levels of Curriculum Integration

You may find it useful to think of integrating the curriculum in terms of levels. These levels of content integration fall at different places on a continuum from least integrated to most integrated.

ACTIVITY 9.4

Experimenting with Integrated Teaching

Identify a teacher in a content area that can in some way be coordinated with yours. Talk to this teacher about experimenting with an integrated unit. Following the steps outlined above, create and implement the unit.

Level 1 represents the traditional organization of the content instruction where teachers plan their subjects in relative isolation and usually teach alone. Students must make any connections with other content areas on their own.

Level 2 involves students using learning with a theme approach rather than a pure topic outline. They may have some minimal input into the planning, and teachers may teach alone or with another teacher. In this step, teachers are integrating content somewhat but keeping their subjects separate. Some experts call this *infusion*.

Level 3 is where students are learning two or more of their content areas around a common theme. Teachers may agree on a common theme and then deal separately with that theme in their own classrooms. Therefore, the content the students learn in one classroom might be connected to what they are learning at the same time in another subject. This may be subject focused, theme focused, or project focused. Some refer to this as a *coordinated curriculum*.

Level 4 is when teachers and students collaborate on a common theme and when content boundaries disappear.

Level 5 is when teachers and students have collaborated on a common theme and the content to be studied. Discipline boundaries are blurred and teachers of several subjects and grades teach toward common understanding of a certain theme.

Many educators believe that, in a perfect world, all content areas would be designed in tandem with all others so that the connections for students would be clear. It will take more time and effort to create these kinds of learning experiences and the students will benefit immensely. However, other educators, especially at the high school level, are not sure that it is wise to integrate the curriculum. They believe that too much integration might not allow for the appropriate focus on important content knowledge. Also, since each subject has its own way of thinking, it is hard to combine them without sacrificing some of the purity of studying each content area in isolation. As the decision maker, you must decide whether integrating the curriculum is the best way of meeting your curricular goals, and to what extent.

For you as a new teacher, the safest thing to do is to experiment. You will not learn how to integrate the curriculum until you try. And you will not know which methods work best for you until you have tried several.

Steps in Developing an Interdisciplinary Thematic Unit

Assuming you are sold on the idea of trying this approach, how will you go about it? Here are some basic steps you and your colleague(s) will want to take. (This section adapted from Kellough & Kellough, 1999, pp. 229–235.)

1. Agree on the nature of the unit.
2. Discuss subject-specific outlines, goals, and objectives as well as materials.

3. Choose a topic and create a timeline for your own course. Start listing possible topics that lend themselves to being coordinated with other subjects.
4. With the other teachers, set up two timelines. The first is for the teachers and helps to ensure that each participating teacher will meet deadlines for specific work that is to be coordinated. The second timeline is for the students and the teachers. It shows how long the unit will be, when it will start, and so forth.
5. Decide on the scope and sequence of the content and instruction.
6. Share goals and objectives with each teacher involved.
7. Give the unit a name.
8. Share the subject-specific units, lesson plans, and materials.
9. Present the lessons, with each member trading classes from time to time, if appropriate.
10. Evaluate and adjust the unit.

Incorporating Technology

Some Bells and Whistles: How Can Technology Enhance Your Teaching?

Few things will make your content come alive more dramatically than technology. And since many of today's students have become quite expert in the use of all kinds of technology, incorporating it in your classroom is a must. A decade ago, technology was thought of as "any gadget, instrument, machine or device" used by teachers to enhance their lessons (Muffoletto, 1994, p. 25). Teachers needed only a basic understanding of how to use the most commonly available equipment, such as an overhead, a filmstrip and movie projector, a tape recorder, and perhaps a VCR. Other, more sophisticated equipment or learning aids was available in the media center and was operated by someone with special expertise. No longer! While most teachers do use overhead projectors and VCRs regularly, computers have taken over as the technology of choice, and there have been increased efforts to encourage their regular use.

By the time your students have reached secondary school, they have more than likely been exposed to computers in some way for most of their lives. In fact, they are probably a good deal more knowledgeable about them than you are. Don't be intimidated. That's good. It means that you have the opportunity to take advantage of their fascination with computers to enhance your teaching in incredible ways. The real challenge you face may very well be your own comfort level in using this important tool as part of your instruction. You have no choice—if you are not proficient, at least in the basics, become so.

The Basics

Fortunately, you don't have to know *everything* about computers. The nature of your content area will determine which computer skills you must master. Most subject areas, however, require some understanding of the basics (see Activity 9.5). Among the most essential computer skills are word processing, databases, spreadsheets, and the Internet.

Word Processing

Word processing is simply typing on a computer. It can replace any teaching or learning activity that used to be done by handwriting or on a typewriter and is easier and more effective to use than either. For example, errors can be corrected on-screen before being printed, and words or sentences can be inserted, deleted, or moved around. Work can be saved and retrieved again later. It makes reports and homework assignments easier for your students to do and for you to read.

Databases

Database management systems (DBMS) are computerized record-keeping systems that were developed to replace paper. They allow for the storage, organization, and manipulation of information, including both text and numerical data. They are, in effect, electronic filing cabinets. *Database* refers to both the computer program and the product (files) it creates. Database software is most useful in locating information through keyword searches.

Teachers reap the benefits of database software when they use it to assist with the instruction of research and information-management skills. They also find DBMS helpful in teaching higher level concepts such as classification and keyword searching—especially to students who are just learning to use the computer (Jankowski, 1993).

Spreadsheets

Spreadsheets are numerical, computerized record-keeping systems that were originally created to replace paper ledger systems. A spreadsheet is basically a grid (table or matrix) of empty cells, with columns identified by letters and rows identified by numbers.

Spreadsheets have three functions. First, they store information in a particular place (a cell) where it can be retrieved easily. Second, spreadsheets calculate functions such as the numerical contents of any combination of cells. Third, they present information in many ways. Whenever students need to do a calculation, they will discover that setting up a spreadsheet can be most helpful. Teachers most often use spreadsheets as management tools for accounting but find that their use requires a variety of mental processes that result in increased proficiency in organizing information and thinking more deeply (Jonassen, 2000).

Secondary teachers can use spreadsheets to perform functions in various content areas, such as

- Solving a complex chemistry problem. This might involve a wet and dry analysis of flue gases, which may be expanded to include volumetric flow rate, pressure, humidity, dew point, temperature, and combustion temperature, in a course on Mass and Energy Balances (Misovich & Biasca, 1990). (*Chemistry*)
- Facilitating student grading of peer speech performances (Dribin, 1985). (*English*)
- Estimating and comparing data related to various dinosaurs (Karlin, 1988). (*Social studies* or *General science*)
- Analyzing field data on ecology of tree species (Sigismondi & Calise, 1990). (*Botany*)
- Analyzing the results of an experiment on microbial growth rates using simple fermentation equipment (Mills & Jackson, 1997). (*Microbiology*)
- Creating mathematical models such as balance of payments and cost-benefit analysis (Cashien, 1990). (*Economics*)

(Examples from Jonassen, 2000, pp. 88–93)

The Internet

According to Morrison and Lowther (2002), the Internet is the "mother of all networks," linking computers with telephone lines, cables, or radio signals. The Internet encompasses many components. The ones most commonly used by students include the World Wide Web (WWW), e-mail, and chat rooms. The WWW is humankind's largest forum for disseminating information. Having access to the Web can provide students with instant information during the course of a class discussion or as they are doing research in the library.

REALITY CHECK 9.3

You may need to help students determine which Web sites are valuable sources. Remind them that anyone can create a Web site. Therefore, along with the helpful information, there is a lot of trash online.

E-mail allows users to send messages electronically. Increasingly, teachers are communicating in this way with their students as they are completing assignments at home or

Operate a computer system to use software successfully.

Evaluate and use computers and other technologies to support instruction.

Explore, evaluate, and use technology-based applications for communications, presentations, and decision making.

Apply current instructional principles and research and appropriate assessment practices to the use of computers and related technologies.

Demonstrate knowledge of uses of computers for problem solving, data collection, information management, communications, presentations, and decision making.

Develop student learning activities that integrate computers and technology for a variety of student grouping strategies and for diverse student populations.

Evaluate, select, and integrate computer/technology-based instruction in the curriculum in a subject area and/or grade level.

Demonstrate knowledge of uses of multimedia, hypermedia, and telecommunications tools to support instruction.

Demonstrate skills in using productivity tools for professional and personal use, including word processing, database management, spreadsheet software, and print/graphic utilities.

Demonstrate knowledge of equity, ethical, legal, and human issues of computing and technology use as they relate to society, and model appropriate behavior.

Identify resources to keep current in applications of computing and related technologies in education.

Use technology to access information to enhance personal and professional productivity.

Apply computers and related technologies to facilitate emerging roles of learners and educators.

FIGURE 9.2 ISTE/NCATE Required Technology Competencies for All Teachers

Source: Roblyer, M. D., & Edwards, J. (2000). *Integrating Educational Technology* (2nd ed., p. 23). Upper Saddle River, NJ: Merrill/Prentice Hall.

on weekends. Chat rooms allow students to talk with others in real time, much like a telephone conversation. Some teachers have encouraged groups of students to "converse" with each other about a topic and as they work on projects.

While the uses described above are the essentials for almost every teacher, there are other competencies that may be of value as you teach your particular content area. Review the following to determine which skills you should develop. See Figure 9.2.

If you are not proficient in these areas, get assistance from someone who can teach you or take a class or workshop to help you develop these skills. With dozens of computer junkies out there and the emphasis on this technology by school systems, you should have no trouble finding help.

The Computer: A Teaching Tool Whose Time Has Come

Experts (Bork, 1987) predicted that microcomputers would revolutionize the way students were taught. Sadly, they have had little impact. Why? One problem is that they are often used just to *deliver* instruction, a function best reserved for drill and practice, tutorials, and games

Your Personal Technology Competency Inventory

Consider your content area and the technology competencies that will enhance your instruction. Make a master list of the competencies you currently lack using the computer skills listed in the "Basics" section and the ISTE/NCATE Required Technologies Competencies list as guides. Create a plan to become proficient in these areas.

for enrichment (Archer, 1998; Becker, 1991). Such uses are referred to as CAI, and the practice hasn't been all bad. Students do learn from these activities. But using them *exclusively* in place of other forms of instruction is not best practice. It is better to use the computer as a *tool,* a way of enhancing and supplementing basic instruction, rather than replacing it.

Jonassen (2000, p. 3) encouraged teachers to incorporate computers into their planning because computers are cognitive tools ("mindtools") for engaging multiple forms of student thinking. When students use them as supplementary tools, aids, or enhancements to their learning, they are becoming proficient in the same skills they will need in their work lives after graduation. Most colleges and jobs expect everyone to know how to access and examine information and be proficient in word processing. The time has definitely come for computers to play a critical role in student learning.

There are four reasons computers may start to have the impact that was predicted years ago (Morrison & Lowther, 2002):

1. After experimenting with computers in schools for 2 decades, educators are more knowledgeable about what works best.
2. There are simply more computers in schools now than ever before.
3. Teachers, administrators, and parents want new and more effective approaches to using computers.
4. Best practice in teaching today encourages realistic contexts for learning.

Student-Centered Instruction

For all content areas, current best practice now emphasizes instruction that is student centered. What better way to help the individual student than with her own personal workstation and her own computer (tutor)? One reason that integrating computers into your subject area is so effective is that computers provide open-ended learning environments where individuals can learn by themselves or with others. Research suggests that technology-rich classroom environments promote collaborative learning and a constructivist approach to understanding content (Cohen, 2001). Students are able to solve all kinds of problems and answer almost any question as they learn new information. One of the best things about this is that, once you have given the students direction, they can do much learning on their own, with you functioning as a facilitator and resource (Morrison & Lowther, 2002).

Such self-directed learning develops in several ways. First, when teachers create inquiry units, students can learn new concepts by collecting data to find answers. Another approach is "guided design," where students usually work in small groups, each group provided with some background on an issue to research. Once the problem is identified, they seek information and receive specific feedback at each step of the process. Both of these are similar to problem-based learning (PBL), where students use data to solve real-world problems. It is based on the scientific method for compiling information: creating an hypothesis, examining the data, testing the hypothesis, and determining a solution (Barrows & Kelson, 1996).

The NTeQ (iNtegrating Technology for inQuiry) Model

NTeQ is a framework for integrating real-world information and skills through technology. It involves the teacher, the student, the computer, the lesson, and the environment. (This section is a summary of Morrison & Lowther, 2002, pp. 23–39.)

The five basic elements of the NTeQ approach will produce the following results when the model is successfully implemented:

1. Teachers will be technologically competent and function as designers, managers, and facilitators (Lowther, Bassoppo-Moyo, & Morrison, 1998).
2. Students actively engage in the learning process and become technologically competent and effective researchers.

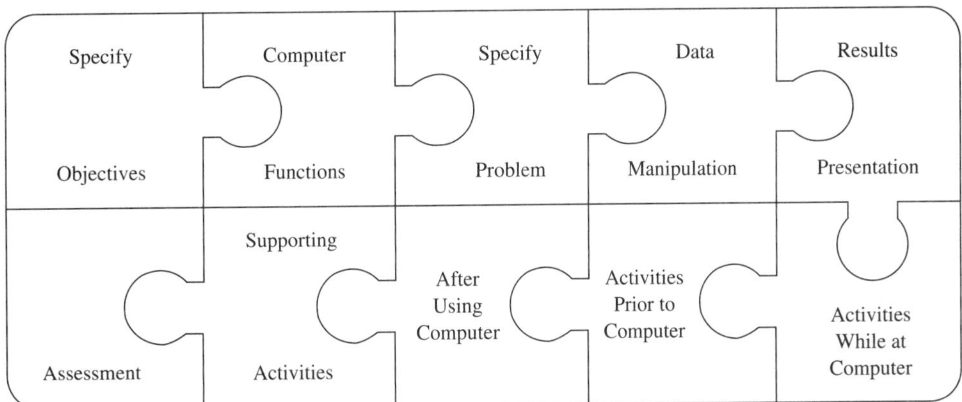

FIGURE 9.3 NTeQ Model

From Gary Morrison and Deborah Lowther, 2002, *Integrating Computer Technology into the Classroom* (2nd ed.), p. 34.

3. Computers are used as tools, as they are in the workplace, to support learning through the use of data to solve problems.
4. Technology is a critical component of lessons that are student centered and problem based.
5. The classroom environment provides a variety of resource-rich activities.

When you prepare for any lesson, there are always some *planning* steps and some *implementing* steps. The following is the NTeQ 10-step recommended model for *planning* an integrated computer lesson (see Figure 9.3). The steps are as follows:

1. Specify Objectives—Consider all of the objectives for everything related to the lesson, not just the ones related to the computer.

2. Computer Functions—Ask yourself what objectives can be met with the use of the computer. Is there a match? Look at the process from the students' point of view. What will they need to do to meet an objective?

3. Specify Problem—It is important that the students understand exactly what the problem is that they will be investigating. They will need to know what the purpose of the lesson is and what resources will be available to help them. They need to be invested in the process of understanding and solving the problem (Moursund, 1996). You can assist them by facilitating discussions that will help them gain clarity.

4. Data Manipulation—You must determine now what your students are going to do with the data they compile. How much instruction they need will depend on how proficient they are in using the computer. Sorting data and making a table are important skills, but what they do with that data is key. Consider providing a "think sheet" that includes pertinent questions to help them interpret data and make predictions (Morrison & Lowther, 2002, p. 73).

5. Results Presentation—How do you want your students to present the information? They might write a report using a word processor that would include a variety of desktop publishing techniques. Perhaps a poster or bulletin board would be best. They might publish their results on a Web page, they might also do a PowerPoint presentation, and so forth (Morrison & Lowther, 2002).

6. Activities While at Computer—You will need to decide how the students will obtain the information and what activities will best make this happen. Will they search the Internet or use a particular database? Will they work in groups or individually?

7. Activities Prior to Computer—What things will students need to do *before* they turn on the computer? This is an important question if you have a limited number of computers available. Preparing a guide that asks them to list basic and related terms they can use to search for information will help them to focus their attention.

8. After Using Computer—You will need to decide what you want them to do with the information they have gathered. Asking the students pertinent questions or preparing another guide sheet may be helpful.

9. Supporting Activities—To have an integrated lesson, you will need to determine what activities, both computer related and other types, will help you to meet your instructional goals. These may be lesson-related activities, activities that relate to an entire unit, or activities that are interdisciplinary in nature (see Activity 9.6).

10. Assessment—Assessment strategies for your integrated computer lesson may take a variety of forms, anything from traditional multiple-choice reviews to be sure that students understand the basic information to creating rubrics to evaluate a presentation to the class.

REALITY CHECK 9.4

Despite the preaching of techies whose passion for technology would have you believe that everything you do should include some work with the computer, you don't have to use computers in every lesson. In fact, many lessons will not lend themselves to the use of this method at all. Decisions about this will depend on the purpose of your instruction as well as the nature of your content.

Implementing Your Lesson

You have *planned* your lesson, but there is more for you to do before implementation. You must now prepare guide sheets, any special technical step-by-step information, and resource handouts so that your students can work as much as possible on their own. Create a rubric to help you evaluate the most important components of your lesson goals. You will then need to turn on computers and open applications, create folders and templates, load specialized software, and bookmark Internet sites (Morrison & Lowther, 2002). All of this needs to be done before the students walk in the door.

In effect, when you create a student-centered and problem-based classroom environment that incorporates the use of computers, you are *facilitating* (assisting, helping, and simplifying for students) rather than *teaching* (formally instructing) in the traditional sense. Having considered the objectives and various components of the lesson, you will now design your lesson approach, which will reflect what you already know about lesson design and selecting appropriate strategies. Again, factors such as

ACTIVITY 9.6

Practicing Computer Activities

Practice creating supporting activities by doing the following:

- Using the Internet, locate three educational shows or videos that would be appropriate for your content area.
- Use database software (such as Appleworks or Microsoft Works) to create a database file that contains a record for each video you choose. Each record will contain five fields: Web site name, URL, content area, show/video title, and description of the show or video.
- Create a columnar report containing all of the fields and records in the database.
- Select one show or video from your database to use as a resource with your students.

how your classroom is arranged and the availability of computers will affect your implementation decisions. Will students need to work in small groups? Will they rotate from computer station to computer station? Are there enough computers for everyone to work individually? Will you choose to demonstrate certain procedures, allow the students to teach each other, provide technology posters with basic instructions, or distribute student handouts with step-by-step instructions (Morrison & Lowther, 2002)?

REALITY CHECK 9.5

If you haven't figured this out already, no matter how proficient you become, you will inevitably run into technical problems. Make friends with a computer person!

Is it more work to incorporate technology into the teaching of your content area? Probably, at least at first, especially if you are learning yourself. But you will get better with time and experience. It is definitely worth the effort. The ways computers can help you in your role as teacher are endless. In addition to enhancing the quality of your instruction, there are numerous resources available for your own information, such as electronic gradebooks, mail merge letters, newsletters, Web pages, and more.

Technology in Specific Content Areas

In teaching your content area, you will want to (a) identify some of the current issues and trends in your subject area that will influence the selection and use of computers, (b) discover some of the common uses for technology in today's curriculum, and (c) create activities that will model content-area integration strategies. To help you get started, the following are some good Internet sites for specific content areas (Roblyer & Edwards, 2000, pp. 229–312). Read these pages for sample integration lessons for each content area, additional resources, and other specific suggestions for integrating technology into your content area.

English and Language Arts

The National Council of Teachers of English http://www.ncte.org/
The National Council of Teachers of English (NCTE) is the leading professional organization for the teaching of English and language arts at all grade levels.

Teachers and Writers Collaborative http://www.twc.org/
Teachers and Writers Collaborative explores the connections between writing and reading literature.

Foreign Language

American Council on the Teaching of Foreign Languages http://www.actfl.org/
This site is the main organization for foreign language teachers.

Language Links—Teaching with the Web http://polyglot.lss.wisc.edu/lss/lang/teach.html
This site presents a compilation of ideas for using WWW resources as a language-teaching tool.

Science

National Science Teachers Association http://www.nsta.org/
This site is the largest organization of science teachers and includes resources, standards, and current issues.

Eisenhower National Clearinghouse (ENC) http://www.enc.org/
Resources included are lesson plans for teachers and activities for students.

Mathematics

National Council of Teachers of Mathematics http://www.nctm.org/index.htm
This site provides many resources related to the implementation of math standards.

PBS Mathline http://www.pbs.org/learn/mathline/index.html
This is a professional development program for teachers.

Social Studies

National Council for the Social Studies http://www.ncss.org/
This site includes resources, professional development activities, and a section devoted to guiding students through Web resources.

Smithsonian Institution http://www.si.edu
Resources include online publications and photographs, historical perspectives, and online tours.

The History Channel http://historychannel.com
This site provides many resources, including audio versions of several great historical speeches, online simulations for students, and a "This Day in History" database.

Art

National Art Education Association http://www.naea-reston.org/
This general arts education site contains useful information about programs and a list of state education department contacts.

Music

Music Educators National Conference http://www.menc.org/

Technology Institute for Music Educators http://www.ti-me.org/
Promotes technology as it applies to music education.

Health and Physical Education

American School Health Association (ASHA) http://ashaweb.org/
Resources for teachers regarding current health issues.

American Alliance for Health, Physical Education, Recreation, and Dance http://www.aahperd.org/
Site offers links to physical education standards and resources.

Special Education

Council for Exceptional Children http://www.cec.sped.org/
The largest international professional organization for teachers of exceptional children.

TIPS from the TRENCHES

The following are suggestions beginning teachers wish they had followed when they began teaching.

For your content area

1. Keep up with the national, state, and local standards for your content area. Because they change, read them at the beginning of every year.

2. Go to meetings and workshops that will give you ideas and information for teaching your subject better.

3. Join the professional organization for your content area.

4. Interact on a regular basis with other teachers who teach your subject.

(Continued)

5. Look for opportunities to work with the departments at your central office that oversee the implementation of the curriculum for your field.

6. Read journals and other publications that are distributed by organizations and groups that relate to your field.

7. Look at catalogs that advertise resources and materials for the teaching of your discipline. Even if you don't order anything, they provide ideas for you to use with your students.

8. Know the state-of-the-art themes and trends in the teaching of your field and carry them through your teaching. For example, one science teacher reports that he reinforces the theme of scientific investigation as a part of every unit, regardless of topic. This way, the students become more aware of the way to think scientifically.

9. Read your text thoroughly before beginning to plan your course. Waiting to read one chapter ahead of the students will prevent you from seeing the big picture as you plan. Besides, there may be chapters you want to skip and others you want to supplement.

For incorporating technology

10. Learn how to use computers in your classroom (even if you think you can teach without them).

11. Find out from your media specialist or curriculum coordinator how much of the budget has been allotted for software and how you should go about getting it.

12. Become proficient in other aspects of technology that are subject specific. For example, if you teach mathematics, you need to be adept in the use of graphing calculators. Many teachers also use PowerPoint presentations.

13. Take workshops to help you develop the necessary skills.

14. Always use a word processor for handouts for students. Hand-written sheets are hard for students to read.

15. Have everything ready for the students when they come in. The beginning of class is no time to start organizing your computer stations.

16. Have a backup lesson plan in case there are technical difficulties with the computers. You don't want to lose valuable class time trying to figure out what went wrong.

17. Don't ever think that there are no new ideas about how to teach your content area. Use the Internet. You will find everything from actual lesson plans to resources and materials.

18. Use e-mail to contact parents and students. It's quick and personal and they love it!

PRAXIS™

Praxis Competencies Related to Your Content Area: Using Resources and Technology to Become an Expert in Your Field

The Praxis Series has content-specific tests to assess whether you have the basic knowledge of your content area and the competencies to be licensed as a teacher of your subject. The tests vary in terms of format, but the material typically covered is what one might find in a bachelor's degree program. States require different tests for different content areas. They usually include a test of pure content knowledge (multiple-choice format) and one on pedagogy, or the teaching of that content area, which is often in essay or constructed-response format.

For example, for the English content area, a candidate might be asked to take both the English Language and Literature test (0040) and the English Language, Literature, and Composition: Pedagogy test (0043). Note the following sample items from English.

Sample Item

His insistence on the pettiness of man and the largeness of nature, on the triviality of the world and the infinite capacities of Walden, is mannered. His boast that he had seen the whole world in his rambles through Concord seems a morose witticism.

In the lines above, Robert Lowell is writing about

(A) Thoreau

(B) James

(C) Faulkner

(D) Whitman

(E) Melville

The correct answer is **A**. Robert Lowell is writing about Henry David Thoreau. Thoreau is best known for *Walden,* a book that recounts his withdrawal to Walden Pond, not far from his Concord birthplace (ETS, 2001, *Test-at-a-Glance*, English, Reading and Communication). The following is a sample question from English Language, Literature, and Composition: Pedagogy (0043). These questions will usually provide you with a teaching scenario and you will be asked to respond as you would in a classroom situation.

Sample Item

The Teaching Situation

Assume that students in your tenth-grade English class are writing essays for a special issue of the school newspaper. The assignment appears below.

The students wrote their first drafts in a 50-minute class period. A new student in your class has asked you to comment on her first draft, which is printed below.

Directions for Your Response

First, read the assignment and the student's draft. Then addressing your comments directly to the student, write a response that

- describes one or two major strengths and weaknesses of the student's writing on the assignment and
- gives the student a strategy for revising the draft.

Student's Assignment

Our class has been asked to write essays for a special edition of the school newspaper on the topic "What I Would Change in My School." Think about some of the things that you think should be changed at school and then choose one to write about. In your essay, explain why it should be changed and how it should be changed. Remember that your audience is other students in the school.

Student's First Draft

What I Would Change If I could change one thing in this school, it would be prejudism. It just seems so senseless to me. Liking someone or not liking someone just because if they're wealth, or race, or religion is stupid. For example, inviting someone to a party because they're rich is not a good reason. You should do it because you really care about them.

I suppose we feel the way we do in school because of the communities in which we live. If adults are prejudiced, then they're children might be, also. I guess the problem goes way beyond one school. It's a problem in society as a whole.

One time I was in the cafeteria at lunch, and I was sitting at a table by myself. My best friend Laura finally joined me. So there were two of us sitting there. Then these two boys from our English class come in and sit down at another table beside us. They started talking about us in voices loud enough for us to hear. They said they liked us. But, they wouldn't sit at the table with us, and they never spoke to us. They also didn't speak to us in class or the halls. Why not? I think the answer is that they are rich and we are not. That is what prejudism is about.

I hope this condition will change one day. I'd like to be a part of the solution.

A sample response that might receive a score of 6 (the highest rating) would include some of the following in the response to the student:

- Praise for the first draft being a good first attempt
- Praise for the use of the example ("inviting someone to a party because they're rich is not a good reason") and how it supports the general idea

- Suggesting that the student elaborate on examples
- Suggesting additional examples (to expand on the references to race and religion)
- Praise of the scene in the lunchroom and asking for more detail—perhaps the exact narrative from the situation
- Suggesting that the reader take the final paragraph a step further and suggest a solution to the problem
- Asking the writer to address the draft to his audience—his peers
- A final word of encouragement

(ETS, 2001, *Test-at-a-Glance,* English, Reading and Communication.)

Clearly, there are problems with the essay. However, the goal is to get the student to improve the essay, not to overwhelm him or her by pointing out every error at once. The teacher has responded to the student in ways that will encourage an effort to rewrite the next draft, focusing on broad content areas that can be addressed first. Mechanics can be addressed in the refinement stage.

The important thing to remember is that the test makers want to know how you will go about using best practice for your content area as you work with students. There is no one right answer—there are many ways to do this and do it well. This is your opportunity to show the people who will read your response that you know what needs to be done with students.

Suggestions for Further Reading

If you have time to read only a couple of sources for the topics in this chapter...

Kellough, R. D., & Kellough, N. G. (1999). *Secondary school teaching: A guide to methods and resources* (chap. 11). Upper Saddle River, NJ: Prentice Hall.

Morrison, G. R., & Lowther, D. L. (2002). *Integrating computer technology into the classroom* (2nd ed.). Upper Saddle River, NJ: Merrill/Prentice Hall.

References

Archer, J. (1998). The link to higher scores. Technology counts '98. *Education Week, 5,* (18) 10–20.

Barrows, H. S., & Kelson, A. M. (1996). Problem-based learning: A total approach to education. Unpublished monograph. Springfield: Southern Illinois School of Medicine. (Cited in Morrison and Lowther, 2002.)

Becker, H. J. (1991). How computers are used in United States schools: Basic data from the 1989 I.E.A. Computers in Education survey. *Journal of Educational Computing Research, 7,* 385–406.

Bork, A. (1987). *Learning with personal computers.* New York: Harper & Row.

Bormuth, J. (1968). The Cloze readability procedure. *Elementary English, 45*(April), 429–436.

Callahan, J. F., Clark, L. H., & Kellough, R. D. (1992). *Teaching in the middle and secondary schools.* New York: Macmillan.

Carroll, D., Alexander, B., Bell S., Chadwick, D., & Rudkin, A. (2002). *English.* Chapel Hill, NC: N.C. Teach.

Cashien, P. (1990). Special sheet investigations in economic teaching. *Economics, 26*(110), Part 2, 73–84.

Clark, L. H., & Starr, I. S. (1996). *Secondary and middle school teaching methods.* Upper Saddle River, NJ: Merrill/Prentice Hall.

Cohen, V. L. (2001). Learning styles and technology in a ninth grade high school population. *Journal of Research on Technology in Education, 33*(4), 586.

Conderman, G., Hatcher, R., & Ikan, P. (1998). Why student-led conferences work. *Kappa Delta Pi Record, 34*(4), 132–134.

DiBiase, W., Boger, D., Cowan, M., Veal, W., & Elliott C. (2002). *Science.* Chapel Hill, NC: N.C. Teach.

Dribin, C. I. (1985). Spreadsheets and performance: A guide for student-graded presentations. *The Computing Teacher, 19*(9), 22–25.

Educational Testing Service (ETS). (2001). *Test-at-a-Glance*—English, Reading and Communication. Princeton, NJ: Author.

Fry, E. (1968). A readability formula that saves time. *Journal of Reading, 11*(April), 587.

Gretes, J., Elliott, C., Goldstein, C., Leonard, M., Bray, M., & Weyker, B. (2002). *Technology.* Chapel Hill, NC: N.C. Teach.

Gulledge, S., Addo, L., Goode, J., Jester, J., Painter, J., Smith., R., & Stapleton, M. (2002). *Social studies.* Chapel Hill, NC: N.C. Teach.

Hollis, R. (1990). Database yearbooks in the second grade. *The Computing Teacher, 17*(6), 14–15.

Jankowski, L. (1993–1994). Getting started with databases. *The Computing Teacher, 21*(4), 8–9.

Jonassen, D. H. (2000). *Computers as mindtools for schools* (2nd ed.). Upper Saddle River, NJ: Merrill.

Karlin, M. (1988). Beyond distance = rate * time. *The Computing Teacher,* (February), 20–23.

Kellough, R. D., & Kellough, N. G. (1999). *Secondary school teaching: A guide to methods and resources.* Upper Saddle River, NJ: Prentice Hall.

Lowther, D. L., Bassoppo-Moyo, T., & Morrison, G. R. (1998). Moving from computer literate to technologically competent: The next reform. *Computers and Human Behavior, 14,* 93–109.

McKenna, N. (1976). Synonymic versus verbatim scoring of the Cloze procedure. *Journal of Reading, 20,* 141–143.

Mills, J., & Jackson, R. (1997). Analysis of microbial growth data using a spreadsheet. *Journal of Biological Education, 31*(1), 34–38.

Misovich, M., & Biasca, K. (1990). The power of spreadsheets in a mass and energy balances course. *Chemical Engineering Education, 24,* 46–50.

Morrison, G. R., & Lowther, D. L. (2002). *Integrating computer technology into the classroom* (2nd ed.). Upper Saddle River, NJ: Merrill/Prentice Hall.

Moursund, D. (1996). *Increasing your expertise as a problem-solver: Some roles of computers* (2nd ed.). Eugene, OR: International Society of Technology in Education.

Muffoletto, R. (1994). Technology and restructuring education: Constructing a context. *Educational Technology, 34*(2), 24–28.

National Council of Teachers of Mathematics. (2002). Principles and Standards for School Mathematics. http://standards.nctm.org/document/Chapter 7/index.htm

Pugalee, D., Bell, K., Hardin, K., Royster, N., McCoy, L., Hernandez, M. (2002). *Mathematics*. Chapel Hill, NC: N.C. Teach.

Roblyer, M. D., & Edwards, J. (2000). *Integrating educational technology* (2nd ed.). Upper Saddle River, NJ: Merrill/Prentice Hall.

Romine, B. (1996). Reading courses for middle and high school content area teachers: A U.S. survey. *Journal of Adolescents and Adult Literacy, 40*(3), 194–198.

Sigismondi, L. A., & Calise, C. (1990). Integrating basic computer skills into science classes: Analysis of ecological data. *The American Biology Teacher, 31*(1), 34–38.

Wright, E., Brown, R., Cooke, N., Dickens, V., Core, M., & Lillie, D. (2002). *Special education*. Chapel Hill, NC: N.C. Teach.

10

Effective Assessment

This should be a pretty easy couple of days for me—no actual teaching. I'll just be giving tests and returning them. It'll be a pain to read them all, but I need some grades before the end of the quarter.

First-year teacher

The teacher above thinks that he has a break from teaching for a few days. Does he? Hopefully, he will soon learn that when he gives tests, he *is* teaching. These tests are an important part of his instruction. More than enabling him to "get some grades," they are an opportunity for his students to have valuable feedback regarding their progress. They all want this—the sooner the better. Just as important, however, *he* can learn from these tests not only how well his students are performing, but also how well he is doing teaching the material. He will also have critical information he needs to decide how he will focus the next lessons. All of this depends on his attitude about assessment and the process he chooses to implement.

This chapter addresses the essentials regarding the topic of assessment. These include the purposes of assessment, the differences in terminology that relate to evaluating students' performance, and a brief discussion of assumptions that will inform your decisions. Two broad categories of assessment are outlined, followed by some factors you may want to consider as you determine the best approach.

The Purpose of Assessment: Why Is This Important?

Are you a good teacher? How do you know? Perhaps you will respond by saying, as many do, that your students tell you they enjoy your classes, or that you get good evaluations from your principal. These are probably two valid measures of your effectiveness. Regardless of your criteria—students, administrators, or other sources—you have accepted *someone*'s evaluation of your performance. Like most people, you need some external indication of how you are doing. Over time, most teachers gain enough experience and perspective to be able to gauge their own performance without anyone telling them whether or not a lesson is good. But individuals new to the teaching profession, as you are, need feedback as they are learning how to define what effective teaching is.

Likewise, your students need input on their performance. This input is usually received as some form of evaluation. It might be a test grade, a comment on a paper, or even a compliment after class. Students want to know, as you do, how they are doing.

One of the hardest things for teachers to do is to evaluate students' work. It takes time and energy to determine the best way to do it, create instruments you want to use, administer the instruments, and then grade them. At the end of the quarter, semester, and year, you are faced with the task of looking over all the work your students have completed and assigning a grade for the report card. Most teachers simply accept this aspect of teaching as a necessary evil and know that, regardless of their attempts to play down this part of school, grades are a major concern for most secondary students.

In this age of accountability, assessment has implications at all levels as never before, in two ways. First, of course, evaluation continues to serve the time-honored purpose of letting the students and their parents know how they are performing. However, it's the increased emphasis on the second function that seems to have a wider impact than ever. This refers to being accountable to others outside your classroom (administrators, college admissions directors, and the public), keeping them informed about how students are doing. Teachers are routinely asked to explain results.

Yes, pressure on teachers has definitely increased tremendously with respect to evaluating students. It sometimes seems that everyone is paying close attention to, questioning, and analyzing the results of every assessment measure from a daily pop quiz to standardized tests. Some teachers say, in fact, that there is now too much attention paid to this component of schooling. Mrs. Williamson is a veteran middle school science teacher. She complains that much of the fun has gone out of her career because she has this concern on her mind at all times. "I am constantly aware of how every lesson will impact the end-of-grade tests. I feel that all I do is prepare students for the next round of tests—either mine, the ones I normally give at the end of chapters, or state-mandated standardized tests. I long for the days when all I had to think about was creating an interesting lesson for students without every assignment and activity needing to be tied directly to a test of some kind."

Although the results of standardized tests are scrutinized by the outside world, you need to keep these concerns in perspective. You'll have your hands full developing good and useful assessment strategies for your students with respect to their day-to-day progress on the lessons at hand. If you focus on this, the results ultimately seen by others will take care of themselves. Keep your eye on what is important. Remember that the purposes of assessment and evaluation are to help students to learn; to discover areas that need to be enhanced, reinforced, or retaught; to provide you with feedback regarding the quality of your teaching; and to let parents know how your students are doing.

Definition of Terms: What's the Difference Between Certain Expressions?

Teachers use several terms related to the topic of assessment interchangeably. However, understanding the subtle differences in these terms that are used in school settings will help you to use them correctly and to refine your thinking with regard to each. The following are among the most common:

1. Grading is the process of determining the value of certain work. When you grade papers, you are reading them and evaluating their worth by assigning them a grade.

2. Testing is the process of administering a formal (written) or informal (not written) measure of a student's mastery of certain content.

3. Norm-referenced tests are tests that compare students to peers. These are usually in the form of standardized tests.

4. Criterion-referenced tests are basically teacher-made tests (where the teacher determines the criterion).

5. High-stakes testing is when the results of tests have significant consequences for test takers and other stakeholders. For example, these tests might determine whether a student is accepted into certain specialized programs.

6. Low-stakes testing is when the results are more useful to the teacher in the classroom for the purposes of improving instruction. These might include a test of student interest in certain areas of the country to assist the teacher in determining appropriate group activities.

7. Assessment is the process of gathering information about a student's performance and may include multiple measures such as written work, observations, as well as a variety of other data. The purpose is to provide an indication of where students' strengths and weaknesses are in understanding concepts taught so that instruction can be modified appropriately.

8. Evaluation is the process of assigning value to student work. Making this determination may include multiple assessments. As the teacher, you are making a judgment about the quality of the data.

9. Authentic (alternative) assessment includes strategies that assess student performance in realistic contexts. These usually include multiple measures with input from the student (Guillaume, 2000).

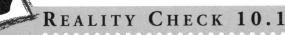

REALITY CHECK 10.1

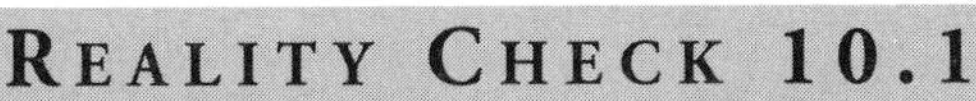

You will hear a lot from other teachers and the administrators in your school about the importance of your students' doing well on standardized tests. Some school systems even offer individual schools and teachers incentives to encourage them to stress achievement in this area. Find the approach that is right for you as you respond to the pressure you may experience regarding testing. True, those tests are important for many reasons. But remember that your students' success and achievement each day in your classroom are *more* important.

Does the use or misuse of these terms really matter in terms of what you do each day? Maybe,

maybe not. But clearly, more attention is being paid to terminology. This is because the stakes are so high in the area of testing and student assessment in every respect, and the implications are great—results translate into funding for districts and public relations for administrators, to name only two.

Guidelines for Assessment: What Assumptions Will Inform Your Decisions?

You will face the issue of evaluating students as long as you are a teacher. Your challenge is to figure out which assessment approaches and strategies best provide you with what you want to know along the way. These will vary somewhat depending on your content area. You must also wade through the many options available to you to evaluate your students. How will you determine the best way to do it? There are several guidelines you should keep in mind:

- Assessment needs to be a reflection of your views of education. Where are you coming from philosophically? You had some indication of this when you completed Activity 1.6 (Determining Your Own Philosophical Approach) in chapter 1. Do you believe that students need to memorize facts or certain specific information? If so, you will tend to give them tests that reinforce that approach. Likewise, if you believe that the most important lessons to be learned are based on the interaction of the students with each other, your measures of their performance in this area should be very different from those who value memorizing specific information.
- Assessment needs to be driven by specific learning goals that you have identified. You are the teacher. Therefore, you will be making the decisions about what is important for your classes and what is not. You will determine the content for which you will hold them accountable. Even if the state curriculum requires you to address particular topics, the ultimate decision is yours about how to teach the topic, how much depth to go into, and how much time to spend on the unit.
- Assessment needs to be systematic and fair. You must make sure your students know what they are expected to master and how they will be held accountable for this mastery. You need to provide them with ample time not only to learn, but also to prepare for the evaluation. While most middle and high school students enjoy surprises, they rarely do when it comes to tests.
- Assessment needs to be connected to your instruction. If your students do poorly on a test, rather than proceed with the next unit, consider reteaching the content or incorporating concepts not mastered into the next unit for reinforcement. Sadly, few teachers do this. Feeling the pressure of time, they often move on, disregarding what their own evaluation measures told them needed to be done.
- Assessment needs to be a reflection of students' learning styles. Paying attention to how your students learn is important not only when deciding about methodology, but also when you are determining the best way to test them. Assume that you have a class where few of the students are comfortable with lecture but the information would most likely lend itself most efficiently to this method of instruction. You have successfully adapted your instruction to include activities that involve group work and other similar forms of learning instead. How much sense does it make then to give the class a written test that requires them to prove they have memorized specific information you so creatively had them learn in a social context? Adapting traditional testing procedures to their learning styles results in higher grades, fewer classroom behavior problems, and more cooperative attitudes (Welch, 1995).
- Assessment needs to be a reflection of student involvement. To the extent possible, try to let students have some say about how they are evaluated. Maybe not every time, but certainly in some cases. High school teacher Shirley Benson (2000) described how she transformed her listless classes into "partnership" classes, with highly motivated students

eager to evaluate their own progress. Student-led conferences have also been found to serve as effective authentic assessment strategies (Conderman, Hatcher, & Ikan, 1998).

- Assessment needs to be part of a total management system. It is critical that you incorporate your assessment procedures as part of your overall management of the class. This would include a system of evaluation that the students understand as well as a consistent approach to the overall process of evaluation that you select based on your goals.

Simplifying Evaluation: When Do You Choose Between Measurement and Authentic Assessment?

On the way to finally evaluating your students, you will be gathering a variety of assessment data. Through the years, many types of assessment strategies have been developed, each with several definitions and numerous variations in implementation. To simplify this complicated topic of evaluating students at the secondary level, it may be easier to think in terms of two broad categories: *measurement* and *authentic assessment.*

Measurement

Tests! Like your students, you are probably most familiar with the traditional form of evaluation, paper-and-pencil tests. The purpose of such tests is to literally measure in some objective way exactly what the students have learned. Teachers generally use different forms of measurement almost exclusively to determine how well students are performing. Typically, these forms of measurement are teacher-made questions or short-answer items, essay (discussion) questions, or both.

There are numerous variations of short-answer items that can be created to determine what specific information students have learned. You will no doubt recognize the following as several of the most common.

Sample Short-Answer Items

Fill-in-the-Blank

These items usually have a sentence or a phrase with one part omitted.

Example: The capital of Peru is ______.

Students are expected to be able to recall certain specific information. Teachers may accept either the exact word(s) needed or synonyms.

True–False Statements

These items require the students to determine the accuracy of statements. To avoid confusing students, teachers should always make sure that the statements are brief and clear and do not contain terminology or content that could possibly be vague or debatable.

Example: True or False: (1) ______ Thomas Jefferson was the third president of the United States. (*clear*)

(2) ______ Thomas Jefferson believed in equality for all people and therefore did not believe in slavery. (*debatable*)

Multiple-Choice Items

These items require the student to complete sentences based on choices provided. Be sure to make the choice options different enough from each other to ensure that the correct answer is evident, but similar enough to require students to discern between choices.

Example: Before becoming president, Bill Clinton was governor of

(A) Alabama
(B) Georgia
(C) Mississippi
(D) Arkansas

You could vary this type of question with such statements as "All of the following are southern states EXCEPT. . . ."

Matching

Matching involves having the student match items in the left column with items in the right column. There should be more items to choose from in the right column than the column on the left.

Example:

1.______ 1954	a. The year John Kennedy was assassinated
2.______ 1961	b. The year Martin Luther King was assassinated
3.______ 1968	c. *Brown v. Board of Education of Topeka*
	d. Year Princess Diana was born
	e. Year Nixon was elected

One thing you will want to consider as you develop short-answer tests is the factor of time. Always take the test yourself and then assume it will take your students double (or even triple) that time.

Sample Essay Questions

Essay questions enable the teacher to determine how well students understand material. These questions require students to use writing and organization skills to go into more depth about content they have studied. Good essay questions are clear and both specific enough to help students focus but broad enough to allow them to elaborate. Essay questions never have one-word responses. Questions should provide any guidelines that will help the student to be focused. For example,

> describe two of the five primary causes leading to the involvement of the United States in World War I. Limit your response to two pages and include the names of important people who contributed to these events.

The short-answer questions take longer to create but take less time to grade. On the other hand, essay questions tend to take a shorter amount of time to create but take longer to evaluate. These tried-and-true approaches serve a valuable purpose if time is spent to develop a solid test that addresses the objectives for lessons clearly. In recent years, there has been a trend toward more open-ended questions that include less traditional variations such as graphic organizers and pictorial representations (Guillaume, 2000).

How do you know when you have developed a good test? A test is considered "good" if it meets the following criteria (Callahan, Clark, & Kellough, 1992):

1. It reflects the content area students are studying.
2. It involves the skills (cognitive, affective, and psychomotor) that are important to the material at hand.
3. It is related to the behavioral objectives of the unit.
4. It is reliable.
5. It is able to be administered in the time allotted.
6. It can separate students on the basis of how well they perform on tests.

REALITY CHECK 10.2

Most teachers want to be fair in their testing practices and choose approaches they think will help them evaluate students objectively. Don't kid yourself. You may think you are choosing to use some form of measurement because it seems more "objective." The truth is that *all* tests, no matter what kind, have some degree of subjectivity. After all, the teacher makes the decisions about which content to test, how it should be tested, and how it should be graded. Your tasks will be to ask yourself why you are making each decision and be able to explain this to students (and others if need be).

Authentic Assessment

Current trends in education stress the importance of making learning more "authentic." This means that educators have encouraged teachers to replace traditional assessment methods with authentic assessments that are more comprehensive in nature and consider the whole student. The purpose is to determine exactly what the students understand, which means they must be involved in the evaluation process. To make sure the assessments are authentic, teachers must make the instrument as true to life as possible and ensure that it reflects the students' deeper comprehension of the content in some meaningful context.

What assessment strategies are considered to be appropriately authentic? Some of the most common include the following examples (Clark & Starr, 1996; Guillaume, 2000).

1. Observation of Students as They Work—This may involve watching students as they engage in activities, work in groups, or work independently. Most teachers find that making notes and writing anecdotal reports helps them to remember important behaviors.

2. Work Samples or Products—Authentic assessment almost always includes samples of student work. This may be in the form of projects, particular assignments, student-made videos, and so forth.

3. Themes—Depending on the content area, themes are often included as examples of student writing as well as of students' abilities to examine concepts in depth.

4. Notebooks—Notebooks are used in many ways by teachers. Students may be required to keep track of daily notes from class, catalog observations of birds for biology, or organize information from research projects. Regardless of the purpose of the assignment, examining notebooks as part of an assessment process is most useful in providing insight relative to how students think and process concepts.

5. Portfolios—Portfolios (files that contain samples of student work) are increasingly used as part of authentic assessment. They can be excellent effective substitutes for formal observations (Phelps, 1997; VanWagenen & Hibbard, 1998). Because portfolios represent a compilation of several types of work, the teacher can get a good sense of the student's overall progress.

6. Performance-Based Rubrics—Rubrics are scales that provide the teacher with a method of evaluating work at different levels of achievement. This approach gives students and teachers a clear understanding of how the quality of a project is determined. The following example might be used to evaluate a written argument for or against a social issue:

A

- The argument is clearly and thoroughly described.
- The argument has support from a minimum of 6 sources.
- The argument is logical and convincing.

B

- The argument is basically described.
- The argument has 3–5 sources for support.
- The argument is somewhat logical and convincing.

C

- The argument is minimally described and somewhat clear.
- The argument has 1–2 sources for support.
- The argument is slightly convincing.

7. Journals and Reflective Writing—Journals and writing that is reflective allow the teacher to become aware of the way students are developing and processing information. It is an excellent way to gauge growth and maturity through a process because it often reflects a time span over which teachers can see growth.

8. Interviews with the Teacher—Conversations with the teacher about a certain learning project can be documented. These talks are an opportunity for teachers to question students about their thinking on a subject. Teachers can encourage students to talk about their reasons for doing things certain ways, ask them to predict outcomes of particular experiments, and so forth.

9. Anecdotal Records—Teachers often find that making a brief record of events that happen with students and including them in an assessment is valuable. They may be as simple as a brief exchange in a small group when a student made a special contribution or a conversation with the media specialist as the student researched a problem. These anecdotes, often on small 3×5 cards, serve to add authenticity to the overall assessment. They credit the student with efforts made in a way that might not be documented at all and otherwise overlooked.

10. Small Group Interaction—Noting small-group interactions serves to round out an authentic assessment. Indications of which students contributed in which particular ways help teachers to complete a picture of exactly how students progressed within the group dynamic.

Determining Your Approach: Which Method Will Best Help You to Evaluate Your Students?

Many beginning teachers find that determining the best process for assessment with their students is one of the most challenging tasks they face. As you begin, ask yourself the following questions:

1. What are my goals and objectives for this unit of study? (What do you want your students to learn?)
2. Generally, what learning styles help each of my classes to learn best?
3. What method of evaluation best reflects items 1 and 2?
4. What strategies will provide me with the best feedback so that I can make informed decisions about what and how to teach next?

The best approach is often a combination of several evaluation techniques, depending on many factors such as the nature of your content and the needs of your students. Experiment with a combination of measurement and authentic assessment strategies and be willing to change whatever is not working (see Activity 10.1). If you see the process of evaluation as part of your teaching, it will become an enriching and essential part of your total instructional program.

ACTIVITY 10.1

Experimenting with Two Approaches to Evaluation

Experiment with at least two different approaches to evaluation with the same unit of study with two classes of the same general ability level. One approach will be some form of measurement and the other some form of authentic assessment. Spend some time analyzing the results. What were the advantages and disadvantages of each method?

TIPS from the TRENCHES

The following are suggestions beginning teachers wish they had followed when they began teaching.

1. Having a "test day" or similar routine for evaluation of any kind. This is helpful for students to plan their study.

2. Use a variety of assessment and testing strategies.

3. Don't try to grade everything you assign.

4. Give tests and other evaluated work back as soon as possible. Students want to know how they did right away.

5. Be careful about grading homework. Base your feedback and comments on effort, not accuracy. This is their chance to practice and make mistakes without it counting against them.

6. Remember that students expect you to be fair. Write down your criteria for grading and share it with your classes.

7. Let students know from the beginning about your attitude toward grading and evaluation.

8. Provide review sheets if there is a lot of material to be covered on a test.

PRAXIS™

Praxis Competencies Related to Effective Assessment

You may see a variety of questions on the Praxis Examination that reflect your understanding of assessment. More than likely, you will be asked to apply what you know about evaluation to a situation, either in a multiple-choice or constructed-response format. Many of the tests refer in their preparatory materials to the issue of student assessment, each reflecting the content area addressed. For example, the Reading Across the Curriculum: Secondary test (0202) requires you to respond to questions related to the following:

Assessment of Reading

- Identify appropriate formal and informal assessment strategies, including criterion referenced tests, standardized tests, running records, anecdotal records, work samples, Informal Reading Inventories (IRIs), portfolios, and self-assessment
- Analyze and interpret assessment information for the purpose of informing reading instruction, advising parents and students, and making referrals to other professionals

(ETS, 2001, *Test-at-a-Glance*—English, Reading and Communication)

In the Principles of Learning and Teaching: Grades 5–9 test (0523), you are asked to

Create or select evaluation strategies that are appropriate for students and are aligned with the goal of the lesson.

- Evaluation plans to assess student progress and instructional effectiveness
- Use of student products for diagnosis
- Methods for establishing multiple records of evidence of student progress (e.g., anecdotal records, observations, checklists, student journals, survey instruments, videotapes, student self-evaluations, parent comments)
- Methods for gathering quantitative data about student learning
- Methods for clear interpretation, reporting, and communication of data to various populations: students, parents, and administrators

(ETS, 2001, *Test-at-a-Glance*—Principles of Learning and Teaching: Grades 5–9 (0523))

Suggestions for Further Reading

If you have time to read only one book . . .

Stiggins, R. J. (2001). *Student-involved classroom assessment* (3rd ed.). Upper Saddle River, NJ: Prentice Hall.

References

Benson, S. (2000). Make mine an A. *Educational Leadership, 57*(5), 30–32.

Callahan, J. F., Clark, L. H., & Kellough, R. D. (1992). *Teaching in the middle and secondary schools.* New York: MacMillan.

Clark, L. H., & Starr, I. S. (1996). *Secondary and middle school teaching methods.* Upper Saddle River, NJ: Merrill/Prentice Hall.

Conderman, G., Hatcher, R., & Ikan, P. (1998). Why student-led conferences work. *Kappa Delta Pi Record, 34*(4), 132–134.

Educational Testing Service (ETS). (2001). *Test-at-a-Glance*—English, Reading and Communication. Princeton, NJ: Author.

Educational Testing Service (ETS). (2001). *Test-at-a-Glance*— Principles of Learning and Teaching. Princeton, NJ: Author.

Guillaume, A. M. (2000). *Classroom teaching: A primer for new professionals.* Upper Saddle River, NJ: Merrill/Prentice Hall.

Phelps, A. (1997). Portfolio assessment in high school chemistry: One teacher's guidelines. *Journal of Chemical Education, 74*(5), 528–531.

VanWagenen, L., & Hibbard, M. (1998). Building teacher portfolios. *Educational Leadership, 55*(5), 26–29.

Welch, D. (1995). Improving student performance through alternative assessment. *Teaching and Change, 2*(4), 369–391.

11

The Reflective Practitioner

Final Thoughts on Becoming a True Professional

Before this year started, I read the entire teacher's edition for the biology text I'm using—I mean from cover to cover. I figured I was ready for just about anything. Boy, was I wrong! That was just the beginning of *a lot* of reading for my class this year.

First-year teacher

It's the night before your first day of school with the students and you can't sleep. You're excited, but also nervous. Questions keep crossing your mind instead of the sheep you've been counting. Will the lessons work? Will the students like you? Are you really cut out to do this?

You are armed with your college education and a desire to be a great teacher. You may even have read the curriculum handbooks and have discussed some methods for teaching with colleagues. Like the teacher above, you think you have everything in place for your first lessons. Right? Not really. All you've really done is *prepare* to *become prepared* as a really good teacher.

If you do everything suggested in this book, you will have the essential competencies to be effective. But doing the minimum will not make you a *true professional* in this field. Becoming a true professional means going beyond what is minimally expected. While you have support, for the most part, teaching is by nature a solitary endeavor. Thus, your continuing development as a teacher is primarily in your hands. Like the individuals in your classes, every teacher is unique. Only you know your gifts—the magic that occurs when you do certain things and behave in particular ways with your students. Likewise, even if some of your areas for improvement are apparent to those who observe your performance, only you really know all of them. Again, the responsibility for becoming a professional in the truest sense is on you. It will remain so throughout your career.

Monitoring Your Own Development: How Will You Continue to Grow as a Professional?

Reflective Practice and Decision Making

The most important step in your development as a true professional is learning to *reflect* on your teaching and the decisions you make each day. Reflection is the process of thinking about the decisions you made before, during, and after your time with the students. Too often, teachers move rapidly to the next lesson or task, never stopping to consider how the previous one went. You may not be able to think deeply about what has happened until the day is over. That's fine. But ask yourself whether the students were responsive. Did they learn what you were trying to teach? Did you meet your goals and objectives for the class? These and similar questions are second nature for truly professional teachers, and they occur spontaneously and regularly throughout the day.

Teachers make countless decisions daily—some small (whether to change the bulletin board today or tomorrow), some big (whether to begin the year with a generic overview or the content in chapter 1 of the text). *Every* decision you make is important because, in some way, it will influence either directly or indirectly how your students respond to you and your class. Thus, these decisions cannot be made carelessly. They should be made after serious and focused reflection. The longer you teach, the more reflection and making good decisions will become automatic. But as a beginner, you must give every decision due consideration when possible. Remember that every decision teachers make impacts every other decision they make.

There are two kinds of decisions that you will face at all times: ones you can deliberate about in advance and ones you can't. As you already know, much of the time you won't have the luxury of pondering the potential outcome of every decision you make in class. Things happen very quickly when you are working with so many secondary students in a variety of circumstances during the day. That's why you must think about many of the decisions you will face *before* the students walk through the door. These usually include the big decisions such as what and how you will teach the class that day, what management system you will incorporate, and what assignments you will require. You must also have considered a plan B for each of these, in case things don't go as expected. For example, what if you had planned to watch a video that would take much of first period, but the equipment you need is unavailable or broken when you arrive at school that morning. What was your plan B? (You *did* have one, didn't you?)

The decisions you can't make in advance are often the most stressful because they depend heavily on your ability to think quickly on your feet. Naturally, with experience, you will get better at making good spur-of-the-moment decisions. When are you most vulnerable to making bad decisions? Most teachers say this happens when they are tired or feeling poorly and when they aren't paying attention to what is happening around them. The solution? Stay healthy, get plenty of sleep, and become a "withit" teacher. Is it really that simple? No. That's why your journey to becoming a true professional depends on your ability to *reflect* on decisions you made.

Being Receptive to Change

Being *really* good at teaching is an ongoing process of changing, one that starts as soon as you decide to teach and ends the day you retire. Begin right away to accept the fact that keeping up with the content in your field and the best ways to teach it are two things that must stay on your to-do list at all times. This is because four things are always changing: the content, the strategies for teaching, the students, and you.

The Content You Teach Always Changes

Experts in every discipline will constantly explore every facet of their content imaginable. The more research they do, the more inevitable it is that they will discover new information about topics in your subject. For example, think about this with respect to history, a subject every student is required to take. Even the study of history—wherein past events would seem fixed—is always in transition. Perhaps an archeological discovery has unearthed an artifact that changes historical perceptions of how people farmed in the 16th century. Even if the data stay constant, there will always be different interpretations of events and their significance. You will find that keeping up with the most current thinking in the content of your field will be helpful.

State-of-the-Art Teaching Strategies for Your Content Area Change

A good history student used to be one who was very good at memorizing facts and reciting the events of a battle as outlined in the chapter. Now students are asked to read and interpret primary source documents. They must answer more thought-provoking questions such as "How did the event impact the social mores of the time?" Less attention is given to the *what, when,* and *where* and more given to the *why*.

Ways of Dealing with Students Change

In the past, teachers had one approach to presenting information and dealing with students. Teachers concerned themselves with the subject matter rather than with the developmental needs of teenagers. No longer! Now, if they are going to be truly effective, teachers must be aware of current research on the nature of adolescents as they plan their lessons and activities. They have learned that knowing both the approaches their students will respond to best and why they work is key to meaningful learning in their classrooms.

You Change

Yes, you. Your teaching style evolves over time and you may find that you like teaching differently from the way you started out. The more you learn about becoming an educator, the more inclined you will be to experiment with new and different methods. Mrs. Henderson says that when she began teaching, she spent most of her class time lecturing. "Not only did I become bored with that, my students didn't seem as engaged as I wanted them to be. After I attended a workshop called 'Ten Ways to Teach the Same Lesson,' I began to experiment. Not only are my students more interested, but they are learning more. Best of all, I am having more fun than ever."

Because the content, the teaching strategies, the students, and you are always changing, you must *embrace* the idea of change as part of the total package. Keep an open mind. It's the teachers who are not aware of changes in these areas or who do not look for indications of when change is warranted who are the least successful teachers. Most experienced teachers have discovered a formula that works for them—perhaps using the same basic outlines, notes, lesson plans, and activities for their classes every year. Even these teachers will regularly adapt their approach to meet the needs of their students, updating information and trying new ways of doing things. That is, they will adapt their approach if they are good. No doubt you have been subjected to your share of teachers who used decades–old notes, lecturing to each class in the same way with no regard for any differences in individuals. Vow not to be one of them.

Paying Attention to What Works for You

As you teach, it is impossible not to become aware of what works for you. Do your jokes go over well, or have you learned that you need to leave the comedy routine to Jerry Seinfeld? Do your students stay on top of the reading assignments because they know you are going to give them random pop tests, or do these pop tests just take up class time? Do you give them too much to do or not enough to do? To determine what is working for you, you must remember what your goals are and ask yourself if they are being met. If so, then what you are doing is working. If not, it's time to rethink how you are going about the business of teaching. The key is to be intentional about reading your students—their faces and expressions, their attitudes toward you and your class, and the progress they are making in learning your material.

The best way to figure this out is to watch your students carefully *as* you are teaching, asking yourself every few minutes, "Is this working?" Good experienced teachers get in the habit early in their careers of asking themselves this question often during class periods and being prepared to switch gears if necessary. If you are like most beginning teachers, you will find yourself somewhat myopic with respect to what is actually going on in your class. You may be so concerned with covering the material in the lesson that you forget to survey the entire situation. Activity 11.1 may provide some guidance in what to look for.

Listening to Feedback with an Open Mind

The term *feedback* affects different people in different ways. To some it means information or suggestions that will serve as motivation to continue to improve. In other words, it's a good and useful thing. To others, the term is a euphemism for criticism. It doesn't feel good and seems more like an attack. It smacks of advice and, being human, some people don't like that. In these cases, well-meaning feedback is often not only rejected but resented. This is exactly why many teachers are reluctant to ask for feedback about their own performance or to give it to others. What a shame. In this field, feedback is absolutely essential if teachers are going to get better and continue to grow professionally.

ACTIVITY 11.1

Videotaping the Students

To focus more intentionally on what's working for you, begin by observing your students and their responses to you and what you say and do very carefully for one day. If it helps, videotape one or two classes (camera on them—not you) so that you can watch them later with more attention to nuances and the ability to play back certain portions. Consider the following as you watch:

1. What are you doing or saying that makes them smile or respond positively?
2. What are you doing or saying that makes them express frustration or irritation?
3. Which activities do they seem to be most engaged in, and which ones are they least interested in?
4. Do they tend to notice the room and the centers, tables, or resources you have around? Do they spend time examining these areas or do they avoid them?
5. Are the comments students make during a class period or over the entire day affirming or critical?
6. Other general observations?

As hard as it may be for you, actively seek insights, information, advice, and opinions about your teaching from anyone and everyone who might be in a position to provide you with useful and constructive suggestions. And more important, *listen to the feedback!* Becoming a master teacher is a long process—longer for some than for others. You are in the early, formative stages on this road. At this point, you *need* positive reinforcement for the things you are doing right and guidance to change the things you are doing wrong. This doesn't mean that every comment another person has regarding your teaching is something you need to agree with or act on. In fact, it may be appropriate to discount some comments altogether. But do so with valid reason and after you have given the advice due consideration.

Granted, no one likes to feel judged, and inevitably feedback can make you feel this way unless you decide right now that you will view comments as attempts to help you improve. Feedback will come to you in three basic forms: from school administrators, from your colleagues, and from your students.

School systems require their administrators to observe and evaluate teachers. Therefore, you can expect to be observed and to receive reports on your progress by your principal or a designee, usually an assistant principal. If the administrators are doing their jobs well, you will get specific comments about your strengths as well as areas in which they believe you can be more effective. Unfortunately, at the secondary level especially, this process isn't always done as thoroughly and with as much thought as it should be. If you get little more than a perfunctory "You're doing fine," look for more meaningful feedback elsewhere.

The "elsewhere" for better feedback can often be found among your colleagues. Many systems now assign mentor teachers whose task it is to participate actively in your development. Other experienced teachers may also be helpful with suggestions. Look especially to those in your own department who teach the same or similar courses. They can help in various ways—through conversations with you about particular concerns you may have or by observing you and helping you to identify areas for improvement. Other teachers are often your *most valuable* resources. After all, they face the same challenges you do each day and have collected many good ideas. Also, a big advantage is that they are not part of the evaluation loop. Thus, you can hear their comments without concern for repercussions on your "report card." The important thing is to seek their advice no matter how uncomfortable it might be at first. The longer you are in this profession, the more evident it will be that most teachers will *want* to help you. *Fact:* Teachers like to teach, whether they are teaching their students or you. They remember what it was like when they started out, and they have a genuine desire to share their wisdom. Don't you imagine you would feel that way if someone asked you for help?

Remember that all opinions are not equal. Some are worth exactly what you paid for them—nothing. This is why you must seek the right people to offer feedback on your performance. The right person is one

1. Who has your best interest as a growing professional at heart
2. Who has nothing to gain or lose from providing you with such a service
3. Whose professional expertise is recognized as valuable
4. Who is honest
5. Who can provide additional suggestions and help for making things better

If you are uncomfortable asking someone with whom you work for advice, try asking a specialist for your content area who has an office at the central administration for suggestions. Likewise, teachers from other schools may seem like a safer choice. It doesn't matter whom you ask—as long as you get the information and help you need.

Valuable feedback comes from your students, assuming you are open to what they have to say. This feedback is available to you in two ways. First, you can get it informally by making a point of watching how they react to you as you teach. Teenagers are pretty clear about how they feel. Are they bored? Are they sleeping, yawning, or talking with their friends? Do they participate in discussions and ask questions? Are they doing well on your tests and assignments? In short, are they learning in your class? Answers to these and similar questions are feedback and will provide you with important indications of how much of an impact you are having or not having.

Second, you can get the feedback formally by giving them evaluation forms to complete at various times throughout the year (so that you can modify your teaching accordingly) or at the end of the year (so you can plan for the next year). As you develop your form, be sure to ask them questions that will give you some direct indications of what you can do better. It will be useless to ask them if they like math. Focus instead on getting at the heart of the learning process by asking such questions as which activities they enjoyed the most and why.

Remember that the students may tell you more than you want to know. Be brave and develop a thicker skin. You have nothing to lose and everything to gain. After all, this is your *real* audience. The effectiveness of their feedback, of course, is dependent on your own willingness to be receptive and take to heart what they are trying to tell you. If they don't tell you what you want to hear, avoid the very human temptation to write them off as a bad class of unmotivated adolescents. Maybe they are, but it's not likely in most situations. There might be something you can change to address the problem. Instead of dismissing them, see what you can do to turn them into a good class of motivated adolescents.

✓ Videotaping Your Teaching and Seeking Input

There is absolutely no better way to analyze your teaching than to videotape yourself teaching (see Activity 11.2). Analyze the tape in three steps, watching the tape first by yourself, watching it with someone else, and then discussing what you see. This process will provide you with a wealth of information about your effectiveness. As you teach, it's hard to concentrate on what you are trying to do and still have your eyes all over the room, assessing your students' reactions. For example, as you teach, you may *think* you are giving the students enough time to answer questions, but the tape may reveal that you are not. You may *think* you are giving everyone a chance to participate but discover that you are calling on the same six students all the time. The possibilities for what you can learn from this are endless, especially if you watch the tape more than once. Having a videotape also means that you can give it to another colleague for feedback if time doesn't permit your watching it together.

Activity 11.2

Videotaping Yourself

Select one or two of your classes to videotape. Try to have the equipment set up in such a way that it will not distract the students or be in your way as you teach. Start taping before the students enter the room.

When the taping is done and you are ready to observe yourself, either by yourself or with someone else, do the following:

1. Have paper ready to take notes. Divide the paper into sections so you can go from section to section as you watch. Section titles might be "Classroom Management," "Presentation," "Monitoring Student Seatwork," "Lab Station Activity," "Answering Questions," and so forth.
2. Go over your notes and make two columns on your paper, listing (a) your teaching behaviors that are effective and (b) those that represent areas for improvement.
3. Focus on the areas for improvement, numbering them in order of importance.
4. Identify strategies to address each.
5. Select no more than two at a time to focus on for the next day. Gradually work up to address all of them.
6. After an appropriate amount of time, tape yourself again, following the same steps.

Observing Other Teachers

Here's a suggestion you may resist. But, in fact, observing other teachers is another activity that will give you more ideas for your own classroom than you can imagine. Whether or not you agree with how others handle certain situations or how they deal with students, you will gain ideas for dealing with your own situation. You may find this useful not only for expanding your list of teaching strategies, but also for dealing with certain students. For example, if John is a real problem in your class but does well in the class next door, you may want to observe him with that teacher. What is she doing to encourage John to be so cooperative? It may be somewhat uncomfortable to ask a teacher if you may observe. Consider doing it anyway.

Begin by talking with another teacher with whom you have a good relationship about a class you would like to observe. Make sure that the teacher knows that you are there to learn, not to judge what is happening. Pick teachers who are considered to be excellent in the particular areas you are interested in learning about. For example, if motivating students is an issue for you, choose a teacher who seems to do especially well in that area. Prior to observing the class, make a list of some of the things you are particularly concerned about. Do you have trouble getting everyone involved? Is classroom management a problem for you? Plan to look closely at how this teacher manages the class. During the class, take notes on what you see, paying special attention to things that will be helpful to you. After the class, find some time to talk about it with the teacher and ask questions about why the teacher chose to conduct the class in that manner.

Resources: What Opportunities Are Available for Your Own Stimulation?

You will find that talking with colleagues and other personnel in your school and school system may be the most direct and constant informal source of learning about ways to become a better teacher. In addition, there will be many formal opportunities from which you can benefit if you make a point of taking advantage of them. Some of the most valuable are joining professional organizations; attending conferences, workshops, and seminars; and taking courses.

Professional Organizations

There are two types of professional organizations that you will want to know about and participate in. First, as mentioned in chapter 9, there are organizations that relate specifically to your content area, such as the National Council for the Social Studies (NCSS). Regardless of your field, there will be at least one professional organization that exists whose purpose is to inform teachers and keep them abreast of the current trends in your discipline. Often, there will also be a state or local affiliate of the same organization, which makes participation easier. Join and become involved! Membership is well worth the money (which is tax deductible) and includes opportunities to attend conferences where the very best teachers and authorities in the field share their latest research. These organizations also publish at least one magazine you will receive regularly, which includes content updates and ideas for teaching your classes.

The other type of organization you will want to find out about is that which includes teachers of all subjects, such as the National Education Association, the American Federation of Teachers, and Classroom Teachers of America. Like the professional organizations, they usually have state and local chapters as well. They also sponsor conferences and offer publications and other perks such as legal benefits. Some school systems provide staff development funds and substitutes to encourage teachers to attend and make presentations when possible. Find out how your system can help you become a part of these groups.

Workshops, Seminars, and Courses

Never pass up a chance to attend a workshop or seminar that might provide you with intellectual stimulation and/or practical tips for how to make your teaching more effective. More than likely, your school system offers these on a regular basis as a part of a total staff development program for their employees. They are not only offered at convenient locations and after school hours, but are free. The intent is usually to address a specific issue such as stress management or improving the writing abilities of your ninth graders. Others may provide teachers who attend with information about content areas or help with a specific concern regarding teaching practices such as cooperative learning. Most facilitators in these sessions try to make the sessions as practical and hands-on as possible.

Colleges and universities in your area will offer courses related to both teaching in general and in your content area. Take advantage of these. College-level courses not only prepare you with a thorough overview of what you are trying to learn, but they are taught by professors who study the content of the course for a living. As a student, you also have access to a large library that will house a plethora of books, journals, and other resources that your school system may not have readily available. Even if you are not a student at the college, it is worth a trip to the library to see what is available and if you can borrow some of those materials for your own use.

Licensing Requirements: What Does Your State/School District Require You to Do to Stay Current?

State Requirements

When you sign a contract to teach, be sure someone in the school system informs you of what you need to do to meet state requirements to obtain a teaching license. School systems seek to attract traditionally licensed teachers who have completed teacher certification programs. However, because of the teacher shortage in many areas in recent years, they are also actively recruiting candidates who will be seeking licensure through alternative means. These individuals may have a college degree in a content area but no formal teacher preparation. Most school systems look at each candidate individually and determine what courses and other requirements need to be completed before licensure can be awarded. If you are in this situation, make sure you understand exactly what you will need to do and ask for it in writing.

Praxis Examinations or Other Testing Requirements

Most states require teachers to take and pass certain tests as one measure of their suitability for employment. Regardless of format or testing approach, all tests of this nature have questions that are designed to assess the teachers' knowledge of the basic content they are expected to teach. They also focus on the fundamentals of teaching principles and best professional practice. This book has focused on one of the most widely used tests, the Praxis Series.

These are not IQ tests. In other words, they are tests that you can and should prepare for. The tests were designed to be general in nature and thus reflect the preparation teachers would have regardless of their teacher education program. If you went through such a program, dust off your textbooks and review what you have already studied relative to both the content itself and teaching methods. For example, the *content*-specific questions will reflect the basic content of the core (required) courses in a major in that field. In other words, these questions will expect a history major to know general trends in U.S. and world history, but probably not the content from a course on women's fashions in the 18th century. You may prepare for questions regarding the *fundamentals of teaching and methods* by reading college textbooks related to the teaching of your content area (e.g., books on methods for teaching secondary English). If you are an alternative licensure candidate and did not go through such a program, no problem. You can still prepare for the tests by obtaining the appropriate textbooks from any college library, a bookstore, or someone you know in a teacher education program. Just make sure that the sources you use are current, published within the last five years.

Renewal Policies

You certainly wouldn't want to go to a physician, an attorney, or a hairdresser who didn't keep up with developments in his or her field, would you? Likewise, teachers are expected to stay in the know. Thus, most school systems require teachers to continue to learn about their content and how to teach it better. Usually this requirement is in the form of "renewal" credit, which is awarded to teachers as they complete coursework at colleges and universities, take seminars and workshops, and advance their knowledge in a variety of other ways. You must accumulate a certain number of credits within a certain time frame. For example, you may need 15 renewal credits every 5 years. You will want to be sure you know what your system expects in this regard and plan your long-range professional development goals accordingly.

Now you have it—the essentials to start your journey to become a great teacher, a true professional. You are ready to begin what is arguably the most important career anyone can have. You are in a position to impact the future as few others will be able to do. The effort you make to become effective as you work with adolescents in this critical time of their intellectual and personal development is vital to your success. Aim high. Don't get discouraged. You know now what you have to do. Welcome to the exciting world of secondary classrooms!

GLOSSARY

Accommodation When people change how they think to receive new information.

Accountability Taking responsibility for what has taken place in the classroom.

Anecdotal records An informal notation of incidences that occur with students during the classroom situation.

Assertive discipline When students choose how to behave in class and must accept the consequences of that choice.

Assimilation When people incorporate new information into what they already know.

Attention Deficit Disorder/Attention Deficit Hyperactivity Disorder (ADD/ADHD) Evident when students are easily distracted and impulsive.

Authentic assessment The process of collecting information and data for the purposes of improving instruction.

Authority The right a teacher has to determine the choices he or she makes available for students.

Block scheduling Extended instructional periods to accommodate a broader approach to teaching the curriculum.

Cliques Small groups of six to eight students who are good friends and talk about activities and plans for social activity.

Conferencing Meetings with students, parents, or other individuals for the purpose of improving student performance.

Constructivism The process wherein students build on previously learned concepts to create new meaning.

Cooperative learning Students working together in a group to complete an educational task.

Culture Habits and skills of a particular group of people, providing guidelines for how those people act and behave in society.

Curriculum The planned organization of learning activities in school.

Differentiation Making instruction different; based on the idea that teachers should accommodate students' unique needs.

Discovery learning Hands-on learning activity that encourage students to draw their own conclusions.

Disequilibrium When students try to figure things out that don't make sense.

Diversity The quality of being different in any way.

Documentation Written evidence of some event or learning situation.

Enculturation The process of acquiring the characteristics of a culture and functioning in accord with its ways of behaving.

Equilibrium When students organize new information in their minds, making sense out of what they already know.

Ethnicity An affiliation with a group distinguished by customs, characteristics, language, and so forth.

Evaluation The process of appraising the value of student performance.

Giftedness Having certain academic or artistic qualities, attributes, or skills that are above that of most students.

Higher order thinking Divergent thinking process where students are looking for more complex understanding of issues.

Homophobia An unreasonable fear of same-sex attractions or of people who have same-sex attractions.

Inclusion Students with disabilities are "included" in the general education classrooms as much as possible.

Individual education plans (IEPs) Documents that indicate the way the educational program will be adapted to meet the specific needs of students who have an exceptionality.

Individuals with Disabilities Education Act (IDEA) (PL 105–17). Provides assurances that the needs of students with disabilities will be met. Students will be educated in the "least restricted environment" to the extent possible.

Integrated curriculum Curriculum that is organized in such a way that academic disciplines are blended together for the purpose of having students make better connections.

Interdisciplinary A combining of subject matter and disciplines.

Interstate New Teacher Assessment and Support Consortium (INTASC) A group of state agencies and national organizations dedicated to the preparation and professional development of teachers.

Learning style The way a person tends to learn.

Least restrictive environment (LRE) Placing exceptional students in classroom situations that reflect as few restrictions related to their specific disability as possible.

Local education agency (LEA) Schools.

Multicultural education Providing educational settings that include activities and attention to issues related to many cultures.

Multiple intelligences Howard Gardner's theory that there are eight different intelligences in individuals. Some intelligences are more dominant than others in most people.

No Child Left Behind Act of 2001 President Bush's law that was designed to require solutions to the problems in education based on accountability, choice, and flexibility in federal education programs.

Normal schools Teacher preparation institutes popular from the mid-19th to the mid-20th centuries. These were often the equivalent to secondary schooling for many women.

Power The ability to exert control over others.

Prejudice An opinion before facts are known.

Race Any of several varieties of people distinguished by certain physical characteristics.

Racism The idea that one race is superior to others.

Referral A process to identify specific exceptionalities. It involves the completion of a referral form provided by the school.

Rubric An evaluation scale that allows students to see what levels of achievement they need to reach to meet certain standards.

Scaffolding Providing support for students as they transition from one level of understanding about a concept to another.

Schools within schools Certain schools have self-contained components with their own programs that operate independently of the larger schools in which they are housed.

Socialization The process of individuals functioning with others in social settings.

Taxonomy A classification of concepts, theories, or ideas.

Tuition tax credits Allows parents to claim tax deductions for part of the tuition they pay to send their children to private schools.

Vouchers Flat grants for parents that represent the student's estimated educational cost or portion of the school budget to be used at any school of their choice (private or public).

Withitness Teachers who are perceived as "with it" by the students have a positive effect on their behavior. These teachers usually have a businesslike, no-nonsense demeanor and are able to anticipate problems, handling them quickly and efficiently.

Zone of proximal development (ZPD) When a student is "stuck" at a certain point but can move ahead with the support of the teacher.

INDEX

T